AF180108

Stakeholder Management and Entrepreneurship in Africa

Building on past research in the broad field of stakeholder management and entrepreneurship, this book pushes a new agenda for more effective stakeholder engagement and management in entrepreneurial firms in Africa.

Adomako, Gyensare, and Ahsan provide a novel lens for entrepreneurs to manage stakeholders in Africa and a sense of current best practices. Issues discussed include how external stakeholders such as government, nongovernmental organizations, media, civil society organizations, and local institutions influence the core business operations of entrepreneurial firms. The book confronts the central challenge of entrepreneurship by providing a comprehensive understanding of how entrepreneurs could identify, select, enroll, and coordinate stakeholders. In addition, it assesses issues such as stakeholder influence on corporate social responsibility strategy, sustainability, and environmental management of entrepreneurial firms.

An essential read for postgraduate students, researchers, and public and private analysts.

Samuel Adomako, PhD, is associate professor of strategy and entrepreneurship at the University of Birmingham. His research focuses on entrepreneurship and innovation and has appeared in leading journals including *Journal of Product Innovation Management, British Journal of Management* and many others.

Michael Asiedu Gyensare, PhD, is a lecturer in management at the University of Kent, United Kingdom. His research straddles the divide between strategic human resource management, organisational behavior and entrepreneurship and has been published in leading journals such as the *Journal of Product Innovation Management and Journal of Business Research.* He is currently an editorial board member for *Industrial and Commercial Training.*

Mujtaba Ahsan, PhD, is professor of management at San Diego State University. His teaching and research interests are in the areas of entrepreneurship, international business, and innovation. Ahsan's work has been published in a number of journals such as *Academy of Management Review and Entrepreneurship Theory and Practice* among others.

Routledge Studies in Entrepreneurship

This series extends the meaning and scope of entrepreneurship by capturing new research and enquiry on economic, social, cultural and personal value creation. Entrepreneurship as value creation represents the endeavours of innovative people and organisations in creative environments that open up opportunities for developing new products, new services, new firms and new forms of policy making in different environments seeking sustainable economic growth and social development. In setting this objective the series includes books which cover a diverse range of conceptual, empirical and scholarly topics that both inform the field and push the boundaries of entrepreneurship.

Entrepreneurship and the Creation of Organization
Daniel Hjorth and Robin Holt

Entrepreneurship in Creative Crafts
Edited by Vanessa Ratten

Dark Sides of the Startup Nation
Winners and Losers of Technological Innovation and Entrepreneurship in Israel
Sibylle Heilbrunn

Skills, Creativity and Innovation in the Digital Platform Era
Analyzing the New Reality of Professions and Entrepreneurship
Anne Kovalainen and Seppo Poutanen

Corruption and Entrepreneurship
Testing the Theory of Planned Behavior
Mohammad Heydari

Stakeholder Management and Entrepreneurship in Africa
Edited by Samuel Adomako, Michael Asiedu Gyensare and Mujtaba Ahsan

For more information about this series please visit: www.routledge.com/Routledge-Studies-in-Entrepreneurship/book-series/RSE

Stakeholder Management and Entrepreneurship in Africa

Edited by Samuel Adomako, Michael Asiedu Gyensare and Mujtaba Ahsan

Routledge
Taylor & Francis Group
LONDON AND NEW YORK

First published 2024
by Routledge
4 Park Square, Milton Park, Abingdon, Oxon OX14 4RN

and by Routledge
605 Third Avenue, New York, NY 10158

Routledge is an imprint of the Taylor & Francis Group, an informa business

© 2024 selection and editorial matter, Samuel Adomako, Michael Asiedu Gyensare, and Mujtaba Ahsan; individual chapters, the contributors

The right of Samuel Adomako, Michael Asiedu Gyensare, and Mujtaba Ahsan to be identified as the authors of the editorial material, and of the authors for their individual chapters, has been asserted in accordance with sections 77 and 78 of the Copyright, Designs and Patents Act 1988.

All rights reserved. No part of this book may be reprinted or reproduced or utilised in any form or by any electronic, mechanical, or other means, now known or hereafter invented, including photocopying and recording, or in any information storage or retrieval system, without permission in writing from the publishers.

Trademark notice: Product or corporate names may be trademarks or registered trademarks, and are used only for identification and explanation without intent to infringe.

British Library Cataloguing-in-Publication Data
A catalogue record for this book is available from the British Library

Library of Congress Cataloging-in-Publication Data
Names: Adomako, Samuel, editor. | Gyensare, Michael Asiedu, editor. | Ahsan, Mujtaba, editor.
Title: Stakeholder management and entrepreneurship in Africa / edited by Samuel Adomako, Michael Asiedu Gyensare and Mujtaba Ahsan.
Description: Abingdon, Oxon ; New York, NY : Routledge, 2024. | Series: Routledge studies in entrepreneurship | Includes bibliographical references and index.
Identifiers: LCCN 2023059230 (print) | LCCN 2023059231 (ebook) | ISBN 9781032187433 (hardback) | ISBN 9781032187440 (paperback) | ISBN 9781032187440 (ebook)
Subjects: LCSH: Business enterprises--Africa--Management. | New business enterprises--Africa--Management. | Entrepreneurship--Africa.
Classification: LCC HD2917 .S73 2024 (print) | LCC HD2917 (ebook) | DDC 330.96--dc23/eng/20240103
LC record available at https://lccn.loc.gov/2023059230
LC ebook record available at https://lccn.loc.gov/2023059231

ISBN: 978-1-032-18743-3 (hbk)
ISBN: 978-1-032-18744-0 (pbk)
ISBN: 978-1-003-25601-4 (ebk)

DOI: 10.4324/9781003256014

Typeset in Galliard
by SPi Technologies India Pvt Ltd (Straive)

Contents

Contributors

Shirley Maud Acheampong is currently pursuing a PhD in management at the University of Birmingham, U.K., focusing on corporate entrepreneurship. She possesses extensive expertise in corporate and retail relationship management with over 15 years of experience in the banking, fintech and retail sectors. She has expertise in formulating strategies, managing corporate and retail banking operations, overseeing client services and implementing financial technology systems. She has an undergraduate degree in BSc banking and finance from the University of Ghana, and an MBA in finance from the Central University, Ghana.

Kweku Adams, PhD, LLM, MBA, SFHEA, is an associate professor in international business and management at the Bradford School of Management. A senior fellow of the Higher Education Academy, he holds an MBA (University of Bedfordshire), a master of laws (University of York), and a PhD (Swansea University), among others. His research has been published in journals including *Tourism Management*, *Journal of International Management, Technological Forecasting & Social Change, IEEE- Transactions on Engineering Management, Journal of Environmental Management, Journal of Business Research* and others. He is on the editorial review boards of the *Thunderbird International Business Review* and the *Africa Journal of Management.*

Adedapo Adebajo is a lecturer (assistant professor) in marketing at Loughborough University, United Kingdom. He is also a visiting assistant professor in social innovation at the University of Rome Tor Vergata. His teaching and research expertice encompass the realms of marketing, innovation, transformative service research and public service management. He received his PhD in management from the University of Edinburgh, United Kingdom, with a thesis on open innovation in public services. He was awarded a doctoral scholarship in co-production by the Centre for Service Excellence and has presented his research works at reputable academic international conferences.

Samuel Adomako, PhD, is an associate professor of strategy and entrepreneurship at the University of Birmingham. His research examines the nexus of strategy and innovation. His research has appeared in leading journals including *Journal of Product Innovation Management, British Journal of Management, International Small Business Journal, International Business Review, R&D Management Journal, International Journal of Entrepreneurial Behavior and Research, Business Strategy and the Environment, Management International Review, Journal of Institutional Economics, Journal of Business Research, Journal of International Management* and many others. He received his PhD from the University of Warwick. He is a fellow of the Higher Education Academy, UK.

Edmund Osei Afriyie is a PhD candidate in management at the University of Birmingham, UK. He completed his MSc in international business at Brunel University London, UK, and pursued his undergraduate program in business administration at Ashesi University, Ghana. At Brunel University London, he gained an understanding of sustainability in Africa during his dissertation period. He is also particularly interested in exploring the triple-bottom-line sustainability development of multinational enterprises throughout Africa. He has over five years of experience across banking, transacting advisory consulting and human resource analytics.

Betty J. Aidoo-Anderson is a PhD student at the University of Bradford School of Management and Law. She is an academic with a keen interest in people management and the broader area of business management with extensive experience in higher education and industry. She has worked in several sectors includin retail, health, engineering, college and currently in higher education. Her PhD research focuses on the interplay of technology and flexible work patterns to facilitate career progression for female academics. Other research interests include gender, career progression and entrepreneurship, organisational support and HR practices in Africa.

Kwame Owusu-Ansah Owusu Afram is a chartered human resource management practitioner and a management consultant. He practices human resources at the Ghana Communication Technology University and has spent almost 12 years working in university administration. Mr. Afram is also an adjunct lecturer at the Ghana Communication Technology University, and his specializations include human resource management, human resource development, management, entrepreneurship, morals and ethics and HR analytics and technology. He has several publications to his credit.

Mujtaba Ahsan, PhD, is a professor of management at San Diego State University. Dr. Ahsan received his PhD in management from the University of Wisconsin–Milwaukee. His teaching and research interests are in the areas of entrepreneurship, international business and innovation. Ahsan's work has been published in a number of journals such as *Academy of Management Review, Entrepreneurship Theory and Practice, International Journal* *of Management Reviews, Journal of Small Business Management, Management International Review, Journal of Business Ethics* and *Journal of International Management* among others.

George Kofi Amoako is the director at the Office of Research Innovation and Consultancy and an associate professor in the Marketing Department of the Faculty of Business at Ghana Communication Technology University Accra; he is an academic practising Chartered Marketer (CIM-UK) with a specialization in marketing sustainability, branding, corporate social responsibility (CSR) and e-business. He was educated at Kwame Nkrumah University of Science and Technology in Kumasi Ghana and at the University of Ghana and the London School of Marketing (UK). He received his PhD at London Metropolitan University UK. He also has a postgraduate certificate in academic practice from Lancaster University. He has considerable research, teaching, consulting and practice experience in marketing theory application.

Emelia Amoako-Asiedu is a senior lecturer in the School of Business at Ghana Communication Technology University, Ghana. She holds a doctor of philosophy in public administration and policy management and a master of philosophy in public administration. Her research interests are public sector performance management and leadership, public policy management, entrepreneurship, women and gender issues and occupational health, safety and environment.

George Oppong Appiagyei Ampong is an associate professor in management at the Business School of Ghana Communication Technology University in Ghana. He holds a PhD in business administration and a PGCert in international higher education academic practice. His research interests include business and sustainability strategies, entrepreneurship and SME development, organizational leadership and so on. His research has been published in reputable journals such as *VINE Journal of Information and Knowledge Management Systems, Journal of Hospitality and Tourism Insights, Journal of Business Research, Society and Business Review Journal* and *Journal of Technological Forecasting and Social Change* among others.

Alex Antwi Agyei is a lecturer in the Department of Marketing and Supply Chain at the Ghana Communication Technology University. Alex holds a PhD from the University of Jiangsu.

Emem Anwana is a lawyer by profession. She is a senior lecturer in the Applied Law Department of the Durban University of Technology. She is currently the faculty research co-coordinator in charge of post-graduate studies in the Faculty of Management Sciences of the university. Her area of expertise is in business law, commercial law, corporate governance, social justice, supply chain management, entrepreneurship and women/gender issues. Her interest also lies in research and higher education development in emerging economies. She has published several articles, conference proceedings and book chapters in the area.

Rexford Attah-Boakye is an Associate Professor of Accounting at the University of Bradford. He is a qualified chartered accountant (ACCA), an associate member of the Institute of Credit Management (AICM), and a certified quantitative risk management expert (CQRM). His speciality is in financial accounting and reporting, auditing, and assurance, environmental accounting, accounting for cyber-security and artificial intelligence, corporate governance, taxation, and risk management. His research has appeared in the *British Journal of Management, International Journal of Finance & Economics, European Journal of Finance, Technological Forecasting and Social Change, IEEE Transactions on Engineering Management, Journal of Environmental Management*, etc.

Afia Nyarko Boakye is a lecturer of human resource management at Ghana Communication Technology University (GCTU). She holds a PhD in human resource management and has eight years of undergraduate and postgraduate teaching. Her research focuses on human resource planning, organizational behavior, leadership, graduate employability studies and gender-related issues. Apart from her academic background, she has been rendering valuable services to the university and the community on women empowerment, youth mentorship and gender advocacy. She has been researching with colleagues on issues related to organizational behavior, higher education, artificial intelligence, green human resources and gender.

Boakye Boampong is a lecturer in international business at the School of Management, University of Bradford, UK. Boakye's research interests include exploring the effects of project risk management on project success particularly in development project environments, stakeholder influence on project risk management, international business expansion and adaptiveness, strategic human resource management and sustainable development. He holds a PhD in development economics from the University of Bradford, an MSc in project planning and management, a PGCE in education, and a BSc (Hons) in land economy.

Emmanuel Kwaw Buah is currently pursuing a PhD in management at the University of Birmingham, United Kingdom. He holds an executive master of business administration (EMBA) in finance from the University of Ghana. Prior to this, he completed his undergraduate studies in geography and resource development at the University of Ghana. He has two decades of experience in finance, commodity trading, health insurance and liquid waste management within the economies of Ghana and Zimbabwe, where he held diverse roles.

Phabion Tichawona Chaza is a part-time research student with the School of Management at the University of Bradford, UK. Phabion is a chartered accountant with extensive management experience in the small and mid-sized business sector and is currently the managing director of a medium-sized logistics group operating in southern Africa. His research interests focus on the consequences of business failure on small to medium-sized businesses and their operators.

Joseph Kwadwo Danquah, PhD, is an assistant professor of human capital development, innovation and entrepreneurship. He holds a PhD in human resource development and a masters in human and organisational capacity for development, both from the University of Bradford–UK. Joseph is a fellow of the Higher Education Academy (HEA) and an academic member of the Chartered Institute of Personnel and Development (CIPD). He is a researcher and currently a lecturer in human resource management and human resource development at the School of Management, Law, and Social Sciences. His research interest focuses on human resource management/development, SME development, managerial effectiveness, innovation, entrepreneurship, and strategic human resource management.

Samuel Narh Dorhetso is a PhD candidate and an economics lecturer at the Accra Institute of Technology. He holds a BSc from the Kwame Nkrumah University of Science and Technology, an executive MBA from the University of Ghana Business School, a post graduate certificate (now MSc) in aeromechanical engineering from the Nigerian Air Force and certifications in aircraft and munitions maintenance from the United States Air Force. He was commissioned into the Ghana Air Force but voluntarily resigned at the rank of a flight lieutenant. He received the best paper award for the 11th Sustainable Education and Development Research Conference (SEDRC 2022).

Robert Kwame Dzogbenuku is a senior lecturer of marketing at Central University, Ghana. He holds an MPhil and MBA degrees in marketing from London Metropolitan University, United Kingdom (UK) and University of Cape Coast, Ghana, respectively, and is a qualified member of the Chartered Institute of Marketing, UK. Before becoming an academic, he spent a decade marketing and managing courier and insurance services in Ghana. Robert currently has 14 Scopus-ranked papers to his credit having published in leading journals like the *International Journal of Emerging Markets, Journal of Hospitality and Tourism Insights, Journal of Hospitality and Tourism Insight, Journal of International Consumer Marketing* and *Marketing Intelligence and Planning* among others. He has presented research papers at international conferences like the annual Academy of Marketing Conferences in the UK.

Antoinette Yaa Benewaa Gabrah is a PhD candidate of the University of Professional Studies Accra. She holds an MPhil in marketing from the University of Ghana. She is currently a faculty at Academic City University College in Accra Ghana. Antoinette has published in Scopus indexed journals. Her research interests include e-business, services marketing and digital marketing strategies.

Michael A. Gyensare, PhD, is a lecturer in management at the University of Kent, United Kingdom. Michael received his PhD in management from Edith Cowan University. His research straddles the divide between strategic HRM/OB and entrepreneurship. Michael's research has been published in leading journals such as the *Journal of Product Innovation Management*, *Journal of Business Research* and *Leadership and Organisation Development Journal*. He is currently an editorial board member for *Industrial and Commercial Training*.

Cai Jin is an international student at Durham University Business School. As a 2023 Laidlaw scholar, Cai combines academic research with practical experience in innovative corporations, fostering cross-cultural teamwork skills. Notably, Cai has assisted strategic advisories for Durham County and Pix Moving, a high-tech start-up in China. With a passion for consulting, Cai aspires to accumulate more experience in the consulting industry. As a promising scholar with a diverse background, Cai looks forward to making a meaningful impact in the business world.

Nomfundo Gladys Khoza is a lecturer at the Central University of Technology, Free State. She holds a master's degree graduate in Business Administration and is studying towards a PhD in entrepreneurship. She is an active member of the Ikudu-COIL project, which emphasizes nurturing innovation, global citizenship and leadership among university students. Her research interests lie in collaborative online internalization learning, digital transformation on SMEs, and online teaching and learning.

Ernest Kumi is a senior lecturer and the head of the Department of Marketing at Sunyani Technical University (STU). He earned both his master's and bachelor's degrees from the University of Ghana, Legon. He obtained his PhD in human resource management at the Kwame Nkrumah University of Science and Technology (KNUST). His research interests include career development, work and life integration, organizational behavior, labor force technology, entrepreneurship and human resource management. He has held a number of positions at STU, including head of the Department of Marketing (2016–2017) and director of the Brong Ahafo Research and Community Engagement Unit (BAREC) from 2017 to 2019.

Samuel Yaw Kusi (PhD, University of Vaasa) is an assistant professor in marketing at the Department of Marketing, Faculty of Management, Law, & Social Sciences, University of Bradford, United Kingdom. Samuel's research interest centers on international marketing, specifically on how internationalizing SMEs can enhance their financial performance by applying appropriate decision-making logic in their branding. Samuel has published his findings in prestigious academic journals including *International Business Review* and *Journal of World Business*, among others.

Mavis Serwah Benneh Mensah, PhD, is an associate professor of entrepreneurship and the founding director of the Centre for Entrepreneurship and Small Enterprise Development, University of Cape Coast, Ghana. She has over 19 years of entrepreneurship teaching and research experience. Her research interests include entrepreneurship and small enterprise development, especially in the areas of innovation, women's entrepreneurship, entrepreneurship education and the entrepreneurial university. She is a KAAD scholar and a recipient of research funding from the Association of African Universities and the Deutsche Gesellschaft für Technische Zusammenarbeit (GTZ) GmbH, now the Deutsche Gesellschaft für Internationales Zusammenarbeit (GIZ).

Michael Mensah is currently a PhD student at the University of Bradford–UK. He holds an MPhil in operations management from the University of Ghana Business School, a bachelor of law and international professional diploma in logistics and transport management from the Ghana Institute of Management and Public Administration and the Chartered Institute of Logistics and Transport–UK. Michael holds a bachelor of arts degree in geography and resource development from the University of Ghana and a diploma in communication studies from the Ghana Institute of Journalism. Michael is the immediate past municipal chief executive officer for Awutu/Senya East Municipal Assembly, Kasoa, Ghana.

Nosiphiwe Mgudlwa is a lecturer in the Department of Business Support Studies at the Central University of Technology, Free State. Mgudlwa holds a master's degree in business administration. Her research interests lie in finance and entrepreneurship, especially its application in small businesses, as well as educational technology. She is currently studying towards a PhD in entrepreneurship.

Gilbert Zana Naab holds a PhD in development economics from the University of Bradford. Dr Gilbert's PhD research focused on the design and implementation of financial services for poverty reduction. Gilbert is an assistant professor in international business at the School of Strategy and Leadership at Coventry University and was previously an associate lecturer at the University of Sunderland (London). Dr Naab has experience in banking, national, and international development, including previous projects with the United Nations Economic Commission for Africa (UNECA), the sub-regional office for Eastern Africa (Rwanda) and the African Union.

Rabake Nana joined Huddersfield Business School in January 2021 as a lecturer in the Department of Management. Prior to that, she was an associate lecturer from 2017 to 2020. Her background is in international business management, where she obtained her MSc degree as well as her PhD. Her thesis looked at corporate community involvement implementation of multinational corporations operating in least-developed countries.

Arinze Christian Nwoba (PhD, University of Leeds) is a lecturer (assistant professor) in marketing at Loughborough Business School, Loughborough University, Loughborough, United Kingdom. Arinze's research centers on international marketing and strategy, social marketing, entrepreneurship and social entrepreneurship, corporate sustainability and emerging markets phenomena. Arinze has published his research findings in the *European Journal of Marketing, International Marketing Review, Production, Planning & Control, Business Strategy and the Environment, Asia Pacific Journal of Management, Telematics* and *Informatics* amongst others.

Theresa Obuobisa-Darko heads the Department of Management Studies at the Ghana Communication Technology University. She holds a PhD in public administration and public policy from the University of Ghana. Theresa's research interest is in the field of human resource management, organizational development and public policy.

Samuel Amponsah Odei holds a doctorate degree in regional and public economics from the University of Pardubice in the Czech Republic. He currently works as a researcher at the Department of Economics at the University of Hradec Králové in the Czech Republic. He lectures the courses International Trade and International Economics. He actively engages in community services and is a member of the Regional Science Association International (RSAI). His research interests are centered on firm-level and territorial innovations, regional growth and development.

James Okrah is a highly skilled research engineer with a postgraduate research certificate in business economics from Ural Federal University. With extensive experience as a research assistant and intern, James has contributed to several publications in peer-reviewed journals, showcasing his expertise in research methodology and academic writing. His research interests focus on entrepreneurship and economic development, with a particular emphasis on exploring innovative ways to foster sustainable growth. As a current member of the research team at Ural Federal University, James is committed to advancing his field and contributing to the academic community through his research endeavors.

Dacosta Omari holds a PhD in management from Durham University Business School, UK. Prior to joining Durham University, Dacosta was a lecturer in the Department of Human Resource Management at the Central Business School (CBS), Central University in Ghana. He holds a master of philosophy (MPhil) in business administration (human resource management option) and a bachelor of arts in psychology with political science, all from the University of Ghana. Dacosta's research interests are in the areas of international human resource management, R&D investment, quality management, innovation management and SMEs.

Priscilla Ntriwaa Otuo is a lecturer in the Department of Marketing and Entrepreneurship at the University of Ghana Business School. She holds a PhD in marketing from the University of Hull, UK. Priscilla's research areas include portfolio entrepreneurship venture start-up and growth in developing economies.

Richard Plange-Rhule is pursuing a PhD in governance, public administration and policy at the Ghana Institute of Management and Public Administration (GIMPA) in Ghana. His expertise covers governance, public administration, strategy, policy and entrepreneurship. He is also the CEO of Datbreau Research Limited. His areas of research include strategy, innovation and business development with an emphasis on MSMEs, SMEs and MNCs.

Mark Kofi Prempeh is an assistant lecturer in statistics at Kumasi Technical University Ghana. Mark is also the head of biostatistics at Komfo Anokye Teaching Hospital, Kumasi Ghana. Mark is interested in research centered on emerging market firms and how they survive in business, considering the institutional voids in the environment.

Patient Rambe is a full professor of entrepreneurship and director of the Centre for Enterprise and Entrepreneurship Studies (CEES) in the Faculty of Management Sciences at the Central University of Technology, Free State. He holds a PhD in business management from the University of the Free State (South Africa) and another PhD in educational technology from the University of Cape Town (South Africa). His works appeared in the *Journal of Innovation and Entrepreneurship* (Springer), *International Journal of Management Education* (Elsevier), *European Journal of Innovation Management* (Emerald), *International Journal of Business and Globalisation* (Elsevier) and *Journal of Social Entrepreneurship* (Taylor and Francis).

William Yamoah is currently a second year PhD student in public administration and policy management at the University of Ghana Business School. He holds a master's in project management from Northeastern University, Boston, USA, and a bachelor of education from the University of Winneba, Ghana. He has over 20 years of working experience, holding managerial positions such as director of finance and administration at the New Patriotic Party Headquarters, deputy director, program manager, and instructor. William is keen to leverage his managerial skills and professional experiences to bring a desired outcome to his role.

Solomon Tawiah Yeboah is a senior lecturer, head of the Department of Entrepreneurship and Agribusiness at Cape Coast Technical University, and owner of Grodesol Group Limited, a small business management consulting firm. He was educated at the University of Ghana, Legon, graduating with a BSC in administration and marketing; an MBA in marketing from the University of Leicester, UK; a certificate in specialized plant and machinery operation and site safety awareness from the Construction Awards Alliance, UK; a professional certificate in IT principles; and a professional certificate in MS Word from Impact International College, Reading, UK; he is also a PhD scholar in management at the Crescent School of Business at the BSA Crescent Institute of Science and Technology, Chennai, India. His research interests include new venture creation, brand strategies, business sustainability and entrepreneurial marketing.

Nadia Zahoor is an associate professor at Queen Mary, University of London, UK. She completed her PhD in management at the University of Huddersfield, UK. Her research interests are strategic alliances, global strategy, innovation and organizational resilience. She is particularly interested in the context of small and medium-sized enterprises in emerging markets. Her research has been published in mainstream journals, including the *Journal of Product Innovation Management, British Journal of Management, International Marketing Review, Journal of Business Research, Business Strategy and the Environment, International Small Business Journal, International Journal of Management Reviews* and *International Business Review* among others. She is serving as a guest editor for the special issues at such leading journals as *R&D Management Journal, European Management Journal* and *International Studies of Management & Organization.*

Stakeholder Management and Entrepreneurship in Africa

An Introduction

Samuel Adomako, Michael Asiedu Gyensare and Mujtaba Ahsan

Africa, a continent of rich cultural diversity and untapped economic potential, stands at the crossroads of entrepreneurship and innovation. With its youthful population, emerging markets and growing middle class, Africa presents a unique landscape for entrepreneurial endeavors. From local startups addressing pressing social challenges to tech-driven enterprises with global ambitions, the entrepreneurial spirit in Africa is thriving. In this evolving ecosystem, effective stakeholder management is paramount. Entrepreneurs in Africa must navigate complex regulatory environments, engage with a diverse array of stakeholders and harness the continent's vast opportunities.

Undoubtedly, the African continent is home to some of the fastest-growing economies in the world (Brookings Institute, 2019), and it is conjectured to be the next frontier for growth and development. Furthermore, empirical evidence indicates that entrepreneurship plays an influential role in the economic growth of African countries (Adusei, 2016). However, African countries are fraught with weak institutional environments, and this heightens the adversity entrepreneurs face. The weak institutional environments create hurdles for firms engaging in entrepreneurial and innovation activities, which the entrepreneurs must overcome to achieve success (Ahsan et al., 2021; Adomako et al., 2021).

Stakeholder management and entrepreneurship in Africa is a critical and dynamic field of study that explores the intricate relationship between entrepreneurs and the diverse stakeholders they engage with on the African continent. This area of research delves into how entrepreneurs in Africa effectively navigate and engage with a wide range of stakeholders, including government bodies, local communities, investors, and customers, to drive business success and foster socioeconomic development. In an environment where entrepreneurship is often the driving force behind innovation, economic growth, and employment, effective stakeholder engagement becomes a linchpin for success. Entrepreneurs, whether they are tackling local issues or aiming for global markets, must navigate a complex web of relationships with stakeholders that can include governments, local communities, investors, and more. Understanding and managing these relationships is crucial for sustainable entrepreneurial ventures and ensuring that the benefits of entrepreneurship are shared

DOI: 10.4324/9781003256014-1

widely across Africa. In this context, exploring the dynamics of stakeholder management within the African entrepreneurial landscape is not only vital but also holds the potential to offer insights and lessons that can contribute to the broader global entrepreneurship literature.

The unique African context presents both opportunities and challenges for entrepreneurship, making this topic a pivotal area for understanding how stakeholder management strategies can lead to sustainable entrepreneurial ventures and inclusive growth across the continent. In the context of Africa, a diverse range of stakeholders such as employees, local communities, national or local government officials, politicians, chiefs, religious leaders, customers, nongovernment/nonprofit entities, civil society organizations, groups with special interests and suppliers are affected by or affect the actions of entrepreneurial firms. Two streams of research are especially pertinent for gaining deeper insights into stakeholder management in African countries. The first stream of research focuses on the actions entrepreneurs undertake in weak institutional environments to acquire necessary resources, reduce time to market, and establish venture legitimacy. For instance, strategic relationships with stakeholders such as politicians and government officials could provide access to valuable information and resources (Acquaah, 2007), enhance the firm's "speed to market" by reducing bureaucratic hurdles (Marquis & Raynard, 2015) and create favorable "rules of the game" (Brown & Huang, 2020), which could lead to competitive advantage. Likewise, astutely managing relationships with nongovernment organizations and local communities could bestow legitimacy to new ventures (Ritchie, 2016).

The second stream of research focuses on the well-being of the stakeholders. In contrast to the instrumental strand that treats stakeholders as "means to an end", the normative perspective adopts a moral and philosophical approach to stakeholder management (Reed, 2002) to ensure the well-being of stakeholders. For instance, firms could engage in practices that harm stakeholders under the guise of "promoting entrepreneurship" (Ahsan, 2020). Scholars suggest that entrepreneurship corrects such inequities existing in a society through "fundamental rearrangements in how resources and stakeholders are combined" (Venkataraman, 2002). However, this might not occur in weak institutional environments as such environments typically lack effective mechanisms to correct inequities and provide little protection to employees and local communities. Scholars suggest that engaging in deeper relationships with stakeholders, irrespective of the institutional requirements, could benefit both firms and stakeholders. For instance, focusing on employees' welfare in environments that have fewer constraints on hiring and firing can improve employees' satisfaction and firms' financial performance (Edmans et al., 2014). Likewise, Lumpkin and Bacq (2019) propose a *civic value-creation* framework that involves stakeholders in the value-creation process and leads to financial and nonfinancial benefits for them. These two streams provide rich opportunities for scholars to examine stakeholder management in the complex and heterogeneous African context (Amankwah-Amoah et al., 2019).

The aim of this book is to take stock of past research in the broad field of stakeholder management and entrepreneurship in context of Africa. This book also pushes a new agenda forward for an effective stakeholder engagement and management in entrepreneurial firms in Africa. This book provides a novel lens for entrepreneurs to manage stakeholders in Africa. It offers a better understanding of good practice in stakeholder engagement and management with major focus on entrepreneurial firms on the African continent. Issues discussed in this book include how external stakeholders such as government, non-governmental organizations, media, civil society organizations, and local institutions influence the core business operations of entrepreneurial firms in Africa. The book presents the central challenge of entrepreneurship by providing a comprehensive understanding of how entrepreneurs could identify, select, enroll and coordinate stakeholders. In addition, the book assesses issues such as stakeholder influence on corporate social strategy, sustainability and environmental management of entrepreneurial firms in Africa. This should be of interest to postgraduate students, researchers and public and private analysts.

Chapter Overviews

The book is structured into three comprehensive parts, each addressing distinct yet interrelated aspects of stakeholder management, entrepreneurship and their diverse dimensions:

Part I: Foundational Insights. In the initial part of the book, readers are provided with a holistic foundation in stakeholder management and entrepreneurship. It covers a wide spectrum of topics, offering a general overview of stakeholder management practices. The section delves into the intricate dynamics of stakeholder integration and its pivotal role in corporate entrepreneurship, firm innovation, and venture growth. Furthermore, it explores the critical balance between exploration and exploitation in new ventures, a key challenge for entrepreneurial endeavors. The discussion extends to the innovative resourcing strategies employed by small African firms and their deliberate use of financial bootstrapping as a cost-escalation strategy, providing a rich understanding of resource allocation in the African entrepreneurial landscape.

Part II: Gender, Sustainability, and Stakeholder Engagement. Part II hones in on the intersection of gender, sustainability, and stakeholder management. It encompasses a wide range of perspectives and issues. The section delves into the complexities of managing institutional stakeholders within the context of entrepreneurship. Additionally, it highlights the challenges and opportunities associated with female entrepreneurship, addressing gender disparities and offering insights into how they can be addressed. Cultural aspects come to the forefront in discussions about gender and stakeholder management, emphasizing the influence of cultural factors on entrepreneurial dynamics. The part also delves into the pressing concern of climate action in Africa, illustrating the critical role entrepreneurs play in sustainable development. Sustainable entrepreneurship is a central theme, exploring how entrepreneurs in Africa can balance economic growth with environmental responsibility.

Part III: Stakeholder Management, Strategies, and Entrepreneurship in Africa. The final part of the book takes a close look at best practices and specialized scenarios in stakeholder management. It presents strategies and insights for effective stakeholder engagement in early-stage ventures, illuminating the unique challenges and opportunities these ventures face. Strategies for managing stakeholders are a significant part of the entrepreneurial landscape, and these are discussed in the context of stakeholder management, providing guidance on maintaining harmonious relationships while navigating the complexities of strategic dynamics. Finally, the section addresses the inevitability of business failure and how proactive stakeholder management can mitigate its impact, emphasizing the importance of responsible entrepreneurship.

Acknowledgment

At Routledge, we want to thank **Kendrick Loo** and **Chelsea Low** for their support and understanding.

References

Acquaah, M. (2007). Managerial social capital, strategic orientation, and organizational performance in an emerging economy. *Strategic Management Journal*, *28*(12), 1235–1255.

Adomako, S., Ahsan, M., Amankwah-Amoah, J., Danso, A., Kesse, K., & Frimpong, K. (2021). Corruption and SME growth: The roles of institutional networking and financial slack. *Journal of Institutional Economics*, *17*(4), 607–624.

Adusei, M. (2016). Does entrepreneurship promote economic growth in Africa? *African Development Review*, *28*(2), 201–214.

Ahsan, M. (2020). Entrepreneurship and ethics in the sharing economy: A critical perspective. *Journal of Business Ethics*, *161*, 19–33.

Ahsan, M., Adomako, S., & Mole, K. (2021). Perceived institutional support and small venture performance: The mediating role of entrepreneurial persistence. *International Small Business Journal*, *39*(1), 18–39.

Amankwah-Amoah, J., Danso, A., & Adomako, S. (2019). Entrepreneurial orientation, environmental sustainability and new venture performance: Does stakeholder integration matter? *Business Strategy and the Environment*, *28*(1), 79–87.

Brookings Institute (2019). Spotlighting opportunities for business in Africa and strategies to succeed in the world's next big growth market. https://www.brookings.edu/research/spotlighting-opportunities-for-business-in-africa-and-strategies-to-succeed-in-the-worlds-next-big-growth-market/

Brown, J. R., & Huang, J. (2020). All the president's friends: Political access and firm value. *Journal of Financial Economics*, *138*(2), 415–431.

Edmans, A., Li, L., & Zhang, C. (2014). *Employee satisfaction, labor market flexibility, and stock returns around the world* (No. w20300). National Bureau of Economic Research. https://www.nber.org/system/files/working_papers/w20300/w20300.pdf

Lumpkin, G. T., & Bacq, S. (2019). Civic wealth creation: A new view of stakeholder engagement and societal impact. *Academy of Management Perspectives*, *33*(4), 383–404.

Marquis, C., & Raynard, M. (2015). Institutional strategies in emerging markets. *Academy of Management Annals*, *9*, 291–335.

Reed, D. (2002). Employing normative stakeholder theory in developing countries: A critical theory perspective. *Business & Society*, *41*(2), 166–207.

Ritchie, H. A. (2016). Unwrapping institutional change in fragile settings: Women entrepreneurs driving institutional pathways in Afghanistan. *World Development*, *83*, 39–53.

Venkataraman, S. (2002). Stakeholder value equilibration and the entrepreneurial process. *The Ruffin Series of the Society for Business Ethics*, *3*, 45–57.

Part I

Stakeholder Management, Innovation and Growth

1 Stakeholder Integration and Corporate Entrepreneurship

Antoinette Yaa Benewaa Gabrah, George Kofi Amoako and Emem Anwana

Introduction

Corporate entrepreneurship entails expanding a company's area of expertise and corresponding opportunities through fresh, in-house resource combinations (Licuanan et al., 2015). This suggests that innovative businesses can encourage profitable inventions by motivating staff to be innovative, risk-takers, and proactive by allowing them the autonomy and flexibility to explore their ideas devoid of bureaucratic lethargy. The corporate entrepreneurship literature shows that corporate entrepreneurship affects organizational performance and confers a competitive advantage (Martín-Rojas et al., 2011). Thus, corporate entrepreneurship has been emphasized as a management innovation process that could improve the strategies of entrepreneurial firms (Boukamcha, 2019; Nair, 2020).

Although the corporate entrepreneurship literature is growing with studies explaining both the antecedents and outcomes, we still do not know enough about how stakeholders affect the processes of corporate entrepreneurship in organizations. For example, relatively little is known about the effects of stakeholder theory on corporate entrepreneurship (Gómez-Haro et al., 2011). Additionally, despite the unique perspective of the stakeholder theory, previous studies on corporate entrepreneurship have mostly used institutional theory, resource-based view, contingency theory, agency theory, and exchange theory (Omotosho & Anyigba, 2019; Kassa & Tsigu, 2021). While the stakeholder theory assumes that the organization and the social environment are interdependent, it emphasizes the interdependence of a company's connections with its clients, partners, employees, and many other parties. Thus, there is a knowledge gap regarding the effective and efficient integration of stakeholders in corporate entrepreneurship. This stresses the necessity to look at how, according to stakeholder theory, stakeholder integration affects corporate entrepreneurship in entrepreneurial enterprises.

This study, therefore, examines the effect of stakeholder integration on corporate entrepreneurship. The work is essentially a nonempirical review of the literature with the development of a conceptual model that can be tested in future studies. The study proposes that stakeholder integration is a strategic

DOI: 10.4324/9781003256014-3

integration capability that makes corporate entrepreneurship successful. It adds that if strategic integration is taken seriously, then it could lead to sustainable competitive advantage and enhance innovation. The research unveils that stakeholder integration allows the entrepreneurial firm to gain legitimacy due to the confidence and trust it gains from relevant stakeholders. The findings of the study extend what is known about stakeholder theory by indicating that the interest and voices of all relevant stakeholders are important and should be integrated to help maintain and sustain corporate entrepreneurship. Furthermore, the findings of the study provide managers of entrepreneurial firms with a vital tool that would create and sustain their competitive edge and foster innovation in the current competitive business environment. The findings of the study provide managers of entrepreneurial firms the framework to encourage the participation and involvement of relevant stakeholders in both decision-making and operations of the firm. The study further portrays the relevance of stakeholder feedback and influence in ensuring effective corporate entrepreneurship.

Literature review

Stakeholder theory

Freeman proposed the stakeholder theory, which argues that a company has stakeholders or people and groups who have an interest in the success or failure of the company (Freeman, 2010). A management strategy known as "stakeholder theory" acknowledges that a company's success depends on the happiness of all of its stakeholders, not just its shareholders. Any organization or person that has the potential to influence or be influenced by a company's decisions is referred to as a stakeholder. Customers, employees, suppliers, shareholders, and the community are some of these stakeholders. According to the notion, a company's long-term viability depends on juggling the interests of all parties involved in a way that adds value to both the business and society at large (Valentinov & Hajdu, 2019). Stakeholder theory comes in a variety of forms, but there are three primary types in terms of theorizing about shareholders or stockholders. The traditional philosophy of corporate management states that a company's primary responsibility is to maximize shareholder value.

The three types of stakeholder theory are descriptive, instrumental, and normative (Donaldson & Preston, 1995). Stakeholder theory that is descriptive explains how businesses handle their connections with stakeholders. Instrumental stakeholder theory contends that considering the interests of multiple stakeholders can improve business performance and generate long-term value for shareholders, it notes that companies frequently consider the interests of multiple stakeholders rather than just shareholders. It implies that to accomplish their objectives, businesses should deliberately manage their relationships with stakeholders. Additionally, according to normative stakeholder theory, businesses are ethically required to consider the interests of all stakeholders, not only shareholders.

This study is underpinned by the assumptions of instrumental stakeholder theory. These presumptions include the following: stakeholder management is both a moral obligation and a business opportunity; companies can gain from considering the interests of all stakeholders rather than just shareholders; the company should have a well-defined process for identifying, evaluating, and managing their stakeholders; by strategically managing relationships with stakeholders, companies can achieve their objectives and produce long-term value for all parties involved.

Corporate entrepreneurship

Corporate entrepreneurship has grown in popularity over the past few decades in both the academic and professional worlds (Chebbi et al., 2020; Provasnek et al., 2017; Yunis et al., 2018). A rising number of researchers have drawn attention to the significance of corporate entrepreneurship in economic growth (Boukamcha, 2019; Chebbi et al., 2020). These earlier studies highlight how corporate entrepreneurship seeks to achieve sustainable competitiveness by encouraging innovation within businesses. It is significant to remember that corporate entrepreneurship lacks a generally acknowledged definition. Corporate entrepreneurship, according to earlier authors like Moriano et al. (2014), is an entrepreneurial approach that entails a series of actions taken to improve product innovation, risk-taking, and proactive reaction to both external and internal constraints (Boukamcha, 2019; Chebbi et al., 2020).

Dimensions of corporate entrepreneurship

CORPORATE VENTURING

Corporate venturing entails launching new enterprises within an existing one. Typically, it springs from fundamental expertise. It is pursuing and entering new markets or product lines that are connected to the company's existing offerings. By adapting the firm's products for current markets or developing new markets for current products, new activities are established within entrepreneurial enterprises that already exist (Boukamcha, 2019). The process of starting and growing new enterprises or ventures—whether through internal expansion or outside acquisition—is referred to in this dimension. In doing so, new company prospects, products or services, and business models can all be developed.

INNOVATION

Pinchot was the first to advocate for intrapreneurship (1985). This involves trying to apply the mindset and behavior that external entrepreneurs employ to start and grow their enterprises inside an already-existing, typically very large corporate environment. Intrapreneurs are the most interested in trying to instill some of these entrepreneurial characteristics into their culture to encourage innovation and uncover new market opportunities (Thornberry, 2003). The development of novel goods, services, and technology is innovation. It is seen as the creation of a fresh production process and the introduction of new, distinctive, and special goods into already existing or brand-new markets (Boukamcha, 2019). A crucial strategic element of business entrepreneurship is innovation (Goldsby et al., 2018). This parameter relates to the process of introducing new or enhanced goods, services, procedures, or business models. This can apply to both new and current firms and can encompass both gradual and dramatic innovation.

STRATEGIC RENEWAL

Strategic renewal emphasizes organizational change, reorganization, and strategy reformulation (Boukamcha, 2019). The entrepreneurial firm's strategic transformation, rejuvenation, or self-renewal are other terms for it. Such a transformation is built on fresh thinking and a strategy shift that incorporates the innovation and reinterpretation of business concepts (Boukamcha, 2019; Moriano et al., 2014). To respond to changes in the external environment, this component refers to the process of revitalizing the organization by implementing new strategies and business models. It requires the capacity to understand when a strategy or business model is no longer working and to create a replacement that is more compatible with the shifting external conditions.

Stakeholder integration

Stakeholder integration has received attention in recent times since integrating stakeholders in corporate decision-making is regarded as both ethical and necessary (Danso et al., 2020). Additionally, it is a priceless strategic asset that gives businesses a competitive edge. The capacity to create a productive collaborative relationship with a wide range of stakeholders is known as stakeholder integration. Both the normative approach and the instrumental approach of stakeholder theory are connected to this. Stakeholder management is a component of stakeholder integration, which is seen as a strategic competence. Stakeholder integration is a morally neutral practice (Danso et al., 2020; et al., 2010). Although Delgado-Ceballos et al. (2012) contend that it can be utilized to assist an employee's interests, stakeholder integration capability is typically used to the advantage of stakeholders.

Stakeholder integration capability and corporate entrepreneurship

The ability of an organization to effectively examine and include the viewpoints and interests of its stakeholders in decision-making processes is referred to as stakeholder integration capability. In numerous aspects, including access to resources, improved decision-making, higher stakeholder support, enhanced reputation, compliance with regulations, and long-term sustainability, this can promote corporate entrepreneurship as seen through the prism of stakeholder theory (Adams et al., 2022). The empirical data suggests that technological know-how and the ability to integrate stakeholders have a significant impact on corporate entrepreneurship. It indicates unequivocally that having the ability to absorb knowledge and advance technologically can lead to the creation of novel and sophisticated procedures that support business entrepreneurship. This goal enables the company to identify market opportunities and turn them into a competitive advantage. It stresses once more that corporate entrepreneurship does improve organizational performance by giving entrepreneurs the responsibility of using resources with the ability to create value more efficiently than rivals (Garcia-Sánchez et al., 2018).

Stakeholder involvement and corporate entrepreneurship

Stakeholder involvement is the process in which the concerns, needs, and values of the public are incorporated into decision-making (Belyaeva et al., 2020). Stakeholder involvement, according to the stakeholder theory, is the collection of interactions made with present or potential customers at various stages of the development process (Pellizzoni et al., 2020). The majority of these studies emphasize the central significance and function of stakeholder involvement as well as how to ensure there is the right level of stakeholder involvement. The literature appears to investigate stakeholder involvement and its relevance to enterprise governance (Larner & Mason, 2014; Fasna & Gunatilake, 2020) and education evaluation (Taut, 2008; Jacobson & Azzam, 2018). Stakeholders may help entrepreneurial enterprises and offer both implicit and explicit support. Therefore, to facilitate the entrepreneurial process and ensure effective corporate entrepreneurship, internal and external stakeholders must be involved (Alonso & Austin, 2018; Belyaeva et al., 2020). It is significant to note that the COVID-19 pandemic has highlighted the necessity of incorporating a wide range of stakeholders and allowing the integration of a large number of stakeholders. These parties contribute actively to integration (Belyaeva et al., 2020; Grunwald et al., 2021). Therefore, the greater the level of stakeholder involvement, the greater the degree of entrepreneurship and creativity, which contribute to the generation of new ideas and the resolution of issues. Consequently, it is accurate to state that corporate entrepreneurship performance is positively correlated with the effective participation of various stakeholders in the decision-making process (Fasna & Gunatilake, 2020). This enables the various stakeholders to pool their resources and expertise to develop ideas and discover answers (Belyaeva et al., 2020; Grunwald et al., 2021).

Stakeholder feedback and corporate entrepreneurship

Stakeholder feedback involves receiving feedback from people whose views are considered helpful and relevant. The degree to which an entrepreneurial firm asks for and includes stakeholder feedback in its decision-making processes is known as stakeholder feedback (Herremans et al., 2016). Stakeholder feedback requests improve the communication loop and highlight the contributions of other project participants. Stakeholder feedback requests demonstrate respect and a desire for improvement. It helps entrepreneurial businesses comprehend and address the requirements of their stakeholders better (Heavey et al., 2020; Mason, 2022). This can take the form of a survey, focus group, or suggestion boxes and hotlines. Firms need to have such systems in place to help collect, analyze, and act on the feedback received.

Stakeholder communications and corporate entrepreneurship

Stakeholder communication is the regular exchange of information between a company and its stakeholders. Therefore, it involves any engagement with pertinent groups, individuals, organizations, and processes. A critical component of ensuring the success of entrepreneurial enterprises is keeping stakeholders informed (Upham & Mills, 2005). Transparency and communication are essential components of stakeholder participation. Entrepreneurial businesses interact with a variety of stakeholders, including the government, suppliers, middlemen, and investors, to manage these relationships for both parties' advantage (Perrigot et al., 2012; Welch & Jackson, 2007). Up until recently, this communication was typically unidirectional or straightforward. When a business communicates with a stakeholder in a one-dimensional way, it does so to them rather than with them. The simple style of communication, on the other hand, suggests that the organization is at the center of the communication structure and communicates with stakeholders at the periphery, with little communication taking place across stakeholder groups. Based on the stakeholder theory, stakeholder communication is an important aspect of stakeholder integration as it enables the company to interact with stakeholders, understand their needs and interests, and manage their expectations. To effectively communicate with stakeholders, a company must engage in a variety of activities, including listening to stakeholders and asking for their feedback, sharing information about its plans and activities with stakeholders, conversing with stakeholders and addressing their concerns, sharing information about its performance and how it affects stakeholders, establishing trust and credibility with stakeholders, and providing forums for stakeholders to express their opinions and grievances. It needs to be well-planned as well (Scholes Clutterbuck, 1998).

Stakeholder influence and corporate entrepreneurship

Stakeholder influence refers to the extent to which stakeholders can influence the decisions and actions of the company. As it ensures that all stakeholders' perspectives and requirements are taken into account when making decisions that affect them, it is a crucial variable in stakeholder integration (Hörisch et al.,

2020). Stakeholder influence can take many different forms, such as direct influence, where stakeholders have a direct say in company decisions, such as through voting or board representation; indirect influence, where stakeholders provide feedback and input on company decisions but do not directly participate in the decision-making process; and pressure, which is when customers, shareholders, or other interested parties put pressure on a business through different tactics, like activism, boycotts, or social media campaigns; legal action, in which stakeholders use their political or economic clout to influence corporate choices; and lobbying, in which stakeholders the use of the legal system by stakeholders to sway corporate choices (Bourne & Walker, 2006; Frooman, 1999). Based on the stakeholder theory, this implies that stakeholder influence is important in ensuring that entrepreneurial firms' decisions consider the perspectives of all stakeholders and not just shareholders. Also, it aids in establishing trust and legitimacy among stakeholders, which can result in improved relationships and more effective stakeholder management. Further, it assists in making sure the business is open and responsible for the choices and actions it takes, which can improve its reputation and social license to operate. In addition, it contributes to ensuring that the business responds to the demands and worries of its stakeholders and that its activities are reasonable and fair (Ontita, & Kinyua, 2020). According to empirical data, stakeholder influence significantly affects stakeholders' expectations for project outcomes as well as the success or failure of the project as a whole (Bourne & Walker, 2005; de Bakker & den Hond, 2008). Therefore, this study proposes that stakeholder influence would positively affect corporate entrepreneurship among entrepreneurial firms.

Stakeholder representation and corporate entrepreneurship

Stakeholder representation is the extent to which different stakeholder groups are represented in the decision-making process of the company. Shareholder representation is critical to ensuring effective corporate entrepreneurship irrespective of the form of corporate entrepreneurship. Based on the instrumental value of engaging stakeholders, a problem can be solved by utilizing a variety of perspectives and skills. It is crucial to remember that having an accurate and suitable representation of stakeholders does not come without difficulties and disagreements from academics and practitioners alike (Mertens, 2008). To support innovation, it is crucial to comprehend how different stakeholders collectively express themselves (Berg et al., 2018). It is crucial to note that the literature contends that having a strategic representation of stakeholders, as opposed to one that is comprehensive, is preferable given their relative levels of interest, influence, and benefit (Reed et al., 2018) although authors Like Selin, Schuett, and Carr (2000), who dispute this claim. Selin et al. (2000) maintain, however, that a broad representation of stakeholders and the leadership's readiness to compromise both positively predict the achievement of the result. To encourage corporate entrepreneurship, there shouldn't be any indication of stakeholder representation surpluses or deficits (Schubert & Willems, 2021). Therefore, to improve collaborative endeavors, entrepreneurial enterprises must work together by developing agreements with effective stakeholder representation. Stakeholder interaction, advisory committee participation, and board representation are examples of this. Based on this, the study conceptualizes that a balanced stakeholder representation will enhance corporate entrepreneurship among entrepreneurial firms.

Stakeholder integration in decision-making

Stakeholder integration in decision-making is a critical component of the success of the innovation process of entrepreneurial firms. It is important to consider all relevant stakeholders when making decisions (Garcia-Sánchez et al., 2018). This is because connecting with and including many stakeholders in an entrepreneurial firm's decision-making process can strengthen the entrepreneurial process. Thus, this acts as a means of establishing and maintaining legitimacy (Adomako et al., 2019). Stakeholder integration is a significant dependent factor when it comes to the relationship between entrepreneurial orientation and new venture performance, according to Amankwah-Amoah et al. (2019). They stress that a stronger level of stakeholder integration strengthens a relationship like this. This reinforces the argument that stakeholder integration capability strongly improves corporate entrepreneurship among entrepreneurial firms (Figure 1.1).

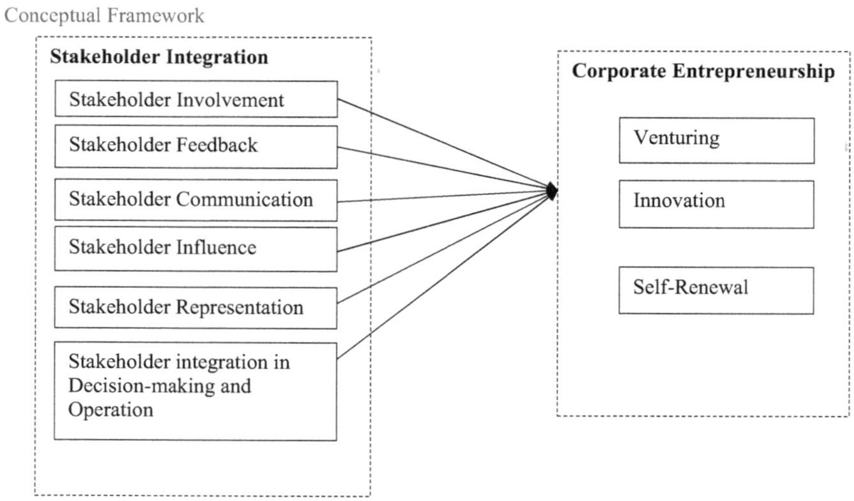

Figure 1.1 A Proposed Conceptual Model.

Implications

First, one of the key implications of stakeholder integration capability on corporate entrepreneurship is for entrepreneurial firms to employ a more participatory approach to decision-making. First, one of the major effects of the ability to integrate stakeholder perspectives on corporate entrepreneurship is that it encourages entrepreneurial firms to use a more participatory style of decision-making. This suggests that stakeholders should actively participate in the decision-making process and that it should not just be a process; it should also consider their opinions or viewpoints. This will assist businesses in locating new business opportunities and creating more creative solutions that, in the long run, can contribute to profitably meeting societal requirements (Ziyae & Sadeghi, 2021). The interests of all key stakeholders should be considered and balanced, hence entrepreneurial enterprises should adopt a stakeholder management approach. This strategy ought to be chosen above the shareholder primacy strategy, which acknowledges that shareholders' interests come first. With a key focus on stakeholders including customers, suppliers, employees, the community, and regulators, this strategy will help entrepreneurial enterprises maintain and sustain corporate entrepreneurship. The relationship between stakeholder integration capability and corporate entrepreneurship also suggests that to achieve sustainability, entrepreneurial firms should adopt a stakeholder management strategy that considers and balances the interests of all stakeholders as well as a participatory approach to decision-making (Spitzeck et al., 2013). This is to say that the main implications of stakeholder integration capability on corporate entrepreneurship are related to how entrepreneurial firms balance the competing interests of different stakeholders to achieve long-term success and sustainability.

The key managerial implications of this research are as follows, First, to build stakeholder networks, it is critical to build and maintain relationships with key stakeholders like employees, customers, suppliers, and regulators. Entrepreneurial enterprises should develop trust with stakeholders to the point that they can be seen as being transparent and honest in their communication as well as in keeping their commitments because these networks are essential to the sustainability of the company. Through mutual respect and understanding, they will be better able to obtain the information and resources they need to seek new business prospects (Ayuso et al., 2006; Han & Park, 2017). Again, partnerships can be used to accomplish this. Second, it follows that entrepreneurial businesses must create a stakeholder management plan. Therefore, entrepreneurial businesses must create and implement a thorough stakeholder management strategy (Jahanshahi et al., 2018). This should spell out how they'll interact with and consider the opinions of all stakeholders. Stakeholder participation typically takes the form of ongoing meetings, questionnaires, or focus groups.

Another key implication is to encourage employee participation. Practices for increasing employee involvement and participation include (1) direct downward communication (newsletters, emails, intranet, and noticeboards); (2) direct two-way communication (team briefings, workplace meetings, staff newsletters, and information cascading via the management team); (3) direct upward feedback (problem-solving groups and suggestion schemes); and (4) direct financial participation (profit-related bonus schemes, deferred profit-sharing schemes, and employee stock options) (Aliyu, 2019). Since employees are likely to provide valuable insights and perspectives on new business prospects, entrepreneurial enterprises should ensure all these employee procedures are present and are properly followed to help employees actively engage in the decision-making process.

One important implication is the necessity of incorporating stakeholder feedback. Stakeholder feedback is a vital tool for getting input from people whose opinions are seen as useful and pertinent. Whenever such feedback is requested, it improves the communication loop and shows that other people's opinions are highly valued. Therefore, entrepreneurial businesses should constantly ask stakeholders for their opinions and take such opinions into account when making decisions. To do this, it is necessary to recognize fresh business prospects and create more creative solutions with major performance ramifications.

Again, the key implication is the need to monitor and measure performance in terms of stakeholder integration, as well as assess the impacts of its actions on stakeholders. To find opportunities for improvement and to make sure they are successfully integrating the viewpoints and interests of all stakeholders, entrepreneurial firms should monitor and measure performance in terms of stakeholder integration. In addition, entrepreneurial enterprises should embrace policies and practices that support and encourage the inclusion of environmental, social, and governance factors in the decision-making process. These steps will improve the company's reputation and image, attracting more new clients, workers, and partners while retaining current clients, workers, and partners. This study's implications regarding the relationship between strategic integration capability and venture capital, innovation, and strategic transformation encourage entrepreneurial firms to engage stakeholders like employees and other pertinent stakeholders in the formulation of strategic collective visions to inspire them to launch new internal innovative projects (Boukamcha, 2019).

Conclusion, limitations, and future research

These propositions should be tested empirically since this research is purely conceptual. The literature suggests stakeholder integration impacts corporate entrepreneurship significantly. Entrepreneurial firms must therefore focus on integrating stakeholders into their decision-making, operations, and other activities to ensure the success of their business innovation both in the short and long term. All stakeholders should be represented, and their feedback is taken into consideration to enhance the entrepreneurial process. Sense of ownership must be encouraged among stakeholders. Research should be expanded on the various components of stakeholder integration, stakeholder integration capability, and the various dimensions of corporate entrepreneurship. This study concludes that stakeholders' value in enhancing entrepreneurial goals among entrepreneurial firms cannot be overemphasized.

References

Adams, D., Adams, K., Attah-Boakye, R., Ullah, S., Rodgers, W., & Kimani, D. 2022. Social and environmental practices and corporate financial performance of multinational corporations in emerging markets: Evidence from 20 oil-rich African countries. *Resources Policy*, *78*, 102756.

Adomako, S., Amankwah-Amoah, J., & Danso, A. 2019. The effects of stakeholder integration on firm-level product innovativeness: Insights from small and medium-sized enterprises in Ghana. *R & D Management*, *49*(5), 734–747.

Aliyu, A. U. L. 2019. Effect of employee participation in decision making in organization performance. *International Journal of Economics and Business*, *3*(2), 255–259.

Alonso, D. A., & Austin, I. P. 2018. Entrepreneurial CSR, managerial role and firm resources: a case study approach. *Competitiveness Review: An International Business Journal*, *28*(4), 368–385.

Amankwah-Amoah, J., Danso, A., & Adomako, S. 2019. Entrepreneurial orientation, environmental sustainability and new venture performance: Does stakeholder integration matter? *Business Strategy and the Environment*, *28*(1), 79–87.

Ayuso, S., Rodríguez, M. Á., & Ricart, J. E. 2006. Using stakeholder dialogue as a source for new ideas: A dynamic capability underlying sustainable innovation. *Corporate Governance: The International Journal of Business in Society*, *6*(4), 475–490.

Belyaeva, Z., Shams, S. R., Santoro, G., & Grandhi, B. 2020. Unpacking stakeholder relationship management in the public and private sectors: The comparative insights. *EuroMed Journal of Business*, *15*(3), 269–281.

Berg, S., Cloutier, L. M., & Bröring, S. 2018. Collective stakeholder representations and perceptions of drivers of novel biomass-based value chains. *Journal of Cleaner Production*, *200*, 231–241.

Boukamcha, F. 2019. The effect of transformational leadership on corporate entrepreneurship in Tunisian SMEs. *Leadership and Organization Development Journal*, *40*(3), 286–304.

Bourne, L., & Walker, D. H. 2005. Visualising and mapping stakeholder influence. *Management Decision*, *43*(5), 649–660.

Bourne, L., & Walker, D. H. 2006. Visualizing stakeholder influence—Two Australian examples. *Project Management Journal*, *37*(1), 5–21.

Chebbi, H., Yahiaoui, D., Sellami, M., Papasolomou, I., & Melanthiou, Y. 2020. Focusing on internal stakeholders to enable the implementation of organizational change towards corporate entrepreneurship: A case study from France. *Journal of Business Research*, *119*, 209–217.

Danso, A., Adomako, S., Lartey, T., Amankwah-Amoah, J., & Owusu-Yirenkyi, D. 2020. Stakeholder integration, environmental sustainability orientation and financial performance. *Journal of Business Research*, *119*, 652–662.

de Bakker, F. G., & den Hond, F. 2008. Introducing the politics of stakeholder influence: A review essay. *Business & Society*, *47*(1), 8–20.

Delgado-Ceballos, J., Aragón-Correa, J. A., Ortiz-de-Mandojana, N., & Rueda-Manzanares, A. 2012. The effect of internal barriers on the connection between stakeholder integration and proactive environmental strategies. *Journal of Business Ethics*, *107*, 281–293.

Donaldson, T., & Preston, L. E. 1995. The stakeholder theory of the corporation: Concepts, evidence, and implications. *Academy of Management Review*, *20*(1), 65–91.

Fasna, M. F. F., & Gunatilake, S. 2020. Involvement of stakeholders in the adoption and implementation of energy retrofits in hotel buildings. *International Journal of Energy Sector Management*, *14*(6), 1239–1253.

Freeman, R. E. 2010. *Strategic Management: A Stakeholder Approach*. Cambridge University Press.

Frooman, J. 1999. Stakeholder influence strategies. *Academy of Management Review*, *24*(2), 191–205.

García-Sánchez, E., García-Morales, V. J., & Martín-Rojas, R. 2018. Analysis of the influence of the environment, stakeholder integration capability, absorptive capacity, and technological skills on organizational performance through corporate entrepreneurship. *International Entrepreneurship and Management Journal*, *14*, 345–377.

Goldsby, M. G., Kuratko, D. F., Bishop, J. W., Kreiser, P. M., & Hornsby, J. S. 2018. Social proactiveness and innovation: The impact of stakeholder salience on corporate entrepreneurship. *Journal of Small Business Strategy*, *28*(2), 1–15.

Gomez-Haro, S., Aragon-Correa, J., & Cordón-Pozo, E. 2011. Differentiating the effects of the institutional environment on corporate entrepreneurship. *Management Decision*, *49*(10), 1677–1693.

Grunwald, G., Schwill, J., & Sassenberg, A. M. 2021. Sustainability project partnerships in times of crisis: Conceptual framework and implications for stakeholder integration. *Journal of Entrepreneurship and Public Policy*, *10*(3), 352–378.

Han, J., & Park, C. M. 2017. Case study on the adoption of new technology for innovation: Perspective of institutional and corporate entrepreneurship. *Asia Pacific Journal of Innovation and Entrepreneurship*, *11*(2), 144–158.

Heavey, C., Simsek, Z., Kyprianou, C., & Risius, M. 2020. How do strategic leaders engage with social media? A theoretical framework for research and practice. *Strategic Management Journal*, *41*(8), 1490–1527.

Herremans, I. M., Nazari, J. A., & Mahmoudian, F. 2016. Stakeholder relationships, engagement, and sustainability reporting. *Journal of Business Ethics*, *138*, 417–435.

Hörisch, J., Wulfsberg, I., & Schaltegger, S. 2020. The influence of feedback and awareness of consequences on the development of corporate sustainability action over time. *Business Strategy and the Environment*, *29*(2), 638–650.

Jacobson, M. R., & Azzam, T. 2018. The effects of stakeholder involvement on perceptions of an evaluation's credibility. *Evaluation and Program Planning*, *68*, 64–73.

Jahanshahi, A. A., Nawaser, K., & Brem, A. 2018. Corporate entrepreneurship strategy: An analysis of top management teams in SMEs. *Baltic Journal of Management*, *13*(4), 528–543.

Kassa, A. G., & Tsigu, G. T. 2021. Corporate entrepreneurship, employee engagement and innovation: A resource-based view and a social exchange theory perspective. *International Journal of Organizational Analysis*, (ahead-of-print).

Larner, J., & Mason, C. 2014. Beyond box-ticking: A study of stakeholder involvement in social enterprise governance. *Corporate Governance*, *14*(2), 181–196.

Licuanan, V. S., Sengupta, K., & Neelankavil, J. P. 2015. Entrepreneurship and innovation initiatives among Asian multinationals: A cross-country analysis. *International Journal of Commerce and Management*, *25*(1), 67–83.

Martín-Rojas, R., García-Morales, V. J., & García-Sánchez, E. 2011. The influence on corporate entrepreneurship of technological variables. *Industrial Management & Data Systems*, *111*(7), 984–1005.

Mason, S. 2022. Disempowerment evaluation and the risks of avoiding stakeholder feedback. *Counseling Outcome Research and Evaluation*, *13*(1), 3–11.

Mertens, D. M. 2008. Stakeholder representation in culturally complex communities. In N. L. Smith & P. R. Brandon (Eds.), *Fundamental Issues in Evaluation* (pp. 41–60). The Guilford Press.

Moriano, J. A., Molero, F., Topa, G., & Lévy Mangin, J. P. 2014. The influence of transformational leadership and organizational identification on intrapreneurship. *International Entrepreneurship and Management Journal*, *10*, 103–119.

Nair, S. R. 2020. The link between women entrepreneurship, innovation and stakeholder engagement: A review. *Journal of Business Research*, *119*, 283–290.

Omotosho, S. I., & Anyigba, H. 2019. Conceptualising corporate entrepreneurial strategy: A contingency and agency collaborative approach. *Journal of Strategy and Management*, *12*(2), 256–274.

Ontita, J., & Kinyua, G. M. 2020. Role of stakeholder management on firm performance: An empirical analysis of commercial banks in Nairobi City County, Kenya. *Journal of Business and Economic Development*, *5*(1), 26–35.

Pellizzoni, E., Trabucchi, D., Frattini, F., Buganza, T., & Di Benedetto, A. 2020. Leveraging stakeholders' knowledge in new service development: A dynamic approach. *Journal of Knowledge Management*, *24*(2), 415–438.

Perrigot, R., Kacker, M., Basset, G., & Cliquet, G. 2012. Antecedents of early adoption and use of social media networks for stakeholder communications: Evidence from franchising. *Journal of Small Business Management*, *50*(4), 539–565.

Pinchot III, G. 1985. Intrapreneuring: Why you don't have to leave the corporation to become an entrepreneur. *University of Illinois at Urbana-Champaign's Academy for Entrepreneurial Leadership Historical Research Reference in Entrepreneurship.*

Plaza-Úbeda, J. A., de Burgos-Jiménez, J., & Carmona-Moreno, E. 2010. Measuring stakeholder integration: Knowledge, interaction and adaptational behaviour dimensions. *Journal of Business Ethics*, *93*, 419–442.

Provasnek, A. K., Schmid, E., Geissler, B., & Steiner, G. 2017. Sustainable corporate entrepreneurship: Performance and strategies toward innovation. *Business Strategy and the Environment*, *26*(4), 521–535.

Reed, M. S., Vella, S., Challies, E., De Vente, J., Frewer, L., Hohenwallner-Ries, D., & van Delden, H. 2018. A theory of participation: What makes stakeholder and public engagement in environmental management work? *Restoration Ecology*, *26*, S7–S17.

Scholes, E., & Clutterbuck, D. 1998. Communication with stakeholders: An integrated approach. *Long Range Planning*, *31*(2), 227–238.

Schubert, P., & Willems, J. 2021. In the name of the stakeholder: An assessment of representation surpluses and deficits by nonprofit leaders. *Nonprofit Management and Leadership*, *31*(4), 639–664.

Selin, S. W., Schuett, M. A., & Carr, D. 2000. Modeling stakeholder perceptions of collaborative initiative effectiveness. *Society & Natural Resources*, *13*(8), 735–745.

Spitzeck, H., Boechat, C., & Leão, S. F. 2013. Sustainability as a driver for innovation-towards a model of corporate social entrepreneurship at Odebrecht in Brazil. *Corporate Governance: International Journal of Business in Society*, *13*(5), 613–625.

Taut, S. 2008. What have we learned about stakeholder involvement in program evaluation? *Studies in Educational Evaluation*, *34*(4), 224–230.

Thornberry, N. E. 2003. Corporate entrepreneurship: Teaching managers to be entrepreneurs. *Journal of Management Development*, *22*(4), 329–344.

Upham, P. J., & Mills, J. N. 2005. Environmental and operational sustainability of airports: Core indicators and stakeholder communication. *Benchmarking: An International Journal*, *12*(2), 166–179.

Valentinov, V., & Hajdu, A. 2019. Integrating instrumental and normative stakeholder theories: A systems theory approach. *Journal of Organizational Change Management*, *34*(4), 699–712.

Welch, M., & Jackson, P. R. 2007. Rethinking internal communication: A stakeholder approach. *Corporate Communications: An International Journal*, *12*(2), 177–198.

Yunis, M., Tarhini, A., & Kassar, A. 2018. The role of ICT and innovation in enhancing organizational performance: The catalysing effect of corporate entrepreneurship. *Journal of Business Research*, *88*, 344–356.

Ziyae, B., Sadeghi, H., Nejad, M. S., & Tajpour, M. 2021. A framework of urban entrepreneurship for women breadwinners. *Foresight*, *23*(5), 597–609.

2 How Stakeholder Management Influences Firm Innovation

Samuel Amponsah Odei and James Okrah

Introduction

The effective implementation of innovation is widely considered a vital determinant of long-term success and competitive advantage for firms (Alegre & Chiva, 2013; Damanpour, 2014). Innovation refers to the creation and implementation of new ideas or improvements in existing products, processes, or services leading to improved profitability and customer satisfaction (Kline & Rosenberg, 2009). Several models have been proposed to enhance innovation, one of the models is the open innovation model which requires firms to collaborate with other stakeholders for successful innovations (Chesbrough, 2012; Gassmann et al., 2010). According to the open innovation model, achieving and sustaining innovation necessitates firms to manage an array of stakeholders who are integral to the process, including customers, suppliers, employees, and partners (Kazadi et al., 2016). Stakeholders comprise individuals or groups that have interests or stakes in an organization, including employees, clients, suppliers, regulators, shareholders, knowledge repositories, and communities (Freeman, 2010). Stakeholder management has been acknowledged as a crucial aspect of innovation management for organizations. Organizations that can effectively and efficiently manage their stakeholders are more likely to achieve innovation success. Scholars have identified three key ways in which effective stakeholder management can influence firms' innovation outcomes: resource provision, shaping the innovation agenda, and alleviating risks (Leonidou et al., 2020).

Stakeholder management is a significant component in the innovation process as well as in firms' strategy. Despite the growing importance of stakeholder management, limited studies have empirically examined the influence of stakeholder relationship capability on firm innovation, especially in Africa. The focus of this chapter is, therefore, to contribute to a further understanding of how stakeholder relational capability relates to firm innovation by reviewing extant literature. This literature review aims to examine how stakeholder management influences firms' innovation, with a focus on the role of different stakeholder groups in driving or hindering innovation. To accomplish this objective, this review is structured as follows: First, we highlight the

DOI: 10.4324/9781003256014-4

stakeholder theory of organizations. Second, we examine the linkage between stakeholder management and how it influences firms' innovations. Third, we review the various ways various stakeholders contribute to innovation. Fourth, we review the various challenges and strategies in stakeholder management for successful innovation. Fifth, we examine the future directions and implications. In the conclusion section, we highlight areas of consensus and contention on the potential for leveraging stakeholder management to boost innovation within African firms.

Overview of stakeholder management

Stakeholder management is a critical factor in achieving organizational success. It involves a systematic approach to identifying, analyzing, and engaging individuals or groups who possess a vested interest or influence in the organization's activities, decisions, and outcomes (Freeman and Evan, 1990; De Colle, 2005). According to Haefner, Palmié, and Leppänen (2023), two streams of literature explain the relationship between stakeholder management and innovation. The first stream is of the view that both stakeholder management and innovation are substitutes as they are both ways for firms to achieve differentiation (see, for instance, Garcia-Castro & Francoeur, 2016). The second stream sees a complementarity between stakeholder management and innovation. According to these scholars, stakeholder management offers vital advantages that allow firms to reap benefits from their innovation activities. Stakeholder management enables businesses to build trustworthy relationships with a range of partners based on distributive, procedural, and interactional justice based on obligations and reciprocity (Flammer & Kacperczyk, 2016).

The significance of stakeholder management in organizational contexts is widely recognized. Freeman (1984) emphasised the active management of stakeholder relationships to create value and achieve long-term success. Mitchell et al. (1997) proposed a framework for stakeholder identification and salience, highlighting the importance of recognizing key stakeholders who wield substantial influence on the organization. This framework provides a systematic approach to identifying and engaging with stakeholders who have the greatest impact. Clarkson (1995) argued that organizations should consider the interests and expectations of various stakeholders and manage their relationships ethically and responsibly. Effective stakeholder management is seen as a means to improve corporate social performance, ensuring that organizations not only pursue financial gains but also fulfill their responsibilities to society and the environment. By engaging with stakeholders and considering their perspectives, organizations can make informed decisions that address the interests and concerns of all relevant stakeholders.

Effective stakeholder management involves applying key principles and strategies supported by the literature. These principles and strategies enable organizations to manage stakeholders effectively, establish positive relationships, and align stakeholder interests with organizational goals. One important principle is stakeholder identification and analysis (Mitchell et al., 1997). It emphasizes identifying and prioritizing key stakeholders based on their significance, influence, and potential impact. The corresponding strategy involves conducting stakeholder mapping and analysis to understand their needs, expectations, and concerns.

Another principle is proactive engagement, which focuses on actively engaging with stakeholders to build relationships, gain insights, and understand their perspectives (Freeman, 1984). This is achieved through various communication channels and platforms, involving stakeholders in decision-making, providing regular updates, and seeking feedback.

Collaboration and partnerships is a principle that highlights the importance of fostering collaborative relationships and partnerships with stakeholders (Selsky & Parker, 2005). This helps create shared value and achieve common goals. The strategy involves establishing strategic alliances, joint initiatives, or partnerships to leverage resources, knowledge, and expertise.

Transparent communication (Boutilier & Thomson, 2011) is another crucial principle. It emphasizes the need to maintain open and transparent communication with stakeholders to build trust, manage expectations, and ensure information sharing. Timely and accurate information provision, addressing concerns and feedback openly, and maintaining consistent messaging are part of the strategy.

Conflict resolution addresses the effective management of conflicts and stakeholder disagreements (Freeman et al., 2007). This principle aims to maintain positive relationships and promote collaboration. Implementing conflict resolution mechanisms, such as negotiation, mediation, or arbitration, helps find mutually beneficial solutions. Ethical and social responsibility is a principle that urges organizations to consider the ethical implications of decisions and actions on stakeholders and society as a whole (Donaldson & Preston, 1995). Integrating ethical considerations and social responsibility into organizational practices, policies, and decision-making processes is the strategy associated with this principle.

Understanding firm-level innovation

Firm-level innovation refers to the ability of a company or organization to introduce new or significantly improved products, processes, services, or business models to the market (Dodgson et al., 2008). It involves the generation, development, and implementation of new ideas or concepts that lead to increased competitiveness, growth, and value creation (Damanpour, 2014). Firm innovation is crucial for organizations to adapt to changing market conditions, stay ahead of competitors, and sustain long-term success (Tidd et al., 2005). Several different forms of firm innovation have been identified and studied in the literature (Dodgson et al., 2008). These forms can be categorized into two broad categories: technological innovation and nontechnological innovation.

- *Technological innovation*: Technological innovation refers to the development and application of new technologies or scientific knowledge to create new products, processes, or services (Tidd et al., 2005). It involves advancements in the physical or technical aspects of a firm's offerings. Some forms of technological innovation include product innovation, process innovation, and service innovation
- Nontechnological innovation: Nontechnological innovation refers to innovation that is not directly related to technological advancements but involves other aspects of the firm's operations (Damanpour, 2014). It encompasses organizational, managerial, marketing, and other strategic innovations. Some forms of nontechnological innovation include organizational innovation, marketing innovation, and strategic innovation. Innovation is essential for driving organizational growth and long-term success. It enables companies to maintain a competitive edge, expand into new markets, improve efficiency and productivity, adapt to changing market conditions, and achieve sustainable growth (Tidd et al., 2005). Continuous innovation allows organizations to differentiate themselves from competitors by introducing new products, services, or business models; attracting customers; and capturing market share. Through innovation, companies can penetrate new markets, diversify their offerings, and expand their customer base. By implementing innovative solutions and processes, organizations can enhance efficiency, reduce costs, and improve productivity (Tidd et al., 2005). Innovation also enables companies to proactively respond to changes in customer preferences, emerging technologies, and regulatory requirements, ensuring their relevance and adaptability. By fostering a culture of continuous improvement and exploration, companies embracing innovation as a core value are better positioned to identify new growth opportunities, adapt to disruptions, and stay ahead of the competition.
- External influences: Understanding market trends, customer needs, and preferences is essential for driving innovation. Companies actively engaging with customers, collecting feedback, and conducting market research are better equipped to develop innovative solutions that meet customer demands (Tellis et al., 2009).
- Collaboration and partnerships: Collaboration with external partners such as suppliers, customers, research institutions, and other firms facilitates knowledge sharing, resource access, and joint innovation efforts. Leveraging external expertise through open innovation strategies enhances a firm's innovation capabilities (Chesbrough, 2003).

Stakeholder management and firm-level Innovation

Stakeholder management has been acknowledged as an essential aspect of innovation management for organizations. Stakeholder engagement and idea generation are essential in fostering innovation within organizations. Firms that are able to effectively manage their stakeholders are more likely to achieve success in innovation performance. Engaging stakeholders, such as employees, customers, suppliers, and communities, allows firms to tap into their knowledge, expertise, and perspectives, thus fostering the development of innovative ideas (Chesbrough, 2003).

Effective stakeholder management ensures resource provision and support critical for innovation. This includes access to financial capital, expertise, and technology. Engaged stakeholders can provide financial support, collaboration opportunities, and other resources necessary for implementing innovative ideas (López-Gamero et al., 2011).

Stakeholder management facilitates collaboration and co-creation between firms and stakeholders. Collaborative relationships enable joint innovation efforts, where multiple parties work together to develop innovative solutions. By leveraging stakeholder involvement, firms benefit from diverse perspectives and collective intelligence (Chesbrough, 2003). Furthermore, engaging stakeholders allows firms to gather valuable feedback on innovative ideas, products, or services. Stakeholder feedback provides insights into market needs, preferences, and trends, informing the direction of innovation efforts. Incorporating stakeholder feedback enhances market orientation and increases the likelihood of successful innovation outcomes (Ganesh et al., 2014).

In summary, effective stakeholder management plays a vital role in promoting firm innovation. It enhances innovation outcomes by fostering idea generation, providing necessary resources and support, facilitating collaboration and co-creation, incorporating stakeholder feedback for market orientation, and mitigating risks associated with innovation. By effectively managing stakeholders, firms create an environment conducive to innovation, increasing the chances of successful innovation outcomes (Figure 2.1) (Freeman et al., 2007; López-Gamero et al., 2011).

In the innovation triangle, the relationship between stakeholders, firm culture, and innovation is depicted, along with the influence of the external environment. "Firm culture" represents the shared values, beliefs, norms, and behaviors within the organization. Firm culture plays a significant role in shaping how innovation is perceived, encouraged, and implemented within the firm (Barney, 1986). The arrow pointing from firm culture to firm innovation indicates that the organization's culture has a direct influence on its ability to

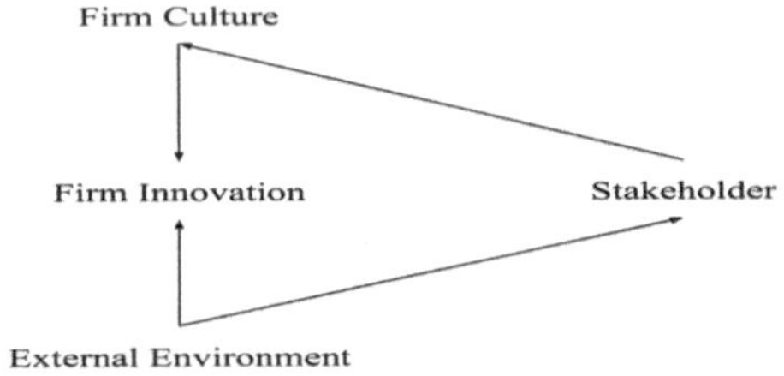

Figure 2.1 The Innovation Triangle.

Source: Authors' elaboration.

innovate (Amabile, 1998). A culture that values creativity, risk-taking, learning, collaboration, and adaptability is more likely to foster innovation and support the development and implementation of new ideas and solutions (Brown & Duguid, 1991).

"Stakeholders" represent the various individuals, groups, or organizations that have an interest in or influence in the firm's activities and outcomes. Stakeholders can include customers, employees, investors, suppliers, government agencies, local communities, and more (Freeman, 1984). The arrow pointing from stakeholders to firm culture represents how stakeholders can shape and influence the organization's culture (Ravasi & Schultz, 2006). Stakeholders' expectations, demands, and feedback can drive changes in the firm's values, practices, and approaches, thereby impacting the culture's receptiveness to innovation (Maitlis & Lawrence, 2007).

"External environment" represents the broader context in which the firm operates. It includes factors such as market dynamics, industry trends, regulatory frameworks, technological advancements, sociocultural influences, and competitive landscape (Barney, 1991). The arrow pointing from the external environment to stakeholders signifies how the external factors can influence and shape the stakeholders' expectations, needs, and demands (DiMaggio & Powell, 1983). The external environment can present opportunities or challenges that require the firm to innovate and adapt to remain competitive and meet stakeholder expectations (Damanpour, 1991). The arrow pointing from external environment to firm innovation indicates that the external environment can both enable and constrain the firm's innovation efforts (Teece, 2007). Factors such as market demand, technological advancements, industry standards, or regulatory changes can drive or impede innovation within the firm (Damanpour & Schneider, 2006).

The diagram captures the interplay between stakeholders, firm culture, and the external environment in shaping and influencing innovation within the organization. It highlights the dynamic and interconnected nature of these factors, emphasizing the importance of managing stakeholder relationships (Donaldson & Preston, 1995), fostering an innovation-supportive culture (Schein, 2010), and staying attuned to the external environment to drive successful innovation outcomes (Eisenhardt & Martin, 2000; Zahra et al., 2006).

Impact of different stakeholders on firm-level innovation

Internal stakeholders, including employees, managers, and shareholders, play a crucial role in fostering a culture of innovation within organizations. Their active involvement and support are essential for creating an environment that encourages and sustains innovation.

Employee involvement and empowerment are key drivers of innovation within organizations (Huczynski & Buchanan, 2013). When employees are encouraged to contribute ideas, take risks, and experiment, they become more engaged in the innovation process. Their diverse knowledge, skills, and experiences contribute to creative problem-solving and the generation of innovative ideas (Amabile, 1998). Creating platforms for idea sharing and providing opportunities for cross-functional collaboration can harness the innovative potential of employees. Recognition and rewards for innovative efforts motivate employees and reinforce the importance of innovation in the organizational culture (Shalley et al., 2004). Employee participation in the innovation process, on the other hand, can present difficulties. Employees may have limited resources or support to pursue new ideas, limiting their potential to contribute to the innovation process (Stock, 2015). As a result, businesses must give employees with the required tools and support, as well as ensure that their innovation initiatives are aligned with the organization's goals.

Managers play a crucial role in creating an environment conducive to innovation. They set the tone for innovation by promoting a supportive and inclusive culture that encourages risk-taking and learning (Amabile et al., 1996; Okrah & Irene, 2023). Managers facilitate innovation by providing resources, removing barriers, and promoting collaboration across different teams and departments (Damanpour & Schneider, 2009). Their leadership style and behaviors significantly influence employees‘ willingness to engage in innovative activities. Effective communication from managers about the importance of innovation, organizational goals, and expectations aligns employees' efforts toward innovation (Shin et al., 2012).

Creating a culture of innovation requires collaboration and alignment among internal stakeholders. Their collective efforts in promoting creativity, providing resources, encouraging risk-taking, and setting the strategic direction can establish a strong foundation for innovation within organizations. One notable example of an organization that has successfully fostered a culture of innovation by engaging its employees as key internal stakeholders is Microsoft. Microsoft encourages its employees to think creatively, take risks, and explore new ideas as part of their work culture. One of the initiatives that Microsoft implemented to promote innovation is the "Hackathon." During this event, employees from different departments and roles are given dedicated time to work on innovative projects outside of their regular job responsibilities. This encourages cross-functional collaboration and empowers employees to experiment and develop new ideas.

External stakeholders, including customers, suppliers, partners, and the government, play a crucial role in driving innovation within organizations. The literature consistently supports the notion that effectively managing these external stakeholders encourages them to contribute technical knowledge, support, resources, new ideas, know-how, and market information, all of which foster innovation (Flammer & Kacperczyk, 2016; Haefner et al., 2023).

Customers provide valuable market insights and feedback that drive innovation. By understanding customer needs, preferences, and emerging trends, organizations can develop innovative solutions that meet their demands (Tellis et al., 2009). Involving customers in the innovation process through co-creation and customer-driven innovation methods enhances product/service development and ensures market relevance. Collaborating with suppliers fosters innovation by enabling knowledge sharing, resource access, and joint problem-solving. Suppliers often possess specialised expertise that contributes to the development of new products, materials, or technologies (Laursen & Salter, 2006). Close partnerships with suppliers enhance a firm's innovation capabilities and expedite the innovation process. However, involving customers in the innovation process can offer challenges. Customers may lack awareness of technical or scientific parts of the innovation process, making it difficult for them to provide relevant feedback.

Factors driving stakeholder management for innovation

Stakeholder management broadly encompasses managing all the expectations and interests of different stakeholders that matter for the innovation process to support the development, adoption, and diffusion of new products, processes or services. Researchers have identified three main ways through which stakeholder management could influence firms' innovation performance: risk reduction, resource provision, and agenda setting (Albats et al., 2020). Stakeholder management for successful innovation can be influenced by a number of factors, including business size and age, industry environment, innovation strategy, and stakeholder characteristics (Haefner et al., 2023). The detailed understanding of these vital factors can help businesses to create effective stakeholder management plans and strategies that can boost and sustain innovation and its related activities.

The size of firms has been proven to be a vital contingency determinant that influence the manner in which they effectiviely and efficiently manage stakeholders for innovation. The linkage is usually with resource endowment connection. Small businesses are usually known to be limited in terms of resources and capabilities to manage stakeholders, albeit they may have more agility and flexibility to manage stakeholder wants and feedback (Haefner et al., 2023). This unique attributes of small businesses mean that their approach to stakeholder management for successful innovation would differ in comparison to large firms. Contrarily, large firms abound in resources and capabilities; therefore, they are more likely to effectively manage stakeholders, although they could also face more difficulties and bureaucracy in handling various stakeholder interests (Vurro et al., 2022). In addition, the industry type could also influence how firms manage various stakeholders relationships for innovation (Coombs & Gilley, 2005). This depends on the nature of the end-products the firm produces. In certain industries, such as those in the pharmaceuticals and biotechnology sectors, stakeholders such as patients, governments, and investors play a crucial role in shaping innovation strategies and process. It is therefore expected that in such sectors, firms may have to deal with several stakeholders. Contrariwise, in industries that deal with consumer products or software, firms would have limited stakeholders such as customers and suppliers to manage for their innovation.

Challenges and strategies in stakeholder management for innovation

Although the extant literature points out that effective stakeholder management plays an essential role in firms' success of innovation, managing the various stakeholders' collaboration in the perspective of innovation can also present daunting challenges (Rankinen et al., 2022). There are several stakeholders that could matter for the innovation process. The first challenge for innovative firms is how they will be able to identify and prioritize the stakeholders of interest. For instance, clients and customers have been shown to be important stakeholder group for firms; however, their involvement in the innovation process could also pose challenges. Clients and customers might not be well-versed in the technical or scientific components of the innovation process, making it challenging for them to offer valuable input for firms' search strategy (Kujala et al., 2010). To overcome the challenge of proper identification and prioritization of stakeholders requires innovative firms to first identify and rank stakeholders according to their influence, importance, and urgency, using stakeholder analysis. Various methods such as the influence-interest grids and stakeholder mapping have been proposed to assess stakeholder importance (Looser & Wehrmeyer, 2015).

The second key challenge in stakeholder management for innovation is that the numerous stakeholder have their respective priorities, competing interests, and expectations, which if not managed properly could impede the innovation process (Oeij et al., 2019). Managing numerous stakeholders with competing interests and priorities can be problematic and could result in conflicts and delays in decision-making. Additionally, it may be challenging for businesses to implement novel ideas since some stakeholders may be averse to change and may oppose creative projects (Alegre & Chiva, 2013). The main strategy therefore for innovative firms to overcome and balance the conflicting interests of multiple stakeholders is to enable open and transparent deliberations to understand and address potential conflicting interests. Negotiate and compromise to reach mutually beneficial agreements, and highlight the shared advantages and long-term value of the innovation. Furthermore, innovative firms could also develop a comprehensive communication plan aimed at tackling stakeholders' interests, provide frequent updates, and highlight the impending benefits of innovation.

Discussion and conclusion

This review has looked at the concept of stakeholder management and its ability to influence firms' innovation. The extant review considered what is meant by stakeholder management, how it potentially influences firms' abilities to innovate, its theoretical backing, what drives it, and what challenges it poses. Overall, the review suggests that effective stakeholder management is crucial for firms seeking to innovate and achieve long-term success (Hall et al., 2010; Flammer & Kacperczyk, 2016), but this depends on the number of stakeholders involved. Firms may navigate complex regulatory frameworks, gain essential knowledge and skills, and develop and implement innovative initiatives by interacting with a variety of stakeholders. While the review revealed that studies on stakeholder management for innovation are gradually gaining scholarly attention in African countries, there is lack of consensus concerning which stakeholders matter for firms' innovations. Furthermore, existing studies have specifically considered this relationship by solely focussed on small and medium scale enterprises and have given limited attention to large firms (Albats et al., 2020). However, managing multiple stakeholders with competing interests can present challenges that firms must address in order to achieve their innovation goals. Furthermore, the review indicates that firms are able to access external knowledge, resources, and expertise from these stakeholders, which could help spur innovations, but these studies have not focused on analyzing the role of organizational capabilities and structure in influencing this relationship (Haefner et al., 2023).

We see that there are varying and inconsistent methods for measuring stakeholder management for innovation. Since stakeholder management is a complicated, multifaceted topic, it is challenging to create measurement methods that are standardized and widely accepted (Greenwood, 2007). Assessing stakeholder management frequently involves using various sets of indicators and tools to measure their effectiveness. While there is no one-size-fits-all measurement approach, various metrics and measures such as stakeholder satisfaction surveys, stakeholder mapping and analysis, stakeholder engagement metrics, reputation, and trust metrics have been used for evaluating stakeholder management (Pedrini & Ferri, 2019). Nevertheless, there is no generally agreed-upon set of measurement indicators or tools (Bhattacharyya & Cummings, 2015), resulting in inconsistencies in measurement practices. However, stakeholder management for innovation is impacted by numerous contextual factors, such as organizational culture, decision-making environment, nature of industry, and characteristics of the stakeholders as well as the regulatory environment. These aforementioned contextual factors can influence the objectives, policies, approaches, and outcomes of effective stakeholder management efforts. Therefore, measurement approaches need to consider and incorporate these contextual factors to provide variations in measurement practices within different contexts. Similarly, innovation is usually also measured differently, comprising of product innovation, process innovation, or general innovation performance (Odei & Hamplová, 2022). These variations in measurement can make it challenging to compare findings across studies and draw definitive conclusions.

References

Albats, E., Alexander, A., Mahdad, M., Miller, K., and Post, G. (2020). Stakeholder management in SME open innovation: Interdependences and strategic actions. *Journal of Business Research*, *119*, pp. 291–301.

Alegre, J., and Chiva, R. (2013). Linking entrepreneurial orientation and firm performance: The role of organizational learning capability and innovation performance. *Journal of Small Business Management*, *51*(4), pp. 491–507.
Amabile, T. M. (1998). How to kill creativity. *Harvard Business Review*, *76*(5), pp. 76–87.
Amabile, T. M., Conti, R., Coon, H., Lazenby, J., and Herron, M. (1996). Assessing the work environment for creativity. *Academy of Management Journal*, *39*(5), pp. 1154–1184.
Barney, J. (1986). Organizational culture: Can it be a source of sustained competitive advantage? *Academy of Management Review*, *11*(3), pp. 656–665.
Barney, J. B. (1991). Firm resources and sustained competitive advantage. *Journal of Management*, *17*(1), pp. 99–120.
Bhattacharyya, A., and Cummings, L. (2015). Measuring corporate environmental performance–stakeholder engagement evaluation. *Business Strategy and the Environment*, *24*(5), pp. 309–325.
Boutilier, R., and Thomson, I. (2011). Communicating corporate social responsibility to internal stakeholders: Walking the walk or just talking the talk? *Management Communication Quarterly*, *25*(4), pp. 550–583.
Brown, J. S., and Duguid, P. (1991). Organizational learning and communities-of-practice: Toward a unified view of working, learning, and innovation. *Organization Science*, *2*(1), pp. 40–57.
Chesbrough, H. (2003). *Open innovation: The new imperative for creating and profiting from technology*. Harvard Business Press.
Chesbrough, H. (2012). Open innovation: Where we've been and where we're going. *Research-Technology Management*, *55*(4), pp. 20–27.
Clarkson, M. B. E. (1995). A stakeholder framework for analyzing and evaluating corporate social performance. *Academy of Management Review*, *20*(1), pp. 92–117.
Coombs, J. E., and Gilley, K. M. (2005). Stakeholder management as a predictor of CEO compensation: Main effects and interactions with financial performance. *Strategic Management Journal*, *26*(9), pp. 827–840.
Damanpour, F. (1991). Organizational innovation: A meta-analysis of effects of determinants and moderators. *Academy of Management Journal*, *34*(3), pp. 555–590.
Damanpour, F. (2014). Footnotes to research on management innovation. *Organization Studies*, *35*(9), pp. 1265–1284.
Damanpour, F., and Schneider, M. (2006). Phases of the adoption of innovation in organizations: Effects of environment, organization and top managers. *British Journal of Management*, *17*(3), pp. 215–236.
Damanpour, F., and Schneider, M. (2009). Characteristics of innovation and innovation adoption in public organizations: Assessing the role of managers. *Journal of Public Administration Research and Theory*, *19*(3), pp. 495–522.
De Colle, S. (2005). A stakeholder management model for ethical decision making. *International Journal of Management and Decision Making*, *6*(3–4), pp. 299–314.
DiMaggio, P. J., and Powell, W. W. (1983). The iron cage revisited: Institutional isomorphism and collective rationality in organizational fields. *American Sociological Review*, *48*(2), pp. 147–160.
Dodgson, M., Gann, D., and Salter, A. (2008). *The management of technological innovation: Strategy and practice*. Oxford University Press.

Donaldson, T., and Preston, L. E. (1995). The stakeholder theory of the corporation: Concepts, evidence, and implications. *Academy of Management Review*, *20*(1), pp. 65–91.

Eisenhardt, K. M., and Martin, J. A. (2000). Dynamic capabilities: What are they? *Strategic Management Journal*, 21(10–11), pp. 1105–1121.

Flammer, C., and Kacperczyk, A. (2016). The impact of stakeholder orientation on innovation: Evidence from a natural experiment. *Management Science*, *62*(7), pp. 1982–2001.

Freeman, R. E. (1984). *Strategic management: A stakeholder approach*. Pitman.

Freeman, R. E. (2010). *Strategic management: A stakeholder approach*. Cambridge University Press.

Freeman, R. E., and Evan, W. M. (1990). Corporate governance: A stakeholder interpretation. *Journal of Behavioral Economics*, *19*(4), pp. 337–359.

Freeman, R. E., Harrison, J. S., Wicks, A. C., Parmar, B. L., and Colle, S. (2007). *Stakeholder theory: The state of the art*. Cambridge University Press.

Ganesh, J., Arnold, M. J., and Reynolds, K. E. (2014). Exploring the impact of market orientation and service orientation on innovation and business performance. *Journal of Service Research*, *17*(4), pp. 428–441.

Garcia-Castro, R., and Francoeur, C. (2016). When more is not better: Complementarities, costs and contingencies in stakeholder management. *Strategic Management Journal*, *37*(2), pp. 406–424.

Gassmann, O., Enkel, E., and Chesbrough, H. (2010). The future of open innovation. *R&D Management*, *40*(3), pp. 213–221.

Greenwood, M. (2007). Stakeholder engagement: Beyond the myth of corporate responsibility. *Journal of Business Ethics*, *74*, pp. 315–327.

Haefner, N., Palmié, M., and Leppänen, P. T. (2023). With (out) a little help from my friends? Reconciling incongruous findings on stakeholder management, innovation, and firm performance. *Entrepreneurship Theory and Practice*, *47*(1), pp. 142–171.

Hall, B. H., Lotti, F., and Mairesse, J. (2010). Innovation and productivity in SMEs: Empirical evidence for Italy. *Small Business Economics*, 39(1), pp. 81–99.

Huczynski, A., and Buchanan, D. (2013). *Organizational behaviour* (8th ed.). Pearson.

Kazadi, K., Lievens, A., and Mahr, D. (2016). Stakeholder co-creation during the innovation process: Identifying capabilities for knowledge creation among multiple stakeholders. *Journal of Business Research*, *69*(2), pp. 525–540.

Kline, S. J., and Rosenberg, N. (2009). An overview of innovation. In N. Rosenberg (Ed.), *Studies on science and the innovation process: Selected works of Nathan Rosenberg* (pp. 173–203). World Scientific Publishing.

Kujala, S., Artto, K., Aaltonen, P., and Turkulainen, V. (2010). Business models in project-based firms–Towards a typology of solution-specific business models. *International Journal of Project Management*, *28*(2), pp. 96–106.

Laursen, K., & Salter, A. (2006). Open for innovation: the role of openness in explaining innovation performance among UK manufacturing firms. *Strategic Management Journal*, *27*(2), pp. 131–150.

Leonidou, E., Christofi, M., Vrontis, D., and Thrassou, A. (2020). An integrative framework of stakeholder engagement for innovation management and entrepreneurship development. *Journal of Business Research*, *119*, pp. 245–258.

Looser, S., and Wehrmeyer, W. (2015). Stakeholder mapping of CSR in Switzerland. *Social Responsibility Journal*, *11*(4), pp. 780–830.

López-Gamero, M. D., Molina-Azorín, J. F., and Claver-Cortés, E. (2011). The whole relationship between environmental variables and firm performance: Competitive advantage and firm resources as mediator variables. *Journal of Environmental Management*, *92*(3), pp. 299–315.

Maitlis, S., and Lawrence, T. B. (2007). Triggers and enablers of sensegiving in organizations. *Academy of Management Journal*, *50*(1), pp. 57–84.

Mitchell, R. K., Agle, B. R., and Wood, D. J. (1997). Toward a theory of stakeholder identification and salience: Defining the principle of who and what really counts. *Academy of Management Review*, *22*(4), pp. 853–886.

Odei, S. A., and Hamplová, E. (2022). Innovations in small businesses: Do public procurement contracts and intellectual property rights matter?. *Heliyon*, *8*(9), pp. e10623.

Oeij, P. R., Van Der Torre, W., Vaas, F., and Dhondt, S. (2019). Understanding social innovation as an innovation process: Applying the innovation journey model. *Journal of Business Research*, *101*, pp. 243–254.

Okrah, J., and Irene, B. (2023). The effect of top managers' years of experience on innovation. *International Journal of Innovation Studies*, *7*(3), pp. 208–217.

Pedrini, M., and Ferri, L. M. (2019). Stakeholder management: A systematic literature review. *Corporate Governance: The International Journal of Business in Society*, *19*(1), pp. 44–59.

Rankinen, J. A., Lakkala, S., Haapasalo, H., and Hirvonen-Kantola, S. (2022). Stakeholder management in PED projects: Challenges and management model. *International Journal of Sustainable Energy Planning and Management*, *34*, pp. 91–106.

Ravasi, D., and Schultz, M. (2006). Responding to organizational identity threats: Exploring the role of organizational culture. *Academy of Management Journal*, *49*(3), pp. 433–458.

Schein, E. H. (2010). *Organizational culture and leadership* (4th ed.). Jossey-Bass.

Selsky, J. W., and Parker, B. (2005). Cross-sector partnerships to address social issues: Challenges to theory and practice. *Journal of Management*, *31*(6), pp. 849–873.

Shalley, C. E., Zhou, J., and Oldham, G. R. (2004). The effects of personal and contextual characteristics on creativity: Where should we go from here? *Journal of Management*, *30*(6), pp. 933–958.

Shin, S. J., Kim, T. Y., Lee, J. Y., and Bian, L. (2012). Cognitive team diversity and individual team member creativity: A cross-level interaction. *Academy of Management Journal*, *55*(1), pp. 197–212.

Stock, R. M. (2015). Is boreout a threat to frontline employees' innovative work behavior?. *Journal of Product Innovation Management*, *32*(4), pp. 574–592.

Teece, D. J. (2007). Explicating dynamic capabilities: The nature and microfoundations of (sustainable) enterprise performance. *Strategic Management Journal*, *28*(13), pp. 1319–1350.

Tellis, G. J., Prabhu, J. C., and Chandy, R. K. (2009). Radical innovation across nations: The preeminence of corporate culture. *Journal of Marketing*, *73*(1), pp. 3–23.

Tidd, J., Bessant, J., and Pavitt, K. (2005). *Managing innovation: Integrating technological, market and organizational change*. John Wiley & Sons.

Vurro, C., Romito, S., and Benassi, M. (2022). Too good to say goodbye? Effect of stakeholder orientation on the survival of large firms. *Long Range Planning*, *55*(5), pp. 102161.

Zahra, S. A., Sapienza, H. J., and Davidsson, P. (2006). Entrepreneurship and dynamic capabilities: A review, model, and research agenda. *Journal of Management Studies*, *43*(4), pp. 917–955

3 Stakeholder Integration, Exploration, and Exploitation in New Ventures

Samuel Adomako

Introduction

An important theme in entrepreneurship research is that for firms to survive the ever-growing competition, they must concurrently engage in opportunity-seeking and advantage-seeking activities (Bingham & Eisenhardt, 2011; Sirmon et al., 2007). The exploration and exploitation of opportunities are crucial for venture performance (Ireland et al., 2001; Parida et al., 2016; Sirmon et al., 2007). Exploration reflects activities to develop new products that deviate from the existing technological range whiles exploitation relates to incremental improvements to existing products utilizing extant technologies (Feng et al., 2019).

Prior research shows that to sustain long-term success, firms must pursue opportunities geared toward the long-term (i.e., engage in exploratory activities) while simultaneously harvesting short-term efficiency benefits stemming from refining existing products and processes (i.e., engaging in exploitative activities) (Feng et al., 2019; Gedajlovic et al., 2012; Kammerlander et al., 2015). However, given that exploration and exploitation require different sets of capabilities, it is often challenging for resource-constrained small firms to engage in both sets of activities (Ireland & Webb, 2009; Mihalache et al., 2014; Vasilchenko & Morrish, 2011; Voss & Voss, 2013). Although some studies have identified several drivers, namely, environment, firm, and top management (Hill & Birkinshaw, 2014; Mihalache et al., 2014) and CEOs' personality (Kammerlander et al., 2015) of a firm's simultaneous engagement in exploration and exploitation, how the drivers relate to levels of a small firm's stakeholder integration are still poorly understood. Specifically, efforts to understand the role of stakeholder integration in driving exploratory and exploitative activities have not yet been either fully conceptualized or tested. In addition, there is very little research on the applicability of stakeholder theory in the ambidexterity literature (García-Sánchez et al., 2018). This is surprising given that stakeholders' involvement in a firm's decision-making and strategies is a valuable strategic resource that offers firms competitive advantages (Plaza-Úbeda et al., 2010; Walsh, 2005). As the conflicting interests of a firm's stakeholders on strategic issues such as opportunity-seeking and

DOI: 10.4324/9781003256014-5

advantage-seeking activities require a firm to develop a specific capability to manage these pressures (Jawahar & McLaughlin, 2001), stakeholder integration capability can help a firm to develop strategies to approach both exploration and exploitation complexities proactively.

In this paper, we draw on the stakeholder theory and focus on stakeholder integration capability, conceptualized as the "ability to establish positive collaborative relationships with a wide variety of stakeholders" (Plaza-Úbeda et al., 2010, p. 419). The concept of stakeholder theory has garnered significant attention to explain firm behavior (Freeman et al., 2010; Knaggård et al., 2019). Applying the stakeholder approach to strategic management (Freeman & McVea, 2005; Freeman et al., 2010) can potentially assist small firms in engaging in both exploratory and exploitative activities, commonly known as ambidexterity. Research suggests that ambidexterity is associated with enhanced performance (Lubatkin et al., 2006; Sirén et al., 2012). With the understanding that stakeholders play a vital role in a firm's strategy (Freeman et al., 2010; Lubatkin et al., 2006; Plaza-Úbeda et al., 2010), we propose that a small firm's ability to pursue exploration and exploitation is influenced by its capacity for stakeholder integration.

However, pursuing both exploratory and exploitative activities concurrently is difficult for new ventures to accomplish given the apparent tensions between exploratory and exploitative entrepreneurial processes. Yet, integrating stakeholder concerns in management practices can help firms to utilize scarce resources for both processes. Both exploratory and exploitative processes compete for scarce resources with different time horizons, yet they cannibalize one another (Mihalache et al., 2014). Thus, by responding to stakeholder expectations to formulate and implement processes that satisfy their demands, firms can explore how they may overcome the hurdles associated with engaging in both exploratory and exploitative activities.

The influence of stakeholder integration capability on both exploratory and exploitative activities may depend on the contextual environment since the pressures of stakeholders, namely competitors, have been a major driver of the implementation of corporate practices (Charan & Murty, 2018) and how well firms achieve their goals. Therefore, we aim to examine the following research questions: (1) how does small firms' stakeholder integration affect their level of exploration and exploitation activities? and (2) how does the competition in the firm's market moderate those linkages?

This paper contributes to the literature in several ways. First, we extend the literature (e.g., Atkins & Lowe, 1994; García-Sánchez et al., 2018; Martin & Javalgi, 2016) by showing how stakeholder integration affects small firms' engagement in both exploratory and exploitative activities. Specifically, the findings of the current study contribute to a better understanding of the drivers of new venture behavior. Moreover, our paper contributes to entrepreneurship research on small firms by revealing further evidence of the role of stakeholder integration in driving small-firm behavior in the early stages of firm development. This contribution is crucial given that exploratory and exploitative activities are often associated with superior venture performance (Lubatkin et al., 2006; Patel et al., 2013).

Second, this paper advances research on organizational ambidexterity (Kammerlander et al., 2015; Mihalache et al., 2014) that focuses on drivers of a firm's engagement in both exploratory and exploitative activities. Specifically, the current paper shows the importance of a small firm's stakeholder integration as a driver of ambidextrous firm activities. As such, the results complement the body of research that has identified firm-level capabilities as drivers of ambidexterity (Mihalache et al., 2014). Third, we enhance stakeholder literature by studying how the influence of stakeholder integration depends on market competition.

Stakeholder management and entrepreneurship in Ghana

Entrepreneurship has been a driving force behind economic growth and development in Ghana (Obeng et al., 2014; Robson et al., 2009). However, the success of entrepreneurs in developing countries such as Ghana is not solely determined by their individual skills and innovative ideas (Ahsan et al., 2023); it heavily relies on effective stakeholder management. Stakeholders are individuals or groups who have a vested interest in the success or failure of a business venture. For entrepreneurs, stakeholders can include customers, suppliers, employees, investors, government agencies, and local communities, among others. Managing these stakeholders is crucial as they can directly or indirectly influence the success of the new entrepreneurial venture.

First, the effective management of stakeholders can create a supportive ecosystem for entrepreneurs (Bischoff et al., 2018; Erina et al., 2017). In Ghana, entrepreneurs often face various challenges such as limited access to capital, infrastructure deficiencies, bureaucratic hurdles, and societal expectations (Adomako et al., 2019b). By engaging and managing stakeholders, entrepreneurs can address these challenges more effectively. For instance, by building strong relationships with investors, entrepreneurs can secure funding for their ventures, while engaging with government agencies can help navigate regulatory frameworks and obtain necessary licenses and permits.

Second, stakeholder management can be critical for fostering trust and credibility, which are essential for the long-term success of any entrepreneurial endeavor (Minoja, 2012; Sundaramurthy, 2008). Gaining the trust of stakeholders, especially customers and local communities, is vital for entrepreneurs to establish a strong market presence. In Ghana, where social networks are prevalent (Kuada, 2009; Robson et al., 2009), positive relationships with customers can lead to increased brand loyalty and business growth. Moreover, entrepreneurs who actively involve local communities in their business activities and contribute to their development can build a positive reputation, leading to enhanced support and cooperation.

Third, when stakeholders are properly managed, it can help in the identification of new entrepreneurial opportunities (Vandekerckhove & Dentchev,

2005 Vershinina et al., 2020). For example, in Ghana, entrepreneurs often encounter dynamic and rapidly changing market conditions (Adomako, 2021). By engaging with diverse stakeholders, entrepreneurs can gather valuable insights and feedback, helping them adapt their products, services, and business models to meet the evolving needs and preferences of their target market. For example, collaboration with suppliers can lead to improved product quality, while feedback from customers can drive innovation and differentiation.

Thus, stakeholder management is important for the success of entrepreneurs in Ghana. By effectively engaging and managing stakeholders, entrepreneurs can overcome challenges, build trust, identify opportunities, and contribute to sustainable development. As Ghana continues to foster its entrepreneurial ecosystem, recognizing and prioritizing stakeholder management will enable entrepreneurs to thrive and contribute to the country's economic growth and social progress.

Theoretical framework and propositions

Stakeholder theory and stakeholder integration

Stakeholder theory explores the importance of satisfying the diverse needs of stakeholders to achieve an organization's objectives (Freeman, 1984; Laplume et al., 2008). It provides a framework for managing relationships with various actors in the environment (Freeman, 1984), emphasizing the simultaneous consideration of the legitimate interests of all relevant stakeholders (Donaldson & Preston, 1995, p. 67). Stakeholder management literature defines stakeholders as groups or individuals who can influence or are affected by the organization's objectives (Freeman, 1984, p. 46). This implies that a firm's stakeholders extend beyond its market and include shareholders, employees, consumer associations, and environmental pressure groups. Stakeholders have an interest in the success or failure of a business as it directly impacts their gains or losses. Stakeholder theory argues that firms should manage their relationship with society by considering the specific actors who can affect or are affected by their objectives (Clarkson, 1995).

Organizational managers often gather information about stakeholder issues to effectively manage relationships with stakeholders (Driessen & Hillebrand, 2013). Therefore, stakeholder integration refers to the extent to which stakeholders' voices are incorporated into the firm's decision-making process (Atkins & Lowe, 1994; Freeman et al., 2010). It encompasses a firm's capability to learn about product lifecycles, design environmentally friendly products and services, and collaborate with suppliers and customers (Hart, 1995). As firms gain a competitive advantage not only through acquiring unique assets but also through their ability to develop capabilities in a socially complex and ambiguous manner (Barney, 1991; Driessen & Hillebrand, 2013; Wernerfelt, 1984), stakeholder integration becomes particularly relevant for exploratory activities like new product development (Hart, 1995). However, research on how stakeholder integration influences exploratory and exploitative activities is still limited. This paper addresses this gap by examining how a firm's level of exploratory and exploitative activities is influenced by its stakeholder integration.

Stakeholder integration and its effect on exploration and exploitation

Given the benefits firms tend to gain from exploration and exploitation activities, researchers are particularly interested in the factors that may drive these activities. One potential driver of exploration and exploitation is firm integration. Stakeholder theory states that the interests of groups of stakeholders must be included in organizational decision-making (Freeman et al., 2010). Stakeholders' integration comprises three main dimensions: the knowledge of stakeholders, the degree of interaction with stakeholders, and the adaptation to stakeholders' claims (Plaza-Úbeda et al., 2010). Firms endowed with resources or capabilities to integrate stakeholders are more likely to understand the demands of their stakeholders and more likely to be able to collaborate with them to identify exploration and exploitative activities to make the organizational and behavioral changes needed to implement the practices identified.

Organizations require specific capabilities and resources to develop strategies that meet the demands of stakeholders and translate them into performance (Plaza-Úbeda et al., 2010). More pressure results in more development of capabilities, and deployment of these capabilities enables improved exploration and exploitation activities in aspects demanded by stakeholders. Consequently, companies around the world are increasingly seeking new ways of incorporating stakeholders while concurrently delivering superior outcomes. Achieving such a balance is a major challenge for many growth-seeking firms (Vargas et al., 2018). Situated within the rubric of stakeholder theory (Freeman, 2010), stakeholder integration encompasses forging closer ties and relationships with different stakeholders to incorporate their concerns and issues at the forefront of organizational strategy (Plaza-Úbeda et al., 2010). This often entails multiple dialogues and communications with different stakeholders to advance an agenda (Salem et al., 2018).

Research under the rubric of stakeholder theory suggests that organizations that seek to incorporate the input of stakeholders often open multiple channels of communication that allow new ideas and insights to diffuse into the focal firm (Danso et al., 2019; Salem et al., 2018). Besides, stakeholder theory suggests that firms tend to prioritize the integration of stakeholders (Savage et al., 1991) because such stakeholders have direct control of resources needed by the firm (e.g., labor, capital, institutional support), and failing to attend to their demands is likely to have severe consequences (Rueda-Manzanares et al., 2008). Thus, by acknowledging and incorporating key stakeholders' interests, organizations are better able to convey a message and impression that they are willing to embrace new ideas and practices (Gupta & Briscoe, 2019) related to exploration and exploitative activities.

P1 *For new ventures, stakeholder integration is positively related to a firm's level of exploration.*

P2 *For new ventures, stakeholder integration is positively related to a firm's level of exploitation.*

Moderating effect of competitive intensity

Competitive intensity captures circumstances and conditions that enhance the rivalry among firms in the marketplace (Estrada-Cruz et al., 2020; Slater & Narver, 1994). The existence of multiple players in the market coupled with limited opportunity for growth often typifies and accelerates competitive intensity (Auh & Menguc, 2005; Kim & Rhee, 2009) and thus creates a more hostile environment for firms seeking growth and higher profit (Chan et al., 2012). In less liberalized industries and less competitive settings, fewer firms experience a decline in performance. Indeed, some firms may maintain their performance despite poor customer service and delays since there is no alternative available. However, in a highly competitive environment, consumers are free to switch from firms that fail to provide superior services and meet their requirements (Chan et al., 2012). As more and more industries are opened to market competition, firms are increasingly required to be more attentive to customers' demands and risk losing them to rival firms. Owing to the greater premium attached to superior performance in competitive environments, firms are motivated to engage with different stakeholders inside and outside to innovate as well as win their support for their products or services (Adomako et al., 2019a).

To succeed in a competitively intense environment, exploration and exploitation activities must be pursued by firms (Auh & Menguc, 2005; Zahra, 1993). Thus, we contend that as competition increases, firms with high levels of stakeholder integration increase their efforts in exploration and exploitation activities to be successful. Accordingly, firms are increasingly under pressure to engage in specific exploration and exploitation activities that allow them to develop a greater affinity for stakeholders and become more attentive to their concerns.

In an industry characterized by intense competition, competitors continually work to imitate and refine products, thereby enhancing the quality and lowering prices (Dickson, 1992; Estrada-Cruz et al., 2020). Given this situation, competitive advantage quickly erodes in such environments. To sustain a continuous competitive advantage, firms need to intensify their exploration and exploitation activities in such a market. Stakeholder integration, therefore, becomes critical for firms in highly competitive environments. For example, advice received from stakeholders is likely to help implement specific measures to bolster product reliability and help the firm to lead the market. Yet, this competitive advantage quickly fades off in an industry characterized by intense competition. Thus, new investments in exploitation activities are required to sustain the firm's market position (Anzenbacher & Wagner, 2020). As firms with stronger stakeholder integration strive to do things based on stakeholders' advice and wish to retain a positive outlook from stakeholders, they are likely to put more effort into explorative and exploitative activities to maintain a temporary competitive advantage when competitive intensity is high instead of low (Lavie et al., 2010). Therefore:

P2a *For new ventures, competitive intensity enhances the positive relationship between stakeholder integration and exploration.*
P2b *For new ventures, competitive intensity enhances the positive relationship between stakeholder integration and exploitation.*

Discussion and conclusion

In this study, we sought to understand how stakeholder integration affects exploration and exploitation in new ventures. Our propositions show a positive influence of stakeholder integration on exploration but no significant relation to exploitation. Besides, we suggest that increases in stakeholder integration and greater degrees of competition are associated with increases in both exploration and exploitation activities. In short, the paper shows that when firms develop greater stakeholders in highly competitive environments, small firms are likely to engage in greater exploratory and exploitative activities. These results allow us to make three important contributions to the entrepreneurship literature.

First, unlike previous studies that examined the effect of CEO personality (Kammerlander et al., 2015) and environment, firm, and top-management characteristics (e.g., Hill & Birkinshaw, 2014; Mihalache et al., 2014) on levels of exploration and exploitation, the current paper uses the stakeholder theory to explain how a firm-level capability (i.e., stakeholder integration) affects firm behavior. This advancement is crucial, as small ventures are typically constrained by resources to engage in exploration and exploitation concurrently (Voss & Voss, 2013; Voss et al., 2008). This paper, therefore, contributes to studies that identify how firms, especially small firms, can remain entrepreneurial (Gedajlovic et al., 2012; Mihalache et al., 2014) by identifying stakeholder integration as an antecedent to exploration activities. Second, we contribute further to the entrepreneurship literature (Martin & Javalgi, 2016) by examining how competitive intensity conditions the stakeholder integration–exploration/exploitation relationship. Consequently, this paper contributes to the emerging stream of research that examines how the influence of stakeholder integration depends on industry characteristics (Adomako et al., 2019b).

Third, by introducing competitive intensity as a moderating factor in the relationship between stakeholder integration and exploration/exploitation, this paper extends the stakeholder management literature beyond the developed markets. More specifically, this paper draws on the contextual idiosyncrasies of developing countries to explain how stakeholder integration affects levels of exploration/exploitation under conditions of intense competition. This contribution implies that when small firms integrate stakeholders into the processes and management of the firm, they stand to benefit when the competition is stronger.

Apart from the preceding theoretical contributions, this paper provides some practical contributions. Our findings show that high levels of stakeholder integration are particularly beneficial for small firms to explore and exploit opportunities. Besides, the influence of stakeholder integration on levels of exploration/exploitation is stronger under conditions of greater competition. This insight is crucial for two types of real-life conditions. First, small-firm owners are encouraged to pay attention to stakeholder management as focusing on stakeholders can be a source of opportunity in the entrepreneurship domain (Kuratko et al., 2007). Second, owner-CEOs are advised to integrate stakeholders in competitive environmental analysis and strategy to reap exploration and exploitation of opportunities.

Limitations and future research

This study has identified several limitations that can serve as avenues for future research. First, we focus on Ghana as a study context, which limits the generalizability of the role of stakeholder integration in levels of exploration and exploitation to other environments. The collectivistic culture of Ghana, characterized by strong values and the active involvement of families and communities in entrepreneurship, may have influenced the results. Therefore, it is important to interpret the findings within the context of collectivistic cultures, and future studies should consider conducting research in multiple countries across Europe, Latin America, and Africa to capture the diverse contextual factors that influence the relationship between stakeholder integration and firm behavior. Despite these limitations, our propositions indicate a positive influence of high levels of stakeholder integration on both exploration and exploitation. Furthermore, we demonstrate that stakeholder integration may play a significant role in driving exploratory and exploitative behaviors, particularly under conditions of increased competition. This study contributes to the development of entrepreneurship theory by shedding light on the specific conditions in which firm-level capabilities, such as stakeholder integration, can positively impact exploration and exploitation behaviors within the unique context of a developing market.

References

Adomako, S. (2021). Resource-induced coping heuristics and entrepreneurial orientation in dynamic environments. *Journal of Business Research*, *122*, 477–487.

Adomako, S., Amankwah-Amoah, J., Dankwah, G. O., Danso, A., & Donbesuur, F. (2019b). Institutional voids, international learning effort and internationalization of emerging market new ventures. *Journal of International Management*, *25*(4), 100666.

Adomako, S., Amankwah-Amoah, J., & Danso, A. (2019a). The effects of stakeholder integration on firm-level product innovativeness: Insights from small and medium-sized enterprises in Ghana. *R&D Management*, *49*(5), 734–747.
Ahsan, M., Adomako, S., Donbesuur, F., & Mole, K. F. (2023). Entrepreneurial passion and product innovation intensity in new ventures: Mediating effects of exploration and exploitation activities. *British Journal of Management*, *34*(2), 849–872.
Anzenbacher, A., & Wagner, M. (2020). The role of exploration and exploitation for innovation success: Effects of business models on organizational ambidexterity in the semiconductor industry. *International Entrepreneurship and Management Journal*, *16*(2), 571–594.
Atkins, M., & Lowe, J. (1994). Stakeholders and the strategy formation process in small and medium enterprises. *International Small Business Journal*, *12*(3), 12–24.
Auh, S., & Menguc, B. (2005). Balancing exploration and exploitation: The moderating role of competitive intensity. *Journal of Business Research*, *58*, 1652–1661.
Barney, J. B. (1991). Firm resources and sustained competitive advantage. *Journal of Management*, *17*(1), 99–120.
Bingham, C. B., & Eisenhardt, K. M. (2011). Rational heuristics: The "simple rules" that strategists learn from process experience. *Strategic Management Journal*, *32*(13), 1437–1464.
Bischoff, K., Volkmann, C. K., & Audretsch, D. B. (2018). Stakeholder collaboration in entrepreneurship education: An analysis of the entrepreneurial ecosystems of European higher educational institutions. *The Journal of Technology Transfer*, *43*, 20–46.
Chan, R. Y., He, H., Chan, H. K., & Wang, W. Y. (2012). Environmental orientation and corporate performance: The mediation mechanism of green supply chain management and moderating effect of competitive intensity. *Industrial Marketing Management*, *41*(4), 621–630.
Charan, P., & Murty, L. S. (2018). Secondary stakeholder pressures and organizational adoption of sustainable operations practices: The mediating role of primary stakeholders. *Business Strategy and the Environment*, *27*(7), 910–923.
Clarkson, M. B. E. (1995). A stakeholder framework for analyzing and evaluating corporate social performance. *Academy of Management Review*, *20*(1), 92–117.
Danso, A., Adomako, S., Lartey, T., Amankwah-Amoah, J., & Owusu-Yirenkyi, D. (2019). Stakeholder integration, environmental sustainability orientation and financial performance. *Journal of Business Research*, *119*, 652–662.
Dickson, P.R. (1992). Toward a general theory of competitive rationality. *Journal of Marketing*, *56*(1), 69–83.
Donaldson, T., & Preston, L. E. (1995). The stakeholder theory of the corporation: Concepts, evidence, and implications. *Academy of Management Review*, *20*(1), 65–91.
Driessen, P. H., & Hillebrand, B. (2013). Integrating multiple stakeholder issues in new product development: An exploration. *Journal of Product Innovation Management*, *30*(2), 364–379.
Erina, I., Shatrevich, V., & Gaile-Sarkane, E. (2017). Impact of stakeholder groups on development of a regional entrepreneurial ecosystem. *European Planning Studies*, *25*(5), 755–771.
Estrada-Cruz, M., Rodriguez-Hernández, N., Verdú-Jover, A. J., & Gómez-Gras, J. M. (2020). The effect of competitive intensity on the relationship between strategic entrepreneurship and organizational results. *International Entrepreneurship and Management Journal*, *18*(1), 1–24.

Feng, Y., Teng, D., & Hao, B. (2019). Joint actions with large partners and small-firm ambidexterity in asymmetric alliances: The mediating role of relational identification. *International Small Business Journal*, *37*(7), 689–712.

Freeman, R. E. (1984). *Strategic management: A stakeholder approach*. Pitman.

Freeman, R. E. (2010). *Strategic management: A stakeholder approach*. Cambridge University Press.

Freeman, R. E., Harrison, J. S., Wicks, A. C., Parmar, B. L., & De Colle, S. (2010). *Stakeholder theory: The state of the art*. Cambridge University Press.

Freeman, R. E., & McVea, J. (2005). A stakeholder approach to strategic management. In M. A. Hitt, E. R. Freeman, & J. S. Harrison (Eds.), *The Blackwell Handbook of Strategic Management* (pp. 183–201). Blackwell.

García-Sánchez, E., García-Morales, V. J., & Martín-Rojas, R. (2018). Analysis of the influence of the environment, stakeholder integration capability, absorptive capacity, and technological skills on organizational performance through corporate entrepreneurship. *International Entrepreneurship and Management Journal*, *14*(2), 345–377.

Gedajlovic, E., Cao, Q., & Zhang, H. (2012). Corporate shareholdings and organizational ambidexterity in high-tech SMEs: Evidence from a transitional economy. *Journal of Business Venturing*, *27*(6), 652–665.

Gupta, A., & Briscoe, F. (2019). Organizational political ideology and corporate openness to social activism. *Administrative Science Quarterly*, *65*(2), 524–563.

Hart, S. L. (1995). A natural resource-based view of the firm. *Academy of Management Review*, *20*(4), 986–1014.

Hill, S. A., & Birkinshaw, J. (2014). Ambidexterity and survival in corporate venture units. *Journal of Management*, *40*(7), 1899–1931.

Ireland, R. D., Hitt, M. A., Camp, S. M., & Sexton, D. L. (2001). Integrating entrepreneurship and strategic management actions to create firm wealth. *Academy of Management Perspectives*, *15*(1), 49–63.

Ireland, R. D., & Webb, J. W. (2009). Crossing the great divide of strategic entrepreneurship: Transitioning between exploration and exploitation. *Business Horizons*, *52*(5), 469–479.

Jawahar, I. M., & G. L. McLaughlin (2001). Toward a descriptive stakeholder theory: An organizational life cycle approach, *Academy of Management Review*, *26*, 397–414.

Kammerlander, N., Burger, D., Fust, A., & Fueglistaller, U. (2015). Exploration and exploitation in established small and medium-sized enterprises: The effect of CEOs' regulatory focus. *Journal of Business Venturing*, *30*(4), 582–602.

Kim, T., & Rhee, M. (2009). Exploration and exploitation: Internal variety and environmental dynamism. *Strategic Organization*, *7*(1), 11–41.

Knaggård, Å., Slunge, D., Ekbom, A., Göthberg, M., & Sahlin, U. (2019). Researchers' approaches to stakeholders: Interaction or transfer of knowledge? *Environmental Science & Policy*, *97*, 25–35.

Kuada, J. (2009). Gender, social networks, and entrepreneurship in Ghana. *Journal of African Business*, *10*(1), 85–103.

Kuratko, D. F., Hornsby, J. S., & Goldsby, M. G. (2007). The relationship of stakeholder salience, organizational posture, and entrepreneurial intensity to corporate entrepreneurship. *Journal of Leadership & Organizational Studies*, *13*(4), 56–72.

Laplume, A. O., Sonpar, K., & Litz, R. A. (2008). Stakeholder theory: Reviewing a theory that moves us. *Journal of Management*, *34*(6), 1152–1189.

Lavie, D., Stettner, U., & Tushman, M. L. (2010). Exploration and exploitation within and across organizations. *Academy of Management Annals*, *4*(1), 109–155.

Lubatkin, M., Simsek, Z., & Veiga, J., (2006). Ambidexterity and performance in small- to medium-sized firms: The pivotal role of top management team behavioral integration. *Journal of Management*, *32*(5), 646–672.

Martin, S. L., & Javalgi, R. R. G. (2016). Entrepreneurial orientation, marketing capabilities and performance: The moderating role of competitive intensity on Latin American International new ventures. *Journal of Business Research*, *69*(6), 2040–2051.

Mihalache, O. R., Jansen, J. J., Van den Bosch, F. A., & Volberda, H. W. (2014). Top management team shared leadership and organizational ambidexterity: A moderated mediation framework. *Strategic Entrepreneurship Journal*, *8*(2), 128–148.

Minoja, M. (2012). Stakeholder management theory, firm strategy, and ambidexterity. *Journal of Business Ethics*, *109*(1), 67–82.

Obeng, B. A., Robson, P., & Haugh, H. (2014). Strategic entrepreneurship and small firm growth in Ghana. *International Small Business Journal*, *32*(5), 501–524.

Parida, V., Lahti, T., & Wincent, J. (2016). Exploration and exploitation and firm performance variability: A study of ambidexterity in entrepreneurial firms. *International Entrepreneurship and Management Journal*, *12*(4), 1147–1164.

Patel, P. C., Messersmith, J. G., & Lepak, D. P. (2013). Walking the tightrope: An assessment of the relationship between high-performance work systems and organizational ambidexterity. *Academy of Management Journal*, *56*(5), 14201442.

Plaza-Úbeda, J. A., de Burgos-Jiménez, J., & Carmona-Moreno, E. (2010). Measuring stakeholder integration: Knowledge, interaction and adaptational behavior dimensions. *Journal of Business Ethics*, *93*(3), 419–442.

Robson, P. J., Haugh, H. M., & Obeng, B. A. (2009). Entrepreneurship and innovation in Ghana: Enterprising Africa. *Small Business Economics*, *32*, 331–350.

Rueda-Manzanares, A., Aragón-Correa, J. A., & Sharma, S. (2008). The influence of stakeholders on the environmental strategy of service firms: The moderating effects of complexity, uncertainty and munificence. *British Journal of Management*, *19*, 185–203.

Salem, M. A., Shawtari, F., Shamsudin, M. F., & Hussain, H. B. I. (2018). The consequences of integrating stakeholder engagement in sustainable development (environmental perspectives). *Sustainable Development*, *26*(3), 255–268.

Savage, G. T., Nix, T. W., Whitehead, C. J., & Blair, J. D. (1991). Strategies for assessing and managing organizational stakeholders. *Academy of Management Perspectives*, *5*(2), 61–75.

Sirén, C.A., Kohtamäki, M., & Kuckertz, A. (2012). Exploration and exploitation strategies, profit performance, and the mediating role of strategic learning: Escaping the exploitation trap. *Strategic Entrepreneurship Journal*, 6(1), 18–41.

Sirmon, D. G., Hitt, M. A., & Ireland, R. D. (2007). Managing firm resources in dynamic environments to create value: Looking inside the black box. *Academy of Management Review*, *32*(1), 273–292.

Slater, S. F., & Narver, J. C. (1994). Does competitive environment moderate the market orientation-performance relationship? *Journal of Marketing*, *58*(1), 46–55.

Sundaramurthy, C. (2008). Sustaining trust within family businesses. *Family Business Review*, *21*(1), 89–102.

Vandekerckhove, W., & Dentchev, N. A. (2005). A network perspective on stakeholder management: Facilitating entrepreneurs in the discovery of opportunities. *Journal of Business Ethics*, *60*, 221–232.

Vargas, N., Lloria, M. B., Salazar, A., & Vergara, L. (2018). Effect of exploitation and exploration on the innovative as outcomes in entrepreneurial firms. *International Entrepreneurship and Management Journal*, *14*(4), 1053–1069.

Vasilchenko, E., & Morrish, S. (2011). The role of entrepreneurial networks in the exploration and exploitation of internationalization opportunities by information and communication technology firms. *Journal of International Marketing*, *19*(4), 88–105.

Vershinina, N., Rodgers, P., Tarba, S., Khan, Z., & Stokes, P. (2020). Gaining legitimacy through proactive stakeholder management: The experiences of high-tech women entrepreneurs in Russia. *Journal of Business Research*, *119*, 111–121.

Voss, G. B., Sirdeshmukh, D., & Voss, Z. G. (2008). The effects of slack resources and environmental threat on product exploration and exploitation. *Academy of Management Journal*, *51*, 147–164.

Voss, G. B., & Voss, Z. G. (2013). Strategic ambidexterity in small and medium-sized enterprises: Implementing exploration and exploitation in product and market domains. *Organization Science*, *24*(5), 1459–1477.

Walsh, J. P. (2005). Book review essay: Taking stock of stakeholder management, *Academy of Management Review*, *30*(2), 426–438

Wernerfelt, B. (1984). A resource-based view of the firm, *Strategic Management Journal*, *5*(2), 171–180.

Zahra, S. A. (1993). Environment, corporate entrepreneurship, and financial performance: A taxonomic approach. *Journal Business Venturing*, *8*(4), 319–340.

4 Stakeholder Legitimacy Perceptions and Firm Innovation

A developing country perspective

Emelia Amoako-Asiedu, Priscilla Ntriwaa Otuo, Theresa Obuobisa-Darko and Alex Antwi-Agyei

Introduction

Stakeholder engagement and innovation has garnered significant attention in the entrepreneurship and innovation literature (Adomako et al., 2019; Leonidou et al., 2020; Nair, 2020). Although the issue of stakeholder legitimacy perceptions is one salient factor influencing stakeholder engagement, it is yet to be fully explored. The limited attention to such fundamental principles of stakeholder engagement is an obstacle to the progress of research in stakeholder engagement (Kujala et al., 2022). Therefore, we draw from the legitimacy theory (Fisher, 2020; Suchman, 1995; Zimmerman & Zeitz, 2002) and stakeholder theory (Freeman, 2015; Friedman & Miles, 2002; Freeman et al., 2010) to explain how stakeholder legitimacy perceptions affect venture innovation. Heeding calls for more research on stakeholders and innovation in different contexts (Adomako et al., 2019; Leonidou et al., 2020), we review extant research on firm innovation and stakeholders in developing countries and attempt to assess ways in which stakeholder legitimacy perceptions influence firm innovation. The core premise of this discussion is that stakeholders' willingness and ability to engage with entrepreneurial ventures and provide resources required for innovative activities depends on their legitimacy perception of the firm. This paper contributes novel insights into the relationship between stakeholder engagement, venture innovation, and stakeholder legitimacy perceptions, focusing on the African context. By extension, our study investigates the influence of diverse stakeholders, such as religious organisations, extended families, and governments, on venture innovation in Africa. To accomplish this, we integrate empirical research and theories on venture legitimacy, firm innovation, and stakeholders within the context of developing countries, with a specific emphasis on Africa.

Our discussion on stakeholder legitimacy and firm innovation proceeds as follows. First, we present a review of the literature on venture innovation in developing economies. Second, we explain stakeholder theory and stakeholder engagement. Third, we examine the literature on venture legitimacy. Fourth, we discuss five key stakeholders, and this analysis provides us with insights to contribute to current research and fill knowledge gaps in the entrepreneurship and innovation literature.

DOI: 10.4324/9781003256014-6

Venture innovation

Innovation is generally conceptualised as anything new concerning products, production processes, markets, supply sources, and organisational methods (Autio et al., 2014; Carelse, 2013; Garud et al., 2013; Schumpeter, 1939). Researchers often categorise innovations into two types, incremental and radical innovation, which represent modifications or breakthrough innovations, respectively (Adomako et al., 2019; Carelse, 2013. In Africa, innovation often falls into the incremental innovation category, signifying that regional innovations are typically gradual and do not lead to dramatic changes (Carelse, 2013).

The existing literature recognises the linkages between innovation, regional development, firm growth, and economic growth. Further, innovation is a fundamental characteristic of entrepreneurial firms. In this regard, scholars suggest that innovation is a "specific instrument of entrepreneurship" (Soriano and Huarng, 2013, p. 1965).

Several factors may affect a firm's ability to innovate. Among these factors, resource access emerges as a critical issue influencing venture innovation, acting as both an incentive and a disincentive. For instance, skills availability and adequate infrastructure could incentivise firms to engage in innovative activities (van Burg et al., 2012). Conversely, limited financial resources can encourage firms to innovate and exercise prudence in utilising their constrained resources (Amankwah-Amoah et al., 2019; Mosakowski, 2002).

Entrepreneurial ventures rely on two primary sources for such resources needed for innovation: internal and external sources. External resources play a crucial role in the activities of ventures. One key finding from the existing research is that stakeholders offer valuable resources that foster entrepreneurship and innovation (Acquaah, 2007; Amankwah-Amoah et al., 2019; Leonidou et al., 2020; Shams et al., 2020). Stakeholder resources encompass financial resources, social capital, knowledge, and skills, all critical for successful innovation. Freeman (1984, p. 25) defines stakeholders as "any group or individual who can affect or is affected by the achievement of the firm's objectives." The resource dependency theory provides the theoretical foundation for understanding firm's reliance on stakeholders for resources (Barney, 2018; Hillman et al., 2009; Davis & Cobb, 2010; Biermann & Harsch, 2017). Resource dependency theory identifies how access to external resources impacts firm performance.

Given the foregoing discussion, scholars argue that innovation and its value-delivery process are independent of the efforts of a single entrepreneur or a business entity. Therefore, entrepreneurs must embrace the reality that relying solely on in-house competencies in planning and implementing the innovation processes necessary for achieving sustainable competitive advantages does not provide the needed results (Bughin et al., 2008; del Vecchio et al., 2018).

Entrepreneurs' and entrepreneurial firms' interaction with their stakeholders offers an essential source of social knowledge and human capital that enhances entrepreneurs' success in innovation management (Smith & Lohrke, 2008). The next section discusses the role of stakeholders in venture innovation in detail.

Stakeholder engagement

The expanding knowledge base on stakeholder engagement and innovation draws heavily on stakeholder theory (Freeman et al., 2017; Kujala et al., 2022). The stakeholder theory suggests that stakeholders play a crucial role in creating value within ventures, as they possess essential resources that entrepreneurial ventures require (Corral & Monagas, 2017; Freeman et al., 2010; Phillips et al., 2003). Hence, the relationship between firms and diverse stakeholders proves advantageous for entrepreneurial firms (Leonidou et al., 2020; Sefiani et al., 2018) and particularly for innovative activities (Leonidou et al., 2018; Vrontis et al., 2017).

Stakeholder engagement, as used in this context, refers to "the aims, activities, and impacts of stakeholder relations in a moral, strategic, and/or pragmatic manner" (Kujala et al., 2022, p. 1139). Stakeholder engagement activities include collaborations and decision-making, partnerships, as well as communication, which can be one-way or reciprocal (Greenwood, 2007; Jolibert & Wesselink, 2012; Kujala et al., 2022). Stakeholder engagement encompasses three dimensions: moral, pragmatic, and strategic (Kujala et al., 2022). The discussion in this chapter will centre on all three dimensions. First, we address the moral dimension of stakeholder engagement by exploring how stakeholders grant legitimacy to firms. Second, we also consider the role of stakeholder engagement in the organisation's goal-oriented activities, specifically innovation. Third, we provide insights into the pragmatic dimension, explained as context-based approaches to stakeholder engagement in developing economies.

Indeed, Hoffecker (2018, p. 2) emphasises the significance of stakeholders, specifically the local African community, to innovation by conceptualising innovation in developing countries using various terms such as "grassroots innovation," "informal innovation," "rural innovation," "pro-poor innovation," "frugal" or jugaad innovation," "local innovation," and "endogenous innovation." These terms reflect that innovation activities in developing economies often intertwine with local contexts. Empirical evidence from several industries in Africa, including the tourism and agricultural sectors studies, lends credence to this assertion (Adekunle et al., 2013; Carlisle et al., 2013; Nambiar, 2019). For example, Adekunle et al. (2013) found that public, private, and nongovernmental stakeholder networks influenced successful agricultural innovation. The authors illustrated that interactions between these stakeholders and agricultural firms led to heightened cooperation and trust, enabling innovation. Likewise, Adomako et al. (2019) concluded that stakeholder integration impacted firm innovation in a study of Ghanaian SMEs. Adomako et al. (2019, p. 739) conceptualised stakeholder engagement as "knowledge of stakeholders, interaction with stakeholders and adaptation to stakeholder demand." The core argument of Adomako et al. (2019) was that certain market conditions (customer demandingness and competitive intensity) moderated the impact of stakeholder integration on firm innovation.

Venture legitimacy

Legitimacy is socially constructed (Harvey & Schaefer, 2001) and how an organisation views a stakeholder's legitimacy may differ from the stakeholder's opinion of its validity (Santana, 2012). There can therefore be positive stakeholder perceptions that reflect and point toward the maintenance of organisational legitimacy, while a negative perception might mean the organisation's legitimacy is at risk (She & Michelon, 2019). A positive stakeholder legitimate perception is therefore crucial for an organisation's success. Thus, gaining legitimacy by aligning an organisation's activities and actions with stakeholder expectations and thus causing them to have a positive legitimacy perception is required to ensure organisational success (Bellucci et al., 2021).

Firms require legitimacy for three main reasons (Yang & Wu, 2016). First, legitimacy enables firms to acquire resources, especially those that are in short supply. Second, stakeholders consider legitimate organisations as more trustworthy than those that are considered illegitimate. Third, organisations may suffer economic, legal, and social consequences if they are perceived as being illegitimate. Importantly, firms in developing economies require legitimacy because of institutional weaknesses, voids, and resource constraints, meaning legitimacy-granting actors such as customers and suppliers become critical to their activities (Adomako et al., 2019).

The dynamics of legitimacy pressures facing firms are diverse. Suchman emphasizes the cognitive and evaluative aspects of a firm's legitimacy (Santana, 2012). Deephouse et al. (2017) propose that venture legitimacy can exist in four states: accepted, proper, debated, and illegitimate. Actions conducted by legitimate firms are considered appropriate, while those perceived as illegitimate necessitate either termination or significant reforms (Villani et al., 2021). Consequently, at the fundamental level, a venture's operations must avoid being deemed illegitimate. Stakeholders may place entrepreneurial ventures in these legitimacy categories by comparing a firm's behaviour with society's expectations. Therefore, as Steyn and Puth (2000: 209) suggest, a venture's legitimacy is not "an inherent characteristic of an organisation but rather a reflection of societal perceptions of corporate behaviour in comparison to societal expectations."

Moreover, new firms often need more internal structures and resources for successful innovation (Villani et al., 2021), making their ability to innovate more difficult. As a solution to this liability, new firms often strive to establish organisational legitimacy (Fisher, 2020). For example, they may pursue strategies enabling them to gain internal and external legitimacy (Rao et al., 2008a, b), such as aligning themselves with already reputable enterprises. During this new venture stage, the founders(s) are crucial as the primary agents seeking legitimacy (Fisher, 2020). Also, aspects of the entrepreneurship literature suggest that firms that are not new also need to maintain and sometimes restore their legitimacy. In the next section, we discuss five important stakeholder groups and how they impact venture innovation.

Stakeholder legitimacy perceptions and firm innovation: Governmental institutions and political authorities

The general understanding is that firms must comply with regulations and laws to establish legitimacy (Zimmerman & Zeitz, 2002). A firm's legal status, such as formal registration, is crucial in evaluating what Assenova and Sorenson (2017) call "sociopolitical legitimacy." Assenova and Sorenson (2017) define sociopolitical legitimacy as the public and resource providers' perception of an organisation's appropriateness and trustworthiness in exchange relationships. When entrepreneurial firms lack perceived governmental recognition, stakeholders such as lenders and investors may perceive them as risky ventures, resulting in a reluctance to provide financial support (Assenova & Sorenson, 2017). This is particularly important for entrepreneurial ventures in developing economies where resource scarcity is common and firms receive little financial support from governmental sources. Furthermore, potential employees may hesitate to work with informal businesses, and customers may be unwilling to purchase from such enterprises. These challenges can hinder growth, competitiveness, and the ability to deliver high-quality products or services. An examination of over 12,000 businesses in 18 businesses across sub-Saharan Africa revealed that firms that were registered from the onset employed more people and enjoyed higher sales levels (Assenova and Sorenson, 2017). The foregoing study suggests a contribution to firm performance but not necessarily to firm innovation. Therefore, connections with individuals in positions of power and political and social capital play a relevant role in accessing resources (Adomako & Danso, 2014) and, consequently, how firms are successful with their innovative activities. However, based on the foregoing, adhering to the laws (formalisation of business activities) is essential. However, more is needed for a firm's access to the resources it requires from African governmental institutions and political authorities. Thus, although formalisation may indicate a venture's legitimacy, it may not allow the firm to gain essential resources for its innovative activities.

Religious organisations

Religion is essential in defining entrepreneurial motivations, practices, networks, foreign direct investment choices, and policy directions (Balog et al., 2014; Dodd & Seaman, 1998; Dodd & Gotsis, 2007; Fernando & Jackson,

2006; Jenkins, 2004; Micheal, 2000). Jenkins (2004, p. 17), for instance, argues that policymakers' market orientation is influenced by

> competing ideological traditions, some of which are of religious origin which share partial claims to potent anti-market orientations or tend to legitimise particular market outcomes based on social norms, cultural beliefs and which enable members to acquire the knowledge and skills required to innovate.

Religion is vital in defining African entrepreneurship both in the continent and elsewhere. For instance, in a qualitative study of Nigerian entrepreneurs, David-West et al. (2018) established that religion plays a significant role in determining the mindset of entrepreneurs. The study concluded that religious beliefs inspired Christian and Muslim entrepreneurs and their decision-making, interactions, and work ethics. Additional research has found that religious organisations in Nigeria support entrepreneurs with social capital, mentoring services, and other resources. Similar findings emerged from a study of African entrepreneurs in the UK. In their research exploring religion and entrepreneurship among Africans in the United Kingdom, Nwankwo et al. (2012) concluded that churches have played significant roles in supporting venture start-ups and promoting entrepreneurship among the African community in the United Kingdom. The research further concluded that members of the churches accumulate social capital, which allows them to start and grow their businesses. Several of the foregoing studies have intimated the role of religious organisations in providing social capital to African entrepreneurs. The entrepreneurship literature has concluded that the types of networks a firm has and its embeddedness in these network relationships impact its capacity to innovate (Molina-Morales et al., 2010). Evidence of the role of religion on innovation in the African context appears limited.

Family and friends

Generally, literature recognises friends and family as vital stakeholders in promoting innovation and entrepreneurship. For example, Davidsson and Honig (2003) found that family and friends strongly influenced opportunity discovery. Davidsson and Honig (2003) further argued that the presence of friends and family as stakeholders in a person's business is strongly associated with an enhanced discovery process, suggesting that family and friends' advice, encouragement, and support may result in opportunity identification. A review of the literature further highlights the influence of the African family on multiple venture start-ups, and the reasons accounting for this in the literature are various. Steel (1991) revealed that some entrepreneurs establish businesses to follow their parents, who were also entrepreneurs. Others, such as Michell (2004), Roy and Wheeler (2006), and Benzing and Chu (2009), indicated that some entrepreneurs in Africa set up businesses to provide financial security and meet the financial needs of their families. Discua Cruz et al. (2019), in a growth study on portfolio entrepreneurs, also intimated the role of the family in creating multiple businesses in the African context. Kiggundu (2002) further contended in his discussion on entrepreneurship studies in Africa that some entrepreneurs with large families set up more businesses to encourage their children or relatives to enter business activities.

However, these commitments to businesses and support for businesses depend on their legitimacy perceptions about the entrepreneurs' businesses and, in some cases, the entrepreneurs who own and manage these businesses. Community norms and values (discussed in the next section) often affect family members' perceptions of entrepreneurs' businesses.

The community

Communities often have their cultures, values, and beliefs, which impact legitimacy perceptions of entrepreneurs' family and friends, and in some cases, religious organisations in the community. Igwe et al. (2020) for instance, write about how the Igbos in Nigeria are considered to be entrepreneurial. Such beliefs may lead to a more positive assessment of a business owned by an Igbo and its ability to make judicious use of resources. Interestingly, entrepreneurship in some parts of Africa, like Ghana, is considered a legitimate profession for women as women dominate the entrepreneurial landscape. The logical conclusion, therefore, is that such communities may recognise entrepreneurship as a legitimate career choice for women.

Competitors

Ayyagari et al. (2011) suggest that the relationship between competition and innovation is unsettled. This is because the relationship which can be positive or negative, depending on specific competition perception and specific innovation activity (Tang, 2006). While research confirms the positive effect of competition on entrepreneurs' innovative behaviour (Galdón-Sánchez and Schmitz Jr, 2002; Sheikh, 2018; Park et al., 2014), others state a negative relationship (Aghion et al., 2009; Liu et al., 2023). Despite these differences, Allen and Gale (2000) suggest that the device to adopt to control agency costs in business in developing countries is the level of intensity of competition. As a result, firms in such countries adopt appropriate strategies to be innovative to be a competitive advantage. The deduction, therefore, is that competition causes entrepreneurs to be highly innovative.

Conclusions

The study adopted the legitimacy perspective to explore stakeholder engagement and venture innovative practices. The study presents a detailed literature review highlighting the importance of stakeholder legitimacy perceptions and how they impact firm innovation. It emphasises the role of stakeholder legitimacy perceptions in shaping resource availability for entrepreneurial ventures and their innovation efforts. The aim was limited in terms of its focus on four stakeholder groups that impact innovation in Africa. This research is a starting point for exploring the literature on how stakeholder legitimacy perceptions influence the willingness of stakeholders to provide resources for venture innovation. Leonidou et al. (2020) highlight that other stakeholder groups, such as competitors, customers, innovation intermediaries, and social media affect venture innovation. Further research may offer insights into how the legitimacy perceptions of these stakeholders impact venture innovation. Existing research also notes how new firms' legitimacy challenges may differ from others. Therefore, the existing knowledge of stakeholders and innovation may benefit from further studies on how stakeholder legitimacy perceptions influence firms' resource access at different stages of the entrepreneurial process. The depth of our analysis was impacted by the lack of evidence on stakeholder engagement and venture innovation in developing economies, revealing a knowledge gap in the area. Hence, like calls by Adomako et al. (2019), there is the need for further research on the subject in developing countries.

References

Acquaah, M. (2007). Managerial social capital, strategic orientation, and organizational performance in an emerging economy. *Strategic Management Journal, 28*(12), 1235–1255.

Adekunle, A. A., Ellis-Jones, J., Ajibefun, I., Nyikal, R. A., Bangali, S., Fatunbi, A. O., & Angé, A. (2013, June). *Agricultural innovation in sub-Saharan Africa: Experiences from multiple stakeholder approaches.* Forum for Agricultural Research in Africa (FARA).

Adomako, S., Amankwah-Amoah, J., & Danso, A. (2019). The effects of stakeholder integration on firm-level product innovativeness: insights from small and medium-sized enterprises in Ghana. *R&D Management, 49*(5), 734–747.

Adomako, S., & Danso, A. (2014). Regulatory environment, environmental dynamism, political ties, and performance: Study of entrepreneurial firms in a developing economy. *Journal of Small Business and Enterprise Development, 21*(2), 212–230.

Aghion, P., Blundell, R., Griffith, R., Howitt, P., & Prantl, S. (2009). The effects of entry on incumbent innovation and productivity. *The Review of Economics and Statistics, 91*(1), 20–32.

Allen, F., & Gale, D. (2000). Bubbles and crises. *The Economic Journal, 110*(460), 236–255.

Amankwah-Amoah, J., Danso, A., & Adomako, S. (2019). Entrepreneurial orientation, environmental sustainability and new venture performance: Does stakeholder integration matter? *Business Strategy and the Environment, 28*(1), 79–87.

Assenova, V. A., & Sorenson, O. (2017). Legitimacy and the benefits of firm formalization. *Organization Science, 28*(5), 804–818.

Autio, E., Kenney, M., Mustar, P., Siegel, D., & Wright, M. (2014). Entrepreneurial innovation: The importance of context. *Research Policy, 43*(7), 1097–1108.

Ayyagari, M., Demirgüç-Kunt, A., & Maksimovic, V. (2011). Small vs. young firms across the world: Contribution to employment, job creation, and growth. *World Bank Policy Research Working Paper*, (5631).

Balog, A. M., Baker, L. T., & Walker, A. G. (2014). Religiosity and spirituality in entrepreneurship: A review and research agenda. *Journal of Management, Spirituality & Religion*, *11*(2), 159–186.

Barney, J. B. (2018). Why resource-based theory's model of profit appropriation must incorporate a stakeholder perspective. *Strategic Management Journal*, *39*(13), 3305–3325.

Bellucci, M., Marzi, G., Orlando, B., & Ciampi, F. (2021). Journal of Intellectual Capital: A review of emerging themes and future trends. *Journal of Intellectual Capital*, *22*(4), 744–767.

Benzing, C., & Chu, H. M. (2009). A comparison of the motivations of small business owners in Africa. *Journal of Small Business and Enterprise Development*, *16*(1), 60–77.

Benzing, C., Chu, H. M., & Kara, O. (2009). Entrepreneurs in Turkey: A factor analysis of motivations, success factors, and problems. *Journal of Small Business Management*, *47*(1), 58–91.

Biermann, R., & Harsch, M., 2017. Resource dependence theory. *Palgrave handbook of inter-organizational relations in world politics* (pp. 135–155). Palgrave Macmillan. https://doi.org/10.1057/978-1-137-36039-7

Bughin, J., Chui, M., & Johnson, B. (2008). The next step in open innovation. *The McKinsey Quarterly*, *4*(6), 1–8.

Carelse, K. (2013). Employees' perceptions towards workplace diversity in a financial institution operating in the Western Cape.

Carlisle, S., Kunc, M., Jones, E., & Tiffin, S. (2013). Supporting innovation for tourism development through multi-stakeholder approaches: Experiences from Africa. *Tourism Management*, *35*, 59–69.

Corral, S., & Monagas, M. C. (2017). Social involvement in environmental governance: The relevance of quality assurance processes in forest planning. *Land Use Policy*, *67*, 710–715.

Davidsson, P., & Honig, B. (2003). The role of social and human capital among nascent entrepreneurs. *Journal of Business Venturing*, *18*(3), 301–331.

David-West, O., Umukoro, I. O., & Onuoha, R. O. (2018). Platforms in sub-Saharan Africa: Startup models and the role of business incubation. *Journal of Intellectual Capital*, *19*(3), 581–616.

Davis, G. F., & Cobb, J. A. (2010). Corporations and economic inequality around the world: The paradox of hierarchy. *Research in Organizational Behavior*, *30*, 35–53.

Deegan, C. M. (2019). Legitimacy theory: Despite its enduring popularity and contribution, time is right for a necessary makeover. *Accounting, Auditing & Accountability Journal*, *32*(8), 2307–2329.

Deephouse, D. L., Bundy, J., Tost, L. P., & Suchman, M. C. (2017). Organizational legitimacy: Six key questions. *The SAGE Handbook of Organizational Institutionalism*, *4*(2), 27–54.

Del Vecchio, P., Mele, G., Ndou, V., & Secundo, G. (2018). Creating value from social big data: Implications for smart tourism destinations. *Information Processing & Management*, *54*(5), 847–860.

Devine, R. A., & Kiggundu, M. N. (2016). Entrepreneurship in Africa: Identifying the frontier of impactful research. *Africa Journal of Management*, *2*(3), 349–380.

Discua Cruz, A., Basco, R., Parada, M. J., Malfense Fierro, A., & Alvarado-Alvarez, C. (2019). Resilience and family business groups in unstable economies. *The Family Business Group Phenomenon: Emergence and Complexities*, 315–352.

Dodd, S. D., & Gotsis, G. (2007). The interrelationships between entrepreneurship and religion. *The International Journal of Entrepreneurship and Innovation*, *8*(2), 93–104.

Dodd, S. D., & Seaman, P. T. (1998). Religion and enterprise: An introductory exploration. *Entrepreneurship Theory and Practice*, *23*(1), 71–86.

Fernando, M., & Jackson, B. (2006). The influence of religion-based workplace spirituality on business leaders' decision-making: An inter-faith study. *Journal of Management & Organization*, *12*(1), 23–39.

Fisher, G., 2020. The complexities of new venture legitimacy. *Organization Theory*, *1*(2). https://doi.org/10.1177/2631787720913881

Freeman, R. E. (1984). *Strategic management: A stakeholder approach*. Pitman.

Freeman, R. E. (2015). *Strategic management: A stakeholder approach*. Cambridge University Press. https://doi.org/10.1017/CBO9781139192675

Freeman, R. E., Harrison, J. S., Wicks, A. C., Parmar, B. L., & De Colle, S. (2010). Stakeholder theory: The state of the art.*The Academy of Management Annals*, *4*(1), 403–445. https://doi.org/10.1080/19416520.2010.495581

Freeman, R. E., Kujala, J., Sachs, S., & Stutz, C. (2017). Stakeholder engagement: Practicing the ideas of stakeholder theory. *Stakeholder Engagement: Clinical Research Cases*, 1–12. https://doi.org/10.1007/978-3-319-62785-4_1

Friedman, A. L., & Miles, S. (2002). Developing stakeholder theory. *Journal of Management Studies*, *39*(1), 1–21.

Galdón-Sánchez, J., & Schmitz Jr, J. A. (2002). Competitive pressure and labor productivity: World iron-ore markets in the 1980's. *American Economic Review*, *92*(4), 1222–1235.

Garud, R., Tuertscher, P., & Van de Ven, A. H. (2013). Perspectives on innovation processes. *Academy of Management Annals*, *7*(1), 775–819. 33.

Greenwood, M. (2007). Stakeholder engagement: Beyond the myth of corporate responsibility. *Journal of Business Ethics*, *74*, 315–327.

Harvey, B., & Schaefer, A. (2001). Managing relationships with environmental stakeholders: A study of UK water and electricity utilities. *Journal of Business Ethics*, *30*, 243–260.

Hillman, A. J., Withers, M. C., & Collins, B. J. (2009). Resource dependence theory: A review. *Journal of Management*, *35*(6), 1404–1427.

Hoffecker, E. (2018). Local Innovation: what it is and why it matters for developing economies. *D-Lab Working Papers: NDIR Working Paper*, *1*.

Igwe, P. A., Ochinanwata, C., Ochinanwata, N., Adeyeye, J. O., Ikpor, I. M., Nwakpu, S. E., … & Umemezia, E. I. (2020). Solidarity and social behaviour: How did this help communities to manage COVID-19 pandemic? *International Journal of Sociology and Social Policy*, *40*(9/10), 1183–1200.

Jenkins, H. (2004). Corporate social responsibility and the mining industry: Conflicts and constructs. *Corporate Social Responsibility and Environmental Management*, *11*(1), 23–34.

Jolibert, C., & Wesselink, A. (2012). Research impacts and impact on research in biodiversity conservation: The influence of stakeholder engagement. *Environmental Science & Policy*, *22*, 100–111.

Kiggundu, M. N. (2002). Entrepreneurs and entrepreneurship in Africa: What is known and what needs to be done. *Journal of Developmental Entrepreneurship*, *7*(3), 239.

Kujala, J., Sachs, S., Leinonen, H., Heikkinen, A., & Laude, D. (2022). Stakeholder engagement: Past, present, and future. *Business & Society*, *61*(5), 1136–1196.

Leonidou, E., Christofi, M., Vrontis, D., & Thrassou, A. (2020). An integrative framework of stakeholder engagement for innovation management and entrepreneurship development. *Journal of Business Research*, *119*, 245–258.

Leonidou, L. C., Aykol, B., Hadjimarcou, J., & Palihawadana, D. (2018). Betrayal in buyer–seller relationships: Exploring its causes, symptoms, forms, effects, and therapies. *Psychology & Marketing*, *35*(5), 341–356.

Liu, H., Yin, X., & Chu, H. (2023). Cultural diversity in intervention design: A Chinese illustrative example. *The Sage Handbook of Mixed Methods Research Design* (p. 434). Sage.

Micheal, K. G. (2000). Sustainability in tourism through government regulations. http://dl.nsf.gov.lk/bitstream/handle/1/14457/ER-26(3-5)-8.pdf?sequence=2

Michell, N. (2004). Stakeholder participation in planning for multiple-use forest management. In Michael John Lawes (Ed.), *Indigenous forests and woodlands in South Africa. Policy, people and practice* (pp. 704–707). University of KwaZulu–Natal Press.

Molina-Morales, F. X., Parra-Requena, Gloria, & García-Villaverde, P. M. (2010). The mediating effect of cognitive social capital on knowledge acquisition in clustered firms. *Growth and Change*, *41*(1), 59–84.

Mosakowski, E. (2002). Overcoming resource disadvantages in entrepreneurial firms: When less is more. In M. A. Hitt, R. D. Ireland, S. M. Camp, & D. L. Sexton, Eds., *Strategic entrepreneurship: Creating a new integrated mindset*, Blackwell Publishing, 106–126.

Nair, S. R. (2020). The link between women entrepreneurship, innovation and stakeholder engagement: A review. *Journal of Business Research*, *119*, 283–290.

Nambiar, E. S. (2019). Tamm review: Re-imagining forestry and wood business: Pathways to rural development, poverty alleviation and climate change mitigation in the tropics. *Forest Ecology and Management*, *448*, 160–173.

Nwankwo, S., Gbadamosi, A., & Ojo, S. (2012). Religion, spirituality and entrepreneurship: The church as entrepreneurial space among British Africans. *Society and Business Review*, *7*(2), 149–167.

Park, D. C., Lodi-Smith, J., Drew, L., Haber, S., Hebrank, A., Bischof, G. N., & Aamodt, W. (2014). The impact of sustained engagement on cognitive function in older adults: The Synapse Project. *Psychological Science*, *25*(1), 103–112. https://doi.org/10.1177/0956797613499592. PMID: 24214244; PMCID: PMC4154531.

Phillips, R., Freeman, R. E., & Wicks, A. C. (2003). What stakeholder theory is not. *Business Ethics Quarterly*, *13*(4), 479–502.

Rao, R. S., Chandy, R. K., & Prabhu, J. C. (2008a). The fruits of legitimacy: Why some new ventures gain more from innovation than others. *Journal of Marketing*, *72*(4), 58–75.

Rao, H. R., Kim, D. J., & Ferrin, D. L. (2008b). A trust-based consumer decision-making model in electronic commerce: The role of trust, perceived risk, and their antecedents. *Decision Support Systems*, *44*(2), 544–564.

Roy, M. A., & Wheeler, D. (2006). A survey of micro-enterprise in urban West Africa: drivers shaping the sector. *Development in Practice*, *16*(5), 452–464.

Santana, A. (2012). Three elements of stakeholder legitimacy. *Journal of Business Ethics*, *105*(2), 257–265.

Schumpeter, J. A. (1939). *Business cycles: A theoretical and statistical analysis of the capitalist process.* McGraw-Hill.

Sefiani, N., Regragui, H.,& Azzouzi, H. (2018, April). Improving performance through measurement: The application of BSC and AHP in healthcare organization. In *2018 International Colloquium on Logistics and Supply Chain Management (LOGISTIQUA)* (pp. 51–56). IEEE.

Shams, S. R., Vrontis, D., Chaudhuri, R., Chavan, G., & Czinkota, M. R. (2020). Stakeholder engagement for innovation management and entrepreneurial development: A meta-analysis. *Journal of Business Research, 119*, 67–86.

She, C., & Michelon, G. (2019). Managing stakeholder perceptions: Organized hypocrisy in CSR disclosures on Facebook. *Critical Perspectives on Accounting, 61*, 54–76.

Sheikh, S. (2018). The impact of market competition on the relation between CEO power and firm innovation. *Journal of Multinational Financial Management, 44*, 36–50.

Smith, D. A., & Lohrke, F. T. (2008). Entrepreneurial network development: Trusting in the process. *Journal of Business Research, 61*(4), 315–322.

Soriano, D. R., & Huarng, K. H. (2013). Innovation and entrepreneurship in knowledge industries. *Journal of Business Research, 66*(10), 1964–1969.

Steel, J. L. (1991). Interpersonal correlates of trust and self-disclosure. *Psychological Reports, 68*(3_suppl), 1319–1320.

Steyn, B., & Puth, G. (2000). *Corporate communication strategy*. Heinemann.

Suchman, M. C. (1995). Managing legitimacy: Strategic and institutional approaches. *Academy of Management Review 20*(3), 571–610.

Tang, C. S. (2006). Perspectives in supply chain risk management. *International Journal of Production Economics, 103*(2), 451–488.

Van Burg, E., Podoynitsyna, K., Beck, L., & Lommelen, T. (2012). Directive deficiencies: How resource constraints direct opportunity identification in SMEs. *Journal of Product Innovation Management, 29*(6), 1000–1011.

Villani, J., Daly, P., Fay, R., Kavanagh, L., McDonagh, S., & Amin, N. (2021). A community-health partnership response to mitigate the impact of the COVID-19 pandemic on travellers and Roma in Ireland. *Global Health Promotion, 28*(2), 46–55.

Vrontis, D., Thrassou, A., Santoro, G., & Papa, A. (2017). Ambidexterity, external knowledge and performance in knowledge-intensive firms. *The Journal of Technology Transfer, 42*, 374–388.

Yang, Y. K., & Wu, S. L. (2016). In search of the right fusion recipe: The role of legitimacy in building a social enterprise model. *Business Ethics: A European Review, 25*(3), 327–343.

Zimmerman, M. A., & Zeitz, G. J. (2002). Beyond survival: Achieving new venture growth by building legitimacy. *Academy of Management Review, 27*(3), 414–431.

5 Stakeholders and New Venture Growth in Africa

Nadia Zahoor and Arinze Christian Nwoba

Introduction

Over the years, entrepreneurship has occupied an important position in the contemporary global economic environment (Wadhwani et al., 2020). It is a complex phenomenon that is often defined as a process and at times a resource (Wang et al., 2023). The entrepreneurship concept has been defined in several ways. Based on Schumpeter (1912), entrepreneurship is the act of initiating creative endeavors and launching new goods onto the market. Kirzner (1973) suggests that entrepreneurship includes the competitive behaviors that propel the market process, seemingly supporting Schumpeter's theory that entrepreneurship is a contest of ideas. Taking a more legalistic view, Dau and Cuervo-Cazurra (2014) define entrepreneurship "as the creation of new businesses, i.e., a stable collection of individuals who coordinate their efforts to generate new value-added economic activity" (p. 670). Taken together, entrepreneurship consists of three parts: coordination of resources, creation of new ventures, and innovation (Naudé, 2011).

Despite the chorus of conflicting opinions that have characterized its definition, entrepreneurship is considered an important tool for economic growth even in uncertain market conditions (Amorós et al., 2021; Urbano et al., 2019; Zahoor et al., 2023). The significance of entrepreneurship extends beyond mere economic enterprise, encompassing the catalytic role it plays in fostering innovation, igniting economic growth, creating employment opportunities, and driving societal transformation (Mmbaga et al., 2020). In the global context, entrepreneurship emerges as a potent force, underpinning the vitality and dynamism of economies across diverse regions (Galindo-Martín et al., 2021). It serves as a crucible of creativity, propelling the development of new businesses, products, and services and fueling competition and technological advancements (Bradley et al., 2021). This virtuous cycle of innovation and competition has become the hallmark of entrepreneurial ecosystems worldwide, leading to enhanced efficiency, productivity, and economic prosperity (Ajayi et al., 2022; Loots et al., 2021).

Within the context of the African continent, entrepreneurship assumes an even greater significance, as it emerges as a linchpin for addressing pressing

DOI: 10.4324/9781003256014-7

socioeconomic challenges and capitalizing on emerging opportunities (Madzikanda et al., 2021; Weber et al., 2023). Africa's demographic profile, characterized by a youthful and rapidly growing population, presents both a unique asset and a formidable challenge (Nachum et al., 2023; Singh et al., 2023). Entrepreneurship stands as an imperative avenue for harnessing the demographic dividend by creating employment opportunities for the youth and mitigating the perils of burgeoning youth unemployment (Ajide et al., 2021; Nyame-Asiamah et al., 2020). Moreover, it offers a pathway toward economic diversification in many African nations that are heavily reliant on a narrow range of sectors, such as natural resources (Atiase et al., 2018).

Indeed, with Africa's burgeoning youth population and high levels of unemployment, entrepreneurship and new ventures serve as engines of job creation, absorbing a considerable portion of the workforce (Kiggundu & Pal, 2018; Robson et al., 2009). Additionally, new ventures often operate in sectors that have the potential for high growth, including technology, agriculture, and renewable energy (Ajayi et al., 2022; Arthur et al., 2020). For example, Nigeria is believed to have had more than 3,360 new businesses in 2022—more than any other country in Africa. Subsequently, in the same year, South Africa recorded about 660 new businesses, whereas Kenya recorded about 1,000. Further, more than 18,000 new registered businesses were forecasted in Ghana, particularly in the technology and financial services sector (Statista, 2022).

This article contributes to entrepreneurship literature on stakeholders' relevance for new ventures in Africa. This contributes to a more comprehensive picture of entrepreneurship in Africa, shedding light on the unique challenges and opportunities faced by startups. Based on a literature review, we have identified different strategies used by stakeholders to support value creation by new ventures. Further, by examining the role of stakeholders, the study informs the development of supportive policies and regulations tailored to African entrepreneurial environments. Policymakers can use the findings to design initiatives that encourage positive stakeholder engagement and foster a conducive ecosystem for startups.

Theoretical background

In 1963, an internal memorandum at the Stanford Research Institute first used the term "stakeholder" (Strand & Freeman, 2015). This memorandum emphasized the idea that a company should consider the interests of all parties or "stakeholders" affected by its actions, not just the shareholders (Friedman & Miles, 2006; Freeman & McVea, 2005; Freeman & Reed, 1983). The concept of stakeholders challenged the traditional notion of shareholder primacy, which argued that a company's primary responsibility was to maximize profits for its shareholders (Smith & Rönnegard, 2016). In the early 1980s, stakeholder theory was proposed as a broader perspective that recognized the interests of various groups, including employees, customers, suppliers, communities, and more (Freeman, 1984). Throughout the 1980s and 1990s, scholars like Freeman and others continued to refine and expand stakeholder theory (Ackermann & Eden, 2011). They developed various models and frameworks to help managers identify, prioritize, and engage with stakeholders. These efforts aimed to address three interconnected business problems, as mentioned in Figure 5.1.

From stakeholder theory, the relationship between a business, individuals, and groups can help to address three problems exhibited in Figure 5.1. First, stakeholder theory considers a business as a set of relationships between groups who are interested in business operations (Freeman, 1984; Walsh, 2005). It is about the interactions between stakeholders including clients, partners, employees, financiers, local communities, and managers to generate value. It is the executive's role to manage and shape these relationships to maximize value for stakeholders and have control over how that value is allocated (Freeman, 1984). The executive must find a means to reframe issues when stakeholder interests clash to consider the needs of a large number of stakeholders. Second, as it raises concerns about morality, freedom of choice, and the potential for harm and benefits for many groups, managing stakeholder relationships well is also a moral undertaking for assisting firms in flourishing under capitalist systems (Phillips, 2003). Finally, a management explanation that places a strong emphasis on the creation, maintenance, and alignment of stakeholder relationships better equips practitioners to create value and avoid moral lapses (Sisodia et al., 2007).

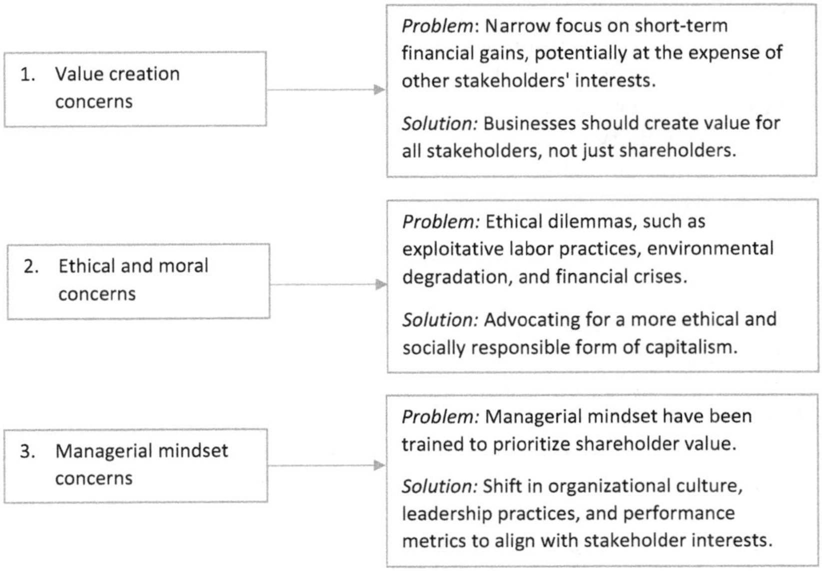

Figure 5.1 Problems at the Core of Stakeholder Theory Development.

Indeed, prior studies highlight the importance of stakeholder theory for entrepreneurship. As shown in Table 5.1, research has uncovered the potential of stakeholder theory in addressing a range of issues in entrepreneurship. For example, literature has identified the key role of collaboration between internal stakeholders (e.g., university affiliates) and external stakeholders (e.g., enterprises, financial institutions, incubators) in an entrepreneurial ecosystem at higher education institutions to support entrepreneurship education (Bischoff et al., 2018; Gianiodis & Meek, 2020). Others have emphasized the significance of stakeholder engagement as a long-term tactic in which stakeholders collaborate to seek goals that benefit both parties, which ought to stimulate creative entrepreneurial endeavors (Riad Shams et al., 2020) including those initiated by women (Nair, 2020).

However, the basic axioms of stakeholder theory, which emphasizes considering the interests of all stakeholders involved in an organization, are well suited for new ventures in the African context. First, stakeholder theory aligns with the goal of inclusive economic development in Africa (Ndaguba & Hanyane, 2019). By acknowledging the diverse array of stakeholders, including marginalized communities, entrepreneurs in Africa can contribute to broader prosperity (Adomako et al., 2021a). Second, in many African nations, natural resources play a pivotal role in economic development. Stakeholder theory emphasizes responsible resource management by engaging with environmental stakeholders, regulatory bodies, and local communities. Entrepreneurs who adopt this approach can contribute to sustainable resource utilization, mitigating the risk of resource depletion and environmental degradation. Third, stakeholder theory reinforces the importance of ethical governance and transparency. In an African context where corruption and governance challenges are not uncommon, entrepreneurs who adhere to ethical principles can contribute to improved business environments. The propositions are divided into different activities from resource acquisition to network formation and sustainability practices. We have chosen these activities to show that determinants are context-specific and the interplay between them will influence the results.

Enhancing access to resources

Emerging markets—especially those in Africa—suffer from institutional voids (Nwoba et al., 2021, 2022). This is due to a lack of infrastructure and specialized intermediaries, absence of market-supporting institutions, high levels of market imperfection, poor and underdeveloped economic and commercial activities, poor communication and transportation services, and a lack of social infrastructures—in turn creating institutional voids (Acquaah, 2006, 2012; Acquaah & Eshun, 2010; Nwoba et al., 2021). In Africa, local community leaders command strong allegiances in their local jurisdictions and serve as a conduit for managers to uncover and extract insights into changing local community expectations and market demands (Nwoba et al., 2021). These local

Table 5.1 Key Studies on the Implications of Stakeholder Theory

Number	*Author(s)*	*Theoretical Perspective Used*	*Methods Used*	*How Has Stakeholder Theory Been Used?*	*Main Findings*
1	Burga and Rezania (2016)	Stakeholder theory	Qualitative; an interview with the founder of FTACC	Demonstrate the importance of stakeholders and social issue management with stakeholder valence	Key stakeholders were recognized and placed according to their combined power, urgency, and legitimacy (PUL) values in the first circle of concentric orbits.
2	Chebbi et al. (2020)	Stakeholder theory; Kotter's change model	Qualitative; ten interviews with members of the organization	Motivate the internal stakeholders to prioritize clients, service quality, and service-mindedness while being proactive and innovative.	To include internal stakeholders in leading a transformation process to adopt a corporate entrepreneurship strategy, top managers can employ various programs.
3	Leonidou et al. (2020)	Stakeholder theory	Systematic review	Integration and management of stakeholders for entrepreneurship development	Mechanisms were explored that link different aspects of the framework and identify interrelations between the stakeholders.
4	Galvão et al. (2020)	Stakeholder theory	Qualitative; ten semi-structured interviews with managers and teachers	Stakeholders' involvement in projects that encourage regional development through entrepreneurial education and training	The creation of a network among stakeholders is important for connecting entrepreneurs, supporting their education, and providing them with training programs within low-density regions.
5	Santoro et al. (2020)	Stakeholder theory; entrepreneurship theory	Quantitative; survey with 117 entrepreneurs	Knowledge and social capital are obtained through stakeholders	Stakeholder engagement moderates the impact of entrepreneurial resilience on entrepreneurs' perceived success

(*Continued*)

Table 5.1 (Continued)

Number	*Author(s)*	*Theoretical Perspective Used*	*Methods Used*	*How Has Stakeholder Theory Been Used?*	*Main Findings*
6	Ramoglou et al. (2023)	Stakeholder theory	Conceptual	Opportunity-actualization perspective in the difficult realm of business venture through stakeholders.	Through the application of strategic opportunity thinking, entrepreneurs can guard against the blind-to-stakeholder mentality that either leads them into nonopportunity areas or keeps them from realizing opportunities that are genuine but challenging to actualize.
7	Bischoff (2021)	Stakeholder theory	Quantitative; survey, 106 participants	Stakeholder support for sustainable entrepreneurship	Sustainable entrepreneurial ecosystems depend on local entrepreneurial cultures, customized support from stakeholders, and collaborative efforts in sustainable entrepreneurship.
8	Haefner et al. (2023)	Stakeholder theory	Fuzzy set qualitative comparative analysis (fsQCA) of 204 publicly listed European firms	Dealing with multiple stakeholders for resource allocation	Innovation and stakeholder management can work as substitutes or complements.
9	Bouguerra et al. (2023)	Stakeholder theory	Stakeholder theory; survey of 249 managers	Entrepreneurial-oriented businesses are more likely to collaborate closely with suppliers to meet sustainability targets.	Entrepreneurial orientation is important for environmental collaboration with suppliers. Further, a high level of work engagement and a low level of market environment complexity moderate this linkage.
10	Gali et al. (2020)	Stakeholder theory	Quantitative; 1156 companies	Businesses with a social conscience are more adept at navigating the intricate webs of stakeholder relationships.	Social performance mediates the direct relationship between social entrepreneurship orientation and financial performance, which is negative.

community leaders include tribal leaders (e.g., local kings and chiefs), religious leaders (e.g., pastors, imams, and reverend fathers/sisters, opinion leaders/activists, and newspaper editors and reporters (Acquaah 2006, 2012; Acquaah & Eshun; 2010). Institutional stakeholders are very influential in garnering resources and providing access to valuable information and knowledge to entrepreneurs (Peng & Luo, 2000; Jones et al. 2018). For instance, as noted by Acquaah (2006), in Ghana—a country in the west of Africa—local community leaders establish ownership, control, maintain, and enforce social norms and values in their communities. Furthermore, Acquaah (2006) posits that even though Ghanaians consider themselves citizens of the Republic of Ghana, they also see themselves as "subjects" of their local community leaders and demonstrate strong allegiance to them. Hence, ties with these important institutional stakeholders enable African entrepreneurs to gain valuable market insights, and resources needed to overcome the institutional voids in the local business environment, in turn driving their innovation process and success.

Proposition 1: Stakeholders play a critical role in providing African entrepreneurs with access to essential resources, including financial capital, infrastructure, and knowledge.

Promoting ethical and s practices

Ethical governance and sustainability are cornerstones of African entrepreneurship (Amankwah-Amoah et al. 2019) Stakeholders, including regulatory bodies, local community leaders, and environmental groups, influence entrepreneurs to adopt ethical and sustainable business practices. These practices enhance reputation, mitigate risks, and contribute to long-term success. For instance, local community leaders and tribal chiefs are interested in the growth and sustainability of their local communities (Acquaah, 2006). Consequently, entrepreneurs would develop sustainable goods and services to solve these social and environmental issues sustainably (Liu et al., 2022; Safi et al., 2023). For example, the Dangote Group, a Nigerian multinational industrial conglomerate, states that one of the key drivers of their ethical and sustainable innovation practices is their close ties with the local communities and tribal leaders where they operate (Dangote, 2023). This has seen the Dangote group win the coveted Most Responsible Business Award in Africa in 2022 at the 16th edition of the Sustainability, Entrepreneurship, and Responsibility Awards (Nairametrics, 2023). This award underlines their pursuit of ethical and sustainable business practices, which are driven by their connections with relevant institutional stakeholders in their host communities.

Proposition 2: Ethical governance and sustainability are cornerstones of African entrepreneurship. Stakeholders, including regulatory bodies, local communities, and environmental groups, influence entrepreneurs to adopt ethical and sustainable business practices.

Facilitating access to networks and markets

Stakeholder engagement expands entrepreneurs' access to networks, both domestically and internationally (Peprah et al. 2023). Entrepreneurs who cultivate relationships with stakeholders can tap into new markets, forge strategic partnerships, and navigate complex regulatory environments more effectively. In Africa, as government officials are in control of economic activities, close ties with government officials would provide entrepreneurs access to important domestic and international networks and resources (International Finance Corporation, 2019; Wang et al., 2022). For example, according to the Tony Elumelu Foundation (2023), Tony Elumelu—a Nigerian economist, entrepreneur, and one of *Time* magazine's most influential people in the world in 2020—maintains close ties with relevant government officials. Such connections and ties have enabled the Tony Elumelu Foundation and business enterprises to expand their reach domestically and to other African countries and meet new business partners and networks (Tony Elumelu Foundation, 2023). The foundation states that the close ties with relevant government stakeholders have removed entry barriers into other African markets and have helped reduce the institutional voids that exist in the market environment in those countries. Hence, close ties with relevant institutional stakeholders in Africa are vital for access to new networks and markets.

Proposition 3: Stakeholder engagement expands entrepreneurs' access to networks, both domestically and internationally.

Enhancing financial inclusion

Stakeholder engagement, particularly with financial institutions and microfinance providers, can enhance financial inclusion for entrepreneurs, especially those in underserved and marginalized communities. This fosters economic empowerment and broader participation in entrepreneurial activities. Close contacts and connections with relevant institutional stakeholders would enable financial institutions to reach the bottom-of-the-pyramid and financially vulnerable customers. M-Pesa is heavily interested in helping Africans (especially those at the bottom of the pyramid) to climb onto the financial ladder, and they operate in many African countries, including Tanzania, South Africa, Lesotho, DRC Congo, Ghana, Mozambique, Egypt, and Ethiopia (M-Pesa, 2023). Currently, M-Pesa is the most successful mobile phone–based financial service in Africa and has linked its success to the close ties and connections it has with relevant institutional stakeholders in its host communities (M-Pesa, 2023). The company states its close contacts and connections with relevant stakeholders in Africa have provided needed resources and information, helped overcome the institutional voids and barriers in many African countries, and in turn, have enabled it to invest in innovation systems that have helped to get more Africans on the financial ladder, in turn ensuring great financial inclusion.

Proposition 4: Stakeholder engagement, particularly with financial institutions and microfinance providers, can enhance financial inclusion for entrepreneurs, especially those in underserved and marginalized communities.

Advocating for entrepreneurial ecosystems

Stakeholders, including industry associations, chambers of commerce, and advocacy groups, have the power to advocate for policies and initiatives that nurture entrepreneurial ecosystems. For instance, in Nigeria, the Wuse Market Traders Association—in the capital city of Abuja—complained that the taxes they were paying to the regional government for the electrification of the market were too high and restricted their entrepreneurial activities (Reuters, 2022). To this end, the group came together and lobbied for the taxes to be reduced. Subsequently, the Nigerian government agreed to their demands and had their taxes lowered. A subsequent follow-up interview by Reuters (2022) revealed that the traders confirmed that the removal of the taxes by the Nigerian government improved their entrepreneurial activities—in turn leading to commercial success. In sum, engaging with these stakeholders can lead to supportive policy reforms and a more conducive business environment for startups.

Proposition 5: Stakeholders, including industry associations, chambers of commerce, and advocacy groups, have the power to advocate for policies and initiatives that nurture entrepreneurial ecosystems.

Building trust and reputation

Trust is a currency of success in African entrepreneurship. Entrepreneurs who actively engage with stakeholders build trust and a positive reputation in the eyes of customers, investors, and communities (USAID, 2023). The Dangote group example listed previously simplifies this point. Due to their ethical and sustainable environmentally friendly practices, they are trusted by the locals in their host communities, who in turn buy their sustainable goods and services. These locals see the company as a good corporate citizen, who is focused on the development of their local communities and enhancing economic and commercial activities (USAID, 2023). Consequently, this enhances the brand reputation of the company, as noted in the numerous business awards they have won. In turn, this trust fosters loyalty and the long-term sustainability of the company.

Proposition 6: Trust is a currency of success in African entrepreneurship. Entrepreneurs who actively engage with stakeholders build trust and a positive reputation in the eyes of customers, investors, and communities.

Conclusion and implications

This chapter underscores the indispensable role of stakeholders in propelling entrepreneurship forward in Africa. The active involvement and support of stakeholders across various dimensions, from resource provision to advocacy and ethical guidance, are key drivers of sustainable entrepreneurial growth. As African entrepreneurship continues to evolve, understanding and harnessing the power of stakeholders becomes not just a strategic choice but a fundamental necessity for a thriving and inclusive entrepreneurial ecosystem on the continent.

Related to theoretical implications, this study uncovers the key role played by stakeholders in the growth of new ventures based in Africa (Freeman, 1984; Mbalyohere & Lawton, 2018). Integration of diverse stakeholders including employees, customers, suppliers, government, and NGOs, among others, allows entrepreneurs to gain market insights, establish distribution channels, and navigate regulatory hurdles, accelerating the process of establishing a presence in new markets. Through sound market presence, entrepreneurs can leverage their relationships with stakeholders, particularly local communities and regulatory authorities, to mitigate political, legal, and social risks that often affect businesses in Africa. For instance, having a constructive discussion with government representatives can present chances to influence laws and policies that promote the expansion and stability of businesses. Furthermore, demonstrating a commitment to local rules and fostering growth in the region's economy promotes goodwill and reduces the likelihood of negative political actions against the venture. A venture's activities in Africa may be impacted by social risks such as unfavorable community attitudes, demonstrations, or cultural misunderstandings. Further, our chapter discussion suggests that African markets often have unique challenges and opportunities that differ from those of developed countries (Adomako et al., 2021b). New ventures can modify their goods to meet these particular needs—whether they have to do with infrastructure, price, or accessibility—by involving stakeholders in the process (Sierra-García et al., 2015). The customization of products according to local needs and culture can enhance their significance for customers in the African continent.

This article has some limitations. First, it focuses on conceptual discussion about the role of stakeholders in new venture growth by drawing insights from literature and other secondary sources. As Africa is a vast and diverse continent with a wide range of economic, cultural, and regulatory contexts, this study struggles to capture the nuances and specific challenges that new ventures face in different African countries or regions. Second, there are diverse stakeholder dynamics in Africa given the changing political, economic, and social conditions. This conceptual chapter fails to fully account for the fluid nature of stakeholder relationships, making it difficult for entrepreneurs to adapt their strategies in real time as conditions evolve. Future studies can go further by exploring the nature of stakeholders in Africa and identifying their contributions to new venture growth. Third, stakeholder theory is evolving, with new perspectives and developments emerging regularly. This conceptual paper lacks the understanding of applicability and advancements in stakeholder theory. Therefore, future studies can empirically validate stakeholder theory in the African continent, potentially leading to gaps or outdated insights in the analysis of stakeholder roles in new venture growth.

References

Ackermann, F., & Eden, C. (2011). Strategic management of stakeholders: Theory and practice. *Long Range Planning*, *44*(3), 179–196. https://doi.org/10.1016/j.lrp.2010.08.001

Acquaah, M. (2006). The impact of managerial networking relationships on organizational performance in sub-Saharan Africa: Evidence from Ghana. *Organization Management Journal*, *3*(2), 115–138.

Acquaah, M. (2012). Social networking relationships, firm-specific managerial experience and firm performance in a transition economy: A comparative analysis of family owned and nonfamily firms. *Strategic Management Journal*, *33*(10), 1215–1228.

Acquaah, M., & Eshun, J.P. (2010). A longitudinal analysis of the moderated effects of networking relationships on organizational performance in a sub-Saharan African economy. *Human Relations*, *63*(5), 667–700.

Adomako, S., Amankwah-Amoah, J., Tarba, S. Y., & Khan, Z. (2021a). Perceived corruption, business process digitization, and SMEs' degree of internationalization in sub-Saharan Africa. *Journal of Business Research*, *123*, 196–207. https://doi.org/10.1016/j.jbusres.2020.09.065

Adomako, S., Ning, E., & Adu-Ameyaw, E. (2021b). Proactive environmental strategy and firm performance at the bottom of the pyramid. *Business Strategy and the Environment*, *30*(1), 422–431. https://doi.org/10.1002/bse.2629

Ajayi, O. O., Mokryani, G., & Edun, B. M. (2022). Sustainable energy for national climate change, food security and employment opportunities: Implications for Nigeria. *Fuel Communications*, *10*, 100045. https://doi.org/10.1016/j.jfueco.2021.100045

Ajide, F. M., Osinubi, T. T., & Dada, J. T. (2021). Economic globalization, entrepreneurship, and inclusive growth in Africa. *Journal of Economic Integration*, *36*(4), 689–717. https://www.jstor.org/stable/27081859

Amankwah-Amoah, J., Danso, A., & Adomako, S. (2019). Entrepreneurial orientation, environmental sustainability and new venture performance: Does stakeholder integration matter? *Business Strategy and the Environment*, *28*(1), 79–87. https://doi.org/10.1002/bse.2191

Amorós, J. E., Cristi, O., & Naudé, W. (2021). Entrepreneurship and subjective well-being: Does the motivation to start-up a firm matter? *Journal of Business Research*, *127*, 389–398. https://doi.org/10.1016/j.jbusres.2020.11.044

Arthur, P., Hanson, K. T., & Puplampu, K. P. (2020). *Disruptive technologies, innovation and development in Africa*. Springer Nature.

Atiase, V. Y., Mahmood, S., Wang, Y., & Botchie, D. (2018). Developing entrepreneurship in Africa: investigating critical resource challenges. *Journal of Small Business and Enterprise Development*, *25*(4), 644–666.

Bischoff, K. (2021). A study on the perceived strength of sustainable entrepreneurial ecosystems on the dimensions of stakeholder theory and culture. *Small Business Economics*, *56*(3), 1121–1140. https://doi.org/10.1007/s11187-019-00257-3

Bischoff, K., Volkmann, C. K., & Audretsch, D. B. (2018). Stakeholder collaboration in entrepreneurship education: an analysis of the entrepreneurial ecosystems of European higher educational institutions. *The Journal of Technology Transfer*, *43*(1), 20–46. https://doi.org/10.1007/s10961-017-9581-0

Bouguerra, A., Hughes, M., Cakir, M. S., & Tatoglu, E. (2023). Linking entrepreneurial orientation to environmental collaboration: A stakeholder theory and evidence from multinational companies in an emerging market. *British Journal of Management*, *34*(1), 487–511. https://doi.org/10.1111/1467-8551.12590

Bradley, S. W., Kim, P. H., Klein, P. G., McMullen, J. S., & Wennberg, K. (2021). Policy for innovative entrepreneurship: Institutions, interventions, and societal challenges. *Strategic Entrepreneurship Journal*, *15*(2), 167–184. https://doi.org/10.1002/sej.1395

Burga, R., & Rezania, D. (2016). Stakeholder theory in social entrepreneurship: A descriptive case study. *Journal of Global Entrepreneurship Research*, *6*(1), 4. https://doi.org/10.1186/s40497-016-0049-8

Chebbi, H., Yahiaoui, D., Sellami, M., Papasolomou, I., & Melanthiou, Y. (2020). Focusing on internal stakeholders to enable the implementation of organizational change towards corporate entrepreneurship: A case study from France. *Journal of Business Research*, *119*, 209–217. https://doi.org/10.1016/j.jbusres.2019.06.003

Dangote. 2023. The Dangote group. https://www.dangote.com/

Dau, L. A., & Cuervo-Cazurra, A. (2014). To formalize or not to formalize: Entrepreneurship and pro-market institutions. *Journal of Business Venturing*, *29*(5), 668–686. https://doi.org/10.1016/j.jbusvent.2014.05.002

Freeman, R. E. (1984). *Strategic management: A stakeholder approach*. Pitman Publishing Inc.

Freeman, R. E., & McVea, J. (2005). A stakeholder approach to strategic management. In *The Blackwell handbook of strategic management* (pp. 183–201) Blackwell.

Freeman, R. E., & Reed, D. L. (1983). Stockholders and stakeholders: A new perspective on corporate governance. *California Management Review*, *25*(3), 88–106. https://doi.org/10.2307/41165018

Friedman, A. L., & Miles, S. (2006). *Stakeholders: Theory and practice*. OUP.

Gali, N., Niemand, T., Shaw, E., Hughes, M., Kraus, S., & Brem, A. (2020). Social entrepreneurship orientation and company success: The mediating role of social performance. *Technological Forecasting and Social Change*, *160*, 120230. https://doi.org/10.1016/j.techfore.2020.120230

Galindo-Martín, M.-Á., Castaño-Martínez, M.-S., & Méndez-Picazo, M.-T. (2021). Effects of the pandemic crisis on entrepreneurship and sustainable development. *Journal of Business Research*, *137*, 345–353. https://doi.org/10.1016/j.jbusres.2021.08.053

Galvão, A. R., Marques, C. S. E., Ferreira, J. J., & Braga, V. (2020). Stakeholders' role in entrepreneurship education and training programmes with impacts on regional development. *Journal of Rural Studies*, *74*, 169–179. https://doi.org/10.1016/j.jrurstud.2020.01.013

Gianiodis, P. T., & Meek, W. R. (2020). Entrepreneurial education for the entrepreneurial university: A stakeholder perspective. *The Journal of Technology Transfer*, *45*(4), 1167–1195. https://doi.org/10.1007/s10961-019-09742-z

Haefner, N., Palmié, M., & Leppänen, P. T. (2023). With(out) a little help from my friends? Reconciling incongruous findings on stakeholder management, innovation, and firm performance. *Entrepreneurship Theory and Practice*, *47*(1), 142–171. https://doi.org/10.1177/10422587211024497

International Finance Corporation. (2019). The unseen sector: A report on the MSME opportunity in South Africa. World Bank Group. https://www.ifc.org/en/insights-reports/2019/msme-opportunity-south-africa

Jones, T. M., Harrison, J. S., & Felps, W. (2018). How applying instrumental stakeholder theory can provide sustainable competitive advantage. *Academy of Management Review*, *43*(3), 371–391. https://doi.org/10.5465/amr.2016.0111

Kiggundu, M. N., & Pal, S. P. (2018). Structure and management of formal and informal business activities in entrepreneurial family and small firms in Africa. *Africa Journal of Management*, *4*(3), 347–388. https://doi.org/10.1080/23322373.2018.1517541

Kirzner, I. M. (1973). *Competition and entrepreneurship*. University of Chicago Press.

Leonidou, E., Christofi, M., Vrontis, D., & Thrassou, A. (2020). An integrative framework of stakeholder engagement for innovation management and entrepreneurship development. *Journal of Business Research*, *119*, 245–258. https://doi.org/10.1016/j.jbusres.2018.11.054

Liu, H., Sinha, A., Destek, M.A., Alharthi, M., & Zafar, M.W. (2022). Moving toward sustainable development of sub-Saharan African countries: Investigating the effect of financial inclusion on environmental quality. *Sustainable Development*, *30*, 2015–2024. https://doi.org/10.1002/sd.2367

Loots, E., Neiva, M., Carvalho, L., & Lavanga, M. (2021). The entrepreneurial ecosystem of cultural and creative industries in Porto: A sub-ecosystem approach. *Growth and Change*, *52*(2), 641–662. https://doi.org/10.1111/grow.12434

Madzikanda, B., Li, C., & Dabuo, F. T. (2021). What determines the geography of entrepreneurship? A comparative study between sub-Saharan Africa and South–East Asia. *Journal of Entrepreneurship and Innovation in Emerging Economies*, *7*(2), 246–262. https://doi.org/10.1177/23939575211023629

Mbalyohere, C., & Lawton, T. C. (2018). Engaging stakeholders through corporate political activity: Insights from MNE nonmarket strategy in an emerging African market. *Journal of International Management*, *24*(4), 369–385. https://doi.org/10.1016/j.intman.2018.04.006

Mmbaga, N. A., Mathias, B. D., Williams, D. W., & Cardon, M. S. (2020). A review of and future agenda for research on identity in entrepreneurship. *Journal of Business Venturing*, *35*(6), 106049. https://doi.org/10.1016/j.jbusvent.2020.106049

M-pesa. (2023). What is M-Pesa? https://www.vodafone.com/about-vodafone/what-we-do/consumer-products-and-services/m-pesa

Nachum, L., Stevens, C. E., Newenham-Kahindi, A., Lundan, S., Rose, E. L., & Wantchekon, L. (2023). Africa rising: Opportunities for advancing theory on people, institutions, and the nation state in international business. *Journal of International Business Studies*, *54*, 938–955. https://doi.org/10.1057/s41267-022-00581-z

Nair, S. R. (2020). The link between women entrepreneurship, innovation and stakeholder engagement: A review. *Journal of Business Research*, *119*, 283–290. https://doi.org/10.1016/j.jbusres.2019.06.038

Nairametrics. (2023). Dangote group emerges "Overall most responsible business" at SERAS 2022 sustainability awards. https://nairametrics.com/2022/12/13/dangote-group-emerges-overall-most-responsible-business-at-seras-2022-sustainability

Naudé, W. (2011). Entrepreneurship is not a binding constraint on growth and development in the poorest countries. *World Development*, *39*(1), 33–44. https://doi.org/10.1016/j.worlddev.2010.05.005

Ndaguba, E. A., & Hanyane, B. (2019). Stakeholder model for community economic development in alleviating poverty in municipalities in South Africa. *Journal of Public Affairs*, *19*(1), e1858. https://doi.org/10.1002/pa.1858

Nwoba, A. C., Boso, N., & Robson, M. J. (2021). Corporate sustainability strategies in institutional adversity: Antecedent, outcome, and contingency effects. *Business Strategy and the Environment*, *30*(2), 787–807.

Nwoba, A. C., Mogaji, E., Zahoor, N., Donbesuur, F., & Alam, G. M. (2022). Obesity, family units and social marketing intervention: Evidence from Nigeria. *European Journal of Marketing*, *56*(11), 2892–2927.

Nyame-Asiamah, F., Amoako, I. O., Amankwah-Amoah, J., & Debrah, Y. A. (2020). Diaspora entrepreneurs' push and pull institutional factors for investing in Africa: Insights from African returnees from the United Kingdom. *Technological Forecasting and Social Change*, *152*, 119876. https://doi.org/10.1016/j.techfore.2019.119876

Peng, M. W., & Luo, Y. (2000). Managerial ties and firm performance in a transition economy: The nature of a micro-macro link. *Academy of Management Journal*, *43*(3), 486–501.

Peprah, A. A., Atarah, B. A., & Kumodzie-Dussey, M. K. (2023). Nonmarket strategy and legitimacy in institutionally voided environments: The case of Jumia, an African e-commerce giant. *International Business Review*, 102169. https://doi.org/10.1016/j.ibusrev.2023.102169

Phillips, R. (2003). *Stakeholder theory and organizational ethics*. Berrett-Koehler Publishers.

Ramoglou, S., Zyglidopoulos, S., & Papadopoulou, F. (2023). Is there opportunity without stakeholders? A stakeholder theory critique and development of opportunity-actualization. *Entrepreneurship Theory and Practice*, *47*(1), 113–141. https://doi.org/10.1177/10422587211043354

Reuters. (2022). Shell to pay 15 million euros in settlement over Nigerian oil spills. https://www.reuters.com/business/energy/shell-pay-15-mln-euros-settlement-over-nigerian-oil-spills-2022-12-23/

Riad Shams, S. M., Vrontis, D., Chaudhuri, R., Chavan, G., & Czinkota, M. R. (2020). Stakeholder engagement for innovation management and entrepreneurial development: A meta-analysis. *Journal of Business Research*, *119*, 67–86. https://doi.org/10.1016/j.jbusres.2020.08.036

Robson, P. J. A., Haugh, H. M., & Obeng, B. A. (2009). Entrepreneurship and innovation in Ghana: enterprising Africa. *Small Business Economics*, *32*(3), 331–350. https://doi.org/10.1007/s11187-008-9121-2

Safi, A., Wei, X., Sansaloni, E. M., & Umar, M. (2023). Breaking down the complexity of sustainable development: A focus on resources, economic complexity, and innovation. *Resource Policy*, 83. https://doi.org/10.1016/j.resourpol.2023.103746

Santoro, G., Bertoldi, B., Giachino, C., & Candelo, E. (2020). Exploring the relationship between entrepreneurial resilience and success: The moderating role of stakeholders' engagement. *Journal of Business Research*, *119*, 142–150. https://doi.org/10.1016/j.jbusres.2018.11.052

Schumpeter, J. (1912). *Theorie der wirtschaftlichen Entwicklung*. Duncker & Humblot.

Sierra-García, L., Zorio-Grima, A., & García-Benau, M. A. (2015). Stakeholder engagement, corporate social responsibility and integrated reporting: An exploratory study. *Corporate Social Responsibility and Environmental Management*, *22*(5), 286–304. https://doi.org/10.1002/csr.1345

Singh, V. K., Abosedra, S., Fakih, A., Ghosh, S., & Kanjilal, K. (2023). Economic volatility and financial deepening in sub-Saharan Africa: evidence from panel cointegration with cross-sectional heterogeneity and endogenous structural breaks. *Empirical Economics*. https://doi.org/10.1007/s00181-023-02415-9

Sisodia, R., Wolfe, D. B., & Sheth, J. N. (2007). *Firms of endearment: The pursuit of purpose and profit*. Pearson Education.

Smith, N. C., & Rönnegard, D. (2016). Shareholder primacy, corporate social responsibility, and the role of business schools. *Journal of Business Ethics*, *134*(3), 463–478. https://doi.org/10.1007/s10551-014-2427-x

Statista. (2022). Economic contribution of small and medium-sized enterprises (SMEs) in Ghana as of 2022, by category. https://www.statista.com/statistics/1322256/economic-contribution-of-smes-in-ghana-by-category/

Strand, R., & Freeman, R. E. (2015). Scandinavian cooperative advantage: The theory and practice of stakeholder engagement in Scandinavia. *Journal of Business Ethics*, *127*(1), 65–85. https://doi.org/10.1007/s10551-013-1792-1

Tony Elumelu Foundation. (2023). AFRICAPITALISM. https://www.tonyelumelufoundation.org/africapitalism

Urbano, D., Aparicio, S., & Audretsch, D. (2019). Twenty-five years of research on institutions, entrepreneurship, and economic growth: What has been learned? *Small Business Economics*, *53*(1), 21–49. https://doi.org/10.1007/s11187-018-0038-0

USAID. (2023). Small business development centers. https://www.usaid.gov/kenya/document/small-business-development-centers

Wadhwani, R. D., Kirsch, D., Welter, F., Gartner, W. B., & Jones, G. G. (2020). Context, time, and change: Historical approaches to entrepreneurship research. *Strategic Entrepreneurship Journal*, *14*(1), 3–19. https://doi.org/10.1002/sej.1346

Walsh, J. P. (2005). Book review essay: Taking stock of stakeholder management.

Wang, C., Hu, Z., & Bao, Z. (2023). Evaluation of the government entrepreneurship support by a new dynamic neutrosophic operator based on time degrees. *Management Decision*, *61*(2), 530–551. https://doi.org/10.1108/MD-03-2022-0305

Wang, D., Cui, L., Vu, T., & Feng, T. (2022). Political capital and MNE responses to institutional voids: The case of Chinese state-owned enterprises in Africa. *Organization Studies*, *43*(1), 105–126. https://doi.org/10.1177/0170840620954011

Weber, C., Fasse, A., Haugh, H. M., & Grote, U. (2023). Varieties of necessity entrepreneurship—New insights from sub Saharan Africa. *Entrepreneurship Theory and Practice*, *47*(5), 1843–1876. https://doi.org/10.1177/10422587221111737

Zahoor, N., Khan, Z., Meyer, M., & Laker, B. (2023). International entrepreneurial behavior of internationalizing African SMEs—Towards a new research agenda. *Journal of Business Research*, *154*, 113367. https://doi.org/10.1016/j.jbusres.2022.113367

6 Stakeholder Management and Entrepreneurial Resourcing of Small African Firms

Financial Bootstrapping as a Cost Escalation Strategy

Patient Rambe, Nosiphiwe Mgudlwa and Nomfundo Gladys Khoza

Introduction

When a firm is construed as a constellation of productive resources paired with an administrative function that coordinates these resources (Penrose, 1959), it is logical to argue that small African firms cannot survive without tapping into the diverse range of stakeholders who serve as owners (e.g., local banks), transmitters (e.g., distribution networks) and dispensers (e.g., spouses friends and family members) of such important strategic resources. Therefore, stakeholder management is deemed critical to availing bootstrapped resources because resource availability depends heavily on the conditions generated by the stakeholders (Wang & Bansal, 2012). Similarly, since financial and nonfinancial resources are the life blood of any enterprising firm, literature demonstrates that the firm cannot afford to neglect any stakeholder entity without undermining its organisational purposes (Xia et al., 2018).

For small firms, financial bootstrapping strategies are understood as cost containment measures arising from leveraging internally generated resources (Grichnik et al., 2014). Financial bootstrapping is defined as financial approaches employed by small firms to acquire and use resources that do not involve raising equity or borrowing money (Patel, Fiet & Sohl, 2011). The reality is whether resources are generated internally or externally by the firms, the claim that bootstrapping is mainly about cost containment (Grichnik et al., 2014) is not a complete argument in developing economies because bootstrapping often escalates costs. For instance, evidence suggests that bootstrapping can be costly and risky when resource providers demand unreasonable or unexpected returns from small firms in the absence of formal agreements or contracts (Patel et al., 2011) or when such firms have weak bargaining power. Moreover, the most pervasive forms of bootstrapping examples such as the use of credit cards may impose prohibitive costs on small firms (Coleman & Robb, 2015). As such, we posed the following questions:

DOI: 10.4324/9781003256014-8

1. Using stakeholder management perspective as an empirical and analytical lens, what are the different bootstrapping strategies employed by small firms, especially in developing countries reported in entrepreneurial literature?
2. As these small firms engage with diverse stakeholders, how can their bootstrapping strategies lead to cost escalation in the context of emerging economies?

By addressing the interface between stakeholder management, African entrepreneurship, and flexible resource mobilisation to eliminate the risk of failure of firms, the chapter extends the body of research on stakeholder management effectiveness by incorporating the way African managers deploy the resources they have at hand in their constrained environment. Such understanding offers new perspectives of (financial) management practices (Rebelo et al., 2016) and decision-making in varied contexts.

Theoretical background

Stakeholder management

For stakeholder theory, an important component of value creation and resources mobilisation in businesses that enhances firms' chances of being successful is their engagement and development of strong relationships with a wide variety of stakeholders (Leonidou et al., 2018; Sefiani, Davies, Bown, & Kite, 2018). Indeed, there is literature on stakeholder theory within the entrepreneurship field that emphasises engaging with various stakeholders to develop some relationships with them in support of entrepreneurship development (Pollack et al., 2017; Leonidou et al., 2018). Negotiating and networking with different stakeholders is central to the emergence, growth, and survival of small African firms (Mishra & Dwivedi, 2012), which are not only dependent on resources they may not own for their survival but are equally challenged by the tragedy of newness and lack of legitimacy in the market. These impediments complicate their access to financial resources. The stakeholder management lens, therefore, not only assists such firms to identify and validate the range of stakeholders who may have a general stake in their operations but also those without whose financial contributions the firms may cease to be economically viable.

Conceptualizing bootstrapping

Resource ownership, resource acquisition, informal access, creativity, and improvisation in resource acquisition are emphasised in definitions of bootstrapping. Ownership definitions include access to resources not owned or controlled by the entrepreneur. Harrison, Mason and Girling (2004) emphasise ownership to define bootstrapping as accessing resources not owned or controlled by the entrepreneur such as those from friends and family networks. Therefore, when SMEs and new ventures do not own or control resources, the entrepreneur team taps into individual (or collective) human and social resources to build organisational, physical and financial resources (Stevenson & Gumpert, 1985).

Resource acquisition tends to emphasise securing internal resources while avoiding external debt. Consistent with this notion, Rutherford, Coombes and Mazzei (2012) define bootstrapping as when entrepreneurs assemble (or acquire) resources and persevere without utilising long-term debt or equity financing from banks and investors.

Creativity and improvisation in resource acquisition emphasise imaginative and innovative access to scarce resources at a minimal cost. The creative element manifests in bootstrapping as a set of processes through which entrepreneurs creatively find resources, increase resource efficiency and minimise explicit costs (Patel et al., 2011).

Role of stakeholders in financial bootstrapping

The literature on bootstrapping highlights that a firm must commit to developing a wide network of relationships—not limited to shareholders, employees or clients—and invest in nurturing them to make them more effective (Pedrini & Ferri, 2019). Similarly, stakeholders are at the heart of the economic enterprise of small firms, and therefore such businesses must be cognizant of the role of stakeholder management in financial bootstrapping to ensure efficient resource mobilisation.

While small enterprises' managers may insist on generating equity from internal stakeholders (e.g., the founder, co-workers and entrepreneurial teams) to avoid dependence on external debt, another internal stakeholder critical to the success of financial bootstrapping is entrepreneurial teams. Existing research (e.g., Leonidou et al., 2018) suggests that entrepreneurial teams are vital conduits of information about the availability of bootstrapped resources as well as the availability and character of products, resources and markets. Apart from availing strategic talent that generates innovative ideas that sustain the firm, entrepreneurial teams can also avail or advance their salaries as loans that ensure the viability of the firm. Similarly, with reference to bootstrapping in family-owned businesses, spouses, daughters and sons can stand in for the founder free of charge or pro-bono during their absence, thereby reducing the wage bill for the firm.

The role of external stakeholders such as retail banks in firms' bootstrapping strategies cannot be conceived outside of stakeholder theory, whose core tenet is organisations' acknowledgement of the validity of diverse stakeholder interests and their response to them within a mutually supportive framework (Aladpoosh, Shaharoun, & Saman, 2012). While borrowing from banks could be the only bootstrapping strategy for small African firms when other options (e.g., families, friends and fools) are untenable, their legitimacy with banks is often derived from their capacity to demonstrate their reasons for existence through the viability of their business plans, their ability to manage funds through financial record management, sustainable revenue streams and their capacity to repay loans.

The method

The study employed a systematic literature review. We sought to provide fresh perspectives on financial bootstrapping, specifically given that in resource-deprived contexts bootstrapping is a germane survival and growth strategy that brings benefits and avoids pernicious costs. Our scoping strategy entailed the identification of relevant research, the selection of studies, quality assessment, data extraction and coding (Shneor & Vik, 2020).

Identification of research

In the identification phase, two rounds of searches were executed. The first round involved conducting research in Ebscohost websites, Google Scholar and Science Direct databases. We restricted our searches to published articles and concentrated on keywords: "Financial bootstrapping + small enterprises" and "financial bootstrapping strategies/techniques + small firms + emerging economies." The search was limited to peer-reviewed articles published in the English language. The initial search in Ebscohost websites retrieved 30 journal articles; in Google Scholar we identified 71 journals, and 15 in Science Direct.

The second round involved merging the lists and removing duplicates and this resulted in a combined list comprising 82 articles. Another search was conducted in the ISI Web of Science database, which led to six journals being identified. The abstracts of these articles were assessed for relevance, completeness and conciseness such as research context, research gap explored, the methodology applied, key findings and implications for theory, policy and practice.

Selection of studies and quality assessment

The inclusion criteria were published manuscripts that were peer-reviewed, and this excluded manuscripts in press, books and book chapters, conference proceeding papers, monographs and public commentary. Out of the 88 published articles, 56 were excluded for (1) their cursory examination of bootstrapping, (2) lack of empirical evidence on the subject matter examined and (3) failure to distinguish bootstrapping from its associated variables. Upon completion of the filtering process, only 32 articles were considered for further analysis.

Data extraction and coding

The selected papers were tabulated in Microsoft Excel to create a database comprising the author's name; journal title; journal name; year published; study purpose; methodology/design/approach; findings; implications for theory, policy or practice; originality and limitations. Other considerations included theories applied, units of analysis and whether the nature of variables analysis coheres with the literature the systematic reviews emphasised (Simba et al., 2021).

Results

Bootstrapping strategies

Improvisation

Improvisation was one of the bootstrapping strategies reported in entrepreneurial literature. Improvisation involves the continual experimentation with new possibilities to create innovative and improved solutions outside current practices (Dyba, 2000). In bootstrapping, this involves small firms exploiting time resources by adjusting their business hours (e.g., opening shops for extended hours; opening shop over weekends and public holidays) to accommodate customers who work all day or are unavailable on weekdays. Other bootstrapping methods involve charging below-market prices for goods and services. The most common forms of improvision employed by the Somali and Bangladesh small firm owners operating in South Africa include segmenting business operation space into retail business premises and makeshift accommodation to reduce rental costs.

Strategising

Strategising involves the development of expedient ways that benefit the firm such as intermingling. Intermingling refers to the use of business assets for the support of the household and/or the use of household assets for the support of the business (Yilmazer & Lyons, 2010). Intermingling is an example of bricolage that cushions the firm owners from resource constraints by deploying nonconventional resources that are integral to supporting business operations. Examples include requesting family members or employees to relieve the entrepreneur at no cost. Other examples of strategising include massive discounts arising from bulk ordering and purchases of goods and services using family income, not having banking accounts and transactions to avoid bank charges and interest payments and bulk transportation of goods ordered by ethically linked entrepreneurs to reduce transportation costs. These survival and competitive strategies are unique to small firms that compete with larger firms and must maintain relative competitiveness (Chebo & Kute, 2019).

Efficiency enhancements

The efficiency enhancement components have manifested in the prevalence of the sharing culture to expedite the efficient operations of firms. Small firms often co-locate with other firms and share employees, raw materials, equity and equipment as a cost containment measure. The appropriation of buildings for multiple purposes such as business operations, laboratories, dining rooms and gymnasia signifies the cost reduction capabilities of emerging firms. Efficiency enhancements can take the form of firms' joint standardizing and sharing of plant, machinery and warehouses with suppliers, ordering supplies jointly with others to secure discounts and sharing buildings during foundational stages of firms (Masesa & Zhou, 2013). In South African contexts, some foreign business owners utilise their premises as makeshift homes, use shared transport for goods and products, jointly order commodities and engage in bulk transportation of jointly purchased goods.

Business informalisation

The informalisation of business may involve deliberate strategies that small firms adopt to resist transition towards formalisation in the mainstream economy. The legalistic school of thought projects informalisation as a deliberate strategy used by small businesses to evade paying taxes and stay under the radar of legal authorities (De Soto, 1989). Closely linked to this argument is the view that excessive bureaucratic red tape and punitive legislation contribute to small business' reluctance to transition from informalisation to the formalisation of their businesses (Maduku & Kaseeram, 2019). The dualist school of thought conceives the informal sector as a consequence of the congregation of low or under-skilled individuals who cannot secure decent jobs in the mainstream economy (International Labour Organisation, 1973) and therefore recede into the shadow economy. The bootstrapping strategies adopted in the informal economy involve payment of uncompetitive or below-market wages to employees, maintaining informality as a tax avoidance strategy and maintaining insulation from labour laws.

Ethnic enclaves

In emerging economy contexts such as South Africa, small businesses operate in former homelands (i.e., townships) that comprise closely knit communities sometimes historically connected by kinship ties, ethnic background, historical affinities, linguistic backgrounds or locational proximity. Kinship ties and ethnic and linguistic backgrounds are marshalled as avenues for facilitating business transactions, exchanging firm resources (e.g., purchase of goods on credit, securing discounts for recurrent purchases) and securing financial resources. For instance, *stokvels* (South African's version of rotating credit and savings schemes) provide a rich funding tapestry that fuels the founding and development of new ventures in townships. High-budget *stokvels* in which individuals save a certain premium, periodically, for future projects (Maduku & Kaseeram, 2019) have potential to bolster the founding of new ventures by mobilising capital (Iwara & Netshandama, 2021).

How bootstrapping strategies may escalate costs

Matshonisas, rotatory savings and credit associations

Extensive borrowing from the ***matshonisas***, ***stokvels*** and micro-financial institutions may exert severe cashflow constraints on the business as these formations charge excessive interest on delayed repayments despite their relaxed borrowing conditions. Since these firms often generate small profits, their cash flow challenges often constrain their growth and long-term sustainability. Therefore, apart from providing income for the poor and safety nets in times of crisis, SMEs make insignificant contribution to income generation that provides bare survival for those on the margins of developing societies without any potential for independent growth (Aurick et al., 2017).

Exploiting cultural enclaves and informalisation strategies

The same way the business may depend on cultural-historical affinities, language-based networks and historical ties for its resource generation strategies, these networks may be burdensome to firms. While such affinities may avail resources (financial capital, human resource and moral support) that accentuate the productivity of firms, the same affinities could constitute customers who either default on payments or pay the business late, leading to serious cash flow problems that suffocate these firms (Masesa & Zhou, 2013). In South Africa, small firms located in proximity to such affinities, networks and ties (especially those located in "townships") are exposed to vandalism, theft, robbery and burglary.

Trade credit

Trade credit is an agreement in which a supplier allows a business to delay payment for goods and services already delivered on credit (Fitzpatrick & Lien, 2013). While trade credit involves access to goods from suppliers on credit, high interest may be charged on such goods. Such interests exert a negative impact on the profitability of small businesses.

Discussion

From a stakeholder management perspective, the business founder and/manager remained the dominant stakeholder in effecting bootstrapping strategies. This view was deemed critical to helping managers in improving the strategic position of their organisation (Mishra & Dwivedi, 2012) by assuming central roles of an efficient resource allocator, the orchestrator of resource management techniques and a bricoleur. Although the business founder remained the main stakeholder on bootstrapping matters by setting the tone for how resources were appropriated and deployed within and beyond firm boundaries, she or he did not act independently and alone. In fact, family members, employees, friends and entrepreneurial teams worked closely with the entrepreneur in facilitating entrepreneurial decisions on strategic allocation of resources. However, banks, trade credit and ethnic networks and the *matshonisas* (loan sharks) were external stakeholders with which the entrepreneurs engaged to make bootstrapping tenable. This collaboration between internal and external stakeholders validates the fact that although internal groups may be key in some resource allocation decision making, external stakeholders cannot be a priori relegated to a subsidiary position (Bailur, 2007) as their withdrawal could damage or undermine firm operations (Mishra & Dwivedi, 2012).

Bootstrapping strategies have been effective and efficient in starting and sustaining small businesses. Literature projected financial bootstrapping as a management technique for managing firms' reliance on resources (Fatoki, 2013). According to the resource dependence theory, firm owners actively employ bootstrapping tactics to lessen the financial ambiguity and dependence of their company. Bootstrapping strategies prominent in literature are improvision through creative innovation, material and design feature enhancements, cashflow management and business process improvement (Dyba, 2000) and strategisation through amalgamation of household and business resources together (Yilmazer & Lyons, 2010). Other strategies include bricolage involving capitalising on business opportunities and underappreciated raw materials, harnessing public subsidies to finance business operations (Masesa & Zhou, 2013) and merging different resources such as grants, internal equity and overdraft facilities (Atherton, 2012).

Evidence from the study demonstrated that different primary and secondary shareholders are not passive bystanders but rather act according to their interests and employ their power to influence the firm in the direction they deem fit (Mishra & Dwivedi, 2012). While internal stakeholders seemed to have a firm grip on the internal operations of the firms regarding its bootstrapping strategies, Clarkson (1995) highlights that external stakeholders had the capacity to shape public opinion in favour or in opposition to the cooperation. In our case, however, the role of external stakeholders such as banks, investors and business networks extended beyond public relations management to include providing or declining funds to small firms depending on their product viability, feasibility and sustainability. Therefore, the notion of a stakeholder extended beyond any entity with a vested interest in the organization's survival and that can affect or be affected by the achievement of the firm's objectives (Freeman, 1984), to include entities with whom the firm interacted and had some interdependencies (Eyiah-Botwe, Aigbavboa, & Thwala, 2016).

Research evidence demonstrates that financial limitations in bootstrapping businesses can stifle further investments and limit subsequent business growth (Vanacker et al., 2011). The authors elaborate that by using bootstrapping tactics, new businesses may be prevented from expanding as quickly as they might otherwise want if they were able to obtain significant sums of external funding. Paradoxically, equity concerns may be crucial for many private organisations such as *matshonisas*, credit associations and trade credit as they provide access to significant sums of funding that enable businesses to experience rapid expansion (Vanacker & Manigart, 2010). Research confirms that businesses with at least some financial slack or a buffer of financial resources experiment more and take more risks, such as extending operating hours that expose them to robberies, which are inimical to their growth and productivity over time (Vanacker et al., 2011).

Implications for theory

Drawing on stakeholder theory, information asymmetries between business owners and investors breed uncertainty about the firm's legitimacy and worth among potential investors that culminate in adverse funding decisions. Deploying efficiency enhancement techniques could improve the financial balance sheets of firms, and when this is provided to potential investors it increases funding opportunities for firms. Therefore, strong signals including firm commitment from entrepreneurs are required if the investment is to be allocated to a project with sustainable returns (Rutherford et al., 2012). To enable all interested parties to perceive, analyse and act on the signal, evidence must be observable or known beforehand, whether expensive or difficult to mimic (Rutherford et al., 2012).

Implications for management

Novel approaches are needed to manage cost escalation. While recognising that cost escalation poses a genuine threat to small firms is the first step to small firms' financial freedom, cost-sensitive budgeting could eliminate wishful thinking that escalation would eventually decline without direct interventions. Applying varying combinations of financial bootstrapping, strategisation and efficiency enhancement may mean that only cost cutting measures are targeted by firms with cashflow challenges while using efficiency to facilitate sustained growth. Therefore, managers could benefit their firms by segmenting owner- and customer-related strategies that eliminate costs, those that enhance cheaper funding options and those innovations that improve efficiency and the value of the firms.

Implications for policy and practice

We have shown that subsidised funding is a useful bootstrapping approach for companies, which improves their future growth, particularly those with aspirations to expand or that have cash flow hurdles. Government agencies in South Africa such as Small Enterprise Development Agency (SEDA) and the Small Enterprise Finance Agency (SEFA) need to raise awareness of subsidies, tax incentives and grants they avail to startups in the entrepreneurial community. Apart from aligning these funding opportunities with firms' bootstrapping techniques, entrepreneurial training and development opportunities on grant proposal writing and exploiting investment opportunities can complement the resources availed via bootstrapping. Since cashflow constraints are prevalent among SMEs, funding agents must link their grant funding to the attainment of specific key performance indicators to ensure good value for money.

Conclusion

The study explored bootstrapping strategies of small firms in Africa, an under-researched context in terms of financial resource generation. The study demonstrated that the use of localised financial bootstrapping tactics enhances the cashflow of startups while simultaneously addressing their need for expansion. Drawing on the stakeholder theory, we highlighted the complexity of generating external funding by small firms, which compels them to over-rely on internally generated funding to support their operations. We clarified the difficult strategic financial decisions that small business entrepreneurs face in addressing their resource constraints, consequently compelling them to implement financial bootstrapping that triggers cost escalation for small businesses.

References

Aladpoosh, H., Shaharoun, A.M., & Saman, M.Z. 2012. Critical features for project stakeholder management: A systematic literature review. *International Journal of Applied Systemic Studies*, *4*(3): 150–167.

Atherton, A. 2012. Cases of start-up financing: An analysis of new venture capialisation structures and patterns. *International Journal of Entrepreneurial Behaviours and Research*, *18*(1): 28–47.

Aurick, M., Munalula, M.,Mundia, L., Mwale, M., & Vincent, K. 2017. Urban informality and small-scale enterprise (SME) development in Zambia: An exploration of theory and practice. *Journal of Behavioural Economics, Finance, Entrepreneurship, Accounting and Transport*, 5(1): 19–29.

Bailur, S. 2007. Using stakeholder theory to analyse telecentre projects. *Information Technologies and International Development*, *3*(3): 61–80.

Chebo, A.K., & Kute, I.M. 2019. Strategic process and small venture growth. The moderating role of environmental scanning and owner-CEO. *Journal of Small Business Strategy*, *29*(3): 60–77.

Clarkson, M. 1995. A stakeholder framework for analysing and evaluating corporate social performance. *Academy of Management Review*, *20*(1): 92–117.

Coleman, S., & Robb, A. 2015. *The next wave: Financing and investing strategies for growth-oriented women entrepreneurs.* California: Stanford University Press.

De Soto, H. 1989. *The other path: The invisible revolution in the third World.* Harper & Row.

Dyba, T. 2000. Improvisation in small software organizations. IEEE Software.

Eyiah-Botwe, E., Aigbavboa, C., & Thwala, D. 2016. Stakeholder management: A literature review of historical development and current trends. *9th Construction Industry Development Board Postgraduate Conference*, February 2–4, 2016, Cape Town, South Africa.

Fatoki, O. 2013. An investigation into the financial bootstrapping methods used by immigrant entrepreneurs in South Africa. *Journal of Economics*, *4*(2): 89–96.

Fitzpatrick, A., & Lien, B. 2013. The use of trade credit by businesses. *Reserve Bank of Australia Bulletin*, 39–46. https://www.rba.gov.au/publications/bulletin/2013/sep/pdf/bu-0913-5.pdf

Freeman, R. E. 1984. *Strategic management: A stakeholder approach*. Pitman.

Grichnik, D., Brinkmann, J., Singh, L., & Manigart, S. 2014. Beyond environmental scarcity: Human and social capital as driving forces of bootstrapping activities. *Journal of Business Venturing*, *29*(2): 310–326.

Harrison, R.T., Mason, C.M., & Girling, P. 2004. Financial bootstrapping and venture development in the software industry. *Entrepreneurship and Regional Development*, *16*: 307–333.

International Labour Organisation. 1973. *Employment, income and equality: A strategy for increasing productivity in Kenya*. Geneva: ILO.

Iwara, I., & Netshandama, V. 2021. Small enterprise capital mobilization and marketing in rural areas. A review synthesis of stokvel model. *Academy of Entrepreneurship Journal*, *27*(2): 1–11.

Leonidou, E., Christofi, M., Vrontis, D., & Thrassou, A. 2018. An integrative framework of stakeholder engagement for innovation management and entrepreneurship development. *Journal of Business Research*, *119*: 245–258.

Maduku, H., & Kaseeram, I. 2019. Maintaining willingness among black owned informal SMMEs in South Africa. *Journal of Emerging Trends in Economics and Management Sciences*, *10*(3): 140–147.

Masesa, A., & Zhou, Y. 2013. Bootstrapping motives in nonfinancially constrained firms: A case study: A firm' s approach to lower operating costs may delay growth and expansion. Master thesis in Entrepreneurship: Lund University.

Mishra, A., & Dwivedi, Y. 2012. Stakeholder theory and applications in information systems. In Y. Dwivedi, M. Wade, & S. Schneberger (Eds.), *Information systems theory: Explaining and predicting our digital society*. Springer. 471–488.

Patel, P.C., Fiet, J.O., & Sohl, J.E. 2011. Mitigating the limited scalability of bootstrapping through strategic alliances to enhance new venture growth. *International Small Business Journal*, *29*(5): 421–447.

Pedrini, M., & Ferri, L. 2019. Stakeholder management: A systematic literature review. *Corporate Governance*, *19*(1): 44–59.

Penrose, E.T. 1959. *The theory of the growth of the firm*. Basil Blackwell.

Pollack, J.M., Barr, S., & Hanson, S. 2017. New venture creation as establishing stakeholder relationships: A trust-based perspective. *Journal of Business Venturing Insights*, *7*: 15–20.

Rebelo, M.F., Santos, G., & Silva, R., 2016. Integration of management systems: Towards a sustained success and development of organizations. *Journal of Cleaner Production*, *127*: 96–111.

Rutherford, M.W., Coombes, S.M.T., & Mazzei, M. J. 2012. The impact of bootstrapping on new venture performance and survival: A longitudinal analysis. *Frontiers of Entrepreneurship Research*, *32*(12): 1–16.

Sefiani, Y., Davies, B. J., Bown, R., & Kite, N. 2018. Performance of SMEs in Tangier: The interface of networking and "wasta". *EuroMed Journal of Business*, *13*(1): 20–43.

Shneor, R., & Vik, A. A. 2020. Crowdfunding success: A systematic literature review 2010–2017. *Baltic Journal of Management*, *15*(2): 149–182.

Simba, A., Ojong, N., & Kuk, G. 2021. Bricolage and MSEs in emerging economies. *The International Journal of Entrepreneurship and Innovation*, *22*(2): 112–123.

Stevenson, H.H., & Gumpert, D.E. 1985. The heart of entrepreneurship. *Harvard Business Review*, *63*: 85–94.

Vanacker, T., Mamigart, S., Meuleman, M., & Sel, L. 2011. The impact of financial bootstrap strategies on value added in new ventures: A longitudinal study [Online]. Available: http://www.gsom.spbu.ru/files/upload/niim/seminar/sophie_manigart_bootstrap_strategies [20 September 2022]

Vanacker, T., & S. Manigart. 2010. Pecking order and debt capacity considerations for high-growth companies seeking financing. *Small Business Economics*, *35*: 53–69.

Wang, T., & Bansal, P. 2012. Social responsibility in new ventures: Profiting from a long-term orientation. *Strategic Management Journal*, *33*(10): 1135–1153.

Xia, N., Zou, P., Griffin, M., Wang, X., & Rui Zhong, R. 2018. Towards integrating construction risk management and stakeholder management: A systematic literature review and future research agendas. *International Journal of Project Management*, *36*: 701–715.

Yilmazer, T., & Lyons, A.C. 2010. Marriage and the allocation of assets in women's defined contribution plans. *Journal of Family and Economic Issues*, *31*: 121–137.

Part II

Gender, Stakeholder Management and Sustainability

7 The Role of Institutional Stakeholders in the Success of New Businesses in Africa

Arinze Christian Nwoba, Samuel Yaw Kusi, Adedapo Adebajo and Mark Kofi Prempeh

Introduction

The African business startup landscape is currently experiencing massive growth (Amaeshi et al., 2018; The Economist, 2022). There has been a surge of successful business startups across various African sectors, leading to the continent becoming a hotspot for entrepreneurial activity, innovation, and investment (Workpay, 2023; Antai & Eze, 2023). In 2022, Nigeria, Kenya, South Africa, Ghana, Morocco, Tunisia, Cameroon, Egypt, and Rwanda were listed among the best countries to start up a business in the world (Oluwole, 2023; Statista, 2023).

Africa's thriving business startup ecosystem can be attributed to its young population (Workpay, 2023; Amankwah-Amoah et al., 2018; Chan-Zuckerberg Initiative, 2023). For instance, 60% of the population of Nigeria (the most populous country Africa, with a population of 212 million citizens) is between 0 and 26 years of age; this is more than 128 million people—which is more than the populations of Spain, France, Germany, and so on (Danns & Danns, 2022; Nwoba et al., 2022). This means that Nigeria has one of the youngest populations in the world (Trading Economics, 2022). With this young population comes an overflowing of imaginative entrepreneurial ideas and concepts—with the central aim of benefiting their local communities (Workpay, 2023; Omotosho, 2023).

Furthermore, Africa's thriving business startup ecosystem can be partly attributed to the increased availability and affordability of technology (Mogaji et al., 2021a). For instance, the rise in the use of mobile phones in many African countries has led to businesses offering mobile-based solutions and services (Mogaji et al., 2021b). M-Pesa—launched in 2007 in Kenya—is a mobile phone-based money transfer, payments, and micro-financing service that has provided a platform for users to deposit money into an account stored on their smartphones, send balances, redeem deposits for regular money, and withdraw money while being charged a small fee for each transaction (M-Pesa, 2023). Over the last decade, M-Pesa has become the most successful mobile-phone-based financial service in Africa and has enabled a lot of Africans (especially those at the bottom of the pyramid) to climb onto the financial ladder in many

DOI: 10.4324/9781003256014-10

African countries including Tanzania, South Africa, Lesotho, DRC Congo, Ghana, Mozambique, Egypt, and Ethiopia (M-Pesa, 2023). In sum, the contribution of African startups to the economy and local communities is noteworthy as they play an important role in the advancement of the local communities while also benefiting the local populace.

According to organisational and sociological theorists, top-level managerial actions of new business founders are embedded within social networks of relationships with relevant institutional stakeholders (Acquaah, 2007; Granovetter, 1973, 1985). Laumann, Galaskiewicz, and Marsden (1978, p. 458) define these social networks of relationships as "a set of nodes (e.g., persons, organizations) linked by a set of social relationships (e.g., friendship, transfer of funds, overlapping memberships) of a specified type." Standing on this premise, proponents of social networks of relationships in business argue that top-level managerial ties with external stakeholders—a micro-level construct—influence an organisation's competitive advantage and performance—a macro-level construct (Peng & Luo, 2000).

Thus, extant empirical studies have failed to consider or have not fully considered other context-relevant institutional stakeholders that can influence an organisation's performance and success, especially in the African region. There is a popular proverb in Nigeria that translates as "Who you know, is better than what you know"—emphasising the importance of social ties, networks, and connections in the community. In turn, considering the unique institutional setting in Africa, it is paramount to investigate the context-specific relevant institutional stakeholders that are paramount for the success of a new business startup. The next section presents a background of the nature of the business environment in Africa, which is then followed by a discussion of the key institutional stakeholders that influence the success of new business startups in Africa.

Characteristics of the African market environment

First, emerging market firms operating in Africa suffer from institutional voids and must face and overcome institutional adversity to survive in business (Khanna & Palepu, 1997; Adomako et al. 2019; Parente et al., 2019; Zahoor et al., 2022). This is due to the absence of market-supporting institutions, lack of infrastructure and specialised intermediaries, weak government regulations and implementation of policies, corruption, constant coups d'état, high levels of market imperfections, and poor communication and transportation services—in turn creating high levels of uncertainty for top-level managers while disrupting the efficient running of new business startups (Acquaah, 2012; Acquaah & Eshun, 2010; Boso et al., 2013; Luiz et al., 2021; Nwoba et al., 2021). Consequently, the levels of institutional development in the emerging markets of Africa, due to the existence of these institutional adversities, are below those of developed economies (Kafouros & Aliyev, 2016; Wu et al., 2016). For instance, while the well-developed market and economic structures determine the nature of economic and commercial activities in developed markets of the West, the institutional voids and adversity create a burden for top-level managers of new business startups in Africa (Nwoba et al., 2021; (Mogaji et al., 2021a). To overcome these challenges, top-level managers of new business startups depend on their social networks and relevant institutional ties to navigate the harsh institutional, economic, and commercial environment in Africa (Acquaah, 2007, 2012; Acquaah & Eshun, 2010). Notwithstanding, extant studies have failed to explicitly consider these context-specific and relevant social networks and institutional stakeholders that affect the performance, competitiveness, and success of new business startups, especially in emerging markets in Africa. These context-specific and relevant institutional stakeholders and the importance of ties with them are discussed in detail in the next section.

Second, emerging market societies in Africa have collectivistic cultures, whereby the extended family and community perform a substantial role in the lives of individuals and organisations (Nwoba et al., 2021; Acquaah, 2012). For instance, in Africa, an individual's family unit is the determining factor in the lifestyle, networks, and connections an individual first associates with (Nwoba et al., 2022).

In light of this unique institutional background in the African market, we posit that the key institutional stakeholder groups that influence the success of new business startups, and thus top-level managers of new business startups, should have strong ties with political and government officials, regulatory officials, local community leaders, and top-level managers at other firms. These institutional stakeholders play a vital role in the functioning of society and thus would help new business startups navigate the institutional voids in the environment, ensuring success. The next section discusses their role in detail, and how they influence the success of new business startups in Africa.

Key institutional stakeholder groups for new business startup success in Africa

Political and government officials

Despite decades of economic liberalisation and growing democratic practices in many countries in Africa, political and government officials at national, regional, local, and city councils still have absolute power and control over societal affairs through rules, policies, and regulations (Acquaah, 2012). This enables political and government officials to structure the nature of economic and commercial activities. While democratic governments hold powers worldwide, the absolute power held by government and political officials in Africa means they can support, approve, or reject new business startup activities that they believe would be a threat to their absolute leadership and control—creating implications for how firms operate in the region and their success (Nwoba et al., 2021). Hence, this creates a situation whereby new business startups depend on government and political directives for their operations, performance, and, in turn, survival (Luiz and Stewart, 2014).

For instance, in Ghana—a country in the west of Africa—government officials control most financial institutions, exclusively determining which companies to award major public contracts to and set economic and commercial regulations and licensing procedures (Acquaah, 2012). These officials are therefore in a position to provide top-level managers of new business startups easy access to funding and financial resources; award major government projects and contracts; provide certification and approval to products and services as meeting government standards; and provide relevant upcoming information that might affect the new business and its industry sector, in turn, leading to higher levels of performance and success (Peng & Luo, 2000; Wang et al., 2022).

There are a number of institutional voids existent in these market environments—the absence of market-supporting institutions, lack of infrastructure and specialised intermediaries, weak government regulations and implementation of policies, high levels of market imperfections, and poor communication and transportation services (Acquaah, 2012; Nwoba, Boso and Robson, 2021). These, in turn create high levels of uncertainty for top-level managers while disrupting the efficient running of new business startups (Acquaah, 2012; Acquaah & Eshun, 2010; Boso et al., 2013). Thus, the ties top-level managers of new business startups' ties have with government and political officials provide access to needed vital resources, information and knowledge that would enable them to navigate the institutional voids in the market environment. Subsequently, this enables them to improve performance and competitiveness, ensuring success and guaranteeing that they survive in business for the long term. To this end, new business startups in Africa whose top-level managers develop and maintain stronger ties with political and government officials will successfully guide their firms to higher performance -leading to success in business.

Regulatory officials

Regulatory officials are in charge of enforcing government policies and regulations to ensure conformance (Acquaah, 2006, 2012; Nwoba et al., 2021). While government and political officials determine the economic and commercial policies and regulations in the society, regulatory officials enforce government directives and ensure that they are being adhered to by businesses. Regulatory officials include officers in government supporting institutions such as the standards board, internal revenue service, government ministries, central bank, and environmental protection agency (Nwoba et al., 2021). They also include officials in industrial and investment institutions (e.g., investment board, export promotion council, and central stock exchange) and permanent secretaries, directors, and commissioners of government bureaus (Nwoba et al., 2021). Regulatory officials control regulatory and licensing procedures such as providing certification and approval and ensuring that products and services meet government standards and directives. For instance, in Nigeria, the National Agency for Food and Drug Administration and Control (NAFDAC) is primed with the responsibility for regulating and controlling the manufacture, importation, exportation, advertisement, distribution, sale, and use of food, drugs, cosmetics, medical equipment, and drinking water (NAFDAC, 2023). Hence, new business startups operating in these sectors must obtain approval and certification from NAFDAC before they can commerce operations. In the same vein, NAFDAC has the powers to stop the operations of any business startup that does not adhere to the government directives, policies, and regulations (NAFDAC, 2023). Therefore, regulatory officials influence business operations in these settings and play a vital role in the success of new business startups.

In a business interview with CNN in 2021 with retail traders in Nigeria, the traders emphasised the importance of these officials in the success of their business startups (CNN Market Place Africa, 2023). According to Mary—a small-scale medium enterprise business owner in Abuja, the capital city of Nigeria—her connection and ties with the market joint task force responsible for ensuring that taxes and levies are paid and that the goods sold in the market meet the government standards helped in the success and survival of her business (CNN Market Place Africa, 2023). In her words:

> I started my business in 2015 here in Wuse Market [the biggest market in Abuja] and I know almost all the Joint Task Force Members. My friendship with them has really helped my business. Sometimes, they inform me of new taxes and levies that the government plan on introducing in the coming months and that information helps me to plan my expenses and savings to ensure I meet them.

Furthermore, Ahmed, another new business owner in the market, noted that:

> It's been three years since we opened, and those joint task force guys have been very helpful to my business. I wanted to import some new malaria drug from India to sell here in Nigeria, but I did not know that the new Nigerian regulations would not allow the drug to be sold in the market, because it contained a substance that has been banned by the government and I had no idea. So, I decided to talk to one of the Joint Task Force members, who happens to be a close friend of mine, and he immediately informed me of the new government ban on that substance that was contained in the malaria drug. That information really helped me as it would have been a deadly business deal if I went ahead to purchase [it] and [then was] now able to sell [it] in Nigeria.

In Africa, especially in sub-Saharan African markets, formal institutional structures are poor and characterised by weak enforcement capacity while the market, and commercial mechanisms for fostering economic exchange, are underdeveloped, in turn creating higher levels of uncertainty for new business startups in their operations (Garrone et al., 2019; Murithi et al., 2020; Pindado et al., 2023). To overcome these institutional voids and adversity, top-level managers of new business startups rely on their social networking relationships, connections, and ties with regulatory officials to provide preferential access to resources, information, and knowledge on impending rules and regulations and their probable interpretation, which would enable them to navigate the high levels of uncertainty in the market environment, which is, in turn, vital in ensuring the success of their business. In addition, ties and connections with regulatory officials would enable new business startups to obtain licensing approval and certification for new innovations.

Local community leaders

Emerging market societies in Africa have a highly collectivistic culture, whereby community living has precedence over an individualistic lifestyle (Nwoba et al., 2022; Nwoba et al., 2021). This community living spirit plays a substantial role in the lives of individuals and, in turn, business operations. To this end, community leaders such as tribal leaders (e.g., local kings, chiefs, and representatives), religious leaders (e.g., pastors, imams, and reverend fathers/sisters), opinion leaders/activists, and newspaper editors/reporters play a very important role in African communities (Nwoba et al., 2021). These local community leaders command strong allegiances in their local jurisdictions and serve as a conduit for top-level managers to uncover and extract insights into changing local community expectations and demands (Ray, 2003).

Due to the underdeveloped market and commercial structures, these local community leaders, therefore, act as links to a broad marketplace, connecting new business startups with their local communities (Ray, 2003). They are very influential in garnering resources and providing access to valuable information and knowledge to new business startups, that is, they help new business startups to understand the needs of the local populace (Nwoba et al., 2021). Ties with community leaders also help new business startups to mitigate against environmental concerns that a community may have as a result of their operational activities, in turn ensuring goodwill among the local community. This enables new business startups to reduce operational costs. As local community leaders act as conduits for the transmission of information and resources, they serve as local bridges between a new business startup and the local community. The relationships developed by the top-level managers of a new business startup with community leaders would provide the startup with valuable access to resources and information as the community leaders endorse the organisation and its activities and recommend it to their communities. This may enable new business startups to obtain financial resources and funding, enter new market segments, and gain access to new customers. This is echoed by Kuanda and Buame's (2000) finding, which posits that social networking ties and connections developed by entrepreneurs with local community and tribal leaders in Ghana provided businesses with information and opportunities, which lead to higher levels of operational and financial performance. To this end, ties with local community leaders would provide new business startups with relevant market information, opportunities, and financial resources, which are vital to the success of new business startups.

Top managers at other firms (business ties)

Another relevant institutional stakeholder group that influences new business startups' success in Africa is ties with top managers at other firms, that is, business ties. Although the impact of business ties on firm performance has been extensively examined in the extant literature (Peng & Luo, 2000; Li et al., 2009; Gao et al., 2008; Wang & Chung, 2013; Gao et al., 2017), there are very few extant studies that have considered the full aspects of business ties in line with the African business settings (e.g., Nwoba et al., 2021; Acquaah, 2012). To capture the full stream of business ties that are relevant to new business startups operating in Africa, we follow Nwoba, Boso, and Robson (2021) to define business ties to include new business startup ties with supplier companies, customer companies, business associations, distributor or marketer firms, and labour/trade unions.

Extant research findings have posited that business ties and connections with top managers at other firms enable businesses to acquire vital resources, valuable information, and knowledge, which are necessary in navigating the institutional voids in Africa (Wu, 2011; Cheng & Yang, 2017; Ritter & Pedersen, 2020). For instance, business ties with customer companies facilitate the creation, acquisition, and exploitation of knowledge (Kim & Choi, 2021; Sharma et al., 2019; Manuel et al., 2021). Such networking connections and relationships also create customer and brand loyalties, and increases sales, which is vital to the success of new business startups (Rungsithong & Meyer, 2020; Yang & Jiang, 2023). In the same vein, business ties with supplier firms will quickly provide access to quality raw materials, superior service, and fast and reliable deliveries (Zhang et al., 2021; Gligor et al., 2021; Yan et al., 2020).

Thus, these business ties would provide new business startups with access to information on latent and expressed market demands that might threaten the status quo in the marketplace, which would in turn lead to the success of the new business startups (Nwoba et al., 2021). Business ties with competitor firms may lead to the sharing of information about how to reduce business operations costs or may lead to collusion to deal with competitive uncertainties in their environment (Zhang et al., 2020; Liu et al., 2022). In the same vein, business ties with labour and trade unions would increase the chances of success of new African business startups. Extant research has shown that failure to effectively deal with labour/trade unions has negative effects on firm productivity and profitability through workers' demands for competitive wages and missing work through strike actions (Acquaah, 2007; Amato et al., 2017). Recently, employee trade unions have been growing in Africa, and in some organisations, all of the employees may be members of a trade union. Therefore, for new business startups, their employees depend on unions or the leadership of employee representatives for collective bargaining on salaries and working conditions. Hence, any disagreement or confrontation between a union and a new business startup would have negative effects on the startup's efficiency and profitability. To counter these negative effects, most businesses are now including labour/trade unions in corporate decisions on working conditions and wages (Acquaah and Eshun, 2010). This has led to improved communication and harmonious and nonadversarial relationship between the two parties. The improvement in communication between top-level managers of new business startups and trade union leaders improves employee productivity and performance, which, in turn, leads to the success of the new business startups. Furthermore, such cordial relationships may enable trade union leaders to provide additional information to top management of new business startups about employee working preferences, in turn, allowing the new businesses to boost employee morale, motivation, and productivity through choosing and combining the best mix of working conditions, workplace rules, wages, and entitlements. In sum, business ties are relevant in the success of new business startups in Africa.

Conclusion

The African business startup landscape is currently experiencing massive growth (Amankwah-Amoah et al., 2018; Amaeshi et al., 2018; The Economist, 2022). Consequently, there has been a surge of successful business startups across various African sectors, leading to the continent becoming a hotspot for entrepreneurial activity, innovation, and investment. Notwithstanding the massive growth in the African business startup ecosystem, Zhou (2023) posits that 80% of new business startups in Africa fail within their first five years of existence and operations. This means that only 20% of new African business startups survive in the long term. Hence, there is a growing interest among academics, practitioners, the media, and general public in understanding the factors that enable new business startups to succeed and survive in the long term in Africa (Amankwah-Amoah et al., 2018; Nwoba et al., 2021). To this end, this chapter conceptually theorises that, due to the unique institutional business settings in Africa, top-level managerial ties with relevant institutional stakeholders—political/government officials, regulatory officials, local community leaders, and top-managers at other firms—support the growth, long-term survival, performance, and, in turn, success of new business startups on the continent. The chapter posits that these context-specific and relevant institutional stakeholders play a vital role in economic and commercial activities on the African continent and, as such, are vital in the success of new business startups.

References

Acquaah, M., 2006. The impact of managerial networking relationships on organizational performance in SubSaharan Africa: Evidence from Ghana. *Organization Management Journal*, *3*(2), pp. 115–138.

Acquaah, M., 2007. Managerial social capital, strategic orientation, and organizational performance in an emerging economy. *Strategic Management Journal*, *28*(12), pp. 1235–1255.

Acquaah, M., 2012. Social networking relationships, firm-specific managerial experience, and firm performance in a transition economy: A comparative analysis of family owned and nonfamily firms. *Strategic Management Journal*, *33*(10), pp. 1215–1228.

Acquaah, M. and Eshun, J. P., 2010. A longitudinal analysis of the moderated effects of networking relationships on organizational performance in a sub-Saharan African economy. *Human Relations*, *63*(5), pp. 667–700.

Adomako, S., Amankwah-Amoah, J., Dankwah, G. O., Danso, A. and Donbesuur, F., 2019. Institutional voids, international learning effort and internationalization of emerging market new ventures. *Journal of International Management*, *25*(4), p. 100666.

Amaeshi, K., Idemudia, U., Amaeshi, K., Okupe, A. and Idemudia, U., 2018. Africapitalism: A management idea for business in Africa. *Africapitalism: Rethinking the Role of Business in Africa*, *1*, p. 19.

Amankwah-Amoah, J., Boso, N. and Debrah, Y. A., 2018. Africa rising in an emerging world: An international marketing perspective. *International Marketing Review*, *35*(4), pp. 550–559.

Amato, C., Baron, R. A., Barbieri, B., Belanger, J. J. and Pierro, A., 2017. Regulatory modes and entrepreneurship: The mediational role of alertness in small business success. *Journal of Small Business Management*, *55*, pp. 27–42.

Antai, I. and Eze, N. L., 2023. Impact of the COVID-19 pandemic on business-to-business relationships in digital ecosystems: An African perspective. *Information Technology & People*, *36*(8), pp. 69–93.

Boso, N., Story, V. M. and Cadogan, J. W., 2013. Entrepreneurial orientation, market orientation, network ties, and performance: Study of entrepreneurial firms in a developing economy. *Journal of Business Venturing*, *28*(6), pp. 708–727.

Chan-Zuckerberg Initiative, 2023. Building a better future for everyone. https://chanzuckerberg.com/

Cheng, C. and Yang, M., 2017. Enhancing performance of cross-border mergers and acquisitions in developed markets: The role of business ties and technological innovation capability. *Journal of Business Research*, *81*, pp. 107–117.

CNN Marketplace Africa, 2023. How businesses survive in Nigeria. https://edition.cnn.com/business/marketplace-africa

Danns, D. E. and Danns, G. K., 2022. Institutional support and the challenges facing youth entrepreneurs in developing countries: A Guyana case study. *International Journal of Entrepreneurship and Small Business*, *46*(2), pp. 139–161.

Gao, C., Zuzul, T., Jones, G. and Khanna, T., 2017. Overcoming institutional voids: A reputation-based view of long-run survival. *Strategic Management Journal*, *38*(11), pp. 2147–2167.

Gao, S., Xu, K. and Yang, J., 2008. Managerial ties, absorptive capacity, and innovation. *Asia Pacific Journal of Management*, *25*(3), pp. 395–412.

Garrone, P., Piscitello, L. and D'Amelio, M., 2019. Multinational enterprises and the provision of collective goods in developing countries under formal and informal institutional voids. The case of electricity in Sub-Saharan Africa. *Journal of International Management, 25*(2), p. 100650.

Gligor, D. M., Gölgeci, I., Newman, C. and Bozkurt, S., 2021. Performance implications of the buyer-supplier market orientation fit. *Industrial Marketing Management, 93*, pp. 161–173.

Granovetter, M. 1973. The strength of weak ties. *American Journal of Sociology, 78*, pp. 1360–1380.

Granovetter, M. 1985. Economic action and social structure: The problem of embeddedness. *American Journal of Sociology, 91*, pp. 481–510.

Kafouros, M. and Aliyev, M., 2016. Institutional development and firm profitability in transition economies. *Journal of World Business, 51*(3), pp. 369–378.

Khanna, T. and Palepu, K., 1997. Why focused strategies. *Harvard Business Review, 75*(4), pp. 41–51.

Kim, Y. and Choi, T. Y., 2021. Supplier relationship strategies and outcome dualities: An empirical study of embeddedness perspective. *International Journal of Production Economics, 232*, p. 107930.

Kuanda, J. and Buame, S. 2000. Social ties and resource leveraging strategies of small enterprises in Ghana. In O. J. Sorensen & E. Arnould (Eds.), *Proceedings of the 7th International Conference on Marketing and Development* (pp. 425–439). University of Ghana.

Laumann, E. O., Galaskiewicz, J. and Marsden, P. V., 1978. Community structure as interorganizational linkages. *Annual Review of Sociology, 4*(1), pp. 455–484.

Li, J. J., Zhou, K. Z. and Shao, A. T., 2009. Competitive position, managerial ties, and profitability of foreign firms in China: An interactive perspective. *Journal of International Business Studies, 40*, pp. 339–352.

Liu, Y., Collinson, S., Cooper, C. and Baglieri, D., 2022. International business, innovation and ambidexterity: A micro-foundational perspective. *International Business Review, 31*(3), 101852.

Luiz, J. M., Magada, T. and Mukumbuzi, R., 2021. Strategic responses to institutional voids (rationalization, aggression, and defensiveness): Institutional complementarity and why the home country matters. *Management International Review, 61*(5), pp. 681–711.

Luiz, J. M. and Stewart, C., 2014. Corruption, South African multinational enterprises, and institutions in Africa. *Journal of Business Ethics, 124*, pp. 383–398.

Manuela, P., Cristina, B. and Molina-Morales, F. X., 2021. I need you, but do I love you? Strong ties and innovation in supplier–customer relations. *European Management Journal, 39*(6), pp. 790–801.

Mogaji, E., Adeola, O., Hinson, R. E., Nguyen, N. P., Nwoba, A. C. and Soetan, T. O., 2021a. Marketing bank services to financially vulnerable customers: Evidence from an emerging economy. *International Journal of Bank Marketing, 39*(3), pp. 402–428.

Mogaji, E., Balakrishnan, J., Nwoba, A. C. and Nguyen, N. P., 2021b. Emerging-market consumers' interactions with banking chatbots. *Telematics and Informatics, 65*, p. 101711.

M-pesa. 2023. What is M-Pesa. Accessed 30 July 2023. Available from https://www.vodafone.com/about-vodafone/what-we-do/consumer-products-and-services/m-pesa

Murithi, W., Vershinina, N. and Rodgers, P. (2020). Where less is more: institutional voids and business families in sub-Saharan Africa. *International Journal of Entrepreneurial Behavior & Research, 26*(1), 158–174.

NAFDAC. 2023. National agency for food and drug administration and control. Accessed 30 July 2023. Available from https://www.nafdac.gov.ng/

Nwoba, A. C., Boso, N. and Robson, M. J., 2021. Corporate sustainability strategies in institutional adversity: Antecedent, outcome, and contingency effects. *Business Strategy and the Environment*, *30*(2), pp. 787–807.

Nwoba, A. C., Mogaji, E., Zahoor, N., Donbesuur, F. and Alam, G. M., 2022. Obesity, family units and social marketing intervention: Evidence from Nigeria. *European Journal of Marketing*, *56*(11), pp. 2892–2927.

Oluwole, V. 2023. Africa's top 10 most entrepreneurial nations. https://africa.businessinsider.com/local/markets/africas-top-10-most-entrepreneurial-nations/mjnbes1

Omotosho, B. J., 2023. Small scale craft workers and the use of social media platforms for business performance in southwest Nigeria. *Journal of Small Business & Entrepreneurship*, *35*(2), pp. 181–196.

Parente, R., Rong, K., Geleilate, J. M. G. and Misati, E., 2019. Adapting and sustaining operations in weak institutional environments: A business ecosystem assessment of a Chinese MNE in Central Africa. *Journal of International Business Studies*, *50*, pp. 275–291.

Peng, M. W. and Luo, Y., 2000. Managerial ties and firm performance in a transition economy: The nature of a micro-macro link. *Academy of Management Journal*, *43*(3), pp. 486–501.

Pindado, E., Alarcón, S., Sánchez, M. and Martínez, M. G., 2023. International entrepreneurship in Africa: The roles of institutional voids, entrepreneurial networks and gender. *Journal of Business Research*, *166*, p. 114109.

Ray, D. I. 2003. Chiefs in their millennium sandals: Traditional authority in Ghana—Relevance, challenges, and prospects. In W. J. Tettey, K. P. Puplampu, & B. J. Berman (Eds.), *Critical Perspectives in Political and Socioeconomic Development in Ghana. African Social Studies Series*, Vol. 6. Leiden, The Netherlands: Boston Brill; 241–271.

Ritter, T. and Pedersen, C. L., 2020. Digitization capability and the digitalization of business models in business-to-business firms: Past, present, and future. *Industrial Marketing Management*, *86*, pp. 180–190.

Rungsithong, R. and Meyer, K. E., 2020. Trust and knowledge sharing in context: A study of international buyer-supplier relationships in Thailand. *Industrial Marketing Management*, *88*, pp. 112–124.

Sharma, A., Kumar, V., Yan, J., Borah, S. B. and Adhikary, A., 2019. Understanding the structural characteristics of a firm's whole buyer–supplier network and its impact on international business performance. *Journal of International Business Studies*, *50*, pp. 365–392.

Statista, 2023. Estimated number of startups in selected African countries in 2023. https://www.statista.com/statistics/1290679/number-of-startups-in-africa-bycountry/#:~:text=The%20number%20of%20startups%20in,in%20the%20same%20year%2C%20respectively

The Economist, 2022. African startups are raising unprecedented amounts. *What next?* https://www.economist.com/middle-east-and-africa/2022/07/21/african-startups-are-raising-unprecedented-amounts-what-next

Trading Economics, 2022. Nigerian population, 1960–2021. www.tradingeconomics.com/nigeria/population

Wang, C. L. and Chung, H. F., 2013. The moderating role of managerial ties in market orientation and innovation: An Asian perspective. *Journal of Business Research*, *66*(12), pp. 2431–2437.

Wang, D., Cui, L., Vu, T. and Feng, T., 2022. Political capital and MNE responses to institutional voids: The case of Chinese state-owned enterprises in Africa. *Organization Studies*, *43*(1), pp. 105–126.

Workpay, 2023. Unlocking Africa's entrepreneurial potential: Supporting small businesses and startups. https://www.myworkpay.com/blogs/unlocking-africas-entrepreneurial-potential-supporting-small-businesses-and-startups

Wu, J., 2011. Asymmetric roles of business ties and political ties in product innovation. *Journal of Business Research*, *64*(11), pp. 1151–1156.

Wu, J., Wang, C., Hong, J., Piperopoulos, P. and Zhuo, S., 2016. Internationalization and innovation performance of emerging market enterprises: The role of host-country institutional development. *Journal of World Business*, *51*(2), pp. 251–263.

Yan, T., Yang, Y., Dooley, K. and Chae, S., 2020. Trading-off innovation novelty and information protection in supplier selection for a new product development project: Supplier ties as signals. *Journal of Operations Management*, *66*(7–8), pp. 933–957.

Yang, Y. and Jiang, Y., 2023. Buyer-supplier CSR alignment and firm performance: A contingency theory perspective. *Journal of Business Research*, *154*, p. 113340.

Zahoor, N., Christofi, M., Nwoba, A. C., Donbesuur, F. and Miri, D., 2022. Operational effectiveness in post-pandemic times: Examining the roles of digital technologies, talent management and employee engagement in manufacturing SMEs. *Production Planning & Control*, pp. 1–14. https://doi.org/10.1080/09537287.2022.2147863

Zhang, C., Du, N. and Zhang, X., 2021. When an interfirm relationship is ending: The dark side of managerial ties and relationship intimacy. *Journal of Business Research*, *125*, pp. 227–238.

Zhang, J. A., O'Kane, C. and Chen, G., 2020. Business ties, political ties, and innovation performance in Chinese industrial firms: The role of entrepreneurial orientation and environmental dynamism. *Journal of Business Research*, *121*, pp. 254–267.

Zhou, L. 2023. The percentage of businesses that fail (statistics & failure rates). https://www.luisazhou.com/blog/businesses-that-fail/#:~:text=24.,first%20five%20years%20of%20existence&text=Africa%20has%20the%20highest%20entrepreneur,within%20their%20first%20half%2Ddecade

8 Challenges of Female Entrepreneurship in Africa

Towards a Typology of Stakeholder Salience

Mavis Serwah Benneh Mensah, Joseph Kwadwo Danquah and Betty J. Aidoo-Anderson

Background

Female entrepreneurship remains a potent, yet less harnessed, avenue for personal and national development. Similar to global trends, female entrepreneurship in Africa is mainly in traditional and low-income sectors (Elam et al., 2021). It is critical for self-employment, which explains why a number of countries in Africa have early total entrepreneurial activity rates (TEA) that are higher than the TEA of advanced economies. For example, in 2019 the TEA of Senegal (36.8%) and Botswana (32.0%) were higher than those in advanced economies such as Canada (13.3%) and Australia (11.5%) (Pinkovetskaia et al., 2019).

In spite of the importance of female entrepreneurship and the potential for growth in Africa, it suffers from numerous problems including gender discrimination, limited growth and skills and funding deficits (Senou & Manda, 2022). Many measures have been initiated to address the challenges of female entrepreneurship in Africa, including the Africa Development Bank $42 billion Affirmative Finance Action for Women in Africa (AFAWA). Research has also shown how skills training and funding positively impact female entrepreneurship (Chirwa, 2008).

As scholars and practitioners continue to search for insights into the obstacles to female entrepreneurship on the continent, we dwell on the tenets of the stakeholder theory (Freeman, 1999; Mitchell et al., 1997) backed by institutional theory (North, 2016) and the resource-based theory (Barney et al., 2021), to analyse the challenges of female entrepreneurship in Africa and proffer a typology of stakeholder salience. Institutions and resources constitute an integral part of stakeholder relationships which female entrepreneurs ought to leverage for positive synergistic effects on their enterprises.

There is a substantial body of research on the challenges of female entrepreneurship in Africa. However, the scholarly literature falls short of adequate systematic reviews that contribute to building a holistic understanding of the situation. In order to contribute towards addressing these research gaps, we conducted a systematic literature review of the challenges of female entrepreneurship in Africa aimed at proposing a typology of stakeholder salience as informed by the following research questions: (1) What challenges do female

DOI: 10.4324/9781003256014-11

entrepreneurs in Africa encounter in their entrepreneurial pursuits? (2) How do the female entrepreneurs manage or cope with the challenges of their profession? (3) Who are the critical stakeholders and what role do they play in creating, or in addressing, the challenges of female entrepreneurship in Africa?

Theoretical framework

The stakeholder theory informed the design of this research with supporting insights from the resource-based theory and institutional theory. Freeman (1984, as cited in Laplume et al., 2008, p. 1160) defines stakeholder as "any group or individual who can affect or is affected by the achievement of the organisation's objectives." Stakeholders include employees, shareholders, customers, suppliers, governments, and competitors (Laplume et al., 2008). For female entrepreneurship in Africa, there is the additional responsibility of managing family members. The stakeholder theory recognises people within and outside the business as central to its advancement. In contrast, the resource-based theory upholds tangible and intangible resources as fundamental to business success (Barney et al., 2021). Consistent with Adomako et al. (2019), this research underscores stakeholders as critical actors through whom businesses can acquire strategic resources, making it imperative for female entrepreneurs in resource-constrained entrepreneurial ecosystems, such as that of Africa, to prioritise and manage their stakeholder relationships for optimum gains.

For entrepreneurs to successfully manage stakeholder relationships, they must comply with the "rules of the game", which are formal or informal institutions (North, 2016; Mensah & Derera, 2023). A myriad of stakeholder classifications has emerged, one example being the stakeholder salience framework (SSF), also called the MAW framework (Mitchell et al., 1997). The concept of stakeholder salience is predicated on three stakeholder attributes (power, legitimacy and urgency) on who or what truly counts in business organisations and how to manage expectations (Mitchell et al., 2011). Another typology is the holistic stakeholder mapping model (Sedereviciute & Valentini, 2011) which identifies concerned influencers and concerned lurkers as alternatives for MAW's definitive and dependent stakeholders.

There are, however, limited insights into stakeholder salience for female entrepreneurship, particularly within the context of Africa. Consequently, using the stakeholder theory and stakeholder salience concept (Mitchell et al., 2011) backed by the resource-based theory and institutional theory, this chapter analyses the challenges of female entrepreneurship in Africa and proffers a typology of stakeholder salience.

Methodology

This research was based on the transformative research paradigm aimed at addressing critical issues of marginalised groups and individuals (Thambinathan & Kinsella, 2021). Globally, and in particular in Africa, women constitute a marginalised segment with limited decision-making power and control over resources (Elam et al., 2021). We employed the qualitative research approach to conduct document analysis of the challenges of female entrepreneurship in Africa and to propose a typology of stakeholder salience. The findings are important for female entrepreneurs and policy makers to address the challenges, especially those that emanate from critical stakeholders who have the power, legitimacy and/or urgency to thwart or support the progress of women's ventures.

The review process

Following the framework-based systematic literature review approach (Xiao & Watson, 2019), the review began with the determination of the search engines, inclusion/exclusion criteria, and retrieval, coding and analysis. We selected relevant literature based on accessibility, coverage and credibility (Paul et al., 2021). The inclusion/exclusion criteria comprised four major guidelines: (1) empirical publication on any or a combination of the 54 countries in Africa; (2) a focus on the challenges of female entrepreneurship; (3) publications within the past 20 years; and (4) publications written in English. In total, 72 publications from 22 African countries (Table 8.1) were reviewed and

Table 8.1 Countries and Total Number of Publications Accepted for the Study

	Country	*Total No. of Publications*
1.	South Africa	4
2.	Benin	1
3.	Egypt	1
4.	Nigeria	13
5.	Ghana	22
6.	Kenya	1
7.	Botswana	3
8.	Ethiopia	5
9.	SSA	2
10.	Gambia	2
11.	Malawi	1
12.	Rwanda	1
13.	Sudan	1
14.	MENA Region	1
15.	SSA	1
16.	Morocco	2
17.	Tanzania	4
18.	Algeria	1
19.	Cameroon	2
20.	DR Congo	1
21.	Lesotho	2
22.	Zimbabwe	1
	Total	72

Source: Authors' compilation (2022).

included in the study. There were limited studies from countries such as Sudan and the DR Congo, while there were relatively more studies that met our inclusion criteria from Nigeria and Ghana (Table 8.1).

Data extraction and analysis

The tenets of institutional theory and the resource-based theory were guiding frameworks for data analysis. We categorised all formal and informal laws, regulations, norms and practices that are inimical to female entrepreneurship into institutional constraints (North, 2016; Mensah & Derera, 2023). Similarly, resource constraints of female entrepreneurship in Africa were analysed under financial resources, market conditions, human resources, infrastructure, personal capabilities and resources in the natural environment (Barney et al., 2021). We employed the three stakeholder-salience attributes of power, legitimacy and urgency to examine the degree of stakeholder salience.

Results and discussions

In order to address the study's research questions, we present the results and discussions under three main sub-sections. We end by proposing a typology of stakeholder salience for female entrepreneurship in Africa.

Challenges of female entrepreneurship in Africa

The review shows that female entrepreneurs in Africa face numerous challenges including institutional and resource endowment constraints.

Institutional constraints

Institutional constraints, within the context of this study, comprise laws in the general business environment and sociocultural norms and practices that negatively affect actors in an entrepreneurship ecosystem. The results show *generic institutional constraints* common to female entrepreneurs in all the countries involved in the study; however, some *country-specific institutional constraints* were identified. The generic institutional constraints include sociocultural barriers that manifest in gender discrimination, limited control over resources or lack of property rights and limited decision-making power.

The results, as shown in Table 8.2, point to gender discrimination as a fundamental *institutional constraint* which empowers society to regard women as subordinate to men in society, in the workplace and in marriage. This hinders the performance and sustainability of women's enterprises and livelihoods (Table 8.2). Deep-seated patriarchal discrimination, for instance in Botswana (Ntseane, 2004) and in northern Ghana (Adom & Anambane, 2020) deprives women of inheriting property and exercising substantial decision-making powers even over funds raised through their businesses. These findings conform to

Table 8.2 Generic Institutional Constraints

Challenges/Problems	*Examples of Countries and Publications*	*Major stakeholders*
Socio-cultural barriers, e.g., gender bias, limited control over resources	1. Ghana: Overå (2003, 2017); Dzisi (2008); Wrigley-Asante (2012); Salia et al. (2018); Adom et al. (2018); Adom and Anambane (2020), etc. 2. Gambia: Della-Giusta and Phillips (2006) 3. Botswana: Ntseane (2004) 4. Nigeria: Mordi et al. (2010) 5. MENA Region: Hattab (2012) 6. Sudan: Welsh et al. (2013) 7. Rwanda: Nsengimana et al. (2017) 8. South Africa: Aneke et al. (2017) 9. Tanzania: Kapinga and Montero (2017); Isaga (2019) 10. Nigeria: Okolie et al. (2021) 11. Nigeria: Oloko et al. (2022) 12. Gambia: Lim et al. (2022)	1. Traditional authority 2. State 3. Husbands 4. Relatives, especially male relatives 5. Religious bodies: churches and other places of worship 6. Women's business associations
Social and family responsibilities and disruptions, multiple role complexities and associated limitations	1. South Africa: Schindehutte et al. (2003) 2. Botswana: Ntseane (2004) 3. Ethiopia: Singh and Belwal (2008); Gudeta and van Engen (2017); Hundera et al. (2019) 4. Gambia: Della-Giusta and Phillips (2006) 5. Lesotho: Chingono (2016) 6. Rwanda: Nsengimana et al. (2017) 7. Tanzania: Kapinga and Montero (2017); Langevang et al. (2018) 8. Ghana: Adom et al. (2018); Salia et al. (2018) 9. Tanzania: Isaga (2019) 10. (2021) 11. Gambia: Lim et al. (2022)	1. Traditional authority 2. State 3. Husbands 4. Children 5. Relatives 6. Female relatives 7. Domestic workers

Source: Authors' compilation (2022).

prior research that have established entrenched discriminatory sociocultural practices as a fundamental bane to women's entrepreneurship globally (Elam et al., 2021).

There is evidence of dual, triple and even multiple role complexities (Table 8.2) of women entrepreneurs in combining family and entrepreneurial responsibilities. The triple role complexities of women entrepreneurs encompass family, social and economic responsibilities in contrast to men who primarily engage in economic responsibilities (Gudeta & van Engen, 2017). Society expects women to take care of the home, children and relatives by cooking, cleaning, offering childcare and caring for aged and sick relatives (Ahl & Marlow, 2021). Additional multiple role challenges are women entrepreneurs' limited time for their entrepreneurial ventures, fatigue, stress and diversion of business funds due to financial pressures from family responsibilities and mismanagement of funds (Welsh et al., 2013). Thus, owning a business can disrupt family life and reduce the time spent with the family (Schindehutte et al., 2003).

Country-specific institutional constraints, that is challenges that we found to emanate from relatively few countries e.g., Bostwana, Ethiopia and Lesotho (Table 8.3), include a lack of acceptance of entrepreneurial career by family and society; security-related constraints; limited government support; business registration and licensing constraints; high taxes; and delays at the ports and in payment by debtors. These country-specific challenges demonstrate variations in the problems of female entrepreneurship in the various African countries and the need for continuous policy-driven research to derive the right policy focus.

Table 8.3 Country-Specific Institutional Constraints

Challenges/Problems	*Examples of Countries and Publications*	*Major stakeholders*
Lack of acceptance of entrepreneurship as a career by family and society	1. Ethiopia: Abagissa (2013) 2. Tanzania: Isaga (2019) 3. Botswana: Mamabolo and Lekoko (2021)	1. Spouses 2. Extended family
Sexual harassment by public officials and other male service providers	1. Nigeria: Mordi et al. (2010) 2. Ghana: Sallah and Caesar (2020) 3. Tanzania: Isaga (2019)	1. Public officers 2. Male service providers
Corruption and exploitation	1. Ethiopia: Singh and Belwal (2008) 2. Ghana: Oteng-Ababio (2018); Sowatey et al. (2018)	Public officers
Theft of goods and damaged goods	1. Botswana: Ama et al. (2014) 2. Lesotho: Chingono (2016)	Thieves

(*Continued*)

Table 8.3 (Continued)

Challenges/Problems	*Examples of Countries and Publications*	*Major stakeholders*
Climate risk	1. Tanzania – Kapinga and Montero (2017) 2. Sub-Saharan Africa – Gannnon et al. (2022)	1. Society 2. Family
Wars/conflicts	1. Sudan: Welsh et al. (2013) 2. MENA Region: Hattab (2012)	1. Society 2. Family
Limited government support and unfriendly regulations	1. Gambia: Della-Giusta and Phillips (2006) 2. Ethiopia: Singh and Belwal (2008) 3. Ghana: Kuada (2009); Peprah et al. (2019) 4. Nigeria: Mordi et al. (2010) 5. Botswana: Mamabolo and Lekoko (2021)	Government institutions
Lack of co-operation and unhealthy competition among female entrepreneurs	1. Malawi: Chirwa (2008) 2. Algeria: Fatima et al. (2014) 3. Lesotho: Chingono (2016) 4. Morocco: Naguib (2024)	Female entrepreneurs
Registration/licensing constraints	1. Ethiopia: Abagissa (2013) 2. Tanzania: Langevang et al. (2018)	BDS providers
High taxes	1. Botswana: Ama et al. (2014) 2. Rwanda: Nsengimana et al. (2017) 3. Ghana: Peprah et al. (2019)	Government
Delays	(A) At the borders: traders 1. Botswana: Ama et al. (2014) (B) In payment by debtors (defaulters as well) 1. Botswana: Ama et al. (2014) 2. Lesotho: Chingono (2016) 3. Ghana: Peprah et al. (2019)	1. Public officers 2. Debtors

Source: Authors' compilation (2022/2024).

Resource constraints

The review revealed several resource constraints with lack or limited access to finance as the most cited resource constraint (Table 8.4a). Another finding is that Woldie et al. (2018) and Senou and Manda (2022) did not establish any significant difference between the chances of men and women securing funds when they apply to financial institutions for assistance. This was not the case in Morocco where no gender-based discriminatory banking practices were found

Table 8.4a Resource Constraints

Challenges/Problems	*Examples of Countries and Publications*	*Major stakeholders*
Lack of capital/ limited access to finance (including high interest rates, small loan sizes, lack of collateral, etc.)	1. Ghana: Overå (2003, 2017); Abor & Biekpe (2007); Dzisi (2008); Ali (2017); Fieve and Chrysostome (2024), etc. 2. Cameroon: Fonjong (2004) 3. Gambia: Della-Giusta and Phillips (2006); Lim et al. (2022) 4. Ethiopia: Singh and Belwal (2008) 5. Nigeria: Mordi et al. (2010); Halkias et al. (2011); Okolie et al. (2021), etc. 6. Ethiopia: Abagissa (2013) 7. Algeria: Fatima et al. (2014) 8. Botswana: Ama et al. (2014); Mamabolo and Lekoko (2021) 9. Rwanda: Nsengimana et al. (2017) 10. South Africa: Garwe and Fatoki (2012); Derera et al. (2014); Aneke et al. (2017) 11. DR Congo: Woldie et al. (2018) 12. Tanzania: Langevang et al. (2018); Isaga (2019) 13. Ghana: Kuada (2009); Peprah et al. (2019) 14. Benin: Senou and Manda (2022) 15. Morocco: Berguiga and Adair (2021); Naguib (2024) 16. Nigeria: Metu and Nwogwugwu (2024)	1. Financial institutions 2. Government 3. Traditional authority 4. Informal credit suppliers 5. Women entrepreneurs 6. Husbands 7. Parents 8. Friends 9. International Development Organisations (IDOs) 10. Non-governmental Organisations (NGOs) 11. Semi-formal micro finance institutions 12. Charity organisations e.g., churches

Source: Authors' compilation (2022/2024).

but rather female entrepreneurs submitted lower loan applications because they disqualified themselves due to their inability to meet loan conditions (Berguiga & Adair, 2021). This is consistent with the extant literature on funding constraints faced by women entrepreneurs in developing countries which is often traced to size and businesses operating in uncompetitive sectors with low turnover; and a lack of control over resources that can be used as collateral or even investment in their ventures (Panda, 2018).

The findings (Table 8.4b) point to poor market conditions which also constitute major resource constraints to female entrepreneurship in Africa. The leading market-related problems include stiff and unfriendly competition coupled with low demand for products, default debtors, high rent charges and input supply problems such as high prices, low quality and delays in supply (Table 8.4b). Researchers (e.g., Lim et al., 2022) trace low demand and stiff competition to women's deliberate choice to operate in less competitive and less demanding sectors that will permit them to fulfil their multiple roles in the family, society and business, thus causing limited growth of their ventures especially when a premium is placed on family responsibilities. This clarification augments similar explanations offered by the Global Report on Women's Entrepreneurship (Elam et al., 2021).

Table 8.4b Resource Constraints

Challenges/Problems	*Examples of Countries and Publications*	*Major Stakeholders*
Marketing challenges/ stiff competition from local and foreign products/lack of market access leading to low demand	1. Gambia: Della-Giusta and Phillips (2006) 2. Ghana: Overå (2017); Oteng-Ababio (2018); Peprah et al. (2019) 3. Ethiopia: Singh and Belwal (2008); Hundera et al. (2019) 4. Malawi: Chirwa (2008) 5. Botswana: Ama et al. (2014); Mamabolo and Lekoko (2021) 6. Lesotho: Rantšo (2016) 7. Tanzania: Kapinga and Montero (2017); Isaga (2019) 8. Gambia: Lim et al. (2022) 9. Ghana: Fieve and Chrysostome (2024)	1. Competitors 2. Customers
High rent charges	1. Nigeria: Mordi et al. (2010) 2. Ethiopia: Abagissa (2013)	Property owners
Input supply challenges	1. Ethiopia: Abagissa (2013); Hundera et al. (2019) 2. Gambia: Lim et al. (2022)	Suppliers

(*Continued*)

Table 8.4b (Continued)

Challenges/Problems	*Examples of Countries and Publications*	*Major Stakeholders*
Slow business growth/ lack of profit	1. Ethiopia: Mersha and Sriram (2019) 2. Ghana: Fieve and Chrysostome (2024)	Female entrepreneurs
Limited or lack of infrastructure including work premises, equipment, etc.	1. Gambia: Della-Giusta and Phillips (2006) 2. Ghana: Overå (2017); Dzisi (2008); Kuada (2009); Peprah et al. (2019) 3. Ethiopia: Abagissa (2013) 4. Tanzania: Isaga (2019) 5. Ghana: Peprah et al. (2019) 6. Zimbabwe: Kabonga et al. (2021) Gambia: Lim et al. (2022)	1. Suppliers of equipment 2. Property owners 3. Local authorities 4. Law enforcement agencies
Transportation problems	1. Botswana: Ama et al. (2014) 2. Nigeria: Seedhouse et al. (2016) 3. Rwanda: Nsengimana et al. (2017) 4. Ethiopia: Hundera et al. (2019) Gambia: Lim et al. (2022)	Private and public transport owners and operators

Source: Authors' compilation (2022/2024).

Three main issues emerged as major physical and technological infrastructure challenges. They are limited access to equipment and tools mostly reported in studies from the Gambia, Ethiopia and Tanzania (Table 8.4b); and limited access to good work premises and high rent charges. The third infrastructure challenges are poor road network/transportation services established in research from five African countries (Table 8.4b). These findings are consistent with those of Panda (2018) on obstacles to female entrepreneurship in developing countries. The key human resource challenges (Table 8.4c) include lack of skilled and dependable labour supply. Abagissa (2013) and Gudeta and van Engen (2017) emphasise the burden labour-related challenges place on women entrepreneurs due to the absence or limited chance for delegation of responsibilities.

Personal challenges closely relate to human resource deficiencies in skills, knowledge, abilities, values and beliefs of women entrepreneurs. The results (Table 8.4c) indicate that women entrepreneurs exhibit less self-belief due to knowledge and skills gaps as well as their multiple role complexities which limit growth of their businesses (Lim et al., 2022). They hardly have knowledge of seasoned female counterparts who can serve as role models or mentors (Langevang et al., 2018). Personal challenges could rank second after institutional constraints because prior research shows that the challenges are a manifestation of the negative effects of institutions, particularly inimical customary laws and sociocultural and religious norms and practices that discriminate

Table 8.4c Resource Constraints

Challenges/Problems	*Examples of Countries and Publications*	*Major Stakeholders*
Lack of skilled and dependable labour	1. Ghana: Kuada (2009) 2. Ethiopia: Abagissa (2013); Gudeta and van Engen (2017) 3. Tanzania: Isaga (2019)	Employees
No education/low levels of education	1. Ghana: Dzisi (2008); Ghana: Fieve and Chrysostome (2024) 2. Gambia: Della-Giusta and Phillips (2006) 3. Malawi: Chirwa (2008) 4. Botswana: Ama et al. (2014) 5. Sudan: Welsh et al. (2013) 6. Tanzania: Kapinga and Montero (2017) 7. Nigeria: Okolie et al. (2021) 8. Nigeria: Oloko et al. (2022)	Female entrepreneurs
Lack of business and entrepreneurial experience and skills	1. Della-Giusta and Phillips (2006) 2. Ethiopia: Singh and Belwal (2008); Mersha and Sriram (2019); Hundera et al. (2019) 3. Botswana: Ama et al. (2014) 4. Rwanda: Nsengimana et al. (2017) 5. Tanzania: Kapinga and Montero (2017); Langevang et al. (2018); Isaga (2019) 6. Gambia: Lim et al. (2022) 7. Ghana: Fieve and Chrysostome (2024)	Female entrepreneurs
Lack of technical/ technological know-how (self-efficacy)	1. Ethiopia: Singh and Belwal (2008) 2. Ghana: Overå (2017) 3. Morocco: Naguib (2024)	1. Government 2. BDS providers
Personal problems e.g., fear of failure; perceiving oneself as weak, not confident	1. MENA Region: Hattab (2012) 2. Ghana: Fieve and Chrysostome (2024)	

(*Continued*)

Table 8.4c (Continued)

Challenges/Problems	*Examples of Countries and Publications*	*Major Stakeholders*
Limited growth orientation/ motivation on the part of the women entrepreneurs	1. Gambia: Della-Giusta and Phillips (2006) 2. Ghana: Adom et al. (2018) 3. Ethiopia: Mersha and Sriram (2019) 4. Gambia: Lim et al. (2022)	Female entrepreneurs
Lack of (knowledge about) role models and career guidance	1. Tanzania: Langevang et al. (2018) 2. Gambia: Lim et al. (2022) 3. Morocco: Naguib (2024)	1. Government 2. BDS providers

Source: Authors' compilation (2022/2024).

against females in terms of education, career development, decision-making and resource control (Ahl & Marlow, 2021).

In the face of the various human resource challenges, access to training and information as well as social capital becomes paramount to the activities of female entrepreneurs. Nonetheless, the findings show limited access to entrepreneurship training and development and information asymmetry (Table 8.4d) as other major resource-related constraints in the general business environment. Social capital constraints consist of problems that women entrepreneurs encounter in their business networking endeavours. The results reveal diverse angles to networking challenges in female entrepreneurship. For instance, studies in Angola, Tanzania and the Gambia established limited networking opportunities as a key inhibitor to female entrepreneurship whereas researchers noted lack of co-operation and unfair competition among women entrepreneurs in The Gambia, Ethiopia, Malawi, Algeria, Lesotho and Morocco (Table 8.4d). The limited access to training, information and social capital are consistent with similar findings by Panda (2018) on developing countries.

Finally, the study identifies climate change as a fundamental challenge to women entrepreneurs whose enterprises rely on the natural environment for

Table 8.4d Resource Constraints

Challenges/Problems	*Coping Strategies*	*Major Stakeholders*
Limited access to entrepreneurship training and development	1. Gambia: Della-Giusta and Phillips (2006) 2. Ethiopia: Abagissa (2013) 3. Algeria: Fatima et al. (2014) 4. Kapinga and Montero (2017) 5. Ghana: Fieve and Chrysostome (2024)	1. Government 2. BDS providers

(*Continued*)

Table 8.4d (Continued)

Challenges/Problems	*Coping Strategies*	*Major Stakeholders*
Information asymmetry	1. Gambia: Della-Giusta and Phillips (2006) 2. Rwanda: Nsengimana et al. (2017) 3. Nigeria: Oloko et al. (2022)	
Limited networking opportunities and other networking challenges	Informal women entrepreneurs forming pressure group to press home demands 1. Gambia: Della-Giusta and Phillips (2006) 2. Ethiopia: Singh and Belwal (2008) 3. Botswana: Ama et al. (2014) 4. Tanzania: Kapinga and Montero (2017); Isaga (2019); Langevang et al. (2018) 5. Gambia: Lim et al. (2022)	1. Women entrepreneurs' network 2. Family and friends
Climate risk	1. Tanzania: Kapinga and Montero (2017) 2. Sub-Saharan Africa: Gannon et al. (2022)	General public

Source: Authors' compilation (2022/2024).

resources such as land, fuelwood and rainfall for agriculture and cooking. The entrepreneurs rely on the mercy of the weather and natural resources to grow crops, and to dry and cook food for commercial purposes. From Table 8.4d, research by Gannon et al. (2022) and Kapinga and Montero (2017) show that climate-induced challenges such as drought and floods deprive female entrepreneurs who depend on the natural environment for their trades/livelihoods. Informed by the foregoing review, the subsequent sections address coping strategies.

Coping strategies

The stakeholder theory underscores the need for managers and entrepreneurs to effectively manage stakeholder relationships in order to leverage the embedded resources, opportunities and obstacles in those relationships for optimum gains. The review results indicate that fewer studies, about 16 out of the 72 publications, provided insights into the strategies that women entrepreneurs in Africa employ to manage the challenges of their profession.

Coping strategies for institutional constraints

We identified four main coping strategies for institutional constraints, mainly in the domain of gender discrimination and associated socio-cultural barriers. These are seeking help in the face of the multiple role complexities; role integration; downplay of gender identity and seeking spiritual reinforcement.

A major coping strategy for female entrepreneurs, per the results of this study, is seeking the support of family members, and in some instances domestic workers, in the execution of household chores and care of children, the elderly and the sick (Table 8.5). In addition, female relatives, children and husbands are very instrumental in relieving the entrepreneurs of some family responsibilities so that they can concentrate on their enterprise. Although the services of domestic workers could be invaluable to female entrepreneurs, research in the field of sociology points to the fact that domestic workers often come with their own problems and, if not properly managed, can place extra burden on women who use their services (Muasya & Martin, 2016).

Table 8.5 Coping Strategies for Generic Institutional Constraints

Challenges/Problems	*Support/Coping Strategies*	*Major Stakeholders*
Sociocultural barriers, e.g., gender bias, limited control over resources	(A) Collaborative networks/credit co-operatives/advocacy groups 1. Gambia: Della-Giusta and Phillips (2006) 2. Tanzania: Kapinga and Montero (2017); Langevang et al. (2018) 3. South Africa: Aneke et al. (2017) 4. Ghana, Nigeria and Cameroon: Kimbu et al. (2019) 5. Botswana: Mamabolo and Lekoko (2021) 6. Nigeria: Oloko et al. (2022) 7. Ghana: Fieve and Chrysostome (2024) (B) Family moral support 1. Sudan: Welsh et al. (2013) 2. Nigeria: Oloko et al. (2022) (C) Spiritual support 1. Lesotho: Chingono (2016) 2. Ghana: Reid et al. (2015); Quagrainie et al. (2018); Lent (2020) 3. Nigeria: Oloko et al. (2022) (D) Downplay of gender identity • Tanzania: Langevang et al. (2018) (E) Partnering with male business owners • Aneke et al. (2017)	1. Traditional authority 2. State 3. Husbands 4. Relatives, especially male relatives 5. Religious bodies: churches and other places of worship 6. Witch doctors 7. Women's business associations

(*Continued*)

Table 8.5 (Continued)

Challenges/Problems	*Support/Coping Strategies*	*Major Stakeholders*
Social and family responsibilities and disruptions and multiple role complexities & associated limitations	(A) Community support for women's businesses 1. Botswana: Ntseane (2004) (B) Female relatives, children & spouses assisting with child care & other household responsibilities 1. Botswana: Ntseane (2004); Ama et al. (2014) 2. Ethiopia: Hundera et al. (2019) (C) Moral support from family • Sudan: Welsh et al. (2013) (D) Role integration: Co-location of business and home/bringing work home, etc. 1. South Africa: Schindehutte et al. (2003) 2. Tanzania: Langevang et al. (2018) 3. Ethiopia: Gudeta and van Engen (2017); Hundera et al. (2019) (E) Involving husbands as business partners • Tanzania: Langevang et al. (2018)	1. Traditional authority 2. State 3. Husbands 4. Children 5. Relatives 6. Female relatives 7. Domestic workers
Lack of acceptance of entrepreneurial career by family and society	Involvement of spouses in business • Tanzania: Langevang et al. (2018)	1. Spouses 2. Extended family

Source: Authors' compilation (2022/2024).

Role integration (Table 8.5) comes in varied forms including co-location of business and or bringing work home, where possible, to permit the fulfilment of the multiple role complexities. A further insight from Tanzania is that some female entrepreneurs engage their spouses as business partners as a strategy to win their acceptance of their entrepreneurial career. This permits them, from time to time, to attend to family and other social responsibilities while their husbands take care of the business.

Another study by Della-Giusta and Phillips (2006) identifies the use of pressure groups by female entrepreneurs to press home their demands in the face of unfair competition and lack of support for women's enterprises. Others (e.g., Lent, 2020; Oloko et al., 2022) report how women entrepreneurs, on the basis of their faith, resort to places of worship and witch doctors for spiritual strength to effectively fulfil their multiple roles and to seek protection (Table 8.5). Lent (2020) notes that it is common practice for women entrepreneurs in Ghana to spend their evening and night hours as well as Sunday worship hours praying.

Langevang et al. (2018) provide insights on how female entrepreneurs in Tanzania address challenges associated with business registration/licensing as

Table 8.6 Coping Strategies for Country-Specific Institutional Constraints

Challenges/Problems	*Coping Strategies*	*Major Stakeholders*
Lack of acceptance of entrepreneurship as a career by family and society	Involvement of spouses in business • Tanzania: Langevang et al. (2018)	1. Spouses 2. Extended family
Limited government support and unfriendly regulations	Collaborative networks/ credit co-operatives • Ghana, Nigeria and Cameroon: Kimbu et al. (2019)	1. Women's business associations 2. Informal credit scheme operators
Registration/licensing constraints	(A) Avoidance: operating informally or semi-formally • Tanzania: Langevang et al. (2018) (B) Seeking assistance of BDS providers • Tanzania: Langevang et al. (2018)	BDS providers
Wars/conflicts	Family moral support • Sudan: Welsh et al. (2013)	1. Society 2. Family

Source: Authors' compilation (2022).

they adopt an avoidance strategy whereby they choose to operate informally or semiformally (Table 8.6). They note that other women entrepreneurs seek the assistance of business development service providers to overcome the registration and licensing hurdles. Langevang et al. (2018) further reveal that some women entrepreneurs psyche themselves for gender discrimination by downplaying, that is overlooking, tendencies for such discrimination to occur in the execution of their entrepreneurial roles.

Coping strategies for resource constraints

The results demonstrate isolated reports on how women entrepreneurs address/manage some resource constraints. The main coping strategies (Table 8.7a) for financial constraints are financial support from women's business associations (WBAs) and credit co-operatives (e.g., Kimbu et al., 2019), family and friends (Mamabolo & Lekoko, 2021) and churches (Quagrainie et al., 2018). Other entrepreneurs bootstrap and plough back profits or use alternative funding mechanisms such as the village development committee and informal sources (Boateng & Poku, 2019).

The findings do not provide evidence of how women entrepreneurs manage poor market conditions except information asymmetry which they rely on their networks for updates (Table 8.7b). Kimbu et al.'s (2019) research also

Table 8.7a Coping Strategies for Resource Constraints

Challenges/Problems	*Coping Strategies*	*Major Stakeholders*
Lack of capital/ Limited access to finance (including high interest rates, small loan sizes, lack of collateral, etc.)	(A) Collaborative networks/credit co-operatives 1. South Africa: Aneke et al. (2017) 2. Ghana, Nigeria and Cameroon: Kimbu et al. (2019) 3. Ghana: Schindler (2010); Fieve and Chrysostome (2024) (B) Financial support from family and friends 1. Cameroon: Fonjong (2004) 2. Nigeria: Okolie et al. (2021) 3. Ghana: Overå (2017) 4. Botswana: Mamabolo and Lekoko (2021) (C) Personal savings 1. Ghana: Kuada (2009); Oteng-Ababio (2018) 2. South Africa: Derera et al. (2014) 3. Botswana: Mamabolo and Lekoko (2021) (D) Starting small and gradually building the enterprise 1. South Africa: Derera et al. (2014) 2. Ghana: Overå (2017) (E) Bootstrapping and ploughing back profit 1. South Africa: Derera et al. (2014) 2. Tanzania: Langevang et al. (2018) (F) Alternative funding mechanisms e.g., village development committee in Tanzania, NGOs, informal sources, foreign donors 1. Cameroon: Fonjong (2004) 2. Ghana: Kuada (2009) 3. Tanzania: Kapinga and Montero (2017); Langevang et al. (2018) 4. Botswana: Mamabolo and Lekoko (2021) (G) Bank savings to build trust for credit 1. South Africa: Derera et al. (2014) 2. Tanzania: Langevang et al. (2018) (H) Charity organisations • Nigeria: Okolie et al. (2021)	1. Financial institutions 2. Government 3. Traditional authority 4. Informal credit suppliers 5. Women entrepreneurs 6. Husbands 7. Parents 8. Friends 9. International Development Organisations (IDOs) 10. Non-governmental Organisations (NGOs) 11. Semi-formal micro finance institutions 12. Charity organisations e.g., churches
Information asymmetry	(A) Collaborative networks/credit co-operatives 1. Ghana, Nigeria and Cameroon: Kimbu et al. (2019) 2. Nigeria: Oloko et al. (2022) (B) Leveraging mobile phone technology • Tanzania: Kapinga and Montero (2017)	Business associations

Source: Authors' compilation (2022/2024).

Table 8.7b Coping Strategies for Resource Constraints

Challenges/Problems	*Coping Strategies*	*Major Stakeholders*
Limited networking opportunities and other networking challenges	Informal women entrepreneurs forming pressure group to press home demands • Gambia: Della-Giusta and Phillips (2006)	1. Women entrepreneurs' network 2. Family and friends
No education /low levels of education	(A) Family moral support • Sudan: Welsh et al. (2013) (B) Social networks • Nigeria: Oloko et al. (2022) (C) Training • South Africa: Aneke et al. (2017)	1. Family and friends 2. Women entrepreneurs' network 3. BDS providers
Lack of business and entrepreneurial experience and skills	(A) Community/network of women entrepreneurs sharing ideas (collaborative networks) 1. Botswana: Ntseane (2004) 2. Tanzania: Langevang et al. (2018) 3. Ghana, Nigeria and Cameroon: Kimbu et al. (2019) (B) Business mentors/business executive • Botswana: Mamabolo and Lekoko (2021) (C) BDS providers • Botswana: Mamabolo and Lekoko (2021) (D) Continuous professional development • Botswana: Mamabolo and Lekoko (2021) (E) Churches • Ghana: Quagrainie et al. (2018)	1. Women entrepreneurs' network 2. Business mentors 3. BDS providers 4. Government 5. Churches
Limited access to entrepreneurship training and development	(A) Business incubation and training • Tanzania: Kapinga and Montero (2017) (B) Training by Credit Co-operative Groups • Ghana: Fieve and Chrysostome (2024)	1. BDS providers 2. Government 3. Co-operatives
Marketing challenges	Accessing international markets • Botswana: Mamabolo and Lekoko (2021)	Competitors

(*Continued*)

Table 8.7b (Continued)

Challenges/Problems	*Coping Strategies*	*Major Stakeholders*
Slow business growth/lack of profit	Reliance on persistence and passion • Tanzania: Langevang et al. (2018)	Female entrepreneurs
High rent charges	Collaborative networks/credit co-operatives • Ghana, Nigeria and Cameroon: Kimbu et al. (2019)	1. Property owners 2. Business associations
Lack of technical/ technological know-how (self-efficacy)	(A) Collaborative networks/credit co-operatives • Ghana, Nigeria and Cameroon: Kimbu et al. (2019) (B) Personal digital skills acquisition • Botswana: Mamabolo and Lekoko (2021)	Business associations
Information asymmetry	(A) Collaborative networks/credit co-operatives 1. Ghana, Nigeria and Cameroon: Kimbu et al. (2019) 2. Nigeria: Oloko et al. (2022) (B) Leveraging mobile phone technology • Tanzania: Kapinga and Montero (2017)	Business associations

Source: Authors' compilation (2022/2024).

provides evidence of how female entrepreneurs operate from home and or unapproved locations such as streets and pavements to avoid high rent charges. These actions, however, create extra problem of harassment from law enforcement agencies (Kabonga et al., 2021).

Some well-established women entrepreneurs venture into international markets to overcome a saturated local market; others rely on business mentors and executive to acquire the needed business and entrepreneurial skills and experience (Table 8.7b). Some women entrepreneurs tap into personal advancement opportunities in their social and business networks to build entrepreneurial and management competencies and to create a common voice to advocate for fair sociocultural norms and practices. The use of this strategy is limited across the continent (Mensah & Derera, 2023).

Towards a typology of stakeholder salience

Addressing the question of who the critical stakeholders are and their role in creating or finding solutions to the challenges, we identified a number of stakeholders. Key stakeholders who enforce the sociocultural norms and practices include husbands, extended family members, traditional authorities and state authorities. From Figure 8.1 and Table 8.8, we categorise these stakeholders as *critical stakeholders* (CS) because the entrenched customary laws and practices, and sanctions for violation, em*power* the stakeholders and give them the *legitimacy* to enforce the institutions. Noncompliance with the norms, customs and practices have dire consequences for female entrepreneurs which spell a sense of *urgency* and criticality in conforming to the institutional requirements that manifest in the multiple role complexities of the entrepreneurs. Critical stakeholders coincide with definitive stakeholders in Mitchell et al.'s (1997) SSF. Both stakeholder types possess the three attributes of power, legitimacy and urgency.

Sexual abusers, insurgents and public officials who extort money from female entrepreneurs (Table 8.8) are described as *derailers (D)* (Figure 8.1). They use coercive power to exploit entrepreneurs. Society frowns upon such actions so there is no legitimacy for their actions. However, the urgency of their actions is critical because they can cause physical, emotional and psychological harm to the female entrepreneurs and rob them of their freedom, health and financial resources. The actions of derailers have a higher tendency

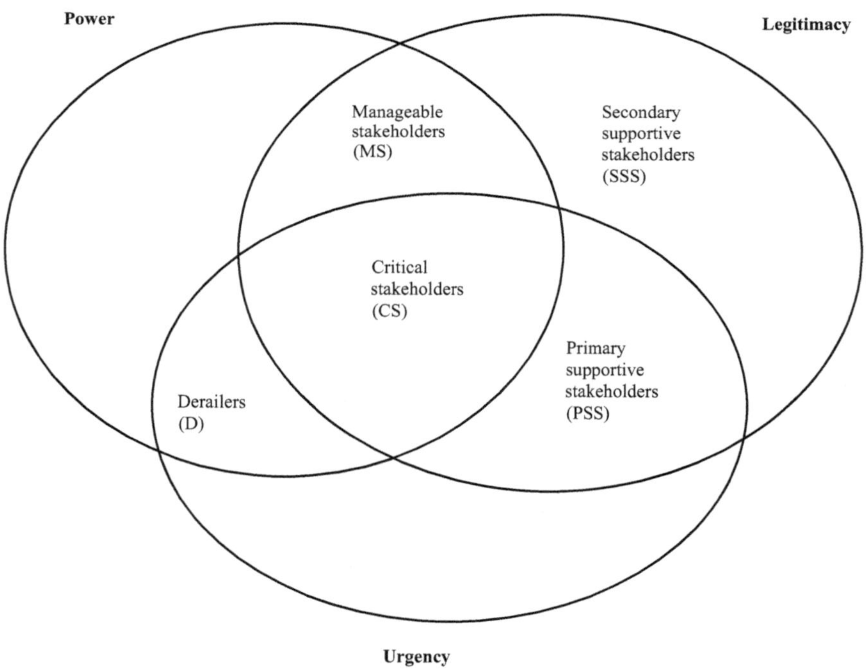

Figure 8.1 Typology of Stakeholder Salience for the Challenges of Female Entrepreneurship in Africa

Source: Authors' compilation (2022).

Table 8.8 Legend to Figure 8.1

Critical Stakeholders (CS)	*Derailers (D)*	*Manageable stakeholders (MS)*	*Primary supportive stakeholders (PSS)*	*Secondary supportive stakeholders (SSS)*
E.g., traditional authority, the state, husbands, parents	E.g., corrupt officials, sexual harassers, destructive competitors, unsupportive employees	E.g., male relatives, suppliers of resources	E.g., female relatives, children, domestic workers, enterprise support organisations, WBAs,	E.g., friends, spiritual directors, witch doctors

Source: Authors' compilation (2022).

to negatively affect the growth of the businesses of female entrepreneurs or lead to the collapse of the businesses.

Stakeholder salience acknowledges the possibility of some stakeholders possessing power and legitimacy (Neubaum et al., 2012). We refer to such stakeholders as ***manageable stakeholders*** (MS), as shown in Table 8.8 and Figure 8.1. They comprise male relatives and suppliers of resources. There is a stronger interplay of *power* and *legitimacy* because society legitimises the expectations that these stakeholders have of female entrepreneurs. Noncompliance will elicit sanctions therefore female entrepreneurs manage these stakeholders by complying with their legitimised expectations/claims. In comparison with the MAW framework (Mitchell et al., 1997, Mitchell et al., 2011), manageable stakeholders are expectant stakeholders, specifically dominant stakeholders.

We further observe from the findings that there are some stakeholders who assist female entrepreneurs in addressing some of their challenges. We classify them into ***primary supportive stakeholders*** (PSS) and ***secondary supportive stakeholders*** (SSS) based on the relative importance of the help that they offer female entrepreneurs (Figure 8.1). PSS include female relatives and children. They offer *legitimate* and *urgent* support to female entrepreneurs to handle multiple role complexities, which makes it possible for the entrepreneurs to devote more time and resources towards business growth and development. Other PSS are enterprise support organisations and WBAs, which serve as important avenues for fund raising, skills training and networking. Friends and spiritual directors (Oloko et al., 2022) tilt more towards SSS (Table 8.8). They provide emotional and psychological support to female entrepreneurs in difficult times when they are consulted for help.

The foregoing results and discussions demonstrate similarities between the MAW framework (Mitchell et al., 1997; Mitchell et al., 2011) and the proposed stakeholder salience typology for addressing the challenges of female entrepreneurship in Africa (Figure 8.1). Although the basis for constructing our framework differs from the MAW framework, this study postulates five types of stakeholders which correspond with five of the seven stakeholder types in the MAW framework.

Conclusion

The aim of this research was to conduct a systematic literature review of the challenges of female entrepreneurship in Africa and to propose a typology of stakeholder salience. At the end of the study, it is evident that female entrepreneurs in Africa grapple with institutional and resource-related constraints with inimical sociocultural norms and practices and inadequate funding as the most cited constraints. Some of the coping strategies female entrepreneurs employ include seeking the support of family members and domestic workers to relieve their multiple role complexities; role integration; spiritual reinforcement; bootstrapping and fundraising. Through a stakeholder salience assessment, we classified stakeholders into five groups, namely critical stakeholders, derailers, manageable stakeholders, PSS and SSS.

We recommend female entrepreneurs pay attention to the activities of their critical stakeholders and manage their demands and expectations to avoid negative repercussions on their businesses due to the stakeholders' power, urgency and legitimacy. Female entrepreneurs should initiate advocacy through special interest groups, which are effective at addressing inimical and unproductive formal and informal institutions. They should also be cautious when dealing with SSS due to the tendency for exploitation.

Future research could focus on possible changes in the status of stakeholders and test our proposed typology of stakeholder salience for female entrepreneurship in Africa.

References

Abagissa, J. (2013). Challenges confronting women in micro and small enterprises in Addis Ababa, Ethiopia. *Ethiopian Journal of Business and Economics*, *3*(1), 95–139.

Abor, J., & Biekpe, N. (2007). Corporate governance, ownership structure and performance of SMEs in Ghana: Implications for financing opportunities. *Corporate Governance: The international Journal of Business in Society*, *7*(3), 288–300.

Adom, K., & Anambane, G. (2020). Understanding the role of culture and gender stereotypes in women entrepreneurship through the lens of the stereotype threat theory. *Journal of Entrepreneurship in Emerging Economies*, *12*(1), 100–124.

Adom, K., Asare-Yeboa, I. T., Quaye, D. M., & Ampomah, A. O. (2018). A critical assessment of work and family life of female entrepreneurs in Sub-Saharan Africa: Some fresh evidence from Ghana. *Journal of Small Business and Enterprise Development*, *25*(3), 405–427.

Adomako, S., Amankwah-Amoah, J., & Danso, A. (2019). The effects of stakeholder integration on firm-level product innovativeness: Insights from small and medium-sized enterprises in Ghana. *R&D Management*, *49*(5), 734–747.

Ahl, H., & Marlow, S. (2021). Exploring the false promise of entrepreneurship through a postfeminist critique of the enterprise policy discourse in Sweden and the UK. *Human Relations*, *74*(1), 41–68.

Ali, M. A. (2017). Stakeholder salience for stakeholder firms: An attempt to reframe an important heuristic device. *Journal of Business Ethics*, *144*, 153–168.

Ama, N. O., Mangadi, K. T., & Ama, H. A. (2014). Exploring the challenges facing women entrepreneurs in informal cross-border trade in Botswana. *Gender in Management: An International Journal*, *29*(8), 502–522.

Aneke, E. O., Derera, E., & Bomani, M. (2017). An exploratory study of challenges faced by women entrepreneurs in the construction industry in South Africa. *International Journal of Business and Management Studies*, *9*(2), 35–51.

Barney, J. B., Ketchen Jr, D. J., & Wright, M. (2021). Resource-based theory and the value creation framework. *Journal of Management*, *47*(7), 1936–1955.

Berguiga, I., & Adair, P. (2021). Funding female entrepreneurs in North Africa: Self-selection vs discrimination? MSMEs, the informal sector and the microfinance industry. *International Journal of Gender and Entrepreneurship*, *13*(4), 394–419.

Boateng, S., & Poku, K. O. (2019). Accessing finance among women-owned small businesses: evidence from lower Manya Krobo municipality, Ghana. *Journal of Global Entrepreneurship Research*, *9*, 1–17.

Chingono, M. (2016). Women, the informal economy and the state in Lesotho. *Journal of Gender and Power*, *6*(2), 51–76.

Chirwa, E. W. (2008). Effects of gender on the performance of micro and small enterprises in Malawi. *Development Southern Africa*, *25*(3), 347–362.

Della-Giusta, M., & Phillips, C. (2006). Women entrepreneurs in the Gambia: Challenges and opportunities. *Journal of International Development: The Journal of the Development Studies Association*, *18*(8), 1051–1064.

Derera, E., Chitakunye, P., & O'Neill, C. (2014). The impact of gender on start-up capital: A case of women entrepreneurs in South Africa. *The Journal of Entrepreneurship*, *23*(1), 95–114.

Dzisi, S. (2008). Entrepreneurial activities of indigenous African women: A case of Ghana. *Journal of Enterprising Communities: People and Places in the Global Economy*, *2*(3), 254–264.

Elam, A.B., Hughes, K.D., Guerrero, M., Hill, S. & Nawangpalupi, C. 2021. Women's entrepreneurship 2020/21. Thriving through crisis. Global Entrepreneurship Research Association. https://www.gemconsortium.org/file/open?fileId=50691

Fatima, M. T., El Amine, M., & Khadidja, H. (2014). Socio-economic determinants of female entrepreneurship in Algeria. *Les Cahiers du Mecas*, *10*(1), 80–90.

Fieve, J. K. D., & Chrysostome, E. V. (2024). Credit cooperative lending loans as challenges and opportunities for women entrepreneurship in Africa: Evidence from Ghana. *Journal of African Business*, *25*(1), 94–114.

Fonjong, L. (2004). Challenges and coping strategies of women food crops entrepreneurs in Fako Division, Cameroon. *Journal of International Women's Studies*, *5*(5), 1–17.

Freeman, R. E. (1999). Divergent stakeholder theory. *Academy of Management Review*, *24*(2), 233–236.

Gannon, K. E., Castellano, E., Eskander, S., Agol, D., Diop, M., Conway, D., & Sprout, E. (2022). The triple differential vulnerability of female entrepreneurs to climate risk in sub-Saharan Africa: Gendered barriers and enablers to private sector adaptation. *Wiley Interdisciplinary Reviews: Climate Change*, *13*(5), 1–23.

Garwe, D. K., & Fatoki, O. (2012). The impact of gender on SME characteristics and access to debt finance in South Africa. *Development Southern Africa*, *29*(3), 448–461.

Gudeta, K. H., & van Engen, M. L. (2017). Work–life boundary management styles of women entrepreneurs in Ethiopia—"Choice" or imposition? *Journal of Small Business and Enterprise Development*, *25*(3), 368–386.

Halkias, D., Nwajiuba, C., Harkiolakis, N., & Caracatsanis, S. M. (2011). Challenges facing women entrepreneurs in Nigeria. *Management Research Review*, *34*(2), 221–235.

Hattab, H. (2012). Towards understanding female entrepreneurship in Middle Eastern and North African countries: A cross-country comparison of female entrepreneurship. *Education, Business and Society: Contemporary Middle Eastern Issues*, *5*(3), 171–186.

Hundera, M. B., Duijsters, G. M., & Naudé, W. A. (2019). How do female entrepreneurs experience and cope with role conflict in Sub-Saharan Africa: Case study from Ethiopia. *International Journal of Entrepreneurship and Small Business*, *38*(1–2), 177–209.

Isaga, N. (2019). Start-up motives and challenges facing female entrepreneurs in Tanzania. *International Journal of Gender and Entrepreneurship*, *11*(2), 102–119.

Kabonga, I., Zvokuomba, K., & Nyagadza, B. (2021). The challenges faced by young entrepreneurs in informal trading in Bindura, Zimbabwe. *Journal of Asian and African Studies*, *56*(8), 1780–1794.

Kapinga, A. F., & Montero, C. S. (2017). Exploring the socio-cultural challenges of food processing women entrepreneurs in Iringa, Tanzania and strategies used to tackle them. *Journal of Global Entrepreneurship Research*, *7*(1), 17.

Kimbu, A. N., Ngoasong, M. Z., Adeola, O., & Afenyo-Agbe, E. (2019). Collaborative networks for sustainable human capital management in women's tourism entrepreneurship: The role of tourism policy. *Tourism Planning & Development*, *16*(2), 161–178.

Kuada, J. (2009). Gender, social networks, and entrepreneurship in Ghana. *Journal of African Business*, *10*(1), 85–103.

Langevang, T., Hansen, M. W., & Rutashobya, L. K. (2018). Navigating institutional complexities: The response strategies of Tanzanian female entrepreneurs. *International Journal of Gender and Entrepreneurship*, *10*(3), 224–242.

Laplume, A. O., Sonpar, K., & Litz, R. A. (2008). Stakeholder theory: Reviewing a theory that moves us. *Journal of Management*, *34*(6), 1152–1189.

Lent, M. (2020). Everyday entrepreneurship among women in northern Ghana: A practice perspective. *Journal of Small Business Management*, *58*(4), 777–805.

Lim, S. S., Sonko, L. K., & Cham, E. (2022). Exploring the supportive factors and inhibitors to the growth propensity of women-owned MSMEs in the Gambia. *Technology Analysis & Strategic Management*, 1–17. https://doi.org/10.1080/09537325.2022.2035348

Mamabolo, A., & Lekoko, R. (2021). Entrepreneurial ecosystems created by woman entrepreneurs in Botswana. *South African Journal of Business Management*, *52*(1), 13.

Mensah, M. S. B., & Derera, E. 2023. Analysis of Ghana's and South Africa's women's entrepreneurship policies. In Henry, C., Coleman, S., Lewis, K. & Foss, L. (eds.). *Women's entrepreneurship policy: a global perspective* (pp. 216–242). Edward Elgar Publishing.

Mersha, T., & Sriram, V. (2019). Gender, entrepreneurial characteristics, and success: Evidence from Ethiopia. *Thunderbird International Business Review*, *61*(2), 157–167.

Metu, A. G., & Nwogwugwu, U. C. (2024). Challenging factors affecting access to finance by female micro entrepreneurs in Anambra State, Nigeria. *Journal of African Business*, *25*(1), 142–154.

Mitchell, R. K., Agle, B. R., Chrisman, J. J., & Spence, L. J. (2011). Toward a theory of stakeholder salience in family firms. *Business Ethics Quarterly*, *21*(2), 235–255.

Mitchell, R. K., Agle, B. R., & Wood, D. J. (1997). Toward a theory of stakeholder identification and salience: Defining the principle of who and what really counts. *Academy of Management Review*, *22*(4), 853–886.

Mordi, C., Simpson, R., Singh, S., & Okafor, C. (2010). The role of cultural values in understanding the challenges faced by female entrepreneurs in Nigeria. *Gender in Management: An International Journal*, *25*(1), 5–21.

Muasya, G., & Martin, J. N. (2016). Conflict in Kenyan households: An exploratory study of professional women and domestic workers. *Howard Journal of Communications*, *27*(4), 385–402.

Naguib, R. (2024). Motivations and barriers to female entrepreneurship: Insights from Morocco. *Journal of African Business*, *25*(1), 9–36.

Neubaum, D. O., Dibrell, C., & Craig, J. B. (2012). Balancing natural environmental concerns of internal and external stakeholders in family and non-family businesses. *Journal of Family Business Strategy*, *3*(1), 28–37.

North, D. C. (2016). Institutions and economic theory. *The American Economist*, *61*(1), 72–76.

Nsengimana, S., Tengeh, R. K., & Iwu, C. G. (2017). The sustainability of businesses in Kigali, Rwanda: An analysis of the barriers faced by women entrepreneurs. *Sustainability*, *9*(8), 1372.

Ntseane, P. (2004). Being a female entrepreneur in Botswana: Cultures, values, strategies for success. *Gender & Development*, *12*(2), 37–43.

Okolie, U. C., Ehiobuche, C., Igwe, P. A., Agha-Okoro, M. A., & Onwe, C. C. (2021). Women entrepreneurship and poverty alleviation: Understanding the economic and socio-cultural context of the Igbo women's basket weaving enterprise in Nigeria. *Journal of African Business*, *22*(4), 448–467.

Oloko, A., Fakoya, K., Ferse, S., Breckwoldt, A., & Harper, S. (2022). The challenges and prospects of women fisherfolk in Makoko, Lagos State, Nigeria. *Coastal Management*, *50*(2), 124–141.

Oteng-Ababio, M. (2018). Crossing conceptual boundaries: Re-envisioning coordination and collaboration among women for sustainable livelihoods in Ghana. *Local Environment*, *23*(3), 316–334.

Overå, R. (2003). Gender ideology and manoeuvring space for female fisheries entrepreneurs. *Institute of African Studies Research Review*, *19*(2), 49–62.

Overå, R. (2017). Local navigations in a global industry: The gendered nature of entrepreneurship in Ghana's oil and gas service sector. *The Journal of Development Studies*, *53*(3), 361–374.

Panda, S. (2018). Constraints faced by women entrepreneurs in developing countries: Review and ranking. *Gender in Management: An International Journal*, *33*(4), 315–331.

Paul, J., Lim, W. M., O'Cass, A., Hao, A. W., & Bresciani, S. (2021). Scientific procedures and rationales for systematic literature reviews (SPAR-4-SLR). *International Journal of Consumer Studies*, *45*(4), O1–O16.

Peprah, V., Buor, D., Forkuor, D., & Sánchez-Moral, S. (2019). Characteristics of informal sector activities and challenges faced by women in Kumasi Metropolis, Ghana. *Cogent Social Sciences*, *5*(1), 1656383.

Pinkovetskaia, I. S., Kryukova, L. I., Campillo, D. F. A., & Rojas-Bahamon, M. J. (2019). Female entrepreneurship: Types of economic activity. *Journal of History Culture and Art Research*, *8*(2), 253–265.

Quagrainie, F. A., Opoku Mensah, A., & Adom, A. Y. (2018). Christian entrepreneurial activities and micro women entrepreneurship development: Church embeddedness in action. *Journal of Enterprising Communities: People and Places in the Global Economy*, *12*(5), 657–676.

Rantšo, T. A. (2016). Factors affecting performance/success of small-scale rural non-farm enterprises in Lesotho. *Journal of Enterprising Communities: People and Places in the Global Economy*, *10*(3), 226–248.

Reid, M., Roumpi, D., & O'Leary-Kelly, A. M. (2015). Spirited women: The role of spirituality in the work lives of female entrepreneurs in Ghana. *Africa Journal of Management*, *1*(3), 264–283.

Salia, S., Hussain, J., Tingbani, I., & Kolade, O. (2018). Is women empowerment a zero sum game? Unintended consequences of microfinance for women's empowerment in Ghana. *International Journal of Entrepreneurial Behavior & Research*, *24*(1), 273–289.

Sallah, C. A., & Caesar, L. D. (2020). Intangible resources and the growth of women businesses: Empirical evidence from an emerging market economy. *Journal of Entrepreneurship in Emerging Economies*, *12*(3), 329–355.

Schindehutte, M., Morris, M., & Brennan, C. (2003). Entrepreneurs and motherhood: Impacts on their children in South Africa and the United States. *Journal of Small Business Management*, *41*(1), 94–107.

Schindler, K. (2010). Credit for what? Informal credit as a coping strategy of market women in northern Ghana. *The Journal of Development Studies*, *46*(2), 234–253.

Sedereviciute, K., & Valentini, C. (2011). Towards a more holistic stakeholder analysis approach. Mapping known and undiscovered stakeholders from social media. *International Journal of Strategic Communication*, *5*(4), 221–239.

Seedhouse, A., Johnson, R., & Newbery, R. (2016). Potholes and pitfalls: The impact of rural transport on female entrepreneurs in Nigeria. *Journal of Transport Geography*, *54*, 140–147.

Senou, M. M., & Manda, J. (2022). Access to finance and rural youth entrepreneurship in Benin: Is there a gender gap? *African Development Review*, *34*(1), 29–41.

Singh, G., & Belwal, R. (2008). Entrepreneurship and SMEs in Ethiopia: Evaluating the role, prospects and problems faced by women in this emergent sector. *Gender in Management: An International Journal*, *23*(2), 120–136.

Sowatey, E., Nyantakyi-Frimpong, H., Mkandawire, P., Arku, G., Hussey, L., & Amasaba, A. (2018). Spaces of resilience, ingenuity, and entrepreneurship in informal work in Ghana. *International Planning Studies*, *23*(4), 327–339.

Thambinathan, V., & Kinsella, E. A. (2021). Decolonizing methodologies in qualitative research: Creating spaces for transformative praxis. *International Journal of Qualitative Methods*, *20*, 1–9.

Thomé, A. M. T., Scavarda, L. F., & Scavarda, A. J. (2016). Conducting systematic literature review in operations management. *Production Planning & Control*, *27*(5), 408–420.

Welsh, D. H., Memili, E., Kaciak, E., & Ahmed, S. (2013). Sudanese women entrepreneurs. *Journal of Developmental Entrepreneurship*, *18*(02), 1–18.

Woldie, A., Laurence, B. M., & Thomas, B. (2018). Challenges of finance accessibility by SMEs in the democratic republic of Congo: Is gender a constraint? *Investment Management and Financial Innovations*, *15*(2), 40–50.

Wrigley-Asante, C. (2012). Out of the dark but not out of the cage: Women's empowerment and gender relations in the Dangme West district of Ghana. *Gender, Place & Culture*, *19*(3), 344–363.

Xiao, Y., & Watson, M. (2019). Guidance on conducting a systematic literature review. *Journal of Planning Education and Research*, *39*(1), 93–112.

9 Gender, Culture, and Stakeholder Management Strategies in Africa

Joseph Kwadwo Danquah, Betty J. Aidoo-Anderson, Boakye Boampong, Gilbert Zana Naab, William Yamoah and Michael Mensah

Introduction

The contributions of women entrepreneurs to African societies have been widely studied. Studies report their utility in reducing child trafficking, prostitution, and crime (Iyiola & Azuh, 2014). They help improve child education and alleviate hunger and poverty (Misango & Ongiti, 2013). Entrepreneurship has been conceptualised as a catalyst for economic growth in Africa (Adusei, 2016); it reduces unemployment and creates jobs, while social entrepreneurs champion environmental and social change.

Even though women entrepreneurs are believed to be resourceful, creative, and capable of building and growing prosperous companies, factors such as gender stereotypes, cultural ideologies, and stakeholder expectations consistently threatens the success of their enterprises. This is evidenced by the extant research which suggests that entrepreneurship is perceived as a man's forte (Jennings & Brush, 2013). Women entrepreneurs tend to have difficulties attaining credibility and may face discrimination. The entrepreneur is rendered masculine attributes such as aggression, competitiveness, individuality, and economic rationality, implying a mismatch between femininity and entrepreneurship (Rudman & Phelan, 2008). Although both male and female entrepreneurs face challenges, Panda (2018, p. 11) argues that "women entrepreneurs face a higher intensity of those challenges due to their gender and personality." This chapter reviews the extant literature on women entrepreneurship, exploring how gender and culture impact women entrepreneurs' approach to stakeholder management and business growth.

Entrepreneurship and women

Entrepreneurship for most women is a choice driven by a complex interplay of various pull and push factors at the micro, meso, and macro levels (Bruin et al., 2007), and the complexity experienced by women entrepreneurs depends on their context (Jamali, 2009). Women entrepreneurs may start business for reasons including greater work–life balance, autonomy, escaping the 'glass ceilings,' and personal growth. Entrepreneurship may afford women the flexibility

DOI: 10.4324/9781003256014-12

needed to carry out their dual responsibilities even though some women in developing economies struggle to find balance. In most African countries, women prioritise motherhood and family responsibilities, spending less time on their businesses, which then negatively impacts their businesses. Although women entrepreneurs may experience greater autonomy than employed women, stakeholder expectations and requirements can constrain this autonomy (Nikina et al., 2015).

The Global Entrepreneurship Monitor (GEM, 2022) reports that more than half of women in developing countries, compared to only 25% in developed countries, recognise entrepreneurship as a path to a better future, confirming the importance of entrepreneurship as a sure route to financial freedom in most developing countries where the rate of employment and wage is low and access to the formal labour market is barricaded to women. Entrepreneurship becomes the best alternative to avoiding joblessness for women. Another driver of entrepreneurship by women in developing countries as observed by GEM is religion, which is pivotal in African communities. The contribution of "charismatics," particularly in Ghana, as advocates for social change and women's empowerment cannot be ignored, although little is known empirically. Their emphasis on prosperity and multiple streams of income has been revolutionary as the anecdotal evidence indicates. It is not surprising that the GEM, 2020 report put women entrepreneurs globally at a significant 42%. In Ghana, 70% of all businesses are owned by women (Abor & Quartey, 2010).

Typically, female entrepreneurs in developing economies, compared to male entrepreneurs, do not engage in value-adding businesses but rather run micro-businesses in the informal sector, with the majority of their workers being unskilled relatives (Chaney, 2014). They are into businesses that are not capital-intensive due to difficulties in accessing capital.

It must be recognised, however, that entrepreneurial drive, support for entrepreneurs, and cultural norms and values is a function of context. Particularly in Africa, institutions have been found to be weak, inefficient, riddled with excessive red tape, offer little protection for entrepreneurs, levy excessive taxes, and have poor infrastructures (Ahsan et al., 2021). Bribery and corruption are the rule of the game, and women are not perceived to be serious businesspeople in the market by customers. Rather, they are sexualised, making stakeholder engagement and management relatively more difficult for women entrepreneurs. Bribes and sex may be demanded for government contracts, licences, and public services. Nonetheless, the impact of 'sanding and greasing' activities on business performance (Goel & Saunoris, 2019) has been found to vary depending on the type of entrepreneur, but the morality and ethical implications of such acts cannot be ignored.

A review of the entrepreneurship literature has shown some differences between men and women entrepreneurs, with others suggesting performance of small businesses irrespective of the gender of the owners. Notwithstanding, women continue to lag in innovative entrepreneurship and sometimes face discrimination. A study by Nambiar et al. (2020) exploring the role of various stakeholders reported that women entrepreneurs experienced gender-based discrimination from stakeholders including staff, customers, suppliers, and competitors. Customers may question the credibility of women entrepreneurs and prey upon them. Women entrepreneurs tend to focus on survival rather than growth.

Culture, gender stereotypes, and women entrepreneurs

The role of norms, values, and assumptions (informal institution—culture) in any business context cannot be downplayed as they communicate what is proper or unacceptable in a particular society and influence behaviour. Culture as stereotypical patterns of learned behaviour (Barnouw, 1985) is not always positive and can disenfranchise other members of society. Women entrepreneurs in Africa and other parts of the world are usually saddled with navigating patriarchy, balancing work and family life, and gender discrimination. Most, if not all, African societies are highly masculine societies, and as per Hofstede's cultural dimension, masculine societies archetypally maintain a sharp role differentiation along gender lines (Peng & Meyer, 2016).

Patriarchal norms ubiquitous in most African societal life require men to hold primary power; women are seen as subservient to men (Panda, 2018). Consequently, successful and independent women entrepreneurs are perceived to be without virtue, resulting in low social recognition and a paucity of legitimacy for such women (De Vita et al., 2014), which is rather ironic because in most African countries, for instance Ghana, idleness is disesteemed. Women are expected to be hard working and support family, but interestingly not independent. Successful women entrepreneurs will therefore make light of their achievements to avoid antagonising male family members or business associates and may not prioritise success, so their spouses don't feel threatened.

Jamali (2009) reasoned that when a married woman launches a business, it affects the role of the husband within the marriage, and the resulting marital adjustment influences the woman and her relationship with the business. Spouses who initially supported their wife's business by contributing to her emotional and mental well-being may withdraw their spousal support when there is perceived neglect of her gender roles (Nikina et al., 2015). This withdrawal may have adverse consequences on women entrepreneurs (Igbanugo et al., 2016). Also, the patriarchal system and cultural values in most African countries limit the freedom and mobility of especially married women. Entrepreneurial wives may be unable to dedicate adequate time to business-related activities such as networking and mentoring, which are imperative for business success (Panda & Dash, 2015), due to the burden of gender roles and responsibilities to their family which impede their ability to socialise or develop the skills needed to run their businesses.

Women in Africa are socialised to be the primary carers for their families, to be good mothers and wives—they also usually have high birth rates, which impede their ability to grow an enterprise (Belwal et al., 2012). A study by

Adom et al. (2018) evaluating the influence of work and family on female entrepreneurs in Ghana found female entrepreneurs' responsibilities to their families negatively impact their ability to generate income from their business and their willingness to expand; they put their family's well-being before business growth.

A dominant social value in most African countries is family, which as Kuada (2009) notes can have a negative impact on business development. The emphasis on family corresponds to Hofstede's collectivist societies, which focus on relatively close ties between individuals and collective accomplishments. An individual's identity is based on the identity of the family or village (Peng & Meyer, 2016). This collectivist mindset can create economic dependence on the few individuals in the family perceived to be economically able (Kuada, 2009). Failure to support members of the family in times of need may incur the wrath of the family (Amine & Staub, 2009). Consequently, business owners put the interests of the extended family over business expansion for family acceptance.

Finally, since entrepreneurship exists within a particular social context, the traditional stereotypes prevalent in this context are likely to permeate and define relationships with stakeholders and cloud the judgement of stakeholders. In most African societies, societal attitudes of not supporting women's work persist (Greene et al., 2013). Women are not adequately recognised or appreciated because a woman is not to be heard. In some regions, women business owners may not have the freedom to relate with male customers (Kalafatoglu & Mendoza, 2017) or employ men, limiting the client base and diversity within the business. Institutions are mainly gendered, and women seeking support from relevant institutions may face discrimination. These gender stereotypes inadvertently hinder women entrepreneurs from seeking support, or they may struggle to negotiate with suppliers, customers, and other stakeholders on issues of price, rent, and office location (Panda, 2018). Government programmes extending financial resources to businesses may prefer male-owned businesses (Halkias et al., 2011).

As discussed, women entrepreneurs face normative challenges encompassing patriarchy, stereotyping of women as mothers and wives, and work–life balance. These challenges can be curtailed primarily through family support including spousal support, religious organisations, opportunities for skill training, education and learning, and policies that offer women equal opportunities (childcare support, educational curriculum, loans, etc). It must, however, be stated that, despite recent studies confirming previous research findings about the influence of the sociocultural context, the narrative is gradually changing, with Africa experiencing the emergence of a category of women entrepreneurs who are more motivated, well-educated, and free from family ties (Aterido & Hallward-Driemeier, 2011). They have also been found to have more managerial experience, moving towards nontraditional sectors, into technology, manufacturing, communication, and transportation, where they were traditionally underrepresented (Bates, 2002). They have rich experiences and resilient networks.

Though recent studies adjudge most women business owners as highly skilled and educated, knowledgeable about social processes and with rich social and cultural capital; customers disregard these attributes (Addo, 2017). Customers may only support entrepreneurs they share similar identities with and patronise businesses they trust (Addo, 2017). The sociocultural influences continue to affect women entrepreneurs adversely in developing countries.

Women entrepreneurs, stakeholder management strategies, and business growth

The challenges uncovered so far in this chapter make it more expedient for women entrepreneurs to adopt strategies to manage stakeholders due to their influence in the success or failure of their enterprises. A stakeholder can be broadly defined as "a group or individual who is affected by or can affect the achievement of an organisation's objectives' Freeman (1984, p. 46) or persons with a legal, financial, or moral stake or interest in the operations and decisions of a business (Carroll, 1991, p. 43). Stakeholders include customers, employees, community, competitors, suppliers, religious/social groups, and institutional officials. Through the stakeholder management process, managers reconcile their own objectives with the claims and expectations made on them by various stakeholder groups (Carroll, 1991). Through engagement with stakeholders, knowledge may be sourced and managed to create innovative and trusted products for stakeholders, as well as building relationships.

Stakeholder management involves identifying stakeholders, analysing their needs or influence, and establishing actions to engage (communicate, involve, develop relationships) and collaborate with them (Yang et al., 2011). It involves allocating resources to satisfy the needs and demands of legitimate stakeholders beyond what is necessary to maintain their voluntary participation in the business. The perceived value or power of a stakeholder may influence the value allocation and depends on the availability of critical resources (Kolk & Pinkse, 2007). Stakeholder management provides opportunities for identifying new business and facilitating market entry (Pollack et al., 2017). Nevertheless, the benefits of managing stakeholders must exceed the costs (Harrison et al., 2010). Stakeholder management can be challenging; the institutional and cultural context affect strategies adopted by companies to grow and sustain an enterprise and can impact attitude towards stakeholder management (Wu & Wokutch, 2015).

For women entrepreneurs, the process can be more nuanced due to the moderating role of extraneous factors such as culture and gender. Women entrepreneurs' approach and attitude may be a departure from mainstream models due to gender role expectations. For instance, as indicated earlier, in some cultures women business owners' access to male customers is restricted, and access to institutional support is limited. Though this scenario may not resonate with all African societies, sexual harassment and undermining of women cut across many, which requires women to be firm, knowledgeable,

Figure 9.1 Women Entrepreneurs, Stakeholder Strategies and Business Growth and Resilience.

articulate, and able to prove they are 'worth their salt.' In some situations, women have little agentic power to negotiate for better deals.

Olander and Landin (2008) focusing on stakeholder management in projects concluded that, effective communication of the benefits and negative consequences of a project (by extension an enterprise) influence the outcome of the stakeholder management process. Engaging and involving stakeholders through effective communication is necessary to avoid resistance to change due to their varied expectations (Walley, 2013).

Essentially, good relationship with stakeholders, employing appropriate strategies (e.g., transparency, providing quality, integrity, and delivery on target) to manage this relationship has the potential to influence the innovation and growth of enterprises. For women entrepreneurs, it may require circumventing the sociocultural factors and attitudes to build a beneficial relationship with predominately, customers, suppliers, and the community. The subsequent section succinctly discusses business growth.

Figure 9.1 models the interdependency between women entrepreneurs and stakeholders and the centrality of gender and culture in determining the management strategies adopted as well as the enterprise growth and resilience.

Business growth and gender

Growth as an outcome of business and a feature of small business success (Costin, 2012) has been measured by the number of employees, increase in sales revenue, assets and profit, turnover, cash flow, customer base, sales, and market share in the extant literature on women entrepreneurship (Prasad et al., 2013). Some contend that, these measures are nebulous, premature, simplistic and inconsistent with entrepreneurial practitioners understanding of growth (Dalborg, Friedrichs & Wincent, 2012). This is because, as Davidsson et al. (2010) posit, growth is not a "homogeneous phenomenon" and not every company will grow when the standard of measurement is turnover, employment, profitability, net worth or fixed assets. Rather, the measures of growth should consider the diversity of business owners, firms, and contexts (Leitch et al., 2010). Research has not found growth to be the goal of most small business owners irrespective of gender. Small business owners' goal is to have a source of livelihood. For most women entrepreneurs, their motivation is flexibility and freedom to juggle work, leisure, and family commitments; growth is not an explicit goal.

Dalborg, Friedrichs, and Wincent (2012) disagree with suggestions that women entrepreneurs' growth ambitions are limited, submitting, however, that growth for women does not follow the conventional terms used to define business growth. Growth is seen as a socially construed phenomenon, resulting in divergent views and misunderstanding of the process and measures of growth in female-owned businesses. Kiviluoto (2013), investigating how key entrepreneurship stakeholders understand growth in Finland, found that entrepreneurs perceive growth as profitability, policymakers and public investors use increased employment as the yardstick, and venture capitalists measure sales growth. From the public and political perspective, growth for entrepreneurs is perceived as increase in employee numbers. For other women entrepreneurs, growth follows sustainability and then profitability. For others resilience is growth.

Some authors also highlight how the different characteristics of female entrepreneurs impact how they run their businesses and pursue growth (Costin, 2012). Costin (2012) investigated the process and measurement of growth in female-owned businesses in Ireland and found female entrepreneurs take proactive steps in pursuit of growth by developing new products, selling to new markets, and expanding advertising and promotion. The majority of participating female entrepreneurs nonetheless indicated they would need support and advice from professional support agencies to pursue the activities, driving home the need for accessible support structures for female entrepreneurs.

Dalborg et al. (2012) presented business growth for women entrepreneurs in five stages. The first stage concentrates on achieving profitability for survival and to earn a living. The second stage of growth focuses on stability, expanding customer base and products; and the next stage is to create work and hire more staff. Stage four is about building reputation and gaining appreciation, and finally personal development and employee skill improvement comprise stage five.

Levie and Lichtenstein (2010), assessing the validity of growth models, could not identify unequivocal consensus on the number of stages in all the models, thereby questioning the theories which model growth as linear and incremental stages. Achtenhagen et al. (2010) proposed internal development (value generation) as a critical indicator of business; this is reflected in the resource base, range, and quality of products. Leitch et al. (2010) added that some common measures of growth like number of employees are not relevant measures for entrepreneurs without considering relevance of the growth process to entrepreneur.

Another perspective to business growth is risk. Some conceptualise that growth leads to loss of the "informal and family-like character" of small business ventures (Davidsson et al., 2010, p. 16); it may erode work–life balance and control, supporting the suggestion that the goal of most business owners is to attain and maintain a comfortable and manageable business size. Thus, business owners are fundamental drivers of growth based on individual characteristics, family situation, and sociocultural and economic context.

Individual characteristics inhibiting women entrepreneurs' businesses

The current literature on women entrepreneurs has largely focused on micro level factors inhibiting women entrepreneurs in comparison to men (De Vita et al., 2014), implying that in fixing the deficiencies of women, they can succeed in business. Researchers have identified individual characteristics such as inadequate education and training of businesswomen and lack of market information, motivation, competence, and networking as some factors limiting women's participation. Women entrepreneurs may be inexperienced and lack financial as well as social capital. Also, women's attitudes and beliefs (risk-aversion, low self-esteem, and 'imposter syndrome') have been cited (Sanford et al., 2015).

The importance of entrepreneurial agency especially of women entrepreneurs has been a subject of interest for researchers. In their research on corruption and SME growth, Adomako et al. (2021) considered how SMEs survive and succeed in a corrupt business environment with their limited resources, submitting that the entrepreneurial agency of SMEs may be definitive in whether they succeed or fail. Such agency includes networking. A review of the extant literature highlights entrepreneurial networking (see Hoang & Yi, 2015, Phillips et al., 2013) with both personal and business ties, as well as institutional networks, as a way of acquiring critical resources, managing and mitigating uncertainties, and receiving special privileges (Adomako et al., 2021). Consequently, Adomako et al. (2021) argue that entrepreneurs may strategically develop ties with government or institutional officials who will protect their ventures in order to achieve success. These connections, however, involve financial resources beyond what is needed for the smooth operation of the business, which may eventually stifle growth. Undeniably, networking has been found to be an effective approach to accessing different information, to tap into potential business opportunities and receive support, knowledge, and distribution channels (Adom et al., 2018).

On the other hand, education has been cited as key to entrepreneurship generally. However, the impact of higher education on the growth of women-owned businesses has generated conflicting conclusions. Some (see: Millan et al., 2014) have established its positive impact on women's entrepreneurial endeavours by assisting in attracting employees while others (e.g. Brush et al., 2017; Prasad et al., 2013) found no connection between the high educational achievement of women and growth of their enterprises (measured as a number of employees, profitability, and income). Likewise, Brush et al. (2017) posit that factors other than high-level education, such as financial capital, network ties, and capability perception, significantly influence growth.

In contrast, a study by Devine et al. (2019) hinted that women's educational attainment can affect business growth but women choose to maintain work–life balance rather than allow their high educational attainment to influence the growth of their enterprises. The existing literature seems to suggest that, although education may influence business success, its influence is not significant. It can be argued that this is because most women entrepreneurs do not engage in businesses which require high technical knowledge.

Prior experience impact on business growth like educational attainment is an area of contradictory findings. Experiences are the skills acquired through observations and handling of different scenarios in the past (Storey & Greene, 2010). While some research reports a positive influence of experience on growth, other sources do not acknowledge the same (see Staniewski, 2016). Women entrepreneurs may exploit existing and emerging markets as well as other opportunities for business growth through their experience either from salaried employment or industry. Women entrepreneurs prior experience can be harnessed to create internal processes that promote business success and growth.

In contrast, Santarelli and Tran (2013) found previous experience may be a barrier for women entrepreneurs since it can make them risk averse, less aggressive, and slow to recognise or take advantage of opportunities to grow in comparison to unexperienced women entrepreneurs. Experience may be effective depending on the stage of the enterprise within the business lifecycle; thus, experience can be relevant at different times in the life of the business (Carter et al., 2003).

Finally, women's ability to access finance has been widely studied in connection to launching and growing a successful business. The criticality of money for women entrepreneurs has been established, including banks' unwillingness to grant loans or instances of banks' discrimination against women. The difficulties women face in raising capital are reported to be a consequence of weak credit history and/or inconsistent earning patterns (Andersson et al., 2007). This results in most women starting their business with personal savings or family support. Bruni et al. (2004) also assert that the limited access women have to financial resources leads them into low capital-intensive ventures in the service sector.

Conclusion

This chapter concisely reviewed how gender and culture influence women entrepreneurs, stakeholder management, and growth of enterprises. Although growth was found to be at the prerogative of the business owner, it was noted that other moderating factors such as societal norms and stereotypes influence the launch, running, interactions with stakeholder, as well as the growth of women businesses. Gender biases and cultural stereotypical ideas which perceive women as unserious businesspeople and typifies entrepreneurship with masculine attributes like aggression may define the relationship between stakeholders. The dominant idea that a man should lead in the African context means women entrepreneurs may not be appreciated or recognised. Notwithstanding the challenges female entrepreneurs in Africa face, the literature points to an emergence of aspirational business owners, well educated, with more entrepreneurial networks, some of whom are inspired by their religious beliefs to impact their communities. This area can be explored further to understand the role of religion (particularly charismatism) and the evolution of societal stereotypes on female entrepreneurs.

References

Abor, J., & Quartey, P. (2010). "Issues in SME development in Ghana and South Africa, *International Research Journal of Finance and Economics*, *39*(6), 215–228.

Achtenhagen, L., Naldi, L., & Melin, L. (2010). Business growth—do practitioners and scholars really talk about the same thing? *Entrepreneurship Theory & Practice*, *34*(2), 289–316.

Addo, P.-A. (2017). Is it entrepreneurship, or is it survival? Gender, community, and innovation in Boston's black immigrant micro-enterprise spaces. *Societies*, *7*(3), 20. https://doi.org/10.3390/soc7030020

Adom, K., Asare-Yeboa, I. T., Quaye, D. M., & Ampomah, A. O., (2018). A critical assessment of work and family life of female entrepreneurs in Sub-Saharan Africa: Some fresh evidence from Ghana. *Journal of Small Business and Enterprise Development*, *25*(3), 405–427.

Adomako, S., Ahsan, M., Amankwah-Amoah, J., Danso, A., Kesse, K., & Frimpong, K. (2021). Corruption and SME growth: the roles of institutional networking and financial slack. *Journal of Institutional Economics*, *17*(4), 607–624.

Adusei, M. (2016). Does entrepreneurship promote economic growth in Africa? *African Development Review*, *28*(2), 201–214.

Ahsan, M., Adomako, S., & Mole, K. (2021). Perceived institutional support and small venture performance: The mediating role of entrepreneurial persistence. *International Small Business Journal*, *39*(1), 18–39.

Amine, L. S., & Staub, K. M. (2009). Women entrepreneurs in sub-Saharan Africa: An institutional theory analysis from a social marketing point of view. *Entrepreneurship and Regional Development*, *21*(2), 183–211.

Andersson, I., Raihan, A., Rivera, M., Sulaiman, I. and Tandon, N. (2007), in Welter, F. (Ed.), Handbook on women-owned SMEs: Challenges and opportunities in policies and programmes, International Organisation for Knowledge Economy and Enterprise Development (IKED) and Global Knowledge Partners (GKP), http://www.iked.org/pdf/Handbook%20on%20Women-owned%20SMEs.pdf

Aterido, R., & Hallward-Driemeier, M. (2011). Whose business is it anyway? *Small Business Economics*, *37*, 443–464.

Barnouw, V. (1985). *Culture and personality*, 4th ed., Homewood, IL: Dorsey Press.

Bates, T. (2002). Restricted access to markets characterises women-owned businesses, *Journal of Business Venturing*, *17*, 313–324.

Belwal, R., Tamiru, M., & Singh, G. (2012). Microfinance and sustained economic improvement: Women small-scale entrepreneurs in Ethiopia. *Journal of international development*, *24*, S84–S99.

Bruine de Bruin, W., Parker, A. M., & Fischhoff, B. (2007). Individual differences in adult decision-making competence. *Journal of Personality and Social Psychology*, *92*(5), 938–956.

Bruni, A., Gherardi, S. & Poggio, B. (2004). "Entrepreneurship-mentality, gender and the study of women entrepreneurs", *Journal for Organisation Change Management*, *17*(3), 256–268.

Brush, C., Ali, A. Kelley, D. and Greene, P. (2017). The influence of human capital factors and context on women's entrepreneurship: Which matters more? *Journal of Business Venturing Insights*, *8*, 105–113.

Carroll, A. B. (1991). The pyramid of corporate social responsibility: Toward the moral management of organizational stakeholders. *Business Horizons*, July–August, 39–48.

Carter, N., Brush, C., Greene, P., Gatewood, E., & Hart, M. (2003). Women entrepreneurs who break through to equity financing: The influence of human, social and financial capital. *Venture Capital: International Journal of Entrepreneurial Finance*, *5*(1), 1–28.

Chaney, A. (2014). Black female entrepreneurs in post-apartheid South Africa: Achieving female economic empowerment in the formal and informal sectors. Doctoral thesis. ProQuest Dissertations and Theses database (UMI No. 3641734).

Costin, Y. (2012). In pursuit of growth: An insight into the experience of female entrepreneurs. *International Journal of Gender and Entrepreneurship*, *4*(2), 108–127.

Dalborg, C., von Friedrichs, Y., & Wincent, J. (2012). Beyond the numbers: Qualitative growth in women's businesses. *International Journal of Gender and Entrepreneurship*, *4*(3), 289–315.

Davidsson, P., Achtenhagen, L., & Naldi, L. (2010). Small firm growth. *Foundations and Trends® in Entrepreneurship*, *6*(2), 69–166.

De Vita, L., Mari, M., & Poggesi, S. (2014). Women entrepreneurs in and from developing countries: Evidence from the literature. *European Management Journal*, *32*(3), 451–460.

Devine, R. A., Molina-Sieiro, G., Holmes Jr., R. M., & Terjesen, S. A. (2019). Female-Led high-growth: Examining the role of human and financial resource management. *Journal of Small Business Management*, *57*(1), 81–109.

Freeman, R. E. (1984). *Strategic management: A stockholder approach*. Pitman.

Global Entrepreneurship Monitor, Smith College. (2022). Women's entrepreneurship 2021/2022 report. https://www.gemconsortium.org/reports/womens-entrepreneurship

Goel, R. K., & Saunoris, J. W. (2019). International corruption and its impacts across 8 entrepreneurship types. https://doi.org/10.1002/mde.3017

Greene, F. J., Han, L., & Marlow, S. (2013). Like mother, like daughter? Analyzing maternal influences upon women's entrepreneurial propensity. *Entrepreneurship Theory and Practice*, *37*(4), 687–711. https://doi.org/10.1111/j.1540-6520.2011.00484.x

Halkias, D., Nwajiuba, C., Harkiolakis, N., & Caracatsanis, S. M. (2011). Challenges facing women entrepreneurs in Nigeria. *Management Research Review*, *34*(2), 221–235.

Harrison, J. S., Bosse, D. A. and Phillips, R. A. (2010). Managing for stakeholders, stakeholder utility functions, and competitive advantage. *Strategic Management Journal*, *31*(1), 58–74.

Hoang, H., & Yi, A. (2015). Network-based research in entrepreneurship: A decade in review. *Foundations and Trends in Entrepreneurship*, *11*(1), 1–54.

Igbanugo, C. and Uzonwanne, M., & Ezenekwe, R., (2016). Small and medium scale enterprises in African setting: The place of women. *International Journal of Economics, Commerce and Management*, *4*(3), 762.

Iyiola, O., & Azuh, D. E. (2014). Women entrepreneurs as small-medium enterprise (SME) operators and their roles in socio-economic development in Ota, Nigeria.

Jamali, D. (2009). Constraints and opportunities facing women entrepreneurs in developing countries: A relational perspective. *Gender in Management: An International Journal*, *24*(4), 232–251.

Jennings, J., & Brush, C. G. (2013). Research on women entrepreneurs: Challenges to (and from) the broader entrepreneurship literature? *The Academy of Management Annals*, *7*(1), 663–715.

Kalafatoglu, T., & Mendoza, X. (2017). The impact of gender and culture on networking and venture creation: An exploratory study in Turkey and MENA region. *Cross Cultural & Strategic Management*, *24*(2), 332–349.

Kiviluoto, N. (2013). Growth as evidence of firm success: Myth or reality? *Entrepreneurship & Regional Development*, *25*(7–8), 569–586.

Kolk, A., & Pinkse, J. (2007). Towards strategic stakeholder management? Integrating perspectives on sustainability challenges such as corporate responses to climate change. *Corporate Governance: The International Journal of Business in Society*, *7*(4), 370–378.

Kuada, J. (2009). Gender, social networks, and entrepreneurship in Ghana. *Journal of African Business*, *10*(1), 85–103.

Leitch, C., Hill, F., & Neergaard, H. (2010). Entrepreneurial and business growth and the quest for a "comprehensive theory": Tilting at windmills?. *Entrepreneurship Theory and Practice*, *34*(2), 249–260.

Levie, J., & Lichtenstein, B. B. (2010). A terminal assessment of stages theory: Introducing a dynamic states approach to entrepreneurship. *Entrepreneurship Theory and Practice*, *34*(2), 317–350.

Millan, J. M., Congregado, E., Roman, C., Van Praag, M., & Van Stel, A. (2014). The value of an educated population for an individual's entrepreneurship success. *Journal of business venturing*, *29*(5), 612–632.

Misango, S. B., & Ongiti, O. K. (2013). Do women entrepreneurs play a role in reducing poverty? A case in Kenya. *International Review of Management and Business Research*, *2*(1), 87.

Nambiar, Y., Sutherland, M., and Scheepers, C. B. (2020). The stakeholder ecosystem of women entrepreneurs in South African townships. *Development Southern Africa*, *37*(1), 70–86.

Nikina, A., Shelton L. M., & LeLoarne, S. (2015). An examination of how husbands, as key stakeholders, impact the success of women entrepreneurs. *Journal of Small Business and Enterprise Development*, *22*(1), 38–62.

Olander, S., & Landin, A. (2008). A comparative study of factors affecting the external stakeholder management process. *Construction Management and Economics*, *26*(6), 553–561.

Panda, S. (2018). Constraints faced by women entrepreneurs in developing countries: Review and ranking. *Gender in Management: An International Journal*, *33*(4), 315–331.

Panda, S., & Dash, S. K. (2015). Friends and strangers: Leveraging the power of networks for new venture success. *Development and Learning in Organizations: An International Journal, 29*(2), 6–9.

Peng, M., & Meyer, K. (2016). *International business* (2nd ed.). Cengage Textbooks.

Phillips, N., Tracey, P., & Karra, N. (2013). Building entrepreneurial tie portfolios through strategic homophily: The role of narrative identity work in venture creation and early growth. *Journal of Business Venturing, 28*(1), 134–150.

Pollack, J. M., Barr, S. & Hanson, S. (2017). New venture creation as establishing stakeholder relationships: A trust-based perspective. *Journal of Business Venturing Insights, 7*, 15–20.

Prasad, V. K., et al. (2013). Women entrepreneurs and business venture growth: An examination of the influence of human and social capital resources in an Indian context. *Journal of Small Business & Entrepreneurship, 26*(4), 341–364.

Rudman, L. A., & Phelan, J. E. (2008). Backlash effects for disconfirming gender stereotypes in organizations. *Research in Organizational Behaviour, 28*, 61–79.

Sanford, A. A., Ross, E. M., Blake, S. J., & Cambiano, R. L. (2015). Finding courage and confirmation: Resisting impostor feelings through relationships with mentors, romantic partners, and other women in leadership. *Advancing Women in Leadership, 35*(1), 31–41.

Santarelli, E., & Tran, H. T. (2013). The interplay of human and social capital in shaping entrepreneurial performance: The case of Vietnam. *Small Business Economics, 40*(2), 435–458.

Staniewski, M. W. (2016). The contribution of business experience and knowledge to successful entrepreneurship. *Journal of Business Research, 69*(11), 5147–5152.

Storey, D. J., & Greene, F. J. (2010). *Small business and entrepreneurship.* Pearson.

Walley, P. (2013). Stakeholder management: The sociodynamic approach. *International Journal of Managing Projects in Business, 6*(3), 485–504.

Wu, J. & Wokutch, R. E. (2015). Confucian stakeholder theory: An exploration. *Business and Society Review, 120*(1). https://doi.org/10.1111/basr.12046

Yang, J. R., Shen, P. Q. G., Bourne, L., Ho, C. M. F. and Xue, X. (2011). A typology of operational approaches for stakeholder analysis and engagement: Findings from Hong Kong and Australia. *Construction Management and Economics, 29*(2), 145–162.

10 Stakeholder Management and Entrepreneurship

A Catalyst for Climate Action in Africa

Robert Kwame Dzogbenuku

Introduction

Globally, entrepreneurs operate as micro, small, and medium-scale enterprises (MSMEs) entities that engage in economic activities at the community level by producing products and services to meet the needs of consumers, thus creating jobs for the unemployed, with profit being the primary goal. Existing literature argues that entrepreneurs are stakeholders of the world and can address socio-economic challenges using a creative mindset with local resources (Luke and Chu, 2013). Indeed, the operations of entrepreneurs can be described as strategic, unique, and distinct, as they mostly aspire to distinguish their operations by leveraging basic management and business principles. In sub-Saharan Africa, entrepreneurs, as transformative stakeholders of change, are labelled as the movers and shakers of rural economies due to their ability to create wealth while mitigating operational risk and championing the attainment of the world's sustainable development goals (SDGs).

The interaction between individuals, SMEs, and the green environment continues to garner a groundswell of attention from the academic community for two major reasons. First, entrepreneurs continue to play special roles in realising the ideals of the SDGs (Kansheba & Wald, 2020; Oppong, 2022) and, secondly, for the fact that human life depends on the ecological environment. Again, entrepreneurs are gradually deploying creative eco-friendly business strategies to protect the ecological environment while pursuing their primary interest in business (Filser et al., 2021; Stam and van de Ven, 2021). The rapid depletion of ecological resources results in severe environmental consequences due to constant interactions between citizens and the ecological environment, a consequence of ecological damage commonly known as climate change (Gast et al., 2017; Cavallo et al., 2019).

Climate change has been defined by Church and White (2006) as the changing patterns of weather and life-threatening weather extremities such as rises in global temperatures, rainfall, and sea levels. Scientists have described the phenomenon as the greatest challenge confronting humanity in recent history (Schoenefeld, 2021; Girona et al., 2023), and it is real. Undeniably, the ramifications of climate change remain dire and widespread with associated

DOI: 10.4324/9781003256014-13

risks: extreme weather conditions, rising sea levels and ocean acidification. This has consequences for agriculture and food production, biodiversity and human health. According to climate experts, human adaptation, a pro-environmental behaviour, is the surest way to mitigate climate action for human survival. In Africa, the consequences of global warming are widespread despite the fact that agricultural sector of the region employs most rural and peri-urban communities for their livelihood (Magesa and Pauline, 2018; Magesa et al., 2023). Unfortunately, the sector is negatively impacted by climate change because farmers of the space depend heavily on rain-fed agriculture. For example, in 2020, 64% of the world's poorest population live sub-Saharan Africa, a development that defies SDG goals 1 and 2 (Kharas and Dooley, 2020).

Stakeholder theory

Stakeholders are individuals, groups of people, or entities who can affect or be affected by the activities of organizations, and they have actual and potential interest in the activities of organizations and communities to which they are connected (Zarewa, 2019). Typically, in the case of entrepreneurs, stakeholders include owners and management of a firm, employees, shareholders, customers, suppliers and intermediaries, competitors, and the media. Other stakeholders include the community, state agencies, and pressure groups in some cases depending on the type of entrepreneurial business and type of operations.

The stakeholder theory suggests that different stakeholder needs are required to meet organisations' objectives irrespective of the sector of operations, and status of the firm (Freeman, 1984; Laplume et al., 2008). The stakeholder theory further argues that organisations that do not manage stakeholder relationships could be described as abstract entities whose survival will be a mirage as they may be affected negatively from achieving their set goals (Clarkson, 1995). In addition, success of organizations irrespective of status, size and role thrives on a sound stakeholder relationship. Therefore, maintaining good relationships among stakeholders calls for careful stakeholder relationship management for mutual benefit, especially if they are closely aligned within the same business environment (Nguyen and Adomako, 2022).

Some of the famous knowledge advancement made in recent times, has been the transformation change drive, a concept that calls for reawakening and revision of mission-led policies to drive rapid changes (Mazzucato, 2015, 2016; Larrue, 2021). Such missions are typically associated with germane stakeholder initiatives (Ergas, 1987) that drive national interest in the quest to fix dreaded social dangers confronting modern societies (Wanzenböck et al., 2020). Climate change at least for now, is a social danger that require transformative ideas from all to fix climate action. The mission therefore requires a careful understanding of the climate change menace through awareness creation at the local, national and the global level, to promote the desired understanding of the causes, consequences including prudent ways to mitigation. To address the menace, the role of the private sector particularly local entrepreneurs cannot be over-emphasized as entrepreneurs have creative mindsets to resolve social challenges at the local level of society using local expertise and resources.

Stakeholder empowerment is a construct that connects a person's strengths and competencies, and proactive behaviours for social policy and social changes (Perkins and Zimmerman, 1995). According to literature, this thought is associated with the power delegation, an authority for decentralization and decision-making at the local community level as it helps to shift responsibility from people seeded with formal power (leaders) to those with less power but responsible for strategy implementation (Conger and Kanungo, 1988). Therefore, an empowered entrepreneur promote assertive behaviour, control of knowledge, and skills that promotes collective participation and action to effect change (Papineau and Kiely, 1996). In management science, power from a stakeholder theory perspective appears under-conceptualized, given the fact that the theory's primary hinged on relational influences and stakeholder engagement. Therefore, local entrepreneurs must be seen as primary agents of development whose support must be sought always to benefit all.

Entrepreneurship

The definition of entrepreneurs or entrepreneurship as a profession is individuals who work and account to themselves while bearing the risk associated with business (Hebert and Link, 1982; Stephan, 2022). Generally, entrepreneurship includes self-employed individuals who are innovative and desperate to create business opportunities for themselves and employ others (Stephan, 2018). Primarily, entrepreneurial motivation is driven by profit each day through self-employment (Welter et al., 2017). In addition, studies have shown that entrepreneurship has a positive relationship with corporate social responsibility (CSR) initiatives because they are affected by activities of communities they operate (Curran, 2017; Tiba et al., 2019). Today, some entrepreneurs are labelled as social entrepreneurs because they focused on social and ecological sustainability concerns, thus incorporating green business strategies in line with their social mission to appeal to the growing green community who are ever concerned about the ecological environment (Hansen and Schaltegger, 2013; Gast et al., 2017; Tabi et al., 2019).

Stakeholder management

Management is simply the process of planning and organising corporate resources and activities for business success using the most effective and efficient methods possible (Bryson, 2018). This implies that managers of organisations must pay special attention to the genuine interests of all stakeholders irrespective of status and interest (Donaldson and Preston, 1995). Again, managers of organizations are deemed to employ prudent management principles to shape the cause of organizations by building the right structure, network and relationship through engagement. Stakeholder engagement permits entities to implement practical management programmes and strategies by deploying innovative measures to overcome operational challenges (Persson and Olander, 2004). Meaning, having a good relationship with stakeholders primarily contributes to the attainment of goals through integration and engagement.

Furthermore, stakeholder integration promotes equal participation of stakeholders irrespective of status as it helps to improve firm performance (Sharma and Vredenburg, 1998; Desai, 2018), a behaviour conceptualized into three-dimensional constructs, namely knowledge of strategic stakeholders, the interaction among stakeholders, and adaptation to stakeholder interest to benefit all (Plaza-Úbeda et al., 2010; Adomako et al., 2019). Thus, African entrepreneurs require a sound knowledge of stakeholders of their environment to shape the operational policy of stakeholder engagement.

Stakeholder engagement denotes the aims, activities, and impacts of stakeholder relations in a moral, strategic, and/or pragmatic manner (Kujala et al., 2022). Participation of stakeholders depends on the nature of the firm's business hence managers must decide on which stakeholder or group they wish to engage depending on the circumstance. Waligo et al. (2013) claim that the views of active stakeholders must be sought at all times for effective execution of corporate activities. It is worth adding that prioritizing the interest of stakeholders in line with the business and ethical environmental values remains supreme for proper stakeholders' engagement, a factor regarded as topmost for prudent business strategy (Ogunsanya et al., 2022; Bahadorestani et al., 2020). This can be achieved by carefully learning and balancing new stakeholder interests for mutual gain and in the interest of the community.

Sustainable environmental development goals are driven by partnerships between environmental stakeholders who have a common worldview of protecting planet Earth from destruction (Scholz and Steiner, 2015; Oonk et al., 2022). Indeed, literature on environment and policy management stresses the fact that stakeholder engagement at all levels of society ought to be prioritised with the hope to protect the environment (Adomako and Nguyen, 2023). This goal is associated with the stakeholder theory that seeks to benefit individuals, organizations, and society at large. In an era of environmental sustainability where positive climate action is valued, all stakeholders of the world are expected to work together seamlessly with a concerted effort for positive climate action.

Organisational and management theories stress that implementing environmentally sustainable policies with an overarching goal of protecting the environment of generations unborn should be part of the aspiration of citizens and organisations (de Grosbois & Fennell, 2022; Hahn & Kühnen, 2013). For example, reports on climate change concerns of organisations, particularly on carbon reporting, have been described as worrying since different stakeholder groups globally have diverse interests, and the result depends on interest and love for one's nation (Daddi et al., 2018).

Climate action

Climate action is all efforts taken by individuals, groups, organizations, and communities to combat climate change and its effects on the environment. The responsibility is to reduce greenhouse gas emissions and/or take critical action to prepare and adjust to both the current effects of climate change to safeguard the interest of future generations through climate adaptation. This is because human activity has reshaped the Earth's climate and ecosystems (Constantino et al., 2022). This can be addressed with a broad range of responses on an unprecedented scale through speed and positive consumer behaviour for social change (Larson et al., 2020; Weber, 2020).

Climate action policy exposes the causes of ongoing climate change emphasising the degree and urgency to meet climate action goals regarding impacts such as global temperature rise, sea level rise, and ocean acidification. In climate action simulation, participants assume leaders from private industry, government, and NGOs combat climate through policy with deliberate positive actions (Rooney-Varga et al., 2020).

Therefore, the stakeholder theory comes in handy to promote sustainable environmental policy, an outcome that depends on all stakeholders to protect the environment (KPMG, 2005, 2008). Furthermore, the stakeholder theory has been applied to identify how organizations respond to stakeholder concerns since stakeholders are interconnected. The theory requires the tacit support of all for short- and long-term success. It also advocates that companies must be flexible to adjust to activities while balancing stakeholders' conflicting interests and demands. Figure 10.1 is a conceptual framework of the study which highlights entrepreneurship, stakeholder management, and positive climate action.

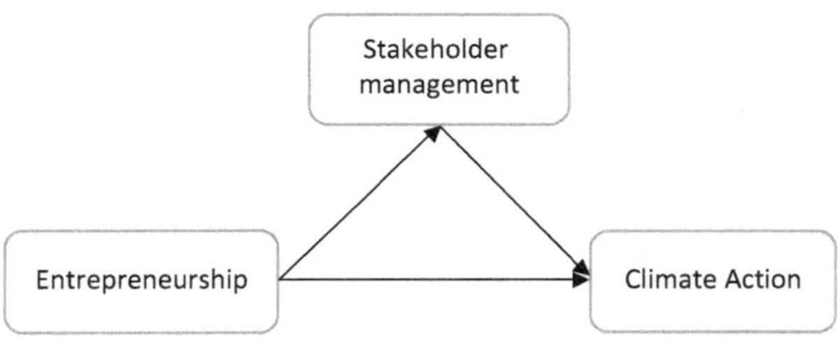

Figure 10.1 Conceptual framework on entrepreneurship, stakeholder management, and climate action.

Research propositions

P1: There is a positive relationship between entrepreneurship and stakeholder management.
P2: There is a positive relationship between stakeholder management and climate action.
P3: There is a positive relationship between entrepreneurship and climate change action.

Methodology

This paper is a conceptual paper based on secondary data. Conceptual research articles are organized into manifolds of varying degree and streams of content as provides notable insight to aid understanding (Chermack and Passmore, 2005). The conceptual research approach was considered to investigate how African entrepreneurs as stakeholders promote climate action initiatives from the perspective of the stakeholder theory. To achieve this, secondary data was from extracted contents of peer-reviewed academic journals that highlight keywords like entrepreneurship, stakeholder theory, environmental sustainability, and climate change. Adopting the methodical literature review style, the researcher read and reviewed existing literature on stakeholder, entrepreneurship stakeholder theory, and climate change. Information obtained from the reviews can be described as exclusive to the keywords under research, thus allowing the researcher to be informed to create new insight and knowledge about the subject reviewed (Torraco, 2005; Chermack and Passmore, 2005; Chanana and Sangeeta, 2021).

Findings of the study

It was identified from the review that entrepreneurs as stakeholders had a proactive mindset to address a social challenge driven profit motives (Janssen et al., 2023). Indeed, social transformation policy which seeks to find a solution to social ills and alter and/or replace the status quo with a tangible remedy, particularly in the social context, can be employed to solve critical social challenges (Haxeltine et al., 2017). This implies that African entrepreneurs as stakeholders ought to be empowered with the desired resources including state resources to promote social challenges like climate change since they are impactful and dominant social actors of social change (Avelino et al., 2022). Indeed, entrepreneurial empowerment is naturally inextricably linked to mainstreaming the responsibility of stakeholders since their primary aim is to up-scale national eco-entrepreneurial activities using innovative ideas (Holscher, 2017).

In the case of African entrepreneurs acting as transformative agents of change, they must be empowered by African governments to actively play the desired stakeholder role through the formulation of workable policies and resources. Often on the African continent, entrepreneurs being transformative agents have been successful through job creation to improve the well-being of other stakeholders and thus can play a leading role in positive climate action. Furthermore, stakeholders' support including the inspiration for local entrepreneurship often engenders socioeconomic growth, thus improving the life of citizens (Sadiq et al., 2021). In addition, African entrepreneurs over the years have demonstrated they have desired capacity to promote national transformative causes. Therefore, climate action initiative through the redevelopment of climate-friendly business policies by entrepreneurs through effective implementation of environmentally friendly market policies are in line with the global quest for climate adaptation.

Therefore, African entrepreneurs who have demonstrated appreciation towards changing life situations are likely to promote positive stakeholder relationships (Alsos et al., 2011; Adomako et al., 2019). Also, entrepreneurs have over the period modernised operational processes by constantly scanning the environment and enhancing or reinventing new ways to relate and integrate their operations to align with other stakeholder demands for cooperation. A finding that is in line with stakeholder theory suggests that different stakeholders align their operations to suit other stakeholders while others exert pressure to obtain what they want by adopting new work styles and practices (Jamali and Karam, 2018).

Implications for eco-entrepreneurs and policymakers

Scholars have for decades argue the role of entrepreneurs in fixing global environmental challenges and the SDGs (Theodoraki et al., 2018; Tipu et al., 2021). This is because entrepreneurial activities are crucial to tackling grand challenges such as poverty, unemployment, reducing energy consumption and carbon emissions, and achieving triple-bottom-line goals (Pacheco et al., 2010). As such, as argued earlier, it is not in doubt that the foundations of the developed and the developing economies are strategically linked to entrepreneurship and the attainment of SDGs to improve the living conditions of global citizens. For the attainment of goal 13 of the SDGs, conscious environmental behaviour of all is required to promote climate action (Moya-Clemente et al., 2020). This implies that, ozone depletion through greenhouse gas, and biodiversity degradation conditions are inimical to the attainment of SDG goal 13 (Iqbal et al., 2021) and must be prioritised over other environmental policies. Therefore, ecological entrepreneurs have a strategic role in tackling climate change forcefully using eco-friendly business strategies across sectors of the global economy (Iqbal et al., 2019).

In the case of African eco-entrepreneurs, there is a need to formulate a workable environmental policy to drive the notable Green Business Policy (GBP), an ecological business framework that deplores marketing strategy anchored on green marketing and environmental sustainability. The green business policy ought to be appreciated and accepted by all green entrepreneurs, by incorporating it into the operational manuals and plans to save the ecological environment. The eco-policy must be carefully designed to promote green products targeted at all, especially green consumers. Furthermore, eco-entrepreneurs are expected to build strong business relationships by working hand-in-hand with suppliers positioned as green input suppliers. Eco-policies of African entrepreneurs also required the buy-in of all stakeholders with the sole aim of forcefully attaining aspiration goal 13 of the SDGs. Implementation of African eco-entrepreneurial policy is dependent on creative influence all stakeholders of the green entrepreneurs with the primary aim of promoting climate action.

Again, the African eco-entrepreneurial policymakers are expected to communicate their motivation and interest in developing green or low carbon products targeted at green consumers by emphasizing on green consumer benefits. This is because green entrepreneurs have been adjudged as stakeholders in green policy formulation and implementation to promote climate action. However, the success of eco-entrepreneurs' quest for climate action is dependent on clear green communication that projects true environmental benefits by adhering to eco-friendly business practices. It is worth adding that the entrepreneurial ecosystem promotes genuineness among stakeholders, which results in knowledge sharing, thus driving entrepreneurial green action (Tiba & Belaid, 2021), which ultimately drives eco-entrepreneurial behaviour (Theodoraki et al., 2022; Chaudhary et al., 2023).

In addition, eco-entrepreneurs must develop the required capacity to negotiate probable concerns that may arise when implementing eco-friendly business policies from the beginning to the end. They must develop and effectively communicate the environmental philosophies to internal and external stakeholders in the contexts of mainstreaming green-focused economy to be acceptable to all stakeholders in the business.

The African entrepreneurial business strategy offers eco-entrepreneurs the bases for the attainment of SDGs to benefit stakeholders and humanity at large (Tolstykh et al., 2021). However, stakeholder interaction will be of benefit by sharing information among all stakeholders beginning from the micro and macro levels of society with requisite resources at hand (Khatami et al., 2021). Ideally, such knowledge and resources must be shared fairly among all stakeholders as envisaged in the eco-policy. However, the success of African eco-entrepreneurs must create new entrepreneurial opportunities and innovative ideas in line with the ideas (Laveren et al., 2020) for the attainment of climate action. Reviewing the existing works on entrepreneurial relationship with previous studies in line with stakeholder theory, the story contributes to existing studies for the advancement of new knowledge on how entrepreneurship and stakeholder management principles contribute to resolving a global challenge like climate change from the African perspective.

References

Adomako, S., Amankwah-Amoah, J., Danso, A., Konadu, R., and Owusu-Agyei, S. (2019), "Environmental sustainability orientation and performance of family and nonfamily firms", *Business Strategy and the Environment*, *28*(6), 1250–1259.

Adomako, S., and Nguyen, N.P., (2023), "Eco-innovation in the extractive industry: Combinative effects of social legitimacy, green management, and institutional pressures." *Resources Policy*, *80*, 103184.

Alsos, G. A., Hytti, U., and Ljunggren, E. (2011), "Stakeholder theory approach to technology incubators", *International Journal of Entrepreneurial Behavior and Research*, *17*(6), 607–625.

Avelino, F., Dumitru, A., Cipolla, C., Kunze, I., and Wittmayer, J. (2022), "Translocal empowerment in transformative social innovation networks," in *The economics of social innovation* (103–125). Routledge.

Bahadorestani, A., Naderpajouh, N., and Sadiq, R. (2020), "Planning for sustainable stakeholder engagement based on the assessment of conflicting interests in projects", *Journal of Cleaner Production*, *242*, 118402.

Bryson, J.M. (2018). Strategic planning. In *Defining public administration* (pp. 208–229). Routledge.

Cavallo, A., Ghezzi, A., and Balocco, R. (2019), "Entrepreneurial ecosystem research: Present debates and future directions", *International Entrepreneurship and Management Journal*, *15*, 1291–1321.

Chanana, N., and Sangeeta. (2021), "Employee engagement practices during COVID-19 lockdown", *Journal of Public Affairs*, *21*(4), e2508.

Chaudhary, S., Kaur, P., Alofaysan, H., Halberstadt, J., and Dhir, A. (2023), "Connecting the dots? Entrepreneurial ecosystems and sustainable entrepreneurship as pathways to sustainability", *Business Strategy and the Environment.*

Chermack, T. J., and Passmore, D. L. (2005), "Using journals and databases in research", *Research in Organizations: Foundations and Methods of Inquiry*, 401–418.

Church, J. A., and White, N.J. (2006) A 20th century acceleration in global sea-level rise. *Geophysical Research Letters*, *33*(1).

Clarkson, M. E. (1995), "A stakeholder framework for analyzing and evaluating corporate social performance", *Academy of Management Review*, *20*(1), 92–117.

Conger, J. A., & Kanungo, R. N. (1988), "The empowerment process: Integrating theory and practice. *Academy of Management Review*, *13*(3), 471–482.

Constantino, S. M., Sparkman, G., Kraft-Todd, G. T., Bicchieri, C., Centola, D., Shell-Duncan, B., Vogt, S., and Weber, E. U. (2022), "Scaling up change: A critical review and practical guide to harnessing social norms for climate action", *Psychological Science in the Public Interest*, *23*(2), 50–97.

Curran, G. (2017), "Social license, corporate social responsibility and coal seam gas: Framing the new political dynamics of contestation", *Energy Policy*, *101*, 427–435.

Daddi, T., Todaro, N. M., De Giacomo, M. R., and Frey, M. (2018), "A systematic review of the use of organization and management theories in climate change studies", *Business Strategy and the Environment*, *27*(4), 456–474.

de Grosbois, D., and Fennell, D. A. (2022), "Determinants of climate change disclosure practices of global hotel companies: Application of institutional and stakeholder theories", *Tourism Management*, *88*, 104404.

Desai, V. M., (2018), "Collaborative stakeholder engagement: An integration between theories of organizational legitimacy and learning", *Academy of Management Journal*, *61*(1), 220–244.

Donaldson, T., and Preston, L. E. (1995), "The stakeholder theory of the corporation: Concepts, evidence, and implications", *Academy of Management Review*, *20*(1), 65–91.

Ergas, Z. (1987), "In search of development in Africa", in *The African State in Transition* (pp. 295–329). Palgrave Macmillan UK.

Filser, M., Kraus, S., Breier, M., Nenova, I., and Puumalainen, K. (2021), "Business model innovation: Identifying foundations and trajectories", *Business Strategy and the Environment*, *30*(2), 891–907.

Freeman, R. E. (1984), "Strategic management: A stakeholder theory", *Journal of Management Studies*, *39*(1), 1–21.

Gast, J., Gundolf, K., and Cesinger, B. (2017), "Doing business in a green way: A systematic review of the ecological sustainability entrepreneurship literature and future research directions", *Journal of Cleaner Production*, *147*, 44–56.

Girona, M. M., Aakala, T., Aquilué, N., Bélisle, A. C., Chaste, E., Danneyrolles, V., and Gauthier, S. (2023), "Challenges for the sustainable management of the boreal forest under climate change", In *Boreal Forests in the face of climate change: Sustainable management* (pp. 773–837). Cham: Springer International Publishing.

Hahn, R., and Kühnen, M. (2013), "Determinants of sustainability reporting: A review of results, trends, theory, and opportunities in an expanding field of research", *Journal of Cleaner Production*, *59*, 5–21.

Hansen, E. G., and Schaltegger, S., (2013), 100 percent organic? A sustainable entrepreneurship perspective on the diffusion of organic clothing. *Corporate Governance*, *15*(5), 583–598.

Haxeltine, A., Pel, B., Wittmayer, J., Dumitru, A., Kemp, R., and Avelino, F. (2017), "Building a middle-range theory of transformative social innovation; theoretical pitfalls and methodological responses", *European Public and Social Innovation Review*, *2*(1), 59–77.

Hebert, R. F., and Link, A. N. (1982), *The entrepreneurs: Mainstream views and radical critiques.* Praeger.

Holscher, H. D. (2017), "Dietary fiber and prebiotics and the gastrointestinal microbiota", *Gut Microbes*, *8*(2), 172–184.

Iqbal, F. M., Lam, K., Sounderajah, V., Clarke, J. M., Ashrafian, H., and Darzi, A. (2021), "Characteristics and predictors of acute and chronic post-COVID syndrome: A systematic review and meta-analysis", *E-Clinical Medicine*, *36*.

Iqbal, N., Tufail, M.S., Mohsin, M. and Sandhu, M.A., (2019), "Assessing social and financial efficiency: the evidence from microfinance institutions in Pakistan", *Pakistan Journal of Social Sciences*, *39*(1), 149–161.

Jamali, D., and Karam, C., 2018. Corporate social responsibility in developing countries as an emerging field of study. *International Journal of Management Reviews*, *20*(1), 32–61.

Janssen, M. J., Wesseling, J., Torrens, J., Weber, K. M., Penna, C., and Klerkx, L. (2023), "Missions as boundary objects for transformative change: Understanding coordination across policy, research, and stakeholder communities", *Science and Public Policy*, *50*, scac080.

Kansheba, J. M. P., and Wald, A. E. (2020), "Entrepreneurial ecosystems: A systematic literature review and research agenda", *Journal of Small Business and Enterprise Development*, *27*(6), 943–964.

Kharas, H., and Dooley, M. (2020), "COVID-19's legacy of debt and debt service in developing countries", *Global Working Paper*, (148).

Khatami, K., Perez-Zabaleta, M., Owusu-Agyeman, I., and Cetecioglu, Z. (2021), "Waste to bioplastics: How close are we to sustainable polyhydroxyalkanoates production?" *Waste Management*, *119*, 374–388.

KPMG (2005), *Survey of corporate responsibility reporting 2005*, KPMG, Amsterdam.

KPMG (2008), *International survey of corporate responsibility reporting 2008*, KPMG, Amsterdam.

Kujala, J., Sachs, S., Leinonen, H., Heikkinen, A., and Laude, D. (2022), "Stakeholder engagement: Past, present, and future", *Business and Society*, *61*(5), 1136–1196.

Laplume, A. O., Sonpar, K., and Litz, R. A. (2008), "Stakeholder theory: Reviewing a theory that moves us", *Journal of Management*, *34*(6), 1152–1189.

Larrue, P. (2021), "The design and implementation of mission-oriented innovation policies: A new systemic policy approach to address societal challenges" *OECD Science, Technology and Industry Policy Papers*, No. 100, OECD Publishing, Paris.

Larson, E., Greig, C., Jenkins, J., Mayfield, E., Pascale, A., Zhang, C., Drossman, J., Williams, R., Pacala, S., Socolow, R., Baik, E., Birdsey, R., Duke, R., Jones, R., Haley, B., Leslie, E., Paustian, K., & Swan, A. (2020). *Net-zero America: Potential pathways, infrastructure, and impacts, interim report*. Princeton University. https://netzeroamerica.princeton.edu/img/Princeton_NZA_Interim_Report_15_Dec_2020_FINAL.pd

Laveren, E., Blackburn, R., Ben-Hafaïedh, C., Díaz-García, C. and González-Moreno, Á. (2020), "An introduction to Sustainable Entrepreneurship and Entrepreneurial Ecosystems", in *Sustainable Entrepreneurship and Entrepreneurial Ecosystems: Frontiers in European Entrepreneurship Research*, 1.

Luke, B., and Chu, V. (2013), "Social enterprise versus social entrepreneurship: An examination of the 'why' and 'how' in pursuing social change", *International Small Business Journal*, *31*(7), 764–784.

Magesa, B., and Pauline, N. (2018), "Analysis of adaptation strategies of water insecure coastal communities of Tanzania by gender: Case of Mlingotini village in Bagamoyo district", *Journal of the Geographical Association of Tanzania*, *39*(1), 118–141.

Magesa, B. A., Mohan, G., Matsuda, H., Melts, I., Kefi, M., and Fukushi, K. (2023), "Understanding the farmers' choices and adoption of adaptation strategies, and plans to climate change impact in Africa: A systematic review", *Climate Services*, *30*, 100362.

Mazzucato, M. (2015), "Building the entrepreneurial state: A new framework for envisioning and evaluating a mission-oriented public sector", *Levy Economics Institute of Bard College Working Paper*, (824).

Mazzucato, M., (2016), "From market fixing to market-creating: a new framework for innovation Policy", *Industry and Innovation*, *23*(2), 140–156.

Moya-Clemente, I., Ribes-Giner, G. and Pantoja-Díaz, O., (2020), "Configurations of sustainable development goals that promote sustainable entrepreneurship over time", *Sustainable Development*, *28*(4), 572–584.

Nguyen, N. P., and Adomako, S. (2022), "Stakeholder pressure for eco-friendly practices, international orientation, and eco-innovation: A study of small and medium-sized enterprises in Vietnam", *Corporate Social Responsibility and Environmental Management*, *29*(1), 79–88.

Ogunsanya, O. A., Aigbavboa, C. O., Thwala, D. W., and Edwards, D. J. (2022), "Barriers to sustainable procurement in the Nigerian construction industry: An exploratory factor analysis", *International Journal of Construction Management*, *22*(5), 861–872.

Oonk, C., Gulikers, J., den Brok, P., and Mulder, M. (2022), "Stimulating boundary crossing learning in a multi-stakeholder learning environment for sustainable development", *International Journal of Sustainability in Higher Education*, *23*(8), 21–40.

Oppong, N. B. (2022), "Sustainable development goals and small and medium enterprises: A comparative study of emerging economies and sub-Saharan Africa", *Global Business Review*, https://doi.org/10.1177/09721509221087848

Pacheco, D. F., Dean, T. J., and Payne, D. S. (2010), "Escaping the green prison: Entrepreneurship and the creation of opportunities for sustainable development", *Journal of Business Venturing*, *25*(5), 464–480.

Papineau, D., & Kiely, M. C. (1996), "Participatory evaluation in a community organization: Fostering stakeholder empowerment and utilization", *Evaluation and Program Planning*, *19*(1), 79–93.

Perkins, D. D., & Zimmerman, M. A. (1995), "Empowerment theory, research, and application", *American Journal of Community Psychology*, *23*(5), 569–579.

Persson, U., and Olander, S. (2004), "September. Methods to estimate stakeholder views of sustainability for construction projects", in *Proceedings of the 21th Conference on Passive and Low Energy Architecture*, 19–22.

Plaza-Úbeda, J. A., de Burgos-Jiménez, J., and Carmona-Moreno, E. (2010), "Measuring stakeholder integration: Knowledge, interaction and adaptational behavior dimensions", *Journal of Business Ethics*, *93*, 419–442.

Rooney-Varga, J. N., Kapmeier, F., Sterman, J. D., Jones, A. P., Putko, M. and Rath, K., (2020), "The climate action simulation", *Simulation & Gaming*, *51*(2), 114–140.

Sadiq, S., Umer, M., Ullah, S., Mirjalili, S., Rupapara, V., and Nappi, M. (2021), "Discrepancy detection between actual user reviews and numeric ratings of Google App store using deep learning", *Expert Systems with Applications*, *181*, 115111.

Schoenefeld, J. J. (2021), "The European Green Deal: What prospects for governing climate change with policy monitoring?" *Politics and Governance*, *9*(3), 370–379.

Scholz, R. W., and Steiner, G. (2015), "Trans-disciplinarity at the crossroads", *Sustainability Science*, *10*, 521–526.

Sharma, S., and Vredenburg, H. (1998), "Proactive corporate environmental strategy and the development of competitively valuable organizational capabilities", *Strategic Management Journal*, *19*(8), 729–753.

Stam, E., and Van de Ven, A. (2021), "Entrepreneurial ecosystem elements", *Small Business Economics*, *56*, 809–832.

Stephan, U., (2018), "Entrepreneurs' mental health and well-being: A review and research agenda", *Academy of Management Perspectives*, *32*(3), 290–322.

Stephan, U., (2022), "Cross-cultural innovation and entrepreneurship", *Annual Review of Organizational Psychology and Organizational Behavior*, 9, 277–308.

Theodoraki, C., Dana, L. P., and Caputo, A. (2022), "Building sustainable entrepreneurial ecosystems: A holistic approach", *Journal of Business Research*, *140*, 346–360.

Theodoraki, C., Messeghem, K., and Rice, M. P. (2018), "A social capital approach to the development of sustainable entrepreneurial ecosystems: An explorative study", *Small Business Economics*, *51*, 153–170.

Tiba, S., and Belaid, F. (2021), "Modeling the nexus between sustainable development and renewable energy: The African perspectives", *Journal of Economic Surveys*, *35*(1), 307–329.

Tiba, S., van Rijnsoever, F. J., and Hekkert, M. P. (2019). Firms with benefits: A systematic review of responsible entrepreneurship and corporate social responsibility literature. *Corporate Social Responsibility and Environmental Management*, *26*(2), pp. 265–284.

Tipu, M. M. H., Masud, M. M., Jahan, R., Baroi, A., and Hoque, A. K. M. A. (2021), "Identification of citrus greening based on visual symptoms: A grower's diagnostic toolkit", *Heliyon*, *7*(11).

Tolstykh, T., Gamidullaeva, L., and Shmeleva, N. (2021), "Universities as knowledge integrators and cross-industry ecosystems: Self-organizational perspective", *Sage Open*, *11*(1), 2158244020988704.

Torraco, R. J. (2005), "Writing integrative literature reviews: Guidelines and examples", *Human Resource Development Review*, *4*(3), 356–367.

Waligo, V. M., Clarke, J. and Hawkins, R., (2013), "Implementing sustainable tourism: A multi-stakeholder involvement management framework," *Tourism Management*, *36*, 342–353.

Wanzenböck, I., Wesseling, J. H., Frenken, K., Hekkert, M. P., and Weber, K. M. (2020), "A framework for mission-oriented innovation policy: Alternative pathways through the problem–solution space", *Science and Public Policy*, *47*(4), 474–489.

Weber, E. U. (2020). "Giving the future a chance: Behavioral economic responses to the dual challenges of COVID-19 and the climate crisis," In A. Samson (Ed.), *Behavioral economics guide 2020.* https://www.behavioraleconomics.com/be-guide/the-behavioral-economics-guide-2020/

Welter, F., Baker, T., Audretsch, D. B., and Gartner, W. B. (2017). Everyday entrepreneurship- A call for entrepreneurship research to embrace entrepreneurial diversity. *Entrepreneurship Theory and Practice*, *41*(3), 311–321.

Zarewa, G. A. (2019), "Barriers to effective stakeholder management in the delivery of multifarious infrastructure projects (MIPs)", *Journal of Engineering, Project, and Production Management*, *9*(2), 85–96.

11 Two Decades of Research on Stakeholder Management and Entrepreneurship in Africa

A Review and Future Research Agenda

Samuel Narh Dorhetso

Introduction

Stakeholder management is a fundamental module to the successful delivery of any project, program or activity. A stakeholder is any person, group or organization that can affect, be affected by or perceive itself to be affected by a project or program. Project stakeholder management is another name for stakeholder management, and it is perceived as a continuous four-step process of identifying stakeholders, determining their influence, developing a communication management plan and influencing stakeholders through engagement. Stakeholder theory states that a pertinent segment of value creation in businesses, which enhances their chances of being successful, is their engagement and development of strong relationships with a wide variety of stakeholders (Harrison et al., 2010; Pollack et al., 2017; Sefiani et al., 2018). Available literature on stakeholder theory within the entrepreneurship knowledge field vividly explains the significant role of engaging with various stakeholders and crafting strong relationships with them for entrepreneurship development (Bresciani et al., 2013; Maxwell & Lévesque, 2014; Pollack et al., 2017; Vandekerckhove & Dentchev, 2005). In the field of economics, an entrepreneur connects the three other factors of production (land, labor, and capital) and is remunerated with profit. The term "entrepreneur" depicts an entity which has the capability to translate inventions or technologies into products and services (Audretsch et al., 2002). Thus, entrepreneurship encapsulates activities of both established firms and start-ups. Entrepreneurship is the creation or extraction of economic value (Alvarez & Busenitz, 2001; Diochon & Anderson, 2011; Gaddefors & Anderson, 2017). There have been several studies on stakeholders, stakeholder management, and entrepreneurship regarding societal engagement and sustainable integration. Contemporary themes of the literature on stakeholder management and entrepreneurship include stakeholder engagement (Amankwah-Amoah et al., 2019), entrepreneurship/entrepreneurialism (Petrolo et al., 2022), stakeholder/stakeholder analysis (Almansour, 2022), social enterprise/social entrepreneurship (England, 2020), sustainable development/SDGs/sustainability (Sansone et al., 2023), stakeholder management (Hiebl & Pielsticker, 2023), and stakeholder

DOI: 10.4324/9781003256014-14

theory (Kansheba et al., 2022). Out of the 52 papers reviewed in this research, only 11 (21.15%) were conceptual and review articles. Thus, it is apparent that more current conceptual and review studies need to be produced in the field, as this would facilitate theory development (Hassan et al., 2022; Mishra et al., 2021). The most recent papers reviewed (only documents published in 2023) with their associated methodologies were case studies (Qi et al., 2023; Sansone et al., 2023), empirical studies (Hiebl & Pielsticker, 2023) and conceptual and review articles (Bailey & Lumpkin, 2023). Bailey and Lumpkin (2023) proposed a stakeholder engagement framework that uses the awareness, desire, knowledge, ability and reinforcement (ADKAR) change methodology to enhance civic wealth creation (CWC) through stakeholders' propensity to participate in the entrepreneurial change processes that create positive social change (PSC). Although their study made a significant contribution to knowledge in the field, it was limited in scope, as it was predominantly focused on PSC. These identified gaps in literature point to the fact that more conceptual review papers geared towards theory development are needed in the continuously evolving field of stakeholder management and entrepreneurship. To the best of the researcher's knowledge, no systematic literature review has been conducted in the specific field from the first article on the subject by von Blottnitz (2006) till now. However, such a study is required for the advancement of theories in the field. To this extent, the purpose of this study was to execute a comprehensive review of the existing literature on stakeholder management and entrepreneurship. Precisely, the specific objective of the study was to answer the following research questions: What theories, theoretical constructs and concepts, contexts and methodologies of interest are interrogated in the existing body of knowledge on stakeholder management and entrepreneurship? What are the current gaps in stakeholder management and entrepreneurship literature? And what are the future directions of research in stakeholder management and entrepreneurship? Several theoretical contributions were made to knowledge in the field through this comprehensive review. Initially, the existing literature was upgraded by proposing a new organizing framework of stakeholder management and entrepreneurship. An organizing framework expedites the incorporation of themes that are identified inductively (Hulland & Houston, 2020). The organizing framework synthesized the antecedents, dimensions and outcomes of stakeholder management and entrepreneurship based on the data available in extant literature. After undergoing various screening procedures, 52 papers were included in this review through the scientific procedures and rationales for systematic literature reviews (SPAR-4-SLR) (Paul et al., 2021) method. A framework-based methodology, the theory–context–characteristics–methodology (TCCM) framework, was used to conduct this review. The TCCM framework was applied due to its usefulness for reviews that aim to make theoretical contributions to a body of knowledge (e.g., Hassan et al., 2022). The current study advances the research on stakeholder management and entrepreneurship through an organization of theories used in the field.

Furthermore, it creates a vivid and pertinent agenda for impactful future research. Consequently, the study would facilitate the establishment of more relevance for stakeholder management and entrepreneurship in strategic management. The outline of the rest of this paper is as follows. The next section provides a detailed summary of the materials and methods used in this research. The third section presents the results of the analysis with respect to theories, context, characteristics and methods. The fourth section offers directions for future research and the fifth section concludes the paper.

Materials and methods

A systematic literature review was considered appropriate for this study, based on its purpose, which was to identify research gaps in literature on stakeholder management and entrepreneurship in order to unveil suggestions for future research. Systematic literature reviews have been extensively used by researchers such as Hassan et al. (2022). There are several types of systematic review documents. These include bibliometric reviews (Dorhetso et al., 2023; Fakhar Manesh et al., 2020) and framework based reviews (Paul & Benito, 2018).

Research domain, search criteria and reporting procedure

Theoretical and empirical journal articles published between the period of 2006 and 2023 were reviewed to synthesize the identified literature on stakeholder management and entrepreneurship in this contemporary review. This study sought to answer the research questions on how stakeholder management and entrepreneurship research literature can be organized to identify developments in research by going through key documents featuring theories, context, characteristics and methods used in extant literature, and performing a gap analysis to prepare a guide for future research in the field. Keywords were painstakingly selected based on the scope of the research and merged with Boolean operators to form a search string that was keyed into the Scopus database. Major keywords such as stakeholder management, stakeholder engagement, stakeholder integration, stakeholder involvement, stakeholder participation, stakeholder networking, entrepreneurship, early-stage ventures, entrepreneurial firms, new businesses in Africa, new ventures, SMEs in Africa, MSMEs, micro firms in Africa, micro small and medium enterprises, and entrepreneurship in Africa were merged to form the search string. The database search on April 7, 2023 initially produced a total number of 148 papers published within the period of 2005 and 2023. The search was then limited to only papers in the field of social sciences, economics, econometrics and finance, business, management and accounting, and this yielded 121 papers. Upon further limitation to only journal articles published in the English language, the search yielded 96 papers. Finally, the search on the Scopus database was limited to only A to C ranked journals on the Australian Business Deans Council (ABDC, 2019) journal quality list, which is extensively used as a benchmark database of journals of international standard (Lu et al., 2016), and this produced a total of 52 journal articles published between 2005 and 2023. Subsequent to the assessment of the articles against these set criteria, the abstracts of the final 52 papers for the period under review were thoroughly read to ascertain if they were meaningfully related to literature in the specific field. All the 52 abstracts read were found to be consistent with the current study and thus were included for further synthesis. The search criteria, procedure and results were reported using the SPAR-4-SLR protocol (Paul et al., 2021) as shown in Figure 11.1.

Discussion

Concepts, theories and theoretical models

Several theories fortified the articles reviewed on stakeholder management and entrepreneurship in this study. The most protuberant concepts, theories and theoretical models applied in the reviewed literature include instrumental stakeholder theory (Laplume et al., 2021), institutional bricolage (Mzembe et al., 2019), critical discourse analysis and framing theory (Kouri & Clarke, 2014), stakeholder theory (Hiebl & Pielsticker, 2023; Sansone et al., 2023; Alonso et al., 2018; Cavazos et al., 2012; Bischoff et al., 2018; Fischer et al., 2020; Kansheba et al., 2022; Khojastehpour & Shams, 2020; Meyer et al., 2020; Bailey & Lumpkin, 2023), concepts of organizational fitness and fitness landscapes (Meyer & Gauthier, 2013), technology acceptance model (Camilleri, 2019); multipolar network theory and stakeholder engagement theory (Kamuhuza et al., 2022), internationalization theory (Khojastehpour & Shams, 2020), actor network theory (Bobadilla et al., 2019) and institutional theory (Hiatt et al., 2018).

Contexts

The contexts of the papers reviewed for this study are evinced in this section by describing the patterns of international research emanating from countries studied in this domain. Thirty (30) countries were affiliated with published research works on stakeholder management and entrepreneurship from 2006 to 2023. The most productive country, based on the standpoint of total number of papers, was the United Kingdom (UK) with 17 articles. The United States and Italy followed with 12 and 7 papers, respectively. In 15 (50 percent) of the countries with publishing associations regarding the topic of stakeholder management and entrepreneurship, none of the authors were involved in international alliances.

Thematic analysis

Research themes in literature on stakeholder management and entrepreneurship straddling the period of 2006 to 2023, which are not intended to be definitive and mutually exclusive, were identified from the articles synthesized

Assembling

Identification

Domain: Stakeholder Management and Entrepreneurship

Research questions:

1. What theories, theoretical constructs and concepts, contexts, and methodologies of interest are interrogated in the existing body of knowledge on stakeholder management and entrepreneurship?

2. What are the current gaps in stakeholder management and entrepreneurship literature?

3. What are the future directions of research in stakeholder management and entrepreneurship?

Source type: Published peer reviewed research journal articles (both final and articles in press)

Source quality: Scopus

Acquisition

Search mechanism and material acquisition: Scopus Database

Search period: 2006 to 2023

Search keywords: Stakeholder management, Stakeholder engagement, Stakeholder integration, Stakeholder involvement, Stakeholder participation, Stakeholder networking, entrepreneurship, early-stage ventures, entrepreneurial firms, new businesses in Africa, new ventures, SMEs in Africa, MSMEs, Micro firms in Africa, Micro small and medium enterprises, and entrepreneurship in Africa.

Total number of items returned from the search: 148

Arranging

Organization

Organizing code: Theories and constructs, contexts, themes, publication outlets (journals), citations, and methodologies.

Organizing framework: Theory–context–characteristics– methodology (TCCM) framework (Paul & Rosado-Serrano, 2019)

Purification

Article type excluded (and total number for each type of exclusion): Articles excluded due to type and language (n=25), field and topic (n=27), not in A to C ranked journals on the ABDC ranking scale (n=44), Inconsistent with literature on CE (n=0).

Article type included (and total number of articles included): Articles addressing stakeholder management and entrepreneurship that were published in A to C ranked journals on the ABDC ranking scale (n=52).

Figure 11.1 The SPAR-4-SLR protocol flow diagram. (Continued)

Assessing

Evaluation

Analysis method: Content analysis

Agenda proposal method: Gap analysis

Reporting

Reporting convention: Tables describing aspects of the TCCM framework followed in the study.

Limitations: Journal type (only A to C ranked journals on the ABDC ranking scale), data type (only journals published in English language)

Source of support: Comments from peers

Figure 11.1 (Continued)

in this review. The themes designate the rate of recurrence of keywords. Keywords help to conjecture the fundamental themes of an author's definition and dimensions (Fetscherin, 2010). The repetition of keywords among documents might be an indicator that the documents convey a collective theme. For the assemblage of papers with similar themes in this study, both author and indexed keywords were used. Only papers with either author keywords or indexed keywords or both keywords with a minimum of five repetitions were nominated for this study. Thus, the current study identified seven main research themes, namely stakeholder engagement (18 papers), entrepreneurship/entrepreneurialism (15 papers), stakeholder/stakeholder analysis (13 papers), social enterprise/social entrepreneurship (11 papers), sustainable development/SDGs/sustainability (8 papers), stakeholder management (6 papers) and stakeholder theory (5 papers).

Journals

The articles were published in a wide collection of journals and reflect almost two decades of research in the field of stakeholder management and entrepreneurship. Amongst the 32 journals, *Journal of Business Research* published the most (8 papers with 15.38 percent), followed by *Journal of Business Ethics* (4 papers with 7.69 percent). The scope of journal coverage depicts the diverse interests of researchers and publishers. The ABDC classification (ABDC, 2019), which gleans from an extensive international coverage, was used to appraise the quality of the research outlets selected for this contemporary study.

Citation analysis

Taking cue from extant literature, as posited by Lu et al. (2016), the impact of scholarly work was assessed by a citation count. Table 11.1 presents the 32 articles (ranking from 1 to 32) with regard to the total number of citations.

Table 11.1 Most cited papers in literature from 2006 to 2023 (citation counts as of April 27, 2023)

S/N	*Authors*	*Type of Article*	*Citation Count*	*Ranking by Citations*
1	Bruneel et al. (2016)	Case study	38	14
2	Mzembe et al. (2019)	Case study	11	30
3	Kouri and Clarke (2014)	Empirical study	20	23
4	Wagner et al. (2021)	Case study	44	12
5	Lorenzo-Afable et al. (2020)	Case study	12	28
6	Vealey and Gerding (2016)	Case study	15	26
7	Soetanto and van Geenhuizen (2007)	Empirical study	17	25
8	Matlay (2011)	Empirical study	59	7
9	Meyer and Gauthier (2013)	Review paper	12	28
10	Matlay (2009)	Empirical study	83	4
11	Riad Shams et al. (2020)	Meta-analysis	21	21
12	Camilleri (2019)	Empirical	33	16
13	Jones and Iredale (2009)	Conceptual review	20	23
14	Retolaza et al. (2009)	Conceptual review	28	19
15	Ferraris et al. (2020)	Mixed study	48	9
16	Nair (2020)	Review article	29	18
17	Fischer et al. (2020)	Case study	36	15
18	Smith and Woods (2015)	Case study	21	21
19	von Blottnitz (2006)	Case study	42	13
20	Altinay et al. (2016)	Case study	102	2
21	Cavazos et al. (2012)	Empirical study	10	31

(*Continued*)

Table 11.1 (Continued)

S/N	*Authors*	*Type of Article*	*Citation Count*	*Ranking by Citations*
22	Agrawal and Hockerts (2021)	Review paper	46	10
23	Amankwah-Amoah et al. (2019)	Empirical study	97	3
24	Bischoff et al. (2018)	Empirical study	79	5
25	Khojastehpour and Shams (2020)	Qualitative study	22	20
26	Fassin and Drover (2017)	Review paper	14	27
27	Chen and Liu (2020)	Empirical study	60	6
28	Leonidou et al. (2020)	Review paper	148	1
29	García-Sánchez et al. (2018)	Empirical study	50	8
30	Hiatt et al. (2018)	Empirical study	30	17
31	Anbarasan and Sushil (2018)	Empirical study	46	10

Note: Papers with citations less than 10 were not included.

Main methodologies used in literature

Based on an analysis of the frequency of reappearance with which different methodologies were used in the papers synthesized, it was evident that case studies were the most popular methodologies used in stakeholder management and entrepreneurship research (38.46 percent), with empirical studies following closely (32.70 percent). However, there were only 11 conceptual and review articles (21.15 percent), and two qualitative analysis papers (3.86 percent). Researchers may consider using alternative data collection methods to explore an understanding of the field from subjective standpoints.

Directions for future research

Theory development

It was evinced by the findings of the theoretical inspection of the literature collected in this review that despite some prominent efforts to study stakeholder management and entrepreneurship, there still lingers a need for more interdisciplinary and multidisciplinary research for theory development and extension of the theories used in the field. To the best of the researchers' knowledge, the existing theories used in stakeholder management and entrepreneurship research did not entirely address the peculiar characteristics of the field until specifically invoked. This finding is a recognized gap which unlocks a door for research in this direction in future. It is recommended that future research should continue to introduce novel theoretical perspectives and integrate theories, potentially presenting new concepts or theoretical models that directly underpin the field. It is noteworthy to recognize *Laplume* et al.'s (2021) addition of an entrepreneurship lens to the business ethics of stakeholder theory to exude how incumbent stakeholder management performance shapes opportunities for entrepreneurs, a largely neglected stakeholder group.

Contexts

The findings of the study revealed that most of the existing research on stakeholder management and entrepreneurship was conducted in developed countries. A huge gap in terms of research emanating from developing countries or in the context of developing economies as found in Africa was found in the literature reviewed. To the best of the researcher's knowledge, only a handful of studies were found from Africa or within an African country setting. Nevertheless, stakeholder management and entrepreneurship issues are rife universally, and Africa is no exception. Furthermore, the emergence of technology and AI makes it more feasible for cross-national and cross-cultural research. Thus, it is suggested that future studies should include cross-national and cross-cultural research to identify any similarities and differences in stakeholder management and entrepreneurship practices across the different geographical settings. Single authored as well as co-authored papers are recommended from either multiple counties or a single developing country.

Thematic perspectives

The current study identified seven main research hotspots that had clouded the stakeholder management and entrepreneurship research space: stakeholder engagement, entrepreneurship/entrepreneurialism, stakeholder/stakeholder analysis, social enterprise/social entrepreneurship, sustainable development/SDGs/sustainability, stakeholder management and stakeholder theory. Based on these findings, it is suggested that future research should be directed towards investigating the links between the identified thematic areas. Future researchers may be encouraged to examine the mediating roles of variables such as stakeholder engagement, stakeholder management and stakeholder integration between stakeholders and variables such as social enterprise, social entrepreneurship, entrepreneurship and sustainability. The moderating roles of stakeholder engagement, stakeholder management and stakeholder integration could also be examined by researchers in future.

Methodological perspectives

It is apparent from the findings that case studies were the most popular methodologies used in the reviewed literature. This was followed closely by empirical articles, suggesting that the field still requires substantive studies. It is also apparent from the results that conceptual and review papers and qualitative analysis had only mediocre representation. Hence, it is recommended that future studies should consider the incorporation of more concepts into research in the field through review methodologies such as systematic literature reviews, using approved frameworks such as the TCCM to identify, select and critically evaluate the field of study to outline an agenda for future research. The field has been in existence for a while, yet it is still evolving and needs more developments in theory to guide future research. Thus, more qualitative analysis, interviews, essays and content analysis should be encouraged in future studies. A qualitative research methodology is more probable to uncover subjective factors that have not been examined but may influence research in the area of stakeholder management and entrepreneurship. It is more likely to provide a more detailed understanding of the field from a peculiar standpoint and make room for inductive reasoning (Creswell, 1998). Additionally, additional empirical studies emanating from developing countries (especially in Africa) should be encouraged for future research.

Conclusion

The purpose of this current study was to contribute to the body of knowledge in stakeholder management and entrepreneurship by way of a systematic literature review of the field. Scholarly papers on the subject for the last 17 years (2006–2023) were identified, selected and scrutinized as a basis for an outline of the state of the art of the research domain. The topmost cited articles and primary outlets for stakeholder management and entrepreneurship research were recognized in this review. Trends in terms of theories, contexts, themes, and main methodologies used in literature were also acknowledged. Concisely, this current study underprops certain gaps identified in the literature on stakeholder management and entrepreneurship and provides new directions for future research with regards to the TCCM framework. However, the limitations of the Scopus database from which the articles for the review were sourced may have implications for the results. Also, the filtering process adopted may have omitted some relevant studies as only selected articles published in ABDC rated academic journals were included in this review.

References

Agrawal A and Hockerts K (2021) Impact investing: Review and research agenda. *Journal of Small Business and Entrepreneurship 33*(2): 153–181.

Almansour M (2022) Business incubators and entrepreneurial training: Leveraging technological innovations and digital marketing. *IEEE Transactions on Engineering Management, 99*: 1–12.

Alonso AD, Sakellarios N, Alexander N and O'Brien S (2018) Corporate social responsibility in a burgeoning industry: A stakeholder analysis. *Journal of Strategy and Management 11*(1): 112–130. https://doi.org/10.1007/s10551-022-05260-5

Altinay L, Sigala M and Waligo V (2016) Social value creation through tourism enterprise. *Tourism Management 54*: 404–417.

Alvarez SA, Busenitz LW (2001) The entrepreneurship of resource-based theory. *Journal of Management 27*(6): 755–775. https://doi.org/10.1177/014920630102700609

Amankwah-Amoah J, Danso A and Adomako S (2019) Entrepreneurial orientation, environmental sustainability and new venture performance: Does stakeholder integration matter? *Business Strategy and the Environment 28*(1): 79–87.

Anbarasan P and Sushil P (2018) Stakeholder engagement in sustainable enterprise: Evolving a conceptual framework, and a case study of ITC. *Business Strategy and the Environment 27*(3): 282–299.

Audretsch DB, Bozeman BC, Kathryn L., Feldman M, Link AN, Siegel DS, Stephan P, Tassey G and Wessner C (2002) The economics of science and technology. *The Journal of Technology Transfer 27*(2):157. https://doi.org/10.1023/A:1014382532639

Australian Business Deans Council (2019). *ABDC journal quality list 2019*. https://abdc.edu.au/abdc-journal-quality-list/ (accessed on February 5, 2023).

Bailey RC and Lumpkin GT (2023) Enacting positive social change: A civic wealth creation stakeholder engagement framework. *Entrepreneurship: Theory and Practice 47*(1): 66–90.

Bischoff K, Volkmann CK and Audretsch DB (2018) Stakeholder collaboration in entrepreneurship education: An analysis of the entrepreneurial ecosystems of European higher educational institutions. *Journal of Technology Transfer 43*(1): 20–46.

Bobadilla N, Goransson M and Pichault F (2019) Urban entrepreneurship through art-based interventions: Unveiling a translation process. *Entrepreneurship and Regional Development 31*(5–6): 378–399.

Bresciani S, Thrassou A, and Vrontis D (2013). Change through innovation in family businesses: Evidence from an Italian sample. *World Review of Entrepreneurship, Management and Sustainable Development 9*: 195. https://doi.org/10.1504/WREMSD.2013.052359

Bruneel J, Moray N, Stevens R and Fassin Y (2016) Balancing competing logics in for-profit social enterprises: A need for hybrid governance. *Journal of Social Entrepreneurship 7*(3): 263–288

Camilleri MA (2019) The SMEs' technology acceptance of digital media for stakeholder engagement. *Journal of Small Business and Enterprise Development 26*(4): 504–521.

Cavazos DE, Patel P and Wales W (2012) Mitigating environmental effects on new venture growth: The critical role of stakeholder integration across buyer and supplier groups. *Journal of Business Research 65*(9): 1243–1250.

Chen J and Liu L (2020) Customer participation, and green product innovation in SMEs: The mediating role of opportunity recognition and exploitation. *Journal of Business Research 119*: 151–162.

Creswell JW. (1998). *Qualitative inquiry and research design: Choosing among five traditions*. Thousand Oaks, CA: Sage.

Diochon M and Anderson AR (2011) Ambivalence and ambiguity in social enterprise; narratives about values in reconciling purpose and practices. *International Entrepreneurship and Management Journal 7*(1): 93–109. https://doi.org/10.1007/s11365-010-0161-0.hdl:10059/613

Dorhetso SN, Boakye LY and Welbeck DNO (2023) Innovation performance and efficiency of research and development intensity as a proportion of GDP: A bibliometric review. In *Sustainable education and development–Sustainable industrialization and innovation*. ARCA 2022. Springer. https://doi.org/10.1007/978-3-031-25998-2_20

England LE (2020) Managing making and makers in open-access craft studios: The case of Turning Earth. *Social Enterprise Journal 16*(2): 159–177.

Fakhar Manesh M, Pellegrini MM, Marzi G and Dabic M (2020) Knowledge management in the fourth industrial revolution: Mapping the literature and scoping future avenues. *IEEE Transactions on Engineering Management*. https://doi.org/10.1109/TEM.2019.2963489

Fassin Y and Drover W (2017) Ethics in entrepreneurial finance: Exploring problems in venture partner entry and exit. *Journal of Business Ethics 140*(4): 649–672.

Ferraris A, Belyaeva Z and Bresciani S (2020) The role of universities in the Smart City innovation: Multistakeholder integration and engagement perspectives. *Journal of Business Research 119*: 163–171.

Fetscherin M (2010) The determinants and measurement of a country brand: The country brand strength index. *International Marketing Review 27*(4):466–479.

Fischer D, Brettel M and Mauer R (2020) The three dimensions of sustainability: A delicate balancing act for entrepreneurs made more complex by stakeholder expectations. *Journal of Business Ethics 163*(1): 87–106.

Gaddefors J, Anderson AR (2017) Entrepreneursheep and context: When entrepreneurship is greater than entrepreneurs. *International Journal of Entrepreneurial Behavior & Research 23*(2):267–278. https://doi.org/10.1108/IJEBR-01-2016-0040

García-Sánchez E, García-Morales VJ and Martín-Rojas R (2018) Analysis of the influence of the environment, stakeholder integration capability, absorptive capacity, and technological skills on organizational performance through corporate entrepreneurship. *International Entrepreneurship and Management Journal 14*(2): 345–377.

Harrison JS, Bosse DA, and Phillips RA (2010) Managing for stakeholders, stakeholder utility functions, and competitive advantage. *Strategic Management Journal 31*: 58–74. https://doi.org/10.1002/smj.801

Hassan SM, Rahman Z and Paul J (2022) Consumer ethics: A review and research agenda. *Psychology & Marketing 39*(1): 111–130.

Hiatt SR, Carlos WC and Sine WD (2018) Manu Militari: The institutional contingencies of stakeholder relationships on entrepreneurial performance. *Organization Science 29*(4): 633–652.

Hiebl MRW and Pielsticker DI (2023) Automation, organizational ambidexterity and the stability of employee relations: New tensions arising between corporate entrepreneurship, innovation management and stakeholder management. *Journal of Technology Transfer. Springer*, *48*(6): 1978–2006.

Hulland J and Houston MB (2020). Why systematic review papers and meta-analyses matter: an introduction to the special issue on generalizations in marketing. *Journal of the Academy of Marketing Science 48*, 351–359. https://doi.org/10.1007/s11747- 020-00721-7

Jones B and Iredale N (2009) Entrepreneurship education and Web 2.0. *Journal of Research in Marketing and Entrepreneurship 11*(1): 66–77.

Kamuhuza W, Wu J, Lodorfos G, McClelland Z and Rodgers H (2022) The tripartite partnership between female entrepreneurs, banks and governments in female entrepreneurship-development: A case study of Zambia. *International Journal of Organizational Analysis 30*(2): 606–626.

Kansheba JMP, Marobhe MI and Wald AE (2022). Cushioning the Covid-19 economic consequences on entrepreneurial ecosystems: The role of stakeholders' engagement, collaboration, and support. *Journal of African Business.* https://doi.org/10.1080/15228916.2022.2078933

Khojastehpour M and Shams SMR (2020) Addressing the complexity of stakeholder management in international ecological setting: A CSR approach. *Journal of Business Research 119*: 302–309.

Kouri R and Clarke A (2014) Framing 'Green Jobs' discourse: Analysis of popular usage. *Sustainable Development 22*(4): 217–230.

Laplume A, Walker, K, Zhang, Z and Yu, X (2021) Incumbent stakeholder management performance and new entry. *Journal of Business Ethics 174*(3): 629–644.

Leonidou E, Christofi M, Vrontis D and Thrassou A (2020) An integrative framework of stakeholder engagement for innovation management and entrepreneurship development. *Journal of Business Research 119*: 245–258.

Lorenzo-Afable D, Lips-Wiersma M and Singh S (2020) 'Social' value creation as care: The perspective of beneficiaries in social entrepreneurship. *Social Enterprise Journal 16*(3): 339–360.

Lu IRR, Heslop LA, Thomas DR and Kwan E (2016) An examination of the status and evolution of country image research, *International Marketing Review 33*(6): 825–850.

Matlay H (2009) Entrepreneurship education in the UK: A critical analysis of stakeholder involvement and expectations. *Journal of Small Business and Enterprise Development 16*(2): 355–368.

Matlay H (2011) The influence of stakeholders on developing enterprising graduates in UK HEIs. *International Journal of Entrepreneurial Behaviour and Research 17*(2): 166–182.

Maxwell AL and Lévesque M (2014). Trustworthiness: A critical ingredient for entrepreneurs seeking investors. *Entrepreneurship Theory and Practice 38*(5), 1057–1080.

Meyer and Gauthier (2013) Navigating challenging fitness landscapes: Social entrepreneurship and the competing dimensions of sustainability. *Journal of Social Entrepreneurship 4*(1): 23–39.

Meyer CR, Cohen DG and Gauthier J (2020) Social entrepreneurship, stakeholder management, and the multiple fitness elements of sustainability: Where cash is no longer king. *Journal of Small Business and Entrepreneurship 32*(5): 431–455.

Mishra R, Singh RK and Koles B (2021). Consumer decision-making in omnichannel retailing: Literature review and future research agenda. *International Journal of Consumer Studies 45*(2), 147–174. https://doi.org/10.1111/ijcs.12617

Mzembe AN, Novakovic Y, Melissen F and Kamanga G (2019) Institutional bricolage as an antecedent of social value creation in a developing country's tourism and hospitality industry. *Corporate Social Responsibility and Environmental Management 26*(4): 997–1008.

Nair SR (2020) The link between women entrepreneurship, innovation and stakeholder engagement: A review. *Journal of Business Research 119*: 283–290.

Paul J and Benito GRG (2018) A review of research on outward foreign direct investment from emerging countries, including China: What do we know, how do we know and where should we be heading. *Asia Pacific Business Review 24*(1):90–115.

Paul J, Lim WM, O'Cass A, Hao AW and Bresciani S (2021) Scientific procedures and rationales for systematic literature reviews (SPAR-4-SLR). *International Journal of Consumer Studies 45*(45):1–16. https://doi.org/10.1111/ijcs.12695

Petrolo D, Fakhar Manesh M, Pellegrini MM and Flamini G (2022) Agri-food entrepreneurship. Harvesting, growing and reseeding the orchard through a bibliometric study. *British Food Journal 124*(7): 2396–2426.

Pollack JM, Barr S and Hanson S (2017) New venture creation as establishing stakeholder relationships: A trust-based perspective. *Journal of Business Venturing Insights 7*, 15–20. https://doi.org/10.1016/j.jbvi.2016.12.003

Qi B, Tian M and Wu Y (2023) The micromechanism of "co-beneficial" cooperation between government and business in the context of Chinese transition economy: The case of "Daqing–Geely mode". *Chinese Management Studies 17*(2): 290–319.

Retolaza JL, Ruiz M and San-Jose L (2009) CSR in business start-ups: An application method for stakeholder engagement. *Corporate Social Responsibility and Environmental Management 16*(6): 324–336.

Riad Shams SM, Vrontis D, Chaudhuri R, Chavan G and Czinkota MR (2020) Stakeholder engagement for innovation management and entrepreneurial development: A meta-analysis. *Journal of Business Research 119*: 67–86.

Sansone G, Santalucia F, Viglialoro D and Landoni P (2023) Blockchain for social good and stakeholder engagement: Evidence from a case study. In *Corporate Social Responsibility and Environmental Management.* John Wiley & Sons, Inc.

Sefiani Y, Davies BJ, Bown R and Kite N (2018) Performance of SMEs in tangier: The Interface of networking and wasta. *EuroMed Journal of Business 13*: 20–43. https://doi.org/10.1108/EMJB-06-2016-0016

Smith L and Woods C (2015) Stakeholder engagement in the social entrepreneurship process: Identity, governance and legitimacy. *Journal of Social Entrepreneurship 6*(2): 186–217.

Soetanto DP and van Geenhuizen M (2007) Technology incubators and knowledge networks: A rough set approach in comparative project analysis. *Environment and Planning B: Planning and Design 34*(6): 1011–1029.

Vandekerckhove W, & Dentchev NA (2005). A network perspective on stakeholder management: Facilitating entrepreneurs in the discovery of opportunities. *Journal of Business Ethics 60*(3): 221–232.

Vealey KP and Gerding JM (2016) Rhetorical work in crowd-based entrepreneurship: Lessons learned from teaching crowdfunding as an emerging site of professional and technical communication. *IEEE Transactions on Professional Communication 59*(4): 407–427.

von Blottnitz H (2006) Promoting active learning in sustainable development: Experiences from a 4th year chemical engineering course. *Journal of Cleaner Production 14*(9–11): 916–923.

Wagner M, Schaltegger S, Hansen EG and Fichter K (2021) University-linked programmes for sustainable entrepreneurship and regional development: How and with what impact? *Small Business Economics 56*(3): 1141–1158.

12 Stakeholder Management Challenges and the Complexities of Promoting Sustainable Entrepreneurship in Africa

Rabake Nana, Kweku Adams and Rexford Attah-Boakye

Introduction

In recent years, stakeholder management has gained significant importance as a field of study and practice, focusing on the intricate connections between organizations and the individuals and groups who possess the ability to greatly influence their actions or be influenced by them. Although there has been notable progress in stakeholder management literature, our understanding of the concept remains relatively limited, particularly in African contexts. Despite being recognised as the next frontier for development and growth, with some of the world's fastest-growing economies located on the continent, Africa still lacks comprehensive research on stakeholder management. Additionally, evidence indicates that entrepreneurship plays a vital role in propelling economic growth in African countries. Despite significant progress in stakeholder management, African countries are recognized as the next frontier for growth and development. However, there is still a limited understanding of the phenomenon as the continent is experiencing remarkable economic growth (Brown & Huang, 2020). According to Adusei (2016), entrepreneurship also plays a key role in spurring economic growth in African nations.

Due to weak institutional environments, African countries face significant challenges in managing stakeholder relationships (Ahsan, 2020; Adomako et al., 2021). As a result of weak institutional environments, entrepreneurs face complex stakeholder management landscapes. In such a context, stakeholder management becomes even more important. As part of stakeholder management in Africa, a wide range of stakeholders participate, including employees, local communities, government officials, politicians, chiefs, religious leaders, customers, nongovernmental/nonprofit organisations, civil society organizations, and suppliers. Entrepreneurship or firm actions can impact or be influenced by each stakeholder (Leonidou et al., 2020). Understanding how stakeholders contribute to the growth of entrepreneurial ventures in Africa is imperative to sustainable and responsible business practices.

Therefore, this chapter aims to provide unique insights that can spur future research into stakeholder management in the complex and heterogeneous African context. Case studies discussion is employed in this chapter to provide

DOI: 10.4324/9781003256014-15

an in-depth understanding of the relationship between stakeholders and entrepreneurship in Africa. It will address questions related to "How do entrepreneurial firms overcome challenges associated with weak institutional environments" in Africa? And "Which stakeholders are critical for developing and growing entrepreneurial firms?" Africa is widely regarded as the next frontier for development and growth and is home to some of the world's fastest-growing economies (Leonidou et al., 2020). The stakeholder management literature has made considerable progress, but its understanding remains relatively limited in the African context. Furthermore, evidence indicates that entrepreneurship plays a crucial role in driving economic growth in African countries (Adusei, 2016). This chapter, therefore, addresses the following questions: What pressures do entrepreneurial firms in Africa experience from various stakeholders when operating in an institutionally weak framework? How do they effectively manage their network of stakeholders to maximize outcomes for the SMEs as well as the various stakeholders?

Literature review

Entrepreneurship from a network perspective

Stakeholders' groups and individuals in this chapter can be defined as those who can influence a firm's strategic outcomes (Freeman, 2010). The stakeholder concept can be rendered meaningless (Donaldson & Preston, 1995; Phillips, 2003), as it can be interpreted in such a broad way. As a result, several studies have taken a network perspective on stakeholder management (Rowley, 1997). Thus, the classical hub model, which emphasizes dyadic stakeholder relationships and the firm as a nexus of contracts, has been abandoned (Vandekerckhove & Dentchev, 2005). Rowley (1997) pioneered the use of social network analysis in the development of stakeholder theory influence beyond the dyadic relationships between an organisation and its stakeholders. Because stakeholder interactions are interdependent, there is a need to be incorporated into the theory to reflect how stakeholders interact not just with the firm but also with one another. Freedman and Evan originally argued for this in their statement that stakeholder relationships are based on multilateral agreements between stakeholders. As a result, firms do not simply respond to each stakeholder individually; they respond to the interactions between multiple stakeholders' influences Rowley (1997). It represented a shift in perspective from the hub-model that Freedman presented initially.

The focal organisation goes further, claiming it is not only the central point of its stakeholders but also all the other focal points in the relevant social system in which it operates (Rowley, 1997). This means that stakeholders have second-order shareholders as well, and integrating these third-order shareholders more completely represents the value chain of entrepreneurship (Freeman & Liedtka, 1997). In our view, such a complex representation of the entrepreneurial environment cannot be achieved due to the "need for independence" and "locus of control" personal qualities. A person who places a lot of importance on achievement might also question the relevance of second-order stakeholders in terms of recognition on a personal or professional level. entrepreneurship will no longer serve as an interconnecting hub for all stakeholders in a graphical representation of a firm's stakeholder network. As a result, instead of envisioning entrepreneurship as the focal organisation, the "stakeholder environment" depicts both direct and indirect stakeholders.

The different network characteristics of entrepreneurship

Using network theory, Rowley (1997) examined how stakeholder relationships influence an entrepreneur's behaviour in a stakeholder environment. Based on network characteristics, ***density and centrality***, Rowley suggested that strategies to manage direct and indirect entrepreneurial stakeholders should be based on the stakeholder's environment. An environment's interconnectedness can be measured by network density, which is the proportion of ties linking actors in the network. This is calculated by multiplying the number of relationships in the network by the number of potential ties of every network member connected to every other member of the network (Rowley, 1997). ***A higher density*** results in more efficient communication across the network and the production of shared behavioural expectations. In this sense, the entrepreneurial "need for independence" characteristic would not lead to communicative isolation from other stakeholders. Network centrality refers to an individual stakeholder actor's power in a network deriving from their position relative to others.

Rowley (1997) defines three types of centralities. The first definition is the ***degree of centrality*** of an actor in a network. The second definition is the degree of centrality of an actor in a network based on the ***number of ties*** it has with other actors in the network. In addition, ***betweenness centrality*** describes the degree to which the focal actor acts as an intermediary between other actors. Entrepreneurs that are positioned as the focal point of a network are more likely to resist stakeholder pressures due to their centrality. Despite the notion that entrepreneurs should pursue high centrality, this does not imply that entrepreneurs should be solely responsible or dominant. A network that has a ***lower density*** and a higher centrality is more similar to Freeman's hub model. This would make an ideal situation for an entrepreneur who would have the power to resist stakeholder influences. Instructively, we argue, however, that a network environment with optimal density and high centrality would most benefit entrepreneurs given the problematic implications of that model, such as conflicting interests and unrealistic entrepreneurial responsibilities. Figure 12.1 presents the entrepreneurial network characteristics and how the degree of density could influence the approach needed to influence and manage them.

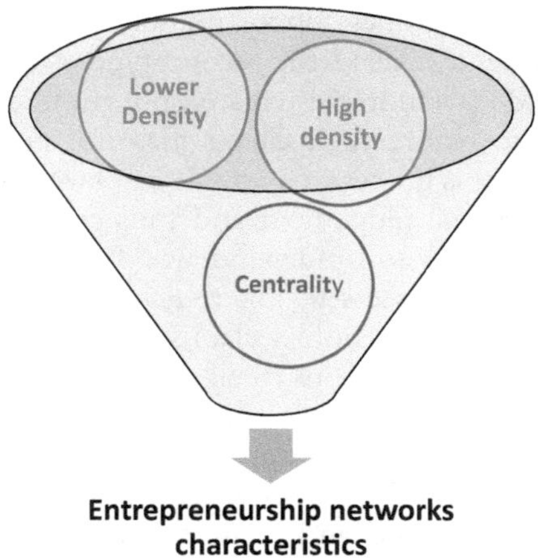

Figure 12.1 Entrepreneurship networks characteristics.

The stakeholder communication structure in a high-density network is efficient, and the behavioural expectations are similar. Having a high centrality within a network allows a firm to influence information flows, giving it a prominent position. A focal organization can influence the creation of expectations, and stakeholders can coordinate their efforts to monitor and punish it (Rowley, 1997, p. 901). While this section sought to explain how entrepreneurs can identify their constituencies by using a network-based approach, the next section examines the prospects for developing networks.

Prospects for network building: Opportunities discovery perspectives

Entrepreneurs' personal limitations in consulting and analysing information in their environments constrain their ability to discover opportunities. In addition, it is argued that entrepreneurs identify with a hub model of their stakeholder environments based on their personal characteristics and how they perceive their relationships with the environment (Vandekerckhove & Dentchev, 2005). It is important, however, to understand how entrepreneurs interact with their stakeholder environment, which plays an important role in finding opportunities. Consequently, we argue that since the network perspective is more realistic than the hub model, it is possible to discover new business opportunities by changing one's stakeholder relationships through network engineering. To find "network opportunities," entrepreneurs must first determine in what specific ways stakeholder relationships should be altered; or what changes need to be made to stakeholder relationships. When new relationships are formed, network opportunities emerge, because these increase the network density.

Nevertheless, Hart and Sharma (2004) suggest that closer involvement is intended to provide a new perspective on stakeholders' activities, resulting in the identification of new business opportunities. Engaging stakeholders in a multistakeholder dialogue leads to the second type of entrepreneurial opportunity. Multistakeholder roundtables create opportunities because they allow diverse stakeholders to realize their claims may not be compatible so as to adjust them. Although this process may result in a favourable outcome, it cannot be based on individual judgement and thus contradicts entrepreneurial notions of locus of control and independence. The purpose is to stimulate creative learning by giving access to different impressions of the interests at play. This process can help stakeholder claims become more stable and viable if it reduces the cognitive limitations of all parties and recasts interpretations of information signals into mutually reinforcing expectations, engagements, and considerations. A second type of opportunity can be identified more effectively if inclusion is enhanced in this sense. To create opportunities for collaborative stakeholder interactions and feasible joint behavioural expectations, stakeholders' selection for inclusion in multistakeholder dialogues cannot be determined by their salience (Mitchell et al., 1997). Rather, creative learning will be instigated by selecting stakeholders with incompatible or unfeasible claims on the firm.

Discussion

Managing stakeholders' legitimate interest

For stakeholder management to serve the narrower interests of legitimate stakeholders, the broad concept of stakeholder management must be further defined (Mitchell, Agle, and Wood, 1997). In such cases, influencing groups with power over the firm may disrupt operations so severely that legitimate claims cannot be met, and new start-ups may not survive (Mitchell et al., 1997). This conceptualisation includes stakeholders most closely associated with the company's operations and objectives considering our interest in competitive performance. Our discussion focuses on stakeholders with interests that are likely to be of high salience practically to firms. Consequently, stakeholders whose objectives are unrelated to the firm's operations (Hillman & Keim, 2001) has not been considered in our discussion. A firm is seen as being at the centre of a complex system of stakeholders (Barringer & Harrison, 2000; Rowley, 1997) that exchanges goods and services, information, technology, talent, influence, money, and other resources. Thus, the stakeholder theory developed by Freeman and subsequent authors (Phillips, 2003) is based on the idea that the market is efficient, while the welfare of the firm takes precedence. It is unlikely that for-profit small businesses that serve stakeholder groups purely for altruistic purposes will prosper or even survive in an efficient market. Stakeholder theory holds that firms maximise their welfare by meeting the needs of their most important stakeholders in a win-win manner (Harrison & St. John, 1996).

A major characteristic of stakeholder management is that firms distribute both value and decision-making authority among a broad spectrum of their primary stakeholders (Freeman et al., 2007). A firm's interest in legitimate stakeholders is always considered at least moderately important (Jones et al., 2007). Hence, entrepreneurs may disregard their standards for handling stakeholders "whenever it is economically advantageous to do so" (Jones et al., 2007) or they may violate those standards whenever it is economically advantageous to do so. As we describe in this chapter, firms tend to treat stakeholders consistently. This may be due to (1) a belief that it is the best way to treat stakeholders, (2) an economic advantage, or (3) a combination of the two. In this chapter, we do not intend to suggest that motivational differences are trivial; however, we intend to examine the possible outcomes of specific types of behaviours rather than their motivations.

As a result, we assume that companies managing stakeholders have fairly accurate information about the minimum requirements for stakeholder participation. Entrepreneurs that know their services are unique to the industry can provide more accurate information, as in our example of a company that provides benefits that are not typically provided. The stakeholder management approach is expected to be more favourable, however, in relation to understanding stakeholder utility functions, as we discuss in a later section. A stakeholder's minimum requirements can then be better understood with this information. In contrast to an arms-length stakeholder management approach, this approach allows for a better understanding of stakeholder needs. A stakeholder is considered an interchangeable economic actor from an arms-length perspective, and power is the primary criterion for determining influence over firm decisions as well as value distribution. Therefore, stakeholder participation is only allowed if it is clearly in the best interests of the firm, and value is allocated following negotiations in which each stakeholder tries to protect their interest (Table 12.1).

Table 12.1 Stakeholder Dynamics in African Industries

Authors	*Industries*	*Illustrations*
Mair, J., & Marti, I. (2006). Social entrepreneurship research: A source of explanation, prediction, and delight	Stakeholder management in agribusiness	The agricultural sector involves various stakeholders, including farmers, suppliers, distributors, consumers, government agencies, and local communities. Effective stakeholder engagement is crucial for addressing the diverse interests and needs of these stakeholders. For example, in Ghana, the Cocoa Abrabopa Association works closely with cocoa farmers, empowering them through training programs, access to finance, and market linkages

(*Continued*)

Table 12.1 (Continued)

Authors	*Industries*	*Illustrations*
Abe, O. (2022). Between control and confrontation: The pitfalls and potential of corporate-community participatory development in Africa's energy and extractive industries	Stakeholder management in the extractive industries	Stakeholders in the extractive industries encompass local communities, indigenous groups, environmental activists, government agencies, and investors. In South Africa, the mining company Anglo American has implemented stakeholder engagement initiatives to address social and environmental issues. Through collaboration with local communities and environmental organizations, the company has established programs for community development, environmental conservation, and sustainable mining practices.
Ajide, F. M. (2020). Financial inclusion in Africa: Does it promote entrepreneurship?	Stakeholder management in the financial sector	The financial sector plays a crucial role in supporting entrepreneurial growth and economic development in Africa. Stakeholders in this sector include banks, microfinance institutions, investors, regulators, and entrepreneurs themselves. In Kenya, the mobile banking platform M-Pesa has revolutionized financial services, providing access to banking services for the unbanked population. By engaging with regulators, telecom companies, and customers, M-Pesa has successfully built trust and created financial inclusion opportunities for millions of people.
Maseno, M., & Wanyoike, C. (2022). Social entrepreneurship as mechanisms for social transformation and social impact in East Africa an exploratory case study perspective	Stakeholder engagement in social enterprises	Social enterprises are emerging as transformative ventures in Africa, combining social impact with sustainable business models. These enterprises operate across sectors such as education, healthcare, and renewable energy, with stakeholders including beneficiaries, investors, government agencies, and nonprofit organizations. For instance, Bridge International Academies, a social enterprise operating in several African countries, engages with local communities, parents, and governments to provide affordable and quality education.

Influence of nonmarket strategies on stakeholders management of entrepreneurial SMEs

The literature has shown that nonmarket strategies (NMS) have a significant impact on both developed and developing market contexts (Adomako et al., 2023; Lawton, McGuire et al., 2013; Rodgers et al., 2019). Although large firms and multinational companies have been analysed, SMEs have received less attention. A growing body of research has revealed that firms use strategies and relationships that go beyond conventional competitive strategies, such as lobbying and other forms of cooperative relationship-building with institutional actors (Rodgers et al., 2019). There has been an increase in research on NMS in emerging markets in recent years (Liedong et al., 2020). According to Rajwani and Liedong, relational strategies can be used to deal effectively with shifting political environments in emerging market economies, and we need to do more studies focusing on development.

Nevertheless, informal institutions can also have an impact on business activity in emerging market contexts alongside formal institutions. According to North (2005), formal institutions consist of written or officially accepted rules and regulations which guide broader society. The informal institutions, on the other hand, encompass traditions, customs, social norms, culture, and unwritten codes of conduct. The norms and values that are passed on from generation to generation may be resistant to change (Bruton et al., 2008). Developing networks and relational strategies is essential for firms in emerging market contexts where informal institutions are more prevalent and dominant. A firm's nonmarket strategies are used to fill institutional voids in emerging markets where institutions are unstable, underdeveloped, or lacking (Marquis & Raynard, 2015).

In the context of institutional constraints, as described previously, large firms have employed strategies such as CPA and/or CSR as a way to navigate them (Rodgers et al., 2019). However, to date, relatively little is known about how resource-constrained SMEs respond to predatory behaviour by implementing NMS (Marquis & Raynard, 2015; Wickert, 2016). SMEs are often unable to engage in mechanisms like lobbying, which are commonly used by multinational corporations. Several factors, including the liabilities of their "newness" and their "smallness," contribute to their lack of capacity to build NMS resources, which stem from the wider set of issues that typically affect SMEs. Aside from this, SMEs are often resource-deprived (Spence, 2007), which can severely hamper the development of NMS. To influence policymakers, large firms possess the necessary nonmarket capabilities and infrastructure, but they lack the necessary nonmarket capabilities and infrastructure. In addition, they lack market power and are often dependent on large firms' supply bases to survive (Street & Cameron, 2007).

Although SMEs are subject to the foregoing constraints, they are still regarded as economic engines in emerging markets (Filatotchev et al., 2009).

Although they make up over 96 percent of private firms in emerging markets, they are not exempt from exchanges with state actors and institutions despite their "smallness." In emerging markets, few studies focus on the direct exchange of SMEs and states. A few studies discuss nonmarket political strategies rather than social strategies. As an example, Soundararajan, Jamali, et al. (2018) examined small garment exporters in India and found that these exporters engaged in mundane evasion work to circumvent and evade the demands for improved working conditions imposed by the state and private sectors. A similar study by Jamali, Lund-Thomsen, and Jeppesen (2017) shows SMEs in India selectively couple with institutional demands and decouple from them. Studies like these suggest that the relationship between SMEs and states in emerging markets is more micro than macro since informal social networks and everyday practices play a larger role. Currently, however, most studies (Jamali et al., 2017; Pastrana & Sriramesh, 2014) focus primarily on CSR practices of small and medium-sized businesses (SMEs) rather than predatory behaviour by state actors and how SMEs respond to it through the establishment of nonprofit management systems.

Understanding the dynamics of managing stakeholder relationships in African contexts

Africa is a diverse continent with a rich tapestry of cultural traditions and practices. These cultural influences significantly impact stakeholder dynamics and require organisations to adapt their approaches accordingly. For example, in many African societies, communal values and collective decision-making are highly valued (Sambala et al., 2020). This places importance on engaging with community leaders, chiefs, and elders as key stakeholders in business ventures. Failure to recognise and respect these cultural norms may result in strained relationships and hinder business success. Conversely, organizations that embrace and align with cultural values can build strong partnerships, gain social acceptance, and leverage local knowledge and networks. Understanding cultural nuances and adapting stakeholder management strategies accordingly can enhance trust and facilitate collaboration with diverse stakeholders.

Social structures and power dynamics play a significant role in stakeholder management in Africa. Traditional hierarchies, social inequalities, and power imbalances can influence stakeholder interactions. For instance, in some African countries, traditional authorities wield considerable influence and are important stakeholders in decision-making processes. Engaging with chiefs, religious leaders, and community elders becomes crucial for navigating social structures and gaining legitimacy (Leonidou et al., 2020). Furthermore, social inequalities and disparities may require organizations to consider inclusive approaches that address the needs of marginalized groups.

The institutional context in Africa significantly influences stakeholder management practices. Weak institutional environments, characterised by limited regulatory frameworks, corruption, and bureaucratic hurdles, pose challenges for organisations (Adams et al., 2019; Adeleye et al., 2020). However, they also create opportunities for entrepreneurial solutions and innovative stakeholder engagement approaches. Organisations operating in such contexts may need to navigate complex regulatory landscapes, build relationships with government officials, and establish collaborative partnerships with civil society organizations. By proactively engaging with institutions and shaping the institutional environment, organizations can drive positive change and foster an enabling environment for stakeholder management.

Implications

Institutional constraints and weak governance in the African context

One of the primary challenges in stakeholder management in Africa is the presence of institutional constraints and weak governance. Weak regulatory frameworks, corruption, and bureaucratic inefficiencies can hinder effective stakeholder engagement and create barriers for organisations seeking to establish transparent and accountable relationships. To address this challenge, it is crucial to advocate for stronger governance mechanisms, promote transparency and accountability, and foster collaborations between the public and private sectors. SMEs can work towards building partnerships with local governments, civil society organisations, and international institutions to strengthen institutional frameworks and create an enabling environment for stakeholder engagement (Ahsan, 2020; Adomako et al., 2021).

Africa is a diverse continent with a wide range of cultural, social, and linguistic dynamics. Managing stakeholders in such diverse contexts requires sensitivity and understanding of the local cultures, norms, and values. Different stakeholders may have varying expectations, priorities, and ways of engagement. Organisations need to adopt context-specific approaches and tailor their stakeholder management strategies accordingly. This may involve engaging community leaders, religious institutions, and cultural influencers to bridge cultural gaps and foster meaningful relationships.

Conclusion

The chapter adopts an interdisciplinary approach, drawing on theories and concepts from stakeholder theory, entrepreneurship, management, and African studies. By including diverse examples, empirical evidence, and theoretical frameworks, the chapter presents a holistic understanding of stakeholder management dynamics in the African context. In addition, this chapter not only contributes to the existing body of knowledge on stakeholder management but also has practical implications for entrepreneurs, policymakers, and organizations operating in Africa. As we conclude this chapter, it is important to acknowledge that stakeholder management is an ongoing process, requiring continuous learning, adaptation, and engagement with stakeholders.

The African context is dynamic and evolving, presenting both opportunities and challenges for stakeholder management. Therefore, further research and exploration of stakeholder management in Africa in relation to entrepreneurship are needed to deepen our understanding and inform future practices.

References

Abe, O. (2022). Between control and confrontation: The pitfalls and potential of corporate-community participatory development in Africa's energy and extractive industries. *The Extractive Industries and Society, 11*, 101095.

Adams, D., Ullah, S., Akhtar, P., Adams, K., & Saidi, S. (2019). The role of country-level institutional factors in escaping the natural resource curse: Insights from Ghana. *Resources Policy, 61*, 433–440.

Adeleye, I., Luiz, J., Muthuri, J., & Amaeshi, K. (2020). Business ethics in Africa: The role of institutional context, social relevance, and development challenges. *Journal of Business Ethics, 161*, 717–729.

Adomako, S., Abdelgawad, S. G., Ahsan, M., Amankwah-Amoah, J., & Liedong, T. A. (2023). Nonmarket strategy in emerging markets: The link between SMEs' corporate political activity, corporate social responsibility, and firm competitiveness. *Journal of Business Research, 160*, 113767.

Adomako, S., Amankwah-Amoah, J., Danso, A., & Dankwah, G. O. (2021). Chief executive officers' sustainability orientation and firm environmental performance: Networking and resource contingencies. *Business Strategy and the Environment, 30*(4), 2184–2193.

Adusei, M. (2016). Does entrepreneurship promote economic growth in Africa? *African Development Review, 28*(2), 201–214.

Ahsan, M. (2020). Entrepreneurship and ethics in the sharing economy: A critical perspective. *Journal of Business Ethics, 161*(1), 19–33.

Ajide, F. M. (2020). Financial inclusion in Africa: Does it promote entrepreneurship? *Journal of Financial Economic Policy, 12*(4), 687–706.

Barringer, B. R., & Harrison, J. S. (2000). Walking a tightrope: Creating value through interorganisational relationships. *Journal of Management, 26*(3), 367–403.

Brown, J. R., & Huang, J. (2020). All the president's friends: Political access and firm value. *Journal of Financial Economics, 138*(2), 415–431.

Bruton, G. D., Ahlstrom, D., & Obloj, K. (2008). Entrepreneurship in emerging economies: Where are we today and where should the research go in the future. *Entrepreneurship Theory and Practice, 32*(1), 1–14.

Donaldson, T., & Preston, L. E. (1995). The stakeholder theory of the corporation: Concepts, evidence, and implications. *Academy of Management Review, 20*(1), 65–91.

Filatotchev, I., Liu, X., Buck, T., & Wright, M. (2009). The export orientation and export performance of high-technology SMEs in emerging markets: The effects of knowledge transfer by returnee entrepreneurs. *Journal of International Business Studies, 40*, 1005–1021.

Freeman, E., & Liedtka, J. (1997). Stakeholder capitalism and the value chain. *European Management Journal, 15*(3), 286–296.

Freeman, R. E. (2010). *Strategic management: A stakeholder approach.* Cambridge University Press.

Freeman, R. E., Harrison, J. S., & Wicks, A. C. (2007). *Managing for stakeholders: Survival, reputation, and success*. Yale University Press.

Harrison, J. S., & St. John, C. H. (1996). Managing and partnering with external stakeholders. *Academy of Management Perspectives*, *10*(2), 46–60.

Hart, S. L., & Sharma, S. (2004). Engaging fringe stakeholders for competitive imagination. *Academy of Management Perspectives*, *18*(1), 7–18.

Hillman, A. J., & Keim, G. D. (2001). Shareholder value, stakeholder management, and social issues: what's the bottom line? *Strategic Management Journal*, *22*(2), 125–139.

Jamali, D., Lund-Thomsen, P., & Jeppesen, S. (2017). SMEs and CSR in developing countries. *Business & Society*, *56*(1), 11–22.

Jones, T. M., Felps, W., & Bigley, G. A. (2007). Ethical theory and stakeholder-related decisions: The role of stakeholder culture. *Academy of Management Review*, *32*(1), 137–155.

Lawton, T., McGuire, S., & Rajwani, T. (2013). Corporate political activity: A literature review and research agenda. *International Journal of Management Reviews*, *15*(1), 86–105.

Leonidou, E., Christofi, M., Vrontis, D., & Thrassou, A. (2020). An integrative framework of stakeholder engagement for innovation management and entrepreneurship development. *Journal of Business Research*, *119*, 245–258.

Liedong, T. A., Rajwani, T., & Lawton, T. C. (2020). Information and nonmarket strategy: Conceptualizing the interrelationship between big data and corporate political activity. *Technological Forecasting and Social Change*, *157*, 120039.

Mair, J., & Marti, I. (2006). Social entrepreneurship research: A source of explanation, prediction, and delight. *Journal of World Business*, *41*(1), 36–44.

Marquis, C., & Raynard, M. (2015). Institutional strategies in emerging markets. *The Academy of Management Annals*, *9*(1), 291–335.

Maseno, M., & Wanyoike, C. (2022). Social entrepreneurship as mechanisms for social transformation and social impact in East Africa an exploratory case study perspective. *Journal of Social Entrepreneurship*, *13*(1), 92–117.

Mitchell, R. K., Agle, B. R., & Wood, D. J. (1997). Toward a theory of stakeholder identification and salience: Defining the principle of who and what really counts. *Academy of Management Review*, *22*(4), 853–886.

North, D. C. (2005). Institutions and the performance of economies over time. In C. Ménard & M. M. Shirley (Eds.), *Handbook of New Institutional Economics*. Springer.

Pastrana, N. A., & Sriramesh, K. (2014). Corporate social responsibility: Perceptions and practices among SMEs in Colombia. *Public Relations Review*, *40*(1), 14–24.

Phillips, R. (2003). *Stakeholder theory and organizational ethics*. Berrett-Koehler Publishers.

Rodgers, P., Stokes, P., Tarba, S., & Khan, Z. (2019). The role of non-market strategies in establishing legitimacy: The case of service MNEs in emerging economies. *Management International Review*, *59*, 515–540.

Rowley, T. J. (1997). Moving beyond dyadic ties: A network theory of stakeholder influences. *Academy of Management Review*, *22*(4), 887–910.

Sambala, E. Z., Cooper, S., & Manderson, L. (2020). Ubuntu as a framework for ethical decision making in Africa: Responding to epidemics. *Ethics & Behavior*, *30*(1), 1–13.

Soundararajan, V., Jamali, D., & Spence, L. J. (2018). Small business social responsibility: A critical multilevel review, synthesis and research agenda. *International Journal of Management Reviews*, *20*(4), 934–956.
Spence, L. J. (2007). CSR and small business in a European policy context: The five "C" s of CSR and small business research agenda 2007. *Business and Society Review*, *112*(4), 533–552.
Street, C. T., & Cameron, A. F. (2007). External relationships and the small business: A review of small business alliance and network research. *Journal of Small Business Management*, *45*(2), 239–266.
Vandekerckhove, W., & Dentchev, N. A. (2005). A network perspective on stakeholder management: Facilitating entrepreneurs in the discovery of opportunities. *Journal of Business Ethics*, *60*, 221–232.
Wickert, C. (2016). "Political" corporate social responsibility in small- and medium-sized enterprises: A conceptual framework. *Business & Society*, *55*(6), 792–824.

Part III

Stakeholder Management, Strategies and Entrepreneurship in Africa

13 Stakeholder Management Best Practices in Entrepreneurship

George Oppong Appiagyei Ampong, Richard Plange-Rhule, Afia Nyarko Boakye and Kwame Owusu-Ansah Owusu Afram

Introduction

Engaging stakeholders is complex in early-stage ventures because some ventures may encounter legal and other urgent issues (Mitchell et al., 1997; Yiapanas & Thrassou, 2022). For instance, early-stage ventures' operations must address customer issues related to product safety and diversity in the workplace (Berman et al., 1999; Freeman et al., 2020). Some studies have noted that stakeholder interactions have internal, explicit, or implicit characteristics (Aerts et al., 2022). Findings from these studies have consequently demonstrated that stakeholder engagement is complex. Thus, entrepreneurial managers must adopt effective approaches to address stakeholder engagement (Adomako & Tran, 2022; Freeman, 1984; Mitchell et al., 1997).

Although the literature has examined the role of stakeholders in entrepreneurship (Govender & Abratt, 2016; Yamahaki & Frynas, 2016), insights into how stakeholder management/engagement influences new ventures in Africa is limited. This study, thus, proposes a framework to enhance stakeholder management in Africa—the three variants stakeholder management approach. Also, the study emphasizes avenues to support stakeholder management in early-stage ventures in the African context. This was achieved by focusing on the key stakeholder management approach, its optimization, and the main challenges confronting effective stakeholder management among early-stage ventures.

The study posits that stakeholders are key drivers of new venture success. It further demonstrates that the management of early-stage ventures must employ appropriate and effective means to optimize stakeholder management in entrepreneurial ventures. The study reveals that a key challenge faced in stakeholder management is the inability to utilize an effective stakeholder management approach. It reinforces the principle of the stakeholder theory that suggests that stakeholders' interests are crucial since their drive is important for early-stage business growth.

In the subsequent paragraphs, attention is given to conflict complexity and how to understand the complexities of conflict and founder-stakeholder

DOI: 10.4324/9781003256014-17

friction. Also, the relationship between stakeholders and early-stage ventures, stakeholders and the survival of early ventures, stakeholder engagement, and stakeholder management approaches are discussed. Finally, some effective stakeholder management approaches that could improve the survival of new ventures in Africa, as well as the challenges and theoretical and practical contributions of the paper, are highlighted.

Conflict complexities

Engaging stakeholders sometimes leads to conflicts between stakeholders and ventures (Verbeke & Tung, 2013). This conflict may be attributed to value allocation on the part of an early-stage venture due to managerial inexperience and failure to meet the expectations or demands of stakeholders (Bacq & Aguilera, 2022; Harrison et al., 2010). It has been noted that some form of conflict arises when early-stage ventures fail to allow stakeholders to contribute to organizational goals (Harrison & Freeman, 1999; Harrison et al., 2010; Jenson, 2001; Post et al., 2002; Vaitoonkiat & Charoensukmongkol, 2020).

Conflicts can also be triggered by failure to fulfil the needs of stakeholders and the firm. Early-stage ventures face issues of stakeholder disagreements, thus affecting the attainment of organizational goals. Freeman (1984) notes that stakeholders play key roles in achieving an organization's objectives (Bacq & Aguilera, 2022; Mitchell et al., 1997). This disagreement might result in stakeholders turning deaf ears during an organizational crisis, especially for an early-stage firm (Nop et al., 2023; Rust et al., 2022; Svendsen & Laberge, 2005). It must be noted that the opinions of stakeholders and an organization in seeking solutions to challenges may vary.

Understanding complexities of conflict

Several studies have revealed that the failure of early-stage ventures results from the differences in opinion among these ventures and their stakeholders regarding expectations. Organizational strategies that can meet the expectations of different stakeholders, therefore, lead to the success and growth of a business (Pirozzi, 2021; Wu, 2013). It has been noted that a firm's poor managerial skills contribute immensely to the failure of early-stage ventures. For example, in a developing country such as Ghana, the lack of stakeholder management strategies has led to the failure of several projects (Masson et al., 2022; Zhang et al., 2022).

It has been extensively proved that time mismanagement and cost considerations have led to the failure of several projects (Lauesen, 2020; Mugumbate & Kruger, 2021). It is, therefore, prudent for organizations to consider how to effectively manage their stakeholders (Mitchellet al., 1997). This is because ineffective stakeholder management strategies cause project failures (Eyiah-Botwe et al., 2016).

Complexities of founder-stakeholder friction

Founders or managers of early-stage ventures usually encounter misunderstandings in their attempt to satisfy the interests of their stakeholders. This is, however, resolved when a consensus is reached (Berman et al., 1999; Berti & Pitelis 2022). Eventually, consensus building that favors the interest of stakeholders such as competitors, government regulatory agencies, suppliers, customers, managers, and shareholders must always be prioritised as the business grows (Freeman 2004; Verbeke & Tung, 2013). Therefore, founders of early-stage ventures or organizations should strive to achieve their objectives and mission and create value for shareholders and stakeholders (Ontita & Kinyua, 2020; Verbeke & Tung, 2013).

A key strategy for meeting stakeholders' needs is utilizing firm resources (Hillman & Keim, 2001). Further, commitment plays a pivotal role in the misunderstandings encountered by early-stage ventures. This usually stems from stakeholders' varied demands and the associated pressure they exert on available resources (Muller et al., 2022; Verbeke & Tung, 2013). However, stakeholders' interests must be considered during commitment since some decisions taken by a firm may impact the operations of management and stakeholders (Ganson et al., 2022; Hillman & Keim, 2001; Hristov & Appolloni, 2022). The scope of commitment is an enterprise with several stakeholder relationships and communication platforms (Verbeke & Tung, 2013). Globally, corporate citizenship or corporate social performance focuses on the responsibility of organizations to communities (Hillman & Keim, 2001; Vázquez-Maguirre & Benito, 2022).

Stakeholders and early venture firm survival

The absence of stakeholders will render the operations of early-stage ventures unsuccessful. In particular, the failure of early-stage ventures to manage their stakeholders usually leads to unforeseen circumstances (Bal et al., 2013; Louder et al., 2021). In essence, stakeholders define the success or failure of an organization or firm (Bhatt & Sable, 2022; Eyiah-Botwe et al., 2016). In contributing to organizational success, stakeholders fund valuable resources, which creates resource heterogeneity (Verbeke & Tung, 2013). They also position a firm to grow its resources (Adams et al., 2022; Le & Behl, 2022; Verbeke & Tung, 2013). Likewise, they help a firm to design their strategies (Barakat et al., 2022; Wu, 2013) and enable adjustments toward the homogeneity of resources (Adams et al., 2022; Le & Behl, 2022; Verbeke & Tung, 2013). This emphasizes the assertion that the ability of early-stage ventures to manage stakeholder relationships give them a competitive advantage (Berman et al., 1999; Freeman, 1984; Varajão et al., 2022; Verbeke & Tung, 2013).

Stakeholder engagement

An effective stakeholder management approach is associated with the appropriate use of resources (Annesi et al., 2021; Verbeke & Tung, 2013). It can be argued that this approach must focus on stakeholders' life quality and comfort

(Bal et al., 2013; Barakat et al., 2022). Stakeholder management approach must be skewed towards effectiveness before it can be effective. For a stakeholder management approach to be effective, it must meet stakeholders' needs and satisfy them (Eyiah-Botwe et al., 2016; Ghareeb & Sameh, 2022). This approach is effective because it increasingly reflects the interest and character of target stakeholders (Verbeke & Tung, 2013). Hence, the nature of the method adopted by early-stage venture firms determines the level of their effectiveness. For instance, the contingency approach is hypothetically ideal for managing different groups of stakeholders (Donkor et al., 2021). Also, a systematic approach or consideration is ideal for managing broader groups of stakeholders (Harrison et al., 2010; Wu, 2013). Thus, the stakeholder management approach can either be effective or not.

Three variant stakeholder management approach for Africa

In the United Kingdom, relationship management has been identified as a variant of the stakeholder management approach that has been applied in the construction sector (Chinyio & Akintoye, 2008). An interactive stakeholder management approach is useful for addressing stakeholders' needs in education in the United Kingdom, Hong Kong, Kazakhstan, the United States, Vietnam, and Qatar. Multi-stakeholder management approaches or inputs have been effective for the retailers' global supply chain system and equitable access to telehealth and schools (Bridoux & Stoelhorst, 2022; Hughes, 2001). Considering the complexities of stakeholder management in Africa, one approach could focus on the stakeholder. Such an approach will concentrate on the policies and actions that highlight the ethics of stakeholders (Carroll & Buchholtz, 1996; McVea & Freeman, 2005); thus, exploring stakeholders' potential and options for integration is crucial (McVea & Freeman, 2005). The broader guideline is value creation and protection, as explained in the stakeholder theory (Freeman, 1984; Wu, 2013).

Another variant approach of stakeholder management is one based on resources. Resource heterogeneity is a social construct in the domain of stakeholders, and the pressures of its utilization are noteworthy (Verbeke & Tung, 2013). Resource value and benefit for all contexts must be prioritized in decision-making (McVea & Freeman, 2005). The most convincing variant of the stakeholder management approach for early-stage venture founders is one based on the benefits of the organization. However, this approach could be suitable in developed countries (Eyiah-Botwe et al., 2016). The focus of the approach on the benefits of an organization may be over-ambitious but could serve as a sustainable framework for project success (Eyiah-Botwe et al., 2016). In the African context, this approach could positively impact early-stage firms in financial terms (Eyiah-Botwe et al., 2016; Hillman & Keim, 2001).

Moreover, these different stakeholder management approaches have implications for the stakeholder theory focusing on the values and morals of an organization's decisions or choices and who is affected (Ferrero et al., 2014).

Thus, it is about an early-stage enterprise building a relationship between its organization and its stakeholders. Meeting the needs and satisfying the interests of all stakeholders will ensure success for the enterprise (Freeman, 2004). The early-stage start-up's stakeholder theory constitutes the responsibility of an organization to care for its stakeholders. In contrast, the agency theory constitutes the effect of entrepreneurial activities on the people employed in the enterprise. The stakeholders' theory, as described by Freeman, thus poses a challenge to early-stageventures. Since Freeman's theory emphasizes the need to target and engage stakeholders, it becomes challenging for early-stage ventures to identify efficient and appropriate stakeholders without negative externalities.

Optimizing stakeholder management approaches for survival

These stakeholder management approaches are critical for the survival of early start-up firms. For an early-stage venture to survive, it needs to optimize stakeholder development approaches. The stakeholder management approach can be descriptive (Jawahar & McLaughlin, 2001; Yang et al., 2009), normative (Yang et al., 2009) and instrumental (Jones, 1995; Yang et al., 2009). To optimize stakeholder management for the maximum benefit, early-stage ventures should prioritize their operations (Berman et al., 1999; Donaldson & Preston, 1995; Eyiah-Botwe et al., 2016). Resource capitalization should always be approached with a standard approach (Grunwald & Fischer, 2022; Verbeke & Tung, 2013). In effect, the best means of optimizing stakeholder management is to embrace and develop good policies (Eyiah-Botwe et al., 2016).

Resource management on the part of founders of early-stage ventures serves as an appropriate means of optimized stakeholder management. Optimized means of stakeholder management based on relationships include positively utilizing the intrinsic stakeholder commitment model to manage stakeholders (Berman et al., 1999). This enables early venture firms to create optimized stakeholder management by building an effective network of stakeholders that impacts value and decision-making (Harrison et al., 2010; Ruvalcaba et al., 2022).

Further, optimizing stakeholder management based on relationships naturally leads to another management approach based on fulfilling stakeholder interests. Over the years, various banking institutions have implemented measures that ensure the need to focus on stakeholders' interests and interact with them (Hutsaliuk et al., 2020; Ontita & Kinyua, 2020). It is, therefore, possible to have diversified approaches for different stakeholders (Eyiah-Botwe et al., 2016; Parmar et al., 2022). It can be noted that the best means of optimizing stakeholder management is challenging for firms (Eyiah-Botwe et al., 2016). However, early venture founders are confronted by the reality that they cannot meet project delivery targets without engaging their stakeholders (Situmorang & Yen, 2022).

Challenges of implementing an approach

A major issue with stakeholder management is determining the underlying difficulty. It is, therefore, important to understand the stakeholder management approach selected in relation to stakeholders' behavior (Ontita & Kinyua, 2020). A systematic approach to engaging with stakeholders toward sustainability remains a challenge since the approaches used over the years have remained the same (Bal et al., 2013). Moreover, why these changes occur over time is yet to be explained (Vandenbussche, 2018; Verbeke & Tung, 2013). A review of all relevant changes, including the behavior of stakeholders, must be assessed when managing stakeholders. This will help to resolve consistently evolving and changing stakeholder management approaches (Sunita, 2021).

Implications

The study makes an original contribution by proposing stakeholder management strategies and the challenges faced in implementing a responsive stakeholder management approach based on the principles of stakeholder theory. The study notes the importance of stakeholder management approaches and suggests ways to optimize such approaches to ensure the benefit of early-stage ventures. Also, the study recognizes that there is a relationship between the perspectives of stakeholders and firm survival.

The research provides insight into the challenges firms encounter in integrating stakeholders and the different stakeholder management approaches they deploy for the survival of early start-up firms or early-stage ventures. It reveals that early start-ups must take a proactive approach to stakeholder management to ensure their success. It is, therefore, proposed that stakeholder interest and interaction are focused on to ensure the success of new ventures. It was observed that it is ethically right to integrate stakeholders in a firm's activities, even though it is challenging for early-stage ventures. The results of the study demonstrate that the satisfaction of all stakeholders is likely to ensure success.

Conclusion

This chapter considers differing categories of stakeholder management and acknowledges the significance of an approach for early-stage ventures in the developing world. Guided by value creation, value protection, and a review of constantly evolving and changing stakeholder management approaches, the study postulates that effective stakeholder management is applicable to the African context to address the underlying difficulty of stakeholder management. Also, focusing on stakeholders is key to optimizing stakeholder management for the best approaches in Africa. Attention should be given to the three variants of the stakeholder management approach to ensure the effectiveness of stakeholder management in Africa since stakeholder drive is important for early-stage business growth. Adopting this three-variant approach to stakeholder management will establish a consensus between the founder of an early-stage venture and its stakeholders. In this direction, early-stage ventures would thrive due to the harmonious relationship between ventures and stakeholders on key issues to promote the attainment of entrepreneurial goals.

Bibliography

Adams, D., Adams, K., Attah-Boakye, R., Ullah, S., Rodgers, W., and Kimani, D. 2022. Social and environmental practices and corporate financial performance of multinational corporations in emerging markets: Evidence from 20 oil-rich African countries. *Resources Policy*, *78(C)*, p. 102756.

Adomako, S., and Tran, M. D. 2022. Stakeholder management, CSR commitment, corporate social performance: The moderating role of uncertainty in CSR regulation. *Corporate Social Responsibility and Environmental Management*, *29*(5), 1414–1423.

Aerts, G., Cauwelier, K., de Pape, S., Jacobs, S., and Vanhondeghem, S. 2022. An inside-out perspective on stakeholder management in university technology transfer offices. *Technological Forecasting and Social Change*, *175*, pp. 121291.

Annesi, N., Battaglia, M., and Frey, M. (2021). Stakeholder engagement by an Italian water utility company: Insight from participant observation of dialogism. *Utilities Policy*, *72*, pp. 101270.

Bacq, S., and Aguilera, R. V. 2022. Stakeholder governance for responsible innovation: A theory of value creation, appropriation, and distribution. *Journal of Management Studies*, *59*(1), pp. 29–60.

Bal, M., Bryde, D., Fearon, D., and Ochieng, E. 2013. Stakeholder engagement: Achieving sustainability in the construction sector. *Sustainability*, *5*(2), pp. 695–710.

Barakat, S. R., Boaventura, J. M. G., and Gabriel, M. L. 2022. Organizational capabilities and value creation for stakeholders: Evidence from publicly traded companies. *Management Decision*, *60*(8), pp. 2311–2330.

Berman, S. L., Wicks, A. C., Kotha, S., and Jones, T. M. 1999. Does stakeholder orientation matter? The relationship between stakeholder management models and firm financial performance. *Academy of Management Journal*, *42*(5), pp. 488–506.

Berti, M., and Pitelis, C. 2022. Open team production, the new cooperative firm, and hybrid advantage. *Academy of Management Review*, *47*(2), pp. 309–330.

Bhatt, M. K., and Sable, R. 2022. A study on impact of emotional, leadership and managerial competencies on project stakeholder management. *Journal of Positive School Psychology*, *6*(3), pp. 8894–8903.

Bridoux, F., and Stoelhorst, J. W. 2022. Stakeholder theory, strategy, and organization: Past, present, and future. *Strategic Organization*, *20*(4), pp. 797–809.

Carroll, A. B., and Buchholtz, A. K. 1996. *Ethics and stakeholder management*. South-Western.

Chinyio, E. A., and Akintoye, A. 2008. Practical approaches for engaging stakeholders: Findings from the UK. *Construction Management and Economics*, *26*(6), pp. 591–599.

Donaldson, T., and Preston, L. E. 1995. The stakeholder theory of the corporation: Concepts, evidence, and implications. *Academy of Management Review*, *20*(1), pp. 65–91.

Donkor, F., Papadopoulos, T., and Spiegler, V. 2021. The supply chain integration–Supply chain sustainability relationship in the UK and Ghana pharmaceutical industry: A stakeholder and contingency perspective. *Transportation Research Part E: Logistics and Transportation Review*, *155*, pp. 102477.

Eyiah-Botwe, E., Aigbavboa, C. O., and Thwala, D. W. 2016. Stakeholder management: A literature review of historical development and current trends. In *Emerging Trends in Construction Organisational Practices and Project Management Knowledge Area–9th CIDB Postgraduate Conference*, Cape Town (pp. 337–347).

Ferrero, I., Michael Hoffman, W., and McNulty, R. E. 2014. Must Milton Friedman embrace stakeholder theory?. *Business and Society Review*, *119*(1), pp. 37–59.

Freeman, R. E. 1984. *Strategic management: A stakeholder approach*. Pitman.

Freeman, R. E. 2004. A stakeholder theory of the modern corporation. *Ethical Theory and Business*, *7*, pp 55–64.

Freeman, R. E., Phillips, R., and Sisodia, R. 2020. Tensions in stakeholder theory. *Business and Society*, *59*(2), pp. 213–231.

Ganson, B., He, T. L., and Henisz, W. J. 2022. Business and peace: The impact of firm–stakeholder relational strategies on conflict risk. *Academy of Management Review*, *47*(2), pp. 259–281.

Ghareeb, A. M. Z., and Sameh, H. S. H. 2022. The role of stakeholder management in reducing the risks associated with value management in construction projects in Egypt. *Innovative Infrastructure Solutions*, *7*(4), pp. 1–15.

Govender, D., and Abratt, R. 2016. Multiple stakeholder management and corporate reputation in South Africa. *International Studies of Management and Organization*, *46*(4), pp. 235–246.

Grunwald, G., and Fischer, K. 2022. Corporate sustainability crisis: Theoretical framework and stakeholder-oriented typology. *Business and Society Review*, *127*(1), pp. 23–48.

Harrison, J. S., Bosse, D. A., and Phillips, R. A. 2010. Managing for stakeholders, stakeholder utility functions, and competitive advantage. *Strategic Management Journal*, *31*(1), pp. 58–74.

Harrison, J. S., and Freeman, R. E. 1999. Stakeholders, social responsibility, and performance: Empirical evidence and theoretical perspectives. *Academy of Management Journal*, *42*(5), pp. 479–485.

Hillman, A. J., & Keim, G. D. (2001). Shareholder value, stakeholder management, and social issues: What's the bottom line? *Strategic Management Journal*, *22*(2), 125–139.

Hristov, I., and Appolloni, A. 2022. Stakeholders' engagement in the business strategy as a key driver to increase companies' performance: Evidence from managerial and stakeholders' practices. *Business Strategy and the Environment*, *31*(4), pp. 1488–1503.

Hughes, A. 2001. Multi-stakeholder approaches to ethical trade: towards a reorganization of UK retailers' global supply chains? *Journal of Economic Geography*, *1*(4), pp. 421–437.

Jawahar, I. M., and McLaughlin, G. L. 2001. Toward a descriptive stakeholder theory: An organizational life cycle approach. *Academy of Management Review*, *26*(3), pp. 397–414.

Jenson, M. C. 2001. Value maximization, stakeholder theory, and the corporate objective function. *Journal of Applied Corporate Finance* 14 (3), pp. 8–9.

Jones, T. M. 1995. Instrumental stakeholder theory: A synthesis of ethics and economics. *Academy of Management Review*, *20*(2), pp. 404–437.

Lauesen, S. 2020. IT project failures, causes and cures. *IEEE Access*, *8*, pp. 72059–72067.

Le, T. T., and Behl, A. 2022. Role of corporate governance in quick response to Covid-19 to improve SMEs' performance: Evidence from an emerging market. *Operations Management Research 15*, pp. 528–550.

Louder, E., Wyborn, C., Cvitanovic, C., and Bednarek, A. 2021. Four guiding principles for choosing frameworks and indicators to assess research impact. *Impact of Social Sciences Blog*.

Masson, L. M., Klove, C. A., and Provenzano, N. 2022. Project management. In *Clinical informatics study guide* (pp. 331–348). Springer, Cham.

McVea, J. F., and Freeman, R. E. 2005. A names-and-faces approach to stakeholder management: How focusing on stakeholders as individuals can bring ethics and entrepreneurial strategy together. *Journal of Management Inquiry*, *14*(1), pp. 57–69.

Mitchell, R. K., Agle, B. R., and Wood, D. J. 1997. Toward a theory of stakeholder identification and salience: Defining the principle of who and what really counts. *Academy of Management Review*, *22*(4), pp. 853–886.

Mugumbate, T., and Kruger, D. 2021. Investigation into South African municipal construction project failures. *Civil Engineering= Siviele Ingenieurswese*, *29*(9), pp. 22–25.

Muller, C. G., Canale, F., and Cruz, A. D. 2022. Green innovation in the Latin American agri-food industry: understanding the influence of family involvement and business practices. *British Food Journal*, *124*, 2209–2238.

Nop, S., Thornton, A., and Tranter, P. 2023. Towards effective stakeholder collaboration in building urban resilience in Phnom Penh: opportunities and obstacles. *Environment, Development and Sustainability*, *25*(1) pp. 297–320.

Ontita, J., and Kinyua, G. M. 2020. Role of stakeholder management on firm performance: An empirical analysis of commercial banks in Nairobi City County, Kenya. *Journal of Business and Economic Development*, *5*(1), pp. 26–35.

Parmar, B. B. L., Wicks, A. C., and Freeman, R. E. 2022. Stakeholder management and the value of human-centred corporate objectives. *Journal of Management Studies*, *59*(2), pp. 569–582.

Pirozzi, M. 2021. The perceived value: a powerful influencer of project success. *PM World Journal*, *10*.

Post, J. E., Preston, L. E., and Sauter-Sachs, S. 2002. *Redefining the corporation: Stakeholder management and organizational wealth*. Stanford University Press.

Rust, N., Lunder, O. E., Iversen, S., Vella, S., Oughton, E. A., Breland, T. A., ... and Reed, M. S. 2022. Perceived causes and solutions to soil degradation in the UK and Norway. *Land*, *11*(1), pp. 131.

Ruvalcaba, C., Akdevelioglu, D., and Schroeder, J. 2022. Stakeholders as value creators: The role of multi-level networks in employee wellness programs. *Journal of Macromarketing*. https://doi.org/10.1177/02761467221084626

Safa, M., Weeks, K., ELHoubi, A., Sharma, N., and MacGillivray, S. 2022. Construction strategic project readiness assessment. *Journal of Engineering, Project, and Production Management*, *12*(1), pp. 13.

Situmorang, R. O. P., and Yen, T. M. 2022. Comparison of benefits, stakeholders, implementation, and locations of community forestry in Taiwan and Indonesia based on experts' views. *Journal of Forest Research 27*, pp. 334–341.

Sunita, P. K. G. (2021). The A Stakeholder Management Conceptual Framework. *Turkish Journal of Computer and Mathematics Education (TURCOMAT)*, *12*(14), pp. 6039–6044.

Svendsen, A. C., and Laberge, M. 2005. Convening stakeholder networks: A new way of thinking, being and engaging. *Journal of Corporate Citizenship*, (19), pp. 91–104.

Vaitoonkiat, E., and Charoensukmongkol, P. 2020. Stakeholder orientation's contribution to firm performance: The moderating effect of perceived market uncertainty. *Management Research Review*, *43*(7), pp. 863–883.

Vandenbussche, L. 2018. Mapping stakeholders' relating pathways in collaborative planning processes; A longitudinal case study of an urban regeneration partnership. *Planning Theory and Practice*, *19*(4), pp. 534–557.

Varajão, J., Marques, R. P., and Trigo, A. 2022. Project management processes–Impact on the success of information systems projects. *Informatica 33*, pp. 421–436.

Vázquez-Maguirre, M., and Benito, A. E. 2022. Impact or outputs? Exploring multinational's CSR activities in Mexico. *Sustainability*, *14*(7), pp. 4140.

Verbeke, A., and Tung, V. 2013. The future of stakeholder management theory: A temporal perspective. *Journal of Business Ethics*, *112*(3), pp. 529–543.

Wu, M. 2013. Towards a stakeholder perspective on competitive advantage. *International Journal of Business and Management*, *8*(4), pp. 20.

Yamahaki, C., and Frynas, J. G. 2016. Institutional determinants of private shareholder engagement in Brazil and South Africa: The role of regulation. *Corporate Governance: An International Review*, *24*(5), pp. 509–527.

Yang, J., Shen, Q., and Ho, M. 2009. An overview of previous studies in stakeholder management and its implications for the construction industry. *Journal of Facilities Management 7*, pp. 159–175.

Yiapanas, G., and Thrassou, A. 2022. Football industry stakeholders' salience and attributes—the case of Cyprus, EU. *Global Business and Economics Review*, *26*(3), pp. 231–251.

14 Towards a 7-S Framework for Effective Stakeholder Engagement and Management in Early-Stage Ventures

A Bibliometric Analysis

Samuel Narh Dorhetso

Introduction

Stakeholder engagement is defined as practices that a firm pursues to involve stakeholders in a positive manner in its activities (Greenwood, 2007). Curzon explicated that stakeholder engagement is often perceived as an interactive process based on dialogue between a firm and its stakeholders. However, stakeholder management is more of a one-sided process leaned towards serving a firm's interest by identifying stakeholders, determining their significance to the firm, and managing them fittingly. Sloan argued that stakeholders were customarily seen as risky to manage, but they are now continuously perceived as active collaborators and partners to be engaged in generation of opportunities for firms. Thus, the positive nature of stakeholder engagement for creating values with benefits to both a firm and its stakeholders cannot be underestimated. Building a relationship with stakeholders may be time consuming, and most of the traits of good relationships (i.e., trust, mutual respect, and understanding) are intangibles that develop and evolve with time, based on personal and collective experiences and interactions. Engaging with stakeholders from the start, as part of a firm's core business strategy, facilitates a proactive cultivation of relationships that can be of capital value during challenging times (IFC, 2007). Stakeholder engagement has been documented as an important determinant for the growth of start-ups (Amankwah-Amoah et al., 2019). However, there seems not to have been a consensus among researchers about what stakeholder engagement means or what should be the characteristics of effective engagement. According to Greenwood, (2007), as with the whole concept of stakeholder thinking, stakeholder engagement is also a field that has not been adequately theorized. The current study aspired to fill this research gap and contribute to the general body of knowledge in the field by developing a theoretical framework on effective stakeholder engagement and management in early-stage ventures. To this extent, the specific objective of this study was to conduct a bibliometric analysis of published documents on effective stakeholder engagement and management in early-stage ventures and set a future research agenda based on a framework developed from a blend of the findings of the bibliographic coupling analysis and

DOI: 10.4324/9781003256014-18

author keyword co-occurrence analysis. A three-prong bibliometric analysis: co-authorship analysis based on countries, keyword co-occurrence analysis based on author keywords, and bibliographic coupling based on documents were performed in this study. This research adopted VOSviewer, a broadly used bibliometric mapping tool to analyze the dissemination of research publications, the scientific community, intellectual structure, and research hotspots. Aside from the theoretical contribution of this study to the existing literature on effective stakeholder engagement and management in early-stage ventures, the results would also help both SME managers and stakeholders to plan on best practices for best firm performance in unison with environmental stakeholder concerns.

Literature review

The word "stakeholder" may have several definitions in extant literature. According to Mitchell et al. (1997), there is only a mediocre scholarly agreement on what exactly constitutes a stakeholder. Stakeholders may be defined as individuals, groups, organizations, or political entities with a specific stake in the outcome of a decision, or impacted by a policy, project, or proposition (UNESCAP, 2018). However, arguments on stakeholder theory, specifically on stakeholder engagement, are often varied and vague as there is no common understanding of the actual meaning of the concept and the characteristics of effective engagement. Several studies on stakeholder engagement (Chen et al., 2017; Freeman et al., 2018; Morrissey et al., 2014; Retolaza et al., 2009; Riad et al., 2020; Romenti, 2010; Smith & Woods, 2015) and stakeholder management (Albats et al., 2020; Amankwah-Amoah et al., 2019; Anbarasan & Sushil, 2018; Hiatt et al., 2018; Khojastehpour & Shams, 2020; Schlierer et al., 2012) are available in extant literature. However, research gaps still remain in the debate on effective stakeholder engagement and management, especially with regard to start-ups as copiously evinced in literature. Although Westrenius et al. specifically analyzed stakeholders for a small business which included start-ups, to the best of the researcher's knowledge, there has not yet been an adequate bibliometric analysis of journal articles on effective stakeholder engagement and management in early-stage ventures found in literature within the field. Thus, the intention of this contemporary research was to conduct a bibliometric analysis of literature on effective stakeholder engagement and management in early-stage ventures and outline a research agenda for future studies in the field based on a framework developed from the identified research gaps. Bibliometric analysis, a tool that has been extensively used by several studies (Dorhetso et al., 2023), is the application of mathematics and statistical methods to study scientific publications (Leydesdorff, 1995). It is a more objective and well-organized tool than traditional qualitative analysis. This study makes ample contributions to the body of knowledge in the field by adding to the existing literature on effective stakeholder engagement and management in early-stage ventures.

Research methodology

Source of data, search criteria, and screening procedure

The Scopus database was the main source of material collected to conduct this study. Search keywords related to effective stakeholder engagement and management in early-stage ventures were identified from a preliminary literature review. The keywords selected based on the scope of the research encapsulated stakeholder engagement, stakeholder management, effective stakeholder engagement, early-stage family business, early-stage ventures, early-stage entrepreneurship, entrepreneurship, nascent entrepreneur, new business, new ventures, SME, and African firms. On April 9, 2023, the retrieval search string was entered by combining the keywords with Boolean operators and the initial results yielded 165 documents, as depicted in Figure 14.1. A few abstracts of the documents were read to be certain that they were documents related to the subject of effective stakeholder engagement and management in early-stage ventures. The search was initially limited to only social sciences, economics, econometrics and finance, business, management, and accounting articles, yielding 136 papers. The search was then limited to only journal articles published in the English language. This stage of the exclusion procedure produced 106 documents that were included in the bibliometric analysis.

Bibliometric analysis and discussion

Bibliometrics analysis is a scientometric technique that was developed over half a century ago for library and information science. This method has since been adopted by other fields of study that require a quantitative assessment of academic articles to determine trends and predict future research scenarios. It has been applied in various fields of literature. Thus, for this contemporary study that intended to develop a framework based on the identified gaps and future

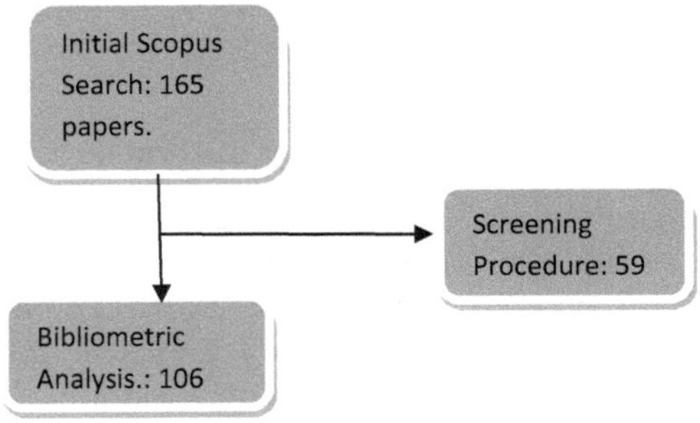

Figure 14.1 Flowchart of document screening process.

Source: Author, 2023.

research agenda, a bibliometric technique was deemed most appropriate. A three-prong bibliometric analysis—co-authorship analysis based on countries, keyword co-occurrence analysis based on author keywords, and bibliographic coupling based on documents—was conducted in this research. This study contributes to the literature by providing bibliometric annals of effective stakeholder engagement and management in early-stage ventures. It also adds to the theoretical body of knowledge with the development of a framework based on the findings of the author keyword co-occurrence analysis, and bibliographic coupling analysis.

Co-authorship Analysis Based on Countries

The findings of the co-authorship analysis based on countries was categorised into 10 clusters: cluster one encapsulated Austria, Burkina Faso, Canada, Congo, Germany, South Africa, and Zimbabwe; cluster two entailed an unknown entity, Czech Republic, Ireland, Italy, Jordan, and the Russian Federation: cluster three captured Brazil, Chile, Israel, Morocco, and Portugal; cluster four contained Belgium, Norway, Spain, Switzerland, and Tanzania; cluster five encapsulated an unknown entity, Cyprus, India, Malaysia, and United States; cluster six contained Denmark, Finland, Ghana, and Indonesia; cluster seven entailed Iran, Malta, UK, and Zambia; cluster eight featured Australia and Bangladesh; cluster nine captured France and Pakistan; and cluster ten encapsulated Malawi and the Netherlands. The findings of the analysis (see Table 14.1, and Figure 14.2 on VOSviewer results) can be explained to mean that authors from the Spain, UK, and United States, as well as other purple coded countries, started publishing on research and issues related to effective stakeholder engagement and management in early-stage ventures much earlier than the others. These current findings are consistent with studies by Peng et al. and Li et al., regarding the UK and United States been ranked as part of the top three countries where the majority of publications emanate from. The missing country from the list is China. The analysis contributes to literature by mapping the geographical context of research on effective stakeholder engagement and management in early-stage ventures in current times.

Keyword co-occurrence analysis based on author keywords

Keywords are the convergence and generalization of the major contents of literature, and their study helps to identify the research hotspots of a particular research area. The co-occurrence of author keywords among papers might be a pointer that they convey a collective theme (Ding et al., 2001). The keyword co-occurrence analysis for this study was hinged on author keywords. From the researcher's perspective, using both author keywords and indexed keywords for retrieval of data for the analysis in this study would have been more resourceful since capturing author keywords only may omit potentially vital

Table 14.1 Results of co-authorship analysis based on countries

Country	*Number of papers*	*Average publication year*	*Average citations*	*Rank by average citation*
United Kingdom	22	2017.82	24.23	10
United States	18	2018.06	30.44	6
Italy	13	2019.00	14.54	14
Australia	8	2018.62	9.00	18
Germany	8	2020.00	27.38	8
India	8	2020.25	12.12	15
Nethelands	7	2018.14	27.48	7
France	6	2018.67	57.83	3
Begium	6	2017.50	15.00	13
Spain	6	2014.00	18.17	12
South Africa	4	2020.00	1.50	24
Canada	4	2019.50	7.50	19
Indonesia	4	2019.25	6.25	20
Switzerland	3	2019.67	32.67	5
Norway	3	2018.67	11.67	16
Brazil	3	2020.67	79.00	2
Ireland	3	2019.67	6.00	21
Cyprus	2	2020.00	84.50	1
Rusian Federation	2	2018.50	24.50	9
Portugal	2	2022.50	1.50	24
Malawi	1	2019.00	11.00	17
Burkina Faso	1	2021.00	6.00	21
Tanzania	1	2022.00	1.00	26
Zambia	1	2022.00	0.00	29
Pakistan	1	2020.00	14.00	14
Monaco	1	2022.00	2.00	23
Chile	1	2023.00	1.00	26
Czech Republic	1	2023.00	0.00	29
Iran	1	2020.00	22.00	11
Malta	1	2019.00	33.00	4
Austria	1	2023.00	0.00	29
Malaysia	1	2018.00	1.00	26
Jordan	1	2022.00	0.00	29

Source: Author, 2023.

themes of the study that were only captured by the indexed keywords. However, the VOSviewer software that facilitated the analysis in this study was confined to author keywords only. Only papers with a minimum number of five occurrences were selected for the analysis. The full results of the keyword co-occurrence analysis based on author keywords is evinced in Table 14.2. From the results, it can be observed that stakeholder engagement, entrepreneurship, stakeholder management, and stakeholders were the topmost four

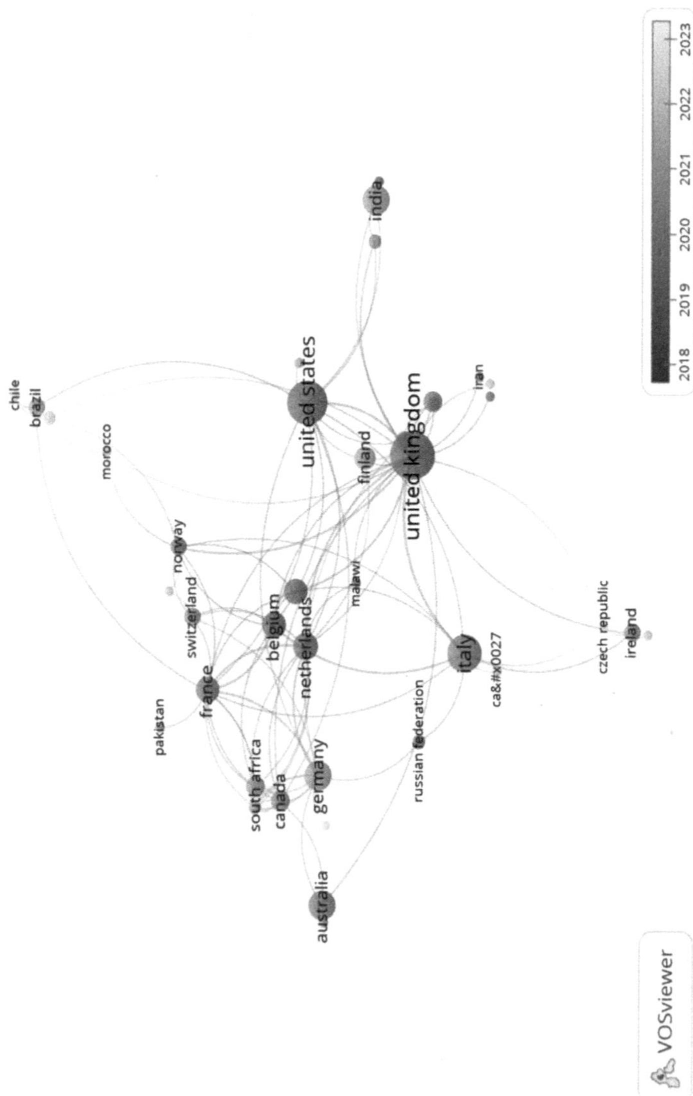

Figure 14.2 VOSviewer results.

Table 14.2 Results of co-authorship analysis based on countries

Keyword	*Occurrences*	*Total link strength*
Stakeholder engagement	24	29
Entrepreneurship	24	25
Stakeholder management	17	15
SMEs	7	10
Social enterprise	7	10
Stakeholders	10	9
Innovation	5	8
CSR	5	7
Social entrepreneurship	8	7
Stakeholder theory	5	7
Sustainability	5	7
Corporate social responsivity	6	6
Sustainable development	5	6

dominant keywords that reoccurred, with frequencies of ten occurrences or more (24, 24, 17 and 10, respectively). However, in terms of link strength, both SME and social enterprise had more links and greater strengths than stakeholders (see Table 14.2). The findings of the analysis, based on the average publication year, revealed that documents in the field of corporate social responsivity were the oldest (n = 2016.00), followed by papers on sustainable development (n = 2016.80), both stakeholder theory and CSR ranked third (n = 2017.80) by this criterion of identifying the oldest papers. It is evident from results of the overlay visualization that papers on stakeholders were relatively the most current (n = 2019.70). This was closely followed by articles on sustainability (n = 2019.60). From the observations made from the findings of the analysis, it can be deduced that stakeholder engagement, entrepreneurship, stakeholder management, and stakeholders were the topmost four research hotspots. These four major themes were closely followed by documents themed on SMEs and social enterprise. The findings of the author keyword co-occurrence analysis partly established the basis for the theoretical framework developed in this study. Based on the findings, it is suggested that future research should focus more on investigating the links between these identified thematic areas. Future studies may also be geared towards developing more theoretical and conceptual frameworks to guide researchers and practitioners on effective ways of stakeholder engagement and management in SMEs and similar start-up businesses. The synopsis of the result off this analysis using VOSviewer is shown in Figure 14.3.

Bibliographic coupling analysis based on documents

Two papers with one or more shared references create a bibliographic couple and may lean towards similar intellectual content. In order to authenticate the consistency of the thematic analysis based on the keyword co-occurrence

Figure 14.3 VOSviewer results.

analysis, bibliographic coupling was used to identify the thematic structure of publications on effective stakeholder engagement and management in early-stage ventures. Only documents that had received at least ten citations were used for the bibliographic coupling analysis in this study, hence only 43 papers were selected. As evinced in the VOSviewer results, the documents were grouped into seven clusters. The contents of these seven clusters are briefly discussed as follows.

Cluster 1 (green cluster)

The cluster contained nine (9) items. The papers in this cluster were hinged on social entrepreneurship (social enterprise, social ventures) and stakeholder engagement. The link between stakeholders and stakeholder engagement (Freeman et al., 2018; Morrissey et al., 2014; Smith & Woods, 2015), social entrepreneurship (Bruneel et al., 2016; Meyer & Gauthier, 2013; Mzembe et al., 2019; Smith & Woods, 2015), and social value creation (Lorenzo-Afable et al., 2020; Mzembe et al., 2019) was strongly exuded in most of these papers, and the most cited document in the cluster focused on impact investing. Agrawal and Hockerts (2021) topped the citation list in this cluster with 46 citations. They argued that, although impact investing has developed greatly, the lack of knowledge about the field coupled with the lack of knowledge production of the field might be dangerous for its future.

Cluster 2 (yellow cluster)

This cluster encapsulated seven items that were focused on stakeholder engagement (Chen et al., 2017), stakeholder management (Khojastehpour & Shams, 2020; Schlierer et al., 2012), small to medium-sized enterprises (SMEs), and start-ups (Camilleri, 2019; Chen et al., 2017; Schlierer et al., 2012), and corporate social responsibility (CSR) (Graafland, 2018; Stewart & Gapp, 2014). Stewart and Gapp (2014) topped the citation list in this cluster with 56 citations. They found that reflective and cyclical learning within a participative environment allowed for the internalization of values, behaviors, beliefs, and actions required for the positive uptake of CSR and sustainable management practice.

Cluster 3 (red cluster)

This cluster captured five articles. The documents were about stakeholder engagement (Riad et al., 2020) and stakeholder management (Albats et al., 2020; Hiatt et al., 2018), and stakeholder theory and entrepreneurial ecosystems (Bischoff et al., 2018; Bischoff & Volkmann, 2018). Bischoff et al. (2018) topped the citation list in this cluster with 76 citations. Their analysis resulted in the development of a set of propositions on stakeholder involvement in the context of entrepreneurship education at higher educational institutions and underscored the importance of stakeholder collaboration from the entrepreneurial ecosystem at the institutions.

Cluster 4 (purple cluster)

This cluster entailed five documents. The main foci of the papers were innovation and stakeholder management (Chen & Liu, 2020; Scholten & Van der Duin, 2015), and stakeholder engagement/integration and sustainable development (Amankwah-Amoah et al., 2019; Anbarasan & Sushil, 2018). The last paper in the cluster, Tang and Tang (2016), studied the impact of competitor–firm power divergence on Chinese SMEs' environmental and financial performance. Amankwah-Amoah et al. (2019) topped the citation list in this cluster with 97 citations. Utilizing using primary data obtained from 242 chief executive officers/entrepreneurs in Ghana, they found that the indirect relationship between entrepreneurial orientation and new venture performance is strengthened at high levels of stakeholder integration.

Cluster 5 (blue cluster)

The fifth cluster encapsulated four papers that revolved around social entrepreneurship (Bandi et al., 2020) and entrepreneurship education (Jones & Iredale, 2009), and stakeholder engagement (Retolaza et al., 2009; Romenti, 2010). Romenti (2010) topped the citation list in this cluster with 36 citations. Romenti (2010) argued that corporate communication reaches its full potential in building corporate reputation, when it moves beyond the influencing of public opinion's perceptions towards the shaping of organizational reality by engaging stakeholders as the main reputation drivers.

Cluster 6 (black cluster)

This cluster contained three documents that hinged on stakeholder engagement (Ferraris et al., 2020; Nair, 2020) and CSR (Penttilä, 2020). Ferraris et al. (2020) topped the citation list in this cluster with 48 citations. They found positive trend in the university integrator role applying a mixed two-step methodology based on online survey of university students and interviews with decision-making stakeholders involved in smart city projects (business, state, entrepreneurs, and academia) in Italy and Russia.

Cluster 7 (pale cluster)

The seventh cluster encapsulated the final grouping of two articles produced from the bibliographic coupling analysis based on documents (Leonidou et al., 2020; Saleem et al., 2020). Leonidou et al. (2020) was the most cited paper in both this cluster and all the seven clusters that were created from the bibliographic coupling analysis. The paper had 148 citations and consolidated the state of scholarly research on stakeholder engagement in innovation management and entrepreneurship development by systematically reviewing relevant literature published in the field.

Cluster summary

From the findings of the bibliographic coupling analysis, it is evident that the major themes of research that have emerged in the study of effective stakeholder engagement and management in early-stage ventures include social entrepreneurship (social enterprise, social ventures) and stakeholder engagement; stakeholders and stakeholder engagement; social entrepreneurship and social value creation; stakeholder engagement, stakeholder management, SMEs and start-ups, and corporate social responsibility; stakeholder engagement and stakeholder management; stakeholder theory and entrepreneurial ecosystems; innovation and stakeholder management; stakeholder engagement/integration and sustainable development; social entrepreneurship and entrepreneurship education; stakeholder engagement; and stakeholder engagement and CSR. It can also be observed from the results, as summarized in Table 14.3, that the second cluster (yellow cluster) had the greatest number of citations (244). This means that articles on stakeholder engagement, stakeholder management, SMEs and start-ups, and CSR have clouded the research space of effective stakeholder engagement and management in early-stage ventures since 2009. Stewart and Gapp (2014) topped the citation list in this cluster with 56 citations of their article on CSR within SMEs. However, in terms of average citations per publication, the seventh cluster (pale cluster) topped (81.00). This may be attributable to the fact that this cluster also produced the most cited document in the entire analysis. Leonidou et al. (2020) consolidated the state of scholarly research on stakeholder engagement in innovation management and entrepreneurship and was cited 148 times. Figure 14.4 shows the VOSviewer results of the network visualization of the bibliographic coupling analysis based on documents.

Theoretical framework development

In order for the theoretical framework to be consistent with the keyword co-occurrence analysis based on author keywords, only themes pinpointed in a minimum number of two published journal articles were included in the framework. The theoretical framework was based on the findings of the bibliographic coupling and author keyword co-occurrence analyses. The theoretical framework, which is purported to guide future research in the field, was synthesised from the results of both analyses. Table 14.4 presents the theoretical outline on effective stakeholder engagement and management in early-stage ventures in order of prominence of the variables studied, according to this contemporary research. Figure 14.4, on the other hand, presents the theoretical framework according to the antecedents of the various variables and how they interact among themselves.

Table 14.3 Cluster summary

Description	*Cluster 1*	*Cluster 2*	*Cluster 3*	*Cluster 4*	*Cluster 5*	*Cluster 6*	*Cluster7*
Period	2013–2021	2012–2020	2018–2020	2015–2020	2009–2020	2020	2020
Total publications (TP)	9	7	5	5	4	3	2
Total citations (TC)	186	244	195	166	94	98	162
TC/TP	20.56	34.86	39.00	33.20	23.50	32.67	81.00

Source: Author, 2023.

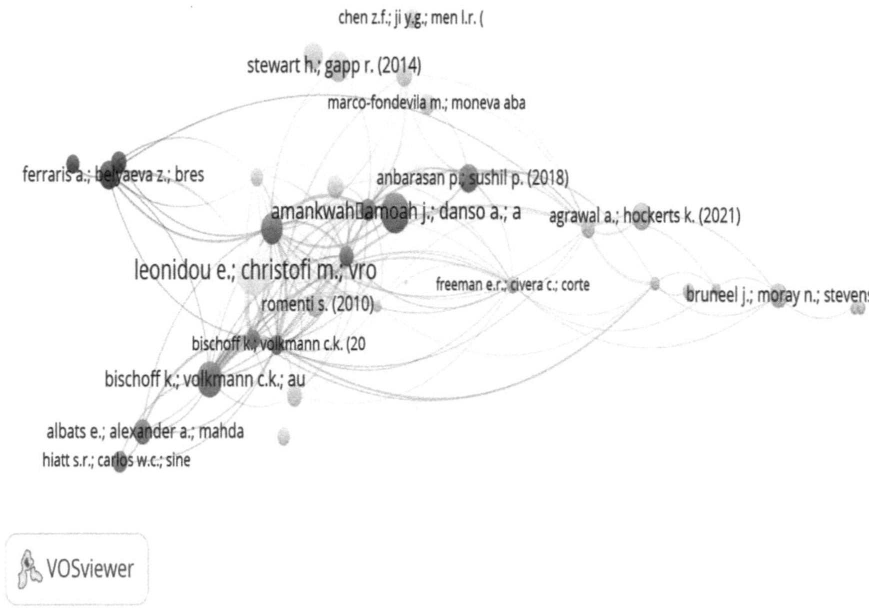

Figure 14.4 VOSviewer results.

Lorenzo-Afable et al. (2020)'s investigation of social value creation based on what beneficiaries care about in their work engagement with social enterprises disclosed that social value creation is a multidimensional and reciprocal process that is shaped as beneficiaries work for social enterprises. As depicted in Figure 14.5, social value creation interacts with the variables: social enterprise/social entrepreneurship/entrepreneurship; and SMEs. Notably, the interaction among these three groups of variables has been isolated in a box as if they were a single group of variables. This single group of variables also concurrently interacts with the group of stakeholders (also conceptualized as a unit of variables) through the media of stakeholder engagement, stakeholder management, and social responsibility.

Future research agenda

Based on the findings of the bibliographic coupling and author keyword co-occurrence analyses, as epitomised in the theoretical framework, it is suggested that future research should focus more on investigating the links between the identified thematic areas. For instance, future studies may examine the mediating roles of variables such as stakeholder engagement, stakeholder management, and social responsibility (CSR) between stakeholders and variables such as social enterprise, social entrepreneurship, entrepreneurship, and social value creation. The moderating roles of stakeholder engagement, stakeholder

Table 14.4 Theoretical framework on effective stakeholder engagement and management in early-stage ventures

Theme	*References*	*Number of studies*	*Ranking*
Stakeholder engagement	Morrissey et al. (2014), Smith and Woods (2015), Freeman et al. (2018), Chen et al. (2017), Riad et al. (2020), Anbarasan and Sushil (2018), Amankwah-Amoah et al. (2019), Retolaza et al. (2009), Romenti (2010), Ferraris et al. (2020), Nair (2020), Leonidou et al. (2020), Saleem et al. (2020).	13	1
Stakeholder management	Schlierer etal. (2012), Khojastehpour and Shams (2020), Hiatt et al. (2018), Albats et al. (2020), Scholten and Van Der Duin (2015), Chen and Liu (2020),	6	2
Social enterprise/social entrepreneurship/ entrepreneurship	Meyer and Gauthier (2013), Smith and Woods (2015), Bruneel et al. (2016), Mzembe et al. (2019), Bandi et al., (2020), Jones and Iredale (2009),	6	2
Stakeholders	Morrissey et al. (2014), Smith and Woods (2015), Freeman et al. (2018).	3	4
SMEs	Schlierer et al. (2012), Chen et al. (2017), Camilleri (2019)	3	4
Corporate social responsibility (CSR)	Stewart and Gapp (2014), Graafland (2018), Penttilä (2020).	3	4
Social value creation	Mzembe et al. (2019), Lorenzo-Afable et al. (2020)	2	7

management, and CSR may also be investigated in diverse fashions in future research. The moderating effect could either be determined between the three enterprise-related variables captured (see Figure 14.5) and stakeholders, or stakeholders and the three enterprise-related variables (i.e., the positions of independent and dependent variables may be swapped to improve research diversity in the field in future). Future studies may also be geared towards developing more theoretical and conceptual frameworks to guide researchers and practitioners on effective ways of stakeholder engagement and management in SMEs and similar start-up businesses at very early stages. As emphasised in extant literature (IFC, 2007; Amankwah-Amoah et al., 2018),

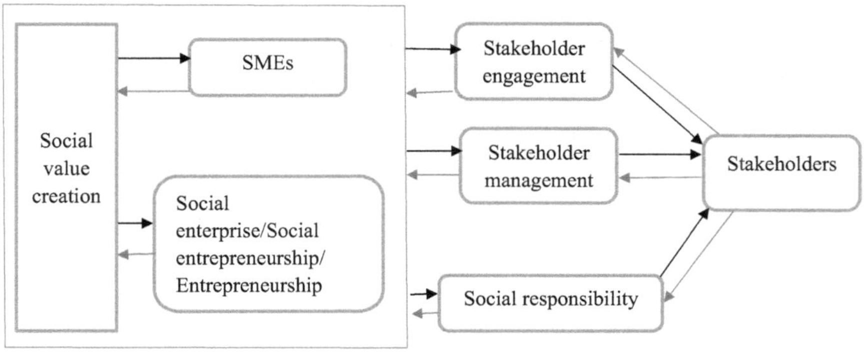

Figure 14.5 Theoretical framework on effective stakeholder engagement and management in early-stage ventures.

engaging with stakeholders from very early stages, as part of an enterprise's core business strategy, facilitates proactive cultivation of relationships that can be of principal value during challenging times.

Conclusion

The purpose of this study was to conduct a bibliometric analysis of the current state of the literature on effective stakeholder engagement and management in early-stage ventures and pinpoint research issues that may be addressed by authors in the future. In this regard, the study filled an identified research gap. However, the documents for the study were sourced from the Scopus database, and its limitations may have repercussions for the results. Hence, the bibliometric analysis conducted was comprehensive but not exhaustive. Also, the database used and the filtering process adopted may have omitted some relevant studies as only journal articles were included in the study. Consequently, conference proceedings, monographs, dissertations, chapters, and books were excluded from the analysis during the data filtering stage. It should be noted that the themes identified in this study are not intended to be definitive and mutually exclusive, as a result of the sample size restrictions in the research stream. In future, researchers may consider developing more theoretical and conceptual frameworks in the field. Authors may also consider using other methods such as systematic literature reviews for future investigations in the field.

References

Agrawal A and Hockerts K (2021) Impact investing: review and research agenda. *Journal of Small Business and Entrepreneurship 3*(2): 153–181.

Albats E, Alexander A, Mahdad M, Miller K and Post G (2020) Stakeholder management in SME open innovation: interdependences and strategic actions. *Journal of Business Research 119*: 291–301.

Amankwah-Amoah J, Danso A and Adomako S (2019) Entrepreneurial orientation, environmental sustainability and new venture performance: does stakeholder integration matter? *Business Strategy and the Environment 28*(1): 79–87.

Anbarasan P and Sushil P (2018) Stakeholder Engagement in Sustainable Enterprise: Evolving a Conceptual Framework, and a Case Study of ITC. *Business Strategy and the Environment 27* (3): 282–299.

Bandi V, Sahrakorpi T, Paatero J and Lahdelma R (2020) Touching the invisible: Exploring the nexus of energy access, entrepreneurship, and solar homes systems in India. *Energy Research and Social Science 69*: 101767.

Bischoff K and Volkmann CK (2018) Stakeholder support for sustainable entrepreneurship—a framework of sustainable entrepreneurial ecosystems. *International Journal of Entrepreneurial Venturing 10*(2): 172–201.

Bischoff K, Volkmann CK and Audretsch DB (2018) Stakeholder collaboration in entrepreneurship education: An analysis of the entrepreneurial ecosystems of European higher educational institutions. *Journal of Technology Transfer 43*(1): 20–46.

Bruneel J, Moray N, Stevens R, and Fassin Y (2016) Balancing competing logics in for-profit social enterprises: A need for hybrid governance. *Journal of Social Entrepreneurship 7*(3): 263–288.

Camilleri MA (2019) The SMEs' technology acceptance of digital media for stakeholder engagement. *Journal of Small Business and Enterprise Development 26*(4): 504–521.

Chen J and Liu L (2020) Customer participation, and green product innovation in SMEs: The mediating role of opportunity recognition and exploitation. *Journal of Business Research 119*: 151–162.

Chen Z F, Ji YG and Men LR (2017) Strategic use of social media for stakeholder engagement in startup companies in China. *International Journal of Strategic Communication 11*(3): 244–267.

Ding Y, Chowdhury GG and Foo S (2001) Bibliometric cartography of information retrieval research by using co-work analysis. *Information Processing and Management 37*(6): 817–842.

Dorhetso SN, Boakye LY and Welbeck DNO (2023) Innovation performance and efficiency of research and development intensity as a proportion of GDP: A bibliometric review. In *Sustainable education and development—Sustainable industrialization and innovation*. ARCA 2022. Springer. https://doi.org/10.1007/978-3-031-25998-2_20

Ferraris A, Belyaeva Z and Bresciani S (2020) The role of universities in the Smart City innovation: Multistakeholder integration and engagement perspectives. *Journal of Business Research 119*: 163–171.

Freeman ER, Civera C, Cortese D and Fiandrino S (2018) Strategizing stakeholder empowerment for effective co-management within fishery-based commons. *British Food Journal 120*(11): 2631–2644.

Graafland J (2018) Does corporate social responsibility put reputation at risk by inviting activist targeting? An empirical test among European SMEs. *Corporate Social Responsibility and Environmental Management 25*(1): 1–13.

Greenwood, M. (2007). Stakeholder engagement: Beyond the myth of corporate responsibility. *Journal of Business Ethics*, *74*, 315–327.

Hiatt SR, Carlos WC and Sine WD (2018) Manu militari: The institutional contingencies of stakeholder relationships on entrepreneurial performance. *Organization Science 29*(4): 633–652.

IFC (2007) *Stakeholder engagement: A good practice handbook for companies doing business in emerging markets.* International Finance Corporation.

Jones B and Iredale N (2009) Entrepreneurship education and Web 2.0. *Journal of Research in Marketing and Entrepreneurship 11* (1): 66–77.

Khojastehpour M and Shams SM (2020) Addressing the complexity of stakeholder management in international ecological setting: A CSR approach. *Journal of Business Research 119*: 302–309.

Leonidou E, Christofi M, Vrontis D and Thrassou A (2020) An integrative framework of stakeholder engagement for innovation management and entrepreneurship development. *Journal of Business Research 119*: 245–258.

Leydesdorff L (1995) *The challenge of scientometrics: The development, measurement and selforganization of scientific communications.* DSWO Press.

Lorenzo-Afable D, Lips-Wiersma M and Singh S (2020) Social value creation as care: The perspective of beneficiaries in social entrepreneurship. *Social Enterprise Journal 16*(3): 339–360.

Meyer CR and Gauthier J (2013) Navigating challenging fitness landscapes: Social entrepreneurship and the competing dimensions of sustainability. *Journal of Social Entrepreneurship 4*(1): 23–39.

Mitchell, R. K., Agle, B. R., & Wood, D. J. (1997). Toward a theory of stakeholder identification and salience: Defining the principle of who and what really counts. *Academy of Management Review, 22*, 853–886.

Morrissey J, Dunphy N and MacSweeney R (2014) Energy efficiency in commercial buildings: Capturing added-value of retrofit. *Journal of Property Investment and Finance 32*(4): 396–414.

Mzembe AN, Novakovic Y, Melissen F and Kamanga G (2019) Institutional bricolage as an antecedent of social value creation in a developing country's tourism and hospitality industry. *Corporate Social Responsibility and Environmental Management 26*(4): 997–1008.

Nair SR (2020) The link between women entrepreneurship, innovation and stakeholder engagement: A review. *Journal of Business Research 119*: 283–290.

Penttilä V (2020) Aspirational talk in strategy texts: A longitudinal case study of strategic episodes in corporate social responsibility communication. *Business and Society 59*(1): 67–97.

Retolaza JL, Ruiz M and San-Jose L (2009) CSR in business start-ups: An application method for stakeholder engagement. *Corporate Social Responsibility and Environmental Management 16*(6): 324–336.

Riad Shams SM, Vrontis D, Chaudhuri R, Chavan G and Czinkota MR (2020) Stakeholder engagement for innovation management and entrepreneurial development: A meta-analysis. *Journal of Business Research 119*: 67–86.

Romenti S (2010) Reputation and stakeholder engagement: An Italian case study. *Journal of Communication Management 14*(4): 306–318.

Saleem I, Siddique I, Ahmed A (2020) An extension of the socioemotional wealth perspective: Insights from an Asian sample. *Journal of Family Business Management 10*(4): 293–312.

Schlierer H, Werner A, Signori S, Garriga E, von Weltzien Hoivik H, van Rossem A and Fassin Y (2012) How do European SME owner-managers make sense of 'stakeholder management'? Insights from a cross-national study. *Journal of Business Ethics 109*(1): 39–51.

Scholten VE and Van der Duin PA (2015) Responsible innovation among academic spin-offs: How responsible practices help developing absorptive capacity. *Journal on Chain and Network Science 15*(2): 165–179.

Smith L and Woods C (2015) Stakeholder engagement in the social entrepreneurship process: Identity, governance and legitimacy. *Journal of Social Entrepreneurship 6*(2): 186–217.

Stewart H and Gapp R (2014) Achieving effective sustainable management: A small-medium enterprise case study. *Corporate Social Responsibility and Environmental Management 21*(1): 52–64.

Tang Z and Tang J (2016) The impact of competitors–firm power divergence on Chinese SMEs' environmental and financial performance. *Journal of Business Ethics 136*(1):147–165.

UNESCAP (2018) *Effective Stakeholder Engagement for The 2030 Agenda Training Reference Material.* United Nations Economic and Social Commission for Asia and the Pacific.

15 Stakeholder Management in Family Business

Emmanuel Kwaw Buah, Shirley Maud Acheampong and Edmund Osei Afriyie

Introduction

This chapter provides an overview, origin, and impact of diverse stakeholder support in family businesses. It further explores the role of internal and external stakeholder relationships and how they create value to ensure family businesses' survival, sustainability, and growth. Family businesses are regarded as the backbone of the global economy and account for a substantial share of the global gross domestic product (Rovelli et al., 2021; Ratten et al., 2017). Beyond their economic impact, family businesses are characterized by their long-term orientation and commitment to employees and communities, thereby becoming more prevalent in the last two decades (Rovelli et al., 2021; Kallmuenzer et al., 2022). Numerous scholars have conceptualized family businesses over the years, defining it as a business organisation in which the family is a significant internal stakeholder through ownership or family ties with family members operating as owners or managers (Hiebl & Li 2020; Mitchell et al., 2011).

Family businesses are characterised by close and frequently inseparable ties between the dominant family and the business and provide specific resources that influence entrepreneurial strategies (Weimann et al., 2021; Duh et al., 2010). These resources include financial, human, and social capital, which are often leveraged to gain a competitive advantage (Osunde, 2017). Decision-making authority resides within the family, and ownership is passed down through generations (Cater III et al., 2014). Members of the same family may hold positions on the board of directors or in executive management and operate with informality and adaptability (Calabrò & Mussolino, 2013). Family businesses place a high emphasis on long-term sustainability, intergenerational continuity, and seamless transition of operations across generations by ensuring that decisions not only benefit the current generation but also secure the future success of the company (Memeli et al., 2018; Randolph, 2019). Instead of prioritising immediate financial benefits, businesses may choose to adopt a longer-term perspective to achieve sustainable growth and profitability (Arrondo-García et al., 2016; Lumpki et al., 2010). This focus on intergenerational continuity allows family businesses to pass down their values, knowledge, and expertise from one generation to the next (Arrondo-García

DOI: 10.4324/9781003256014-19

et al., 2016; Randolph, 2019). Another key characteristic of a family business is the foundation of shared values, which play a pivotal role in shaping the vision and mission of the company (Aronoff & Ward, 2016). Compared to nonfamily businesses, family businesses are more agile with less bureaucratic decision-making processes and have greater emphasis on loyalty, commitment, and trust among family members (Ghee et al., 2015; Duh et al., 2010). Consequently, unravelling the dynamics of stakeholder relationships in family businesses can elucidate best practices, challenges, and opportunities for enhancing stakeholder management in family businesses.

Overview of stakeholder management in Africa

Stakeholder management is an essential element of business initiatives and holds considerable importance in facilitating Africa's socioeconomic progress (Benon-be-isan Nyuur et al., 2014). This overview examines stakeholder management within the African context, considering the distinct challenges, opportunities, and strategies that are pertinent to the region. African societies often emphasize collectivism and the well-being of the community. The Ubuntu philosophy, prevalent in many regions, highlights the importance of interconnectedness (Sarbah & Xiao, 2015; Benon-be-isan Nyuur et al., 2014). Hence, stakeholder engagements incorporate these communitarian ethics rather than individual gains. Stakeholder involvement facilitates the identification of their needs and aspirations, thereby enabling business leaders to develop strategies for sustainable and inclusive development (Waddell, 2017). The African continent exhibits significant diversity, encompassing a multitude of nations, ethnic groups, linguistic variations, and cultural practices (Amaeshi et al., 2016). To achieve effective stakeholder engagement, it is imperative to comprehend the intricacies involved and modify strategies accordingly to uphold local values and traditions (Sarbah & Xiao, 2015). Additionally, power structures and hierarchies within African societies play a significant role in stakeholder engagement (Sarbah & Xiao, 2015; Waddell, 2017). Political, traditional, religious, and community leaders hold substantial influence over decision-making processes (Waddell, 2017). Understanding these power dynamics is essential to effectively navigate regulatory frameworks, obtain support, and cultivate an environment that is conducive to the success of a business (Aguilera & Jackson, 2010; Amaeshi et al., 2016). To effectively manage stakeholders in the African context, businesses must provide continuous stakeholder engagement, integrate sustainable and responsible business practices, and engage in local capacity development, collaborative partnerships, and social responsibility (Eskerod & Jepsen, 2016; Benon-be-isan Nyuur et al., 2014).

Stakeholders in a family business

Stakeholders within a family business are defined as any group or individuals who can affect or be affected by the success of family businesses (Deephouse

& Jaskiewicz, 2013). Thus, it is advantageous for businesses to have trustworthy relationships with their stakeholders (Aragon-Amonarriz & Iturrioz-Landart, 2016) due to their influence on business outcomes. There are 2 main types of stakeholders: internal and external stakeholders. The internal stakeholders include the family owners, nonfamily management, and employees while the external stakeholders include customers, consumers, suppliers, regulators, and local communities. Family businesses' success is prominent when the goals and values of the family owners align with the internal and external stakeholders (Déniz-Déniz et al., 2018; Sorenson et al., 2009). Therefore, family businesses must maintain the right balance between the interests of the family owners and the internal and external stakeholders to ensure their commitment, cooperation, and productivity (Aragon Amonarriz & Iturrioz Landart, 2016; Rovelli et al., 2021; Vandekerkhof et al., 2018). This in turn promotes higher morale and low turnover rates (Edmondson & Mortensen 2021) to enhance performance, sustainability, and long-term growth (Gamble et al., 2021; Gaumer & Shaffer, 2018).

Origin of stakeholders' support in a family business

Preceding World War II, family businesses played an active role in the global economy but were mostly run by family members (Luan et al., 2018; Sharma et al., 2007). The organic growth of family businesses subsequently expanded into new markets, creating new challenges related to cultural differences, regulatory requirements, and competition from local businesses (Ward, 2016; Binachi, 2009). To survive, family businesses started to rely more on external stakeholders, such as consultants and industry associations (Kallmuenzer et al., 2022).

Over the years, the idea of stakeholder support in family businesses became a critical part of running a family business, with its significance becoming increasingly apparent during the 18th and 19th centuries, when business associations and chambers of commerce began to emerge and the size and complexity of family businesses grew (Astrachan & Botero, 2017; Kansikas, 2016). These organisations provided networks with family businesses to share best practices and advocate for policy changes that benefit their industry (Miller et al., 2015; Hansmann & Pargendler 2013).

Forms of stakeholder support on family firms

The following forms of stakeholder assistance are essential for the success and longevity of family businesses:

- *Financial support*: Family members, investors, and creditors provide financial support by investing capital and extending loans or credit. This assistance is indispensable for financing business operations, expansion, and capital expenditures (Siakas et al., 2014).

- *Community support*: Typically, stakeholders such as customers, collaborators, residents, organisations, and authorities provide community support to family businesses that operate within these communities. Positive relationships with the community contribute to the business's survival (Dunham et al., 2006).
- *Employee support*: Nonfamily employees in the business contribute by devoting their skills and knowledge to achieving the organization's goals. Their dedication, productivity, and engagement contribute to the business's overall growth (Luu, 2023; Dawson, 2012).
- *Strategic support*: Stakeholders like family members, advisors, or consultants assist with strategic planning by giving advice and sharing their knowledge in long-term business planning, market research, and strategic decisions (Arsić et al., 2018; Sarbah & Xiao, 2015). Their contributions provide a competitive direction for long-term success (Oudah et al., 2018; Michel & Kammerlander, 2015).

Internal stakeholder support

The presence of family ownership and active management in the operations of a company are critical elements that establish a business as a family business (Ramirez-Lozano et al., 2023; Rovelli et al., 2021). The success and growth of family businesses depend on the extent of stakeholders' support for the business's survival and growth. The heterogeneous nature of family businesses' strategic direction and management style creates diverse family-centred goals that may or may not be in sync with all other stakeholders of the business (Reina et al., 2022; Aragon Amonarriz & Iturrioz Landart, 2016).

Family owners

The owners within a family business play a crucial role as internal stakeholders because they are regarded as the founders and employers (Aragon Amonarriz & Iturrioz Landart, 2016; Sorenson et al., 2009). Family owners provide stability and continuity for the business across different generations by ensuring that the family's values, traditions, and vision are maintained (Rovelli et al., 2021; Zellweger & Nason, 2008). Family businesses tend to have a strong presence of family members on the board of directors and top management roles (Hiebl & Li 2020; Déniz-Déniz et al., 2018). The family members acting as directors and management tend to have diverse socioemotional wealth (SEW), which significantly influences the strategic direction, leadership style, and nonfinancial goals and success of the business (Weimann et al., 2021; Reina et al., 2022). SEW refers to the noneconomic benefits that family owners attach to their businesses, that is, affective needs, family identity, and preservation of family dynasty (Vandekerkhof et al., 2018; Llanos-Contreras et al., 2021).

Where family owners occupy governance and management roles, the issue of conflicts of interest between managers and owners is significantly reduced

(Ramirez-Lozano et al., 2023; Alwadani & Ndubisi, 2020). However, it may promote conflicting interests at the expense of other stakeholders as policies can be adopted to benefit only the family owners (Rovelli et al., 2021; Aragon Amonarriz & Iturrioz Landart, 2016). It is, therefore, vital that family managers actively participate in the day-to-day operations while cultivating a psychologically safe business environment for the long-term success and longevity of the business (Hiebl & Li 2020; Michel & Kammerlander, 2015) This in turn will encourage authentic self-expression, knowledge-sharing, and risk-taking (Edmondson & Mortensen, 2021; Vandekerkhof et al., 2018).

Nonfamily management

Nonfamily management represents the top management members involved in decision-making but has no blood or marital relationship with the owners (Hiebl & Li 2020; Binacci et al., 2016). Their qualifications and experience support industry-specific knowledge to promote competitive advantage and firm growth (Rovelli et al., 2021; Zellweger & Nason, 2008).

Given that family businesses are argued to be less innovative and tend to pursue conservative strategies because of the cost involved in research and innovation (Xiang et al., 2019; Duh et al., 2010), the valuable knowledge, and professional expertise of the nonfamily managers play a fundamental role in driving corporate entrepreneurship (Weimann et al., 2021; Binacci et al., 2016). Their external expertise and objective perspectives contribute to innovative strategic goals without overburdening the business with expensive technological advancements (Ramirez-Lozano et al., 2023; Yong et al., 2022).

Furthermore, nonfamily managers possess broad professional networks that introduce new business prospects, strategic alliances, and access to industry resources and expertise (Hiebl & Li, 2020; Rovelli et al., 2021). Hence, nonfamily managers' contributions to decision-making processes ensure a uniquely diverse and objective business environment with specialized industry expertise that fosters family businesses' long-term success (Déniz-Déniz et al., 2018; Sorenson et al., 2009).

Employees

The employees within family businesses through their specialized knowledge and experience contribute greatly to the continued survival and growth of the family business (Ramirez-Lozano et al., 2023; Alwadani & Ndubisi, 2020). Their commitment and knowledge enhance operational efficiency to provide excellent products or services to meet customer demands (Rovelli et al., 2021; Yong et al., 2022).

Employees who share congruent values with the family owners' strategic direction are more likely to experience a sense of belonging and demonstrate a commitment to upholding its values (Ramirez-Lozano et al., 2023; Zellweger & Nason, 2008). Their loyalty to the family business contributes to shaping the organizational culture with a shared purpose while creating a positive work environment (Déniz-Déniz et al., 2018). Furthermore, employees possess product knowledge and skills that foster professional customer service relationships (Aragon Amonarriz & Iturrioz Landart, 2016; Sorenson et al., 2009), thus establishing customer satisfaction, loyalty, and positive feedback (Yong et al., 2022; Weimann et al., 2021).

Employees by their creative thinking, problem-solving skills, and unique perspectives stimulate innovation and enhance processes to reduce operational costs and improve products and services (Rovelli et al., 2021; Xiang et al., 2019). Consequently, family businesses must invest in employee advancements by nurturing a psychologically safe, supportive, and inclusive workplace culture (Alwadani & Ndubisi, 2020; Sorenson et al., 2009).

Role of external stakeholders

One of the key challenges faced by family businesses pertains to the effective management of external stakeholders to achieve sustainability and long-term success (Gaumer & Shaffer, 2018; Ghee et al., 2015). External stakeholders refer to individuals or entities that hold a vested interest in the prosperity of a business, even though they are not directly engaged in its day-to-day operations (Gamble et al., 2021). They comprise customers, suppliers, creditors, employees, regulators, and the community.

Building and nurturing positive connections with external stakeholders play a pivotal role in the success of a family business (Maloni et al., 2017). When these stakeholders are satisfied with the organization, they are more likely to maintain business relationships and actively support its growth (Xiang et al., 2019). Understanding how external stakeholders contribute to the success of family businesses will provide valuable insights and practical implications for family businesses striving to enhance their stakeholder relationships (Litz et al., 2012).

Suppliers

Suppliers play a critical role in the operations of family businesses by providing the necessary resources and raw materials that enable the production and delivery of goods and services (Maloni et al., 2017). Suppliers range from local vendors and wholesalers to global manufacturers and distributors. In family businesses, the selection and management of suppliers are often influenced by a combination of business needs, relationships, and family dynamics (Gaumer & Shaffer, 2018; Maloni et al., 2017).

Family businesses exhibit a higher propensity for establishing long-term enduring associations with their suppliers (Maloni et al., 2017). Suppliers hold a significant role in the value chain of family businesses by contributing to the overall quality, cost-efficiency, and competitiveness of products and services through favourable pricing, volume discounts, and efficient inventory management (Gaumer & Shaffer, 2018; Gamble et al., 2021).

A timely and reliable supply of materials ensures smooth production processes and product quality leading to customer satisfaction (Zhang et al., 2021; Calabrò et al., 2019). Strategic alliances can be formed with suppliers through mutual trust, collaboration, and shared objectives (Graafland, 2020; Xiang et al., 2019). Thus, family businesses can be shaped by enduring affiliations, interpersonal bonds, and intergenerational trust (Gaumer & Shaffer, 2018).

Communities

Communities encompass the localities and regions where family businesses operate, and these communities provide individuals who may join the organization as employees in the future (Ramirez-Lozano et al., 2023; Gaumer & Shaffer, 2018). Recognizing communities as essential stakeholders acknowledges their influence on the family business and vice versa (Ramirez-Lozano et al., 2023).

The success and sustainability of family businesses are heavily influenced by the involvement of communities and the selection of potential employees. For instance, the Lego Group, a Danish toy company, has maintained 80 years of operations by developing groundbreaking products and a strong dedication to social responsibility that emphasizes sustainability and environmental stewardship (Émilie et al., 2021). The Lego Group's dedication to its local community played a significant role in its success as a global toy industry (Émilie et al., 2021).

Communities provide a supportive environment for business operations by offering resources, infrastructure, and a customer base to enhance reputation and brand perception (Gamble et al., 2021; Adekola & Clelland, 2020). Engagement with communities and potential employees involves establishing mutually beneficial relationships that require understanding their needs, interests, and aspirations to align business activities (Adekola & Clelland, 2020). Engagement strategies may include supporting community events, local initiatives, and educational programs and providing career development prospects (Ramirez-Lozano et al., 2023).

Customers and consumers

Customers and consumers are the purchasers and end-users of products or services (Gaumer & Shaffer, 2018; Calabrò, 2019; Ramirez-Lozano et al., 2023). Customers' buying decisions and recommendations directly impact the brand image, revenue, and profitability of businesses (Gaumer & Shaffer, 2018; Calabrò, 2019) to ensure business survival. Building strong relationships with customers involves establishing trust, delivering value, and meeting their expectations consistently to foster a sense of loyalty and affinity (Ramirez-Lozano et al., 2023; Gaumer & Shaffer, 2018).

Extant research alludes that creating value through customer satisfaction and loyalty is key to repeat purchases, positive referrals, and brand advocacy

(Ramirez-Lozano et al., 2023). By exceeding customer expectations, family businesses can differentiate themselves from competitors and build long-term relationships that generate sustainable revenue streams (Calabrò et al., 2019; Ramirez-Lozano et al., 2023).

Building strong relationships with customers can be achieved through clear communication, delivering on promises, and consistently exceeding customer expectations. Additionally, family businesses can enhance customer experiences by personalizing their services and creating a welcoming atmosphere that makes customers feel valued and appreciated (Gaumer & Shaffer, 2018; Calabrò, 2019; Ramirez-Lozano et al., 2023).

Lawmakers and regulators

Family businesses operate within a regulatory environment that encompasses laws, regulations, and governmental policies that aim to ensure fair competition, protect consumer rights, and maintain social and environmental standards (Xiang et al., 2019; Gorshunov et al., 2020). Understanding the regulatory landscape is essential for family businesses to navigate compliance requirements and engage effectively with lawmakers and regulators to spur their growth (Xiang et al., 2019; Gorshunov et al., 2020).

Lawmakers play a critical role in developing and enforcing legislation and regulations that impact taxation, labour laws, intellectual property rights, environmental standards, and market competition (Xiang et al., 2019). Compliance with these regulations is necessary for family businesses to operate ethically, sustainably, and by legal requirements (Gorshunov et al., 2020; Kim, 2017). Family businesses must establish robust governance frameworks including implementing internal controls, reporting mechanisms, and regular assessments to identify and address compliance gaps to mitigate legal risks (Xiang et al., 2019; Kim, 2017).

Furthermore, developing positive relationships with lawmakers and regulators is essential for family businesses to effectively influence policy decisions and advocate for their interests (Xiang et al., 2019; Doh et al., 2012). Engaging in open and transparent communication, participating in public consultations, and proactively addressing regulatory concerns can help build credibility and trust (Kim, 2017; Doh et al., 2012).

Limitation and future research

Despite the in-depth discussions in this chapter on the impact of stakeholders' support on the survival and growth of family businesses, several limitations are acknowledged leading to future research directions. First, family businesses are not immune to the changes caused by the diffusion of digital technologies. Second, there is an expanding body of research on business model innovation and a fertile area for future research on family businesses (Dangelico et al., 2019). Therefore, future research can concentrate on business model innovative strategies for family businesses to survive, grow, and create wealth. Third, future research can investigate the impact of ownership on family business corporate social responsibilities (CSR). Future research can employ psychological theories to investigate ownership and CSR activities in family businesses (Randolph et al., 2022; Déniz-Déniz et al., 2018). Finally, future research can examine the distinctive characteristics of family businesses such as transgenerational sustainability goals, the pursuit of noneconomic objectives, and strong interpersonal ties (Ferreira et al., 2021).

Conclusion

This chapter highlighted the importance of effective stakeholder management for successful family businesses. The chapter demonstrates the significance of family businesses' survival and growth through internal (family owners, nonfamily management, employee) and external (suppliers, communities, customers/consumers, lawmakers/regulators) stakeholder relationships. Understanding their roles, needs, and expectations is essential for developing effective strategies to manage these stakeholders.

Family owners, nonfamily management, and employees have a significant role to play as the internal stakeholders of the family business by ensuring its success, growth, and survival while nurturing and maintaining a psychologically safe environment with open communication and innovative products to meet the changing demands of customers and consumers (Llanos-Contreras et al., 2021; Alwadani & Ndubisi, 2020).

Suppliers enhance product quality and innovation while customers, consumers, and the community foster trust, loyalty, and a positive brand image (Ramirez-Lozano et al., 2023; Gaumer & Shaffer, 2018). Building positive relationships with lawmakers and regulators allows family businesses to advocate for their interests and influence policy decisions (Kim, 2017; Doh et al., 2012).

By effectively managing the internal and external stakeholders, family businesses can create value, enhance their reputation, and achieve long-term growth (Maloni et al., 2017; Xiang et al., 2019). This success requires a proactive and strategic approach that aligns business objectives with stakeholder interests to foster mutually beneficial relationships (Gamble et al., 2021; Adekola and Clelland, 2020).

References

Adekola, J. and Clelland, D., 2020. Two sides of the same coin: Business resilience and community resilience. *Journal of Contingencies and Crisis Management*, *28*(1), pp. 50–60.

Aguilera, R.V. and Jackson, G., 2010. Comparative and international corporate governance. *The Academy of Management Annals*, 4(1), pp. 485–556.

Alwadani, R. and Ndubisi, N. O., 2020. Sustainable family business: The role of stakeholder involvement, mindful organizing, and contingent human factors. *International Journal of Manpower*, *41*(7), pp. 945–965.

Amaeshi, K., Adegbite, E. and Rajwani, T., 2016. Corporate social responsibility in challenging and non-enabling institutional contexts: Do institutional voids matter?. *Journal of Business Ethics*, *134*, pp. 135–153.

Aragon Amonarriz, C. and Iturrioz Landart, C., 2016. Responsible family ownership in small-and medium-sized family enterprises: an exploratory study. *Business Ethics: A European Review*, *25*(1), pp. 75–93.

Aronoff, C. and Ward, J., 2016. *Family business values: How to assure a legacy of continuity and success*. Springer.

Arrondo-García, R., Fernández-Méndez, C. and Menéndez-Requejo, S., 2016. The growth and performance of family businesses during the global financial crisis: The role of the generation in control. *Journal of Family Business Strategy*, *7*(4), pp. 227–237.

Arsić, S., Banjević, K., Nastasić, A., Rošulj, D. and Arsić, M., 2018. Family business owner as a central figure in customer relationship management. *Sustainability*, *11*(1), p. 77.

Astrachan, C.B. and Botero, I.C., 2017. "We are a family firm": An exploration of the motives for communicating the family business brand. *Journal of Family Business Management*, *8*(1), pp. 2–2.

Benon-be-isan Nyuur, R., F. Ofori, and Debrah, Y. 2014. Corporate social responsibility in sub-Saharan Africa: hindering and supporting factors. *African Journal of Economic and Management Studies*, *5*(1), pp. 93–113.

Bianchi, C., 2009. Retail internationalisation from emerging markets: case study evidence from Chile. *International Marketing Review*, *26*(2), pp. 221–243.

Binacci, M., Peruffo, E., Oriani, R., and Minichilli, A., 2016. Are all non-family managers (NFMs) equal? The impact of NFM characteristics and diversity on family firm performance. *Corporate Governance: An International Review*, *24*(6), pp. 569–583.

Calabrò, A. and Mussolino, D., 2013. How do boards of directors contribute to family SME export intensity? The role of formal and informal governance mechanisms. *Journal of Management and Governance*, *17*, pp. 363–403.

Calabrò, A., Vecchiarini, M., Gast, J., Campopiano, G., De Massis, A. and Kraus, S., 2019. Innovation in family firms: A systematic literature review and guidance for future research. *International Journal of Management Reviews*, *21*(3), pp. 317–355.

Cater III, J.J. and Kidwell, R.E., 2014. Function, governance, and trust in successor leadership groups in family firms. *Journal of Family Business Strategy*, *5*(3), pp. 217–228.

Dangelico, R.M., Nastasi, A. and Pisa, S., 2019. A comparison of family and nonfamily small firms in their approach to green innovation: A study of Italian companies in the agri-food industry. *Business Strategy and the Environment*, *28*(7), pp. 1434–1448.

Dawson, A., 2012. Human capital in family businesses: Focusing on the individual level. *Journal of Family Business Strategy*, *3*(1), pp. 3–11.

Deephouse, D.L. and Jaskiewicz, P., 2013. Do family firms have better reputations than non-family firms? An integration of socioemotional wealth and social identity theories. *Journal of management Studies*, *50*(3), pp. 337–360

Déniz-Déniz, M. D. L. C., Cabrera-Suárez, M. K. and Martín-Santana, J. D., 2018. Family firms and the interests of non-family stakeholders: The influence of family managers' affective commitment and family salience in terms of power. *Business Ethics: A European Review*, *27*(1), pp. 15–28.

Doh, J.P., Lawton, T.C. and Rajwani, T., 2012. Advancing nonmarket strategy research: Institutional perspectives in a changing world. *Academy of Management Perspectives*, *26*(3), pp. 22–39.

Duh, M., Belak, J. and Milfelner, B., 2010. Core values, culture and ethical climate as constitutional elements of ethical behaviour: Exploring differences between family and non-family enterprises. *Journal of Business Ethics*, *97*, pp. 473–489.

Dunham, L., Freeman, R.E. and Liedtka, J., 2006. Enhancing stakeholder practice: A particularized exploration of community. *Business Ethics Quarterly*, *16*(1), pp. 23–42.

Edmondson, A. C., and Mortensen, M., 2021. What psychological safety looks like in a hybrid workplace. *Harvard Business Review*, *3*, pp. 109.

Émilie, R., Gandia, R. and Brion, S., 2021. Orchestrating external user communities and balancing control and autonomy in fast growing community contexts: Lego Group and Ankama. Chapter 12 in P. Cohendet, M. Rao, E. Ruiz, B. Sarazin, & L. Simon (Ed.), *Communities of innovation: How organizations harness collective creativity and build resilience* (pp. 263–283). World Scientific.

Eskerod, P. and Jepsen, A.L., 2016. *Project stakeholder management*. Routledge.

Ferreira, J.J., Fernandes, C.I., Schiavone, F. and Mahto, R.V., 2021. Sustainability in family business–A bibliometric study and a research agenda. *Technological Forecasting and Social Change*, *173*, p. 121077.

Gamble, J.R., Clinton, E. and Díaz-Moriana, V., 2021. Broadening the business model construct: Exploring how family-owned SMEs co-create value with external stakeholders. *Journal of Business Research*, *130*, pp. 646–657.

Gaumer, C.J. and Shaffer, K.J., 2018. Family business succession: impact on supplier relations and customer management. *Human Resource Management International Digest*, *26*(6), pp. 1–4.

Ghee, W.Y., Ibrahim, M.D. and Abdul-Halim, H., 2015. Family business succession planning: Unleashing the key factors of business performance. *Asian Academy of Management Journal*, *20*(2), pp. 103–126.

Gorshunov, M.A., Armenakis, A.A., Feild, H.S. and Vansant, B., 2020. The Sarbanes-Oxley Act of 2002: Relationship to magnitude of financial corruption and corrupt organizational cultures. *Journal of Management*, 21(2), p. 73.

Graafland, J., 2020. Family business ownership and cleaner production: Moderation by company size and family management. *Journal of Cleaner Production*, *255*, p. 120120.

Hansmann, H. and Pargendler, M., 2013. The evolution of shareholder voting rights: separation of ownership and consumption. *Academy of Management Review*, *20*(1), pp. 65–91.

Hiebl, M. R., and Li, Z., 2020. Non-family managers in family firms: review, integrative framework and future research agenda. *Review of Managerial Science*, *14*, pp. 763–807.

Kallmuenzer, A., Tajeddini, K., Gamage, T.C., Lorenzo, D., Rojas, A. and Schallner, M.J.A., 2022. Family firm succession in tourism and hospitality: an ethnographic case study approach. *Journal of Family Business Management*, *12*(3), pp. 393–413.

Kansikas, J., 2016. Career paths in institutional business elites: Finnish family firms from 1762–2010. *Enterprise and Society*, *17*(1), pp.1–38.

Kim, Y., 2017. Consumer responses to the food industry's proactive and passive environmental CSR, factoring in price as CSR tradeoff. *Journal of Business Ethics*, *140*, pp. 307–321.

Litz, R.A., Pearson, A.W. and Litchfield, S., 2012. Charting the future of family business research: Perspectives from the field. *Family Business Review*, *25*(1), pp. 16–32.

Llanos-Contreras, O., Arias, J. and Maquieira, C., 2021. Risk-taking behavior in Chilean listed family firms: A socioemotional wealth approach. *International Entrepreneurship and Management Journal*, *17*, pp. 165–184.

Luan, C.J., Chen, Y.Y., Huang, H.Y. and Wang, K.S., 2018. CEO succession decision in family businesses–A corporate governance perspective. *Asia Pacific Management Review*, *23*(2), pp. 130–136.

Lumpkin, G.T., Brigham, K.H. and Moss, T.W., 2010. Long-term orientation: Implications for the entrepreneurial orientation and performance of family businesses. *Entrepreneurship and Regional Development*, *22*(3–4), pp. 241–264.

Luu, T.D., 2023. Non-family employee strategic renewal in family firms: the transformational leadership role of family board members and psychological ownership. *Journal of Family Business Management*, *13*(2), pp. 272–299.

Maloni, M.J., Hiatt, M.S. and Astrachan, J.H., 2017. Supply management and family business: A review and call for research. *Journal of Purchasing and Supply Management*, 23(2), pp. 123–136.

Memili, E., Fang, H.C., Koc, B., Yildirim-Öktem, Ö. and Sonmez, S., 2018. Sustainability practices of family firms: The interplay between family ownership and long-term orientation. *Journal of Sustainable Tourism*, *26*(1), pp. 9–28.

Michel, A. and Kammerlander, N., 2015. Trusted advisors in a family business's succession-planning process—An agency perspective. *Journal of Family Business Strategy*, *6*(1), pp. 45–57.

Miller, D., Wright, M., Breton-Miller, I.L. and Scholes, L., 2015. Resources and innovation in family businesses: The Janus-face of socioemotional preferences. *California Management Review*, *58*(1), pp. 20–40.

Mitchell, R.K., Agle, B.R., Chrisman, J.J. and Spence, L.J., 2011. Toward a theory of stakeholder salience in family Firms. *Business Ethics Quarterly*, *21*(2), pp. 235–255.

Osunde, C., 2017. Family businesses and its impact on the economy. *Journal of Business and Financial Affairs*, 6(1), pp. 1–3.

Oudah, M., Jabeen, F. and Dixon, C., 2018. Determinants linked to family business sustainability in the UAE: An AHP approach. *Sustainability*, *10*(1), p. 246.

Ramirez-Lozano, J., Peñaflor-Guerra, R. and Sanagustín-Fons, V., 2023. Leadership, communication, and job satisfaction for employee engagement and sustainability of family businesses in Latin America. *Administrative Sciences*, 13(6), p. 137.

Randolph, R.V., Li, Z. and Daspit, J.J., 2019. Toward a typology of family firm corporate entrepreneurship. *Journal of Small Business Management*, *57*(3), pp. 1102–1118.

Randolph, R.V., Memili, E., Koç, B., Young, S.L., Yildirim-Öktem, Ö. and Sönmez, S., 2022. Innovativeness and corporate social responsibility in hospitality and tourism family firms: The role of family firm psychological capital. *International Journal of Hospitality Management*, *101*, p. 103128.

Ratten, V., Ramadani, V., Dana, L.P., Hoy, F. and Ferreira, J., 2017. Family entrepreneurship and internationalization strategies. *Review of International Business and Strategy*, *27*(2), pp. 150–160.

Reina, W., Pla-Barber, J., and Villar, C., 2022. Socioemotional wealth in family business research: A systematic literature review on its definition, roles and dimensions. *European Management Journal*, *41*(6), pp. 1000–1020.

Rovelli, P., Ferasso, M., De Massis, A. and Kraus, S., 2021. Thirty years of research in family business journals: Status quo and future directions. *Journal of Family Business Strategy*, *13*, p. 100422.

Sarbah, A. and Xiao, W., 2015. Good corporate governance structures: A must for family businesses. *Open Journal of Business and Management*, *3*(1), p. 40.

Sharma, P., Hoy, F., Astrachan, J.H. and Koiranen, M., 2007. The practice-driven evolution of family business education. *Journal of Business Research*, *60*(10), pp. 1012–1021.

Siakas, K., Naaranoja, M., Vlachakis, S. and Siakas, E., 2014. Family businesses in the new economy: How to survive and develop in times of financial crisis. *Procedia Economics and Finance*, *9*, pp. 331–341.

Sorenson, R.L., Goodpaster, K.E., Hedberg, P.R. and Yu, A., 2009. The family point of view, family social capital, and firm performance: An exploratory test. *Family Business Review*, *22*(3), pp. 239–253.

Vandekerkhof, P., Steijvers, T., Hendriks, W., and Voordeckers, W., 2018. Socio-emotional wealth separation and decision-making quality in family firm TMTs: The moderating role of psychological safety. *Journal of Management Studies*, *55*(4), pp. 648–676.

Waddell, S., 2017. *Societal learning and change: How governments, business and civil society are creating solutions to complex multi-stakeholder problems*. Routledge.

Ward, J., 2016. *Keeping the family business healthy: How to plan for continuing growth, profitability, and family leadership*. Springer.

Weimann, V., Gerken, M. and Hülsbeck, M., 2021. Old flames never die–the role of binding social ties for corporate entrepreneurship in family firms. *International Entrepreneurship and Management Journal*, *17*(4), pp. 1707–1730.

Xiang, D., Chen, J., Tripe, D. and Zhang, N., 2019. Family firms, sustainable innovation and financing cost: Evidence from Chinese hi-tech small and medium-sized enterprises. *Technological Forecasting and Social Change*, *144*, pp. 499–511.

Yong, C., Firdousi, S. F., Afzal, A., Florjančič, V., and Awais, M., 2022. The influence of internal and external stakeholder mechanisms on entrepreneurial success: the moderating role of digital technology adoption. *Frontiers in Psychology*, *12*, p. 6627.

Zellweger, T. M., and Nason, R. S., 2008. A stakeholder perspective on family firm performance. *Family Business Review*, *21*(3), pp. 203–216.

Zhang, Y., Montenegro-Marin, C.E. and Díaz, V.G., 2021. Holistic cognitive conflict chain management framework in supply chain management. *Environmental Impact Assessment Review*, *88*, p. 106564.

16 Business Failure and Stakeholder Management Relationships in New Ventures

Phabion Tichawona Chaza

Introduction

Entrepreneurship is a vital economic force which is underpinned by strategic managerial behaviour in pursuit of business opportunities (Stevenson, 1983). This continuous and evolving process (Shane, 2003) involves the identification and/or creation of opportunities (Alvarez & Barney, 2010) and their commercialization (Sarasvathy & Venkataraman, 2011). In the process, the identity of the entrepreneur, who is central to the business activity, merges with that of the business venture (Shepherd & Haynie, 2009), forming indistinguishable meanings for the entrepreneur, business venture, and business management.

Business failure may however inflict costs on these resource suppliers, prompting them to seek protections against consequences of possible future venture failure, particularly where a venture re-emerges subsequent to failure. Trust and trustworthiness, good faith, and entrepreneurial apologies, which are significant societal/environmental conditions (Stevenson, 1983), are argued to moderate relationships between management and suppliers of entrepreneurial resources in ventures post failure. Business failure is conceptualized at business and individual levels (Jenkins & McKelvie, 2017; Sarasvathy et al., 2013; Ucbasaran et al., 2013). Failure is defined to exclude business closure where the business shuts its doors and ceases to exist. The discussion also includes the entrepreneur who exits a business when it fails and moves on to engage in a new venture (Jenkins & McKelvie, 2017, Sarasvathy et al., 2013, Ucbasaran et al., 2013). This re-entrepreneur is directly associable (Shepherd & Haynie, 2009) with the failed business and would be percieved accordingly by suppliers of resources.

Who Are Business Stakeholders?

Stakeholders contribute the resources necessary for the establishment and sustenance of business ventures. A business's stakeholders are groups and/or individuals who affect or are affected by the firm's transactions in its efforts to achieve its objectives (Mitchell et al., 1997). In other words, a business's stakeholders benefit from or may be hurt by the business's performance outcomes.

DOI: 10.4324/9781003256014-20

In entrepreneurship, the stakeholder concept challenges unlimited shareowner's rights (Coase, 2013), advocating for the business's multi-fiduciary responsibilities and specifically that the business is restricted against hurting the property rights of others (Pejovich, 1990).

This discussion follows Mitchell and colleagues' stakeholder typology (Mitchell et al., 1997), which categorizes stakeholders based on their power and legitimacy and the urgency of the claim at hand. These three attributes determine the stakeholder's salience to the business, which in turn influences levels of attention a stakeholder deserves and obtains from business management. Stakeholder salience influences strategies deployed by either part in stakeholder management transactions (Frooman, 1999) and may have implications on the stakeholder's ability to reassert and safeguard their claims in ventures established after a business failure.

Successful ventures engage stakeholders equitably (Wheeler et al., 2003) and recognize stakeholders' integral role in the operation of the business (Freeman, 1994). Stakeholder management aligns business goals with stakeholder claims (Carroll & Näsi, 1997), is constrained by stakeholder perceptions of business actions and management behaviour (Brenner & Cochran, 1991), and seeks to balance stakeholder claims on economic, legal and moral assumptions (Brenner & Cochran, 1991) in efforts to achieve equitable gain and harm distribution (Donaldson & Preston, 1995). Superior long-term performance stems from shared values, trust-building, and agility investment (Freeman et al., 2020a; Freeman et al., 2020b).

The foregoing discussion suggests a systemic power imbalance in stakeholder and management relationships, which asymmetry is sustained by the salience of the stakeholders and their diverse interests in a business. Managing stakeholder interests in view of resource indivisibility (Reynolds et al., 2006) requires trade-offs between stakeholder classes for the business's long-term value (Jensen, 2001). It is essential to acknowledge that specific stakeholder interests hold intrinsic value, and that satisfying one group should not disadvantage another (Donaldson & Preston, 1995). Stakeholders in a new post-failure venture may seek assurance that their interests will be fairly managed.

Business is a complex decision-making process within a network of relationships (Holmstrom & Tirole, 1989) which faces diverse and conflicting stakeholder ideologies (Stoney & Winstanley, 2001), contractual constraints (Coase, 2013), and identity orientations (Bridoux & Vishwanathan, 2020). It is against this background that we understand the diversity and complexity of the consequences of failure on stakeholder and management relationships in ventures established after a failure. Failure's consequences may therefore be extensive, leading to post-failure disparities from pre-existing conditions.

Business failure: What is it?

Existing literature defines business failure through various lenses (Jenkins & McKelvie, 2016; Amankwah-Amoah, 2015; Shepherd and Wiklund, 2006;

Ucbasaran et al., 2013). It can be perceived based on financial and economic criteria (Altman et al., 2019) or when the opportunity cost of continuing operations exceeds the business's value. Venture performance below the entrepreneur's expectations, even when resources sufficient for its survival are generated (McGrath, 1999, Ucbasaran et al., 2013), as well as noneconomic disappointments like an unbalanced work/family lifestyle (Khelil, 2016), may define failure. Gillespie and Dietz include harm to stakeholders' interests in their definition of business failure.

Business failure results from a series of events, actions, and responses (Amankwah-Amoah & Debrah, 2014; D'Aveni, 1989; Hambrick & D'Aveni, 1992) associated to risks threatening the business. Literature attributes failure to environmental determinism and/or strategic choice (Mellahi & Wilkinson, 2004). Deterministic factors are external to the business and fall beyond managerial control. Examples of deterministic factors include natural disasters, competition, macroeconomic instability, technology shifts, and market reductions (Mellahi & Wilkinson, 2004; Arditi et al., 2000; Amankwah-Amoah, 2016). The strategic choice perspective focuses on endogenous factors such as management competence, leadership style, and employee skills (Mellahi & Wilkinson, 2004; Arditi et al., 2000). Incompetent management and unskilled workers expose the business to internal failure threats (Amankwah-Amoah, 2016; Xiong & Bharadwaj, 2013).

Endogenous and exogenous factors may interact, leading to business failure. Astute management is crucial in navigating venture challenges and safeguarding the well-being of the business (Xiong & Bharadwaj, 2013). The attributes of top management influence outcomes (Hambrick & D'Aveni, 1992), potentially placing culpability for failure on them in stakeholders' eyes. Equitable stakeholder management aligns interests of the business and stakeholders (Carroll & Näsi, 1997) and failure may portray weak stakeholder management structures and raise questions regarding top management's capabilities and integrity. While negative perceptions arising after business failure affect stakeholder behaviour in post-failure ventures, individual stakeholder experience in assessing the potential for organizational learning may mitigate these effects.

Impact of business failure on stakeholder relationships post failure

Business failure has lasting and significant impacts on stakeholders' financial, personal, and professional relationships (Ucbasaran et al., 2013; Singh et al., 2007; Singh et al., 2015; Shepherd et al., 2009; Harris & Sutton, 1986). The costs of business failure, whether financial, social, or psychological, are interconnected and are reducible to social dimensions (Ucbasaran et al., 2013; Cope, 2011). While investors appear the most exposed to implications of business failure, other stakeholders are equally affected (Cole et al., 2021) with distinctions influenced by the context and extent of their transactions with the failed business (Manzaneque-Lizano et al., 2019).

Extant literature emphasizes that the effectiveness and sustainability of stakeholder relationships are crucial for the survival of new ventures (Phillips et al., 2019; Civera et al., 2019). Cooperation between stakeholders is vital for the success of a new venture (Pollack & Bosse, 2014). Stakeholders affected by a previous failure may terminate relationships, thereby depriving the new venture of critical resources (Freeman, 2010; Clarke & Rhodes, 2020). Such withdrawal may be driven by a desire to avoid future failure costs and/or seek retribution for perceived unfairness relating to the earlier business failure (Clarke & Rhodes, 2020).

Despite potential reluctance, some stakeholders may consider engaging with ventures created after a failure but only under specific conditions. Trust and trustworthiness (Davis et al., 2000; Wicks et al., 1999; Crane, 2020; Greenwood & Van Buren III, 2010), good faith (Dawkins, 2014), and entrepreneurial apologies (Pollack & Bosse, 2014; Ashforth & Gibbs, 1990; Clarke & Rhodes, 2020) emerge as factors influencing stakeholders' willingness to extend relationships to future ventures. While distinct, these factors share a normative foundation which reflects ethical and moral considerations in business and has implications for stakeholder management relationships (Zakhem & Palmer, 2017).

Trust and trustworthiness

Trust is a crucial element in stakeholder relationships and business success (Davis et al., 2000; Wicks et al., 1999; Crane, 2020; Greenwood & Van Buren III, 2010). It fosters cooperative behaviour within businesses (Williams, 2001) and among stakeholder groups (Jensen, 2003). Developing trusting relationships helps businesses save on social and environmental action costs (Peifer & Newman, 2020). To be successful, a business must therefore trust its stakeholders and itself be trustworthy (Gubbins et al., 2018).

Trust serves as a conduit for fulfilling ethical obligations to stakeholders. When a business receives benefits from stakeholders, it has a duty to maximize benefits and minimize harm for the stakeholder (Greenwood & Van Buren III, 2010) in a manner that satisfies distributive justice (Van Buren III, 2001). The business's trustworthiness, which is composed of the trusted party's ability, benevolence, and integrity (Mayer et al., 1995), reflects its capacity to fairly compensate stakeholders (Pirson & Malhotra, 2011; Wicks et al., 1999). Absence of trust occurs when stakeholders lack confidence in the business's trustworthiness and are unwilling to be vulnerable to the business's actions (Greenwood & Van Buren III, 2010). Distrust arises when the business is perceived as pursuing self-interest without ensuring fair benefits and protections for stakeholders (Greenwood & Van Buren III, 2010).

Stakeholder voting and political and economic power may not adequately protect the interests of even the definitive stakeholder. Limitations to the political protections governments are able to offer and the capacity of stakeholders to be represented by governments (Greenwood & Van Buren III, 2010) are examples of when stakeholder powers may be inadequate. The trustworthiness of the business complements the influence of stakeholder salience in cases such as these. The business may however exploit this power imbalance and compromise returns, especially for low-power and vulnerable stakeholders (Phillips, 1997; Greenwood & Van Buren III, 2010).

Trust and trustworthiness contribute to the moral character of the business (Greenwood & Van Buren III, 2010). The business builds a reputation for trustworthiness that influences its transactions with stakeholders in future ventures (Greenwood & Van Buren III, 2010). Businesses with a positive track record of moral duty and fair treatment of stakeholders can expect cooperation in future ventures. Stakeholders' behaviour is influenced by their expectations of the business's conduct in specific circumstances (Greenwood & Van Buren III, 2010). Conversely, a reputation for opportunism and "free-riding" on stakeholder interests may limit cooperation in future business ventures (Axelrod & Hamilton, 1981). The business's treatment of powerless stakeholders may affect whether other stakeholders would want to transact and engage in future exchanges (Crane, 2020). Rebuilding trust after a previous venture failure requires the business to signal trust dimensions (abilities, benevolence, and integrity) as a manner of encouraging stakeholders to re-establish their relationships (Pollack et al., 2017; Shepherd et al., 2000).

Good faith

Business failure's impact on stakeholder relationships is also moderated by substantive stakeholder engagement in good faith (Dawkins, 2014). Good-faith stakeholder management eliminates unfounded suspicions and aligns with fairness principles (Phillips, 1997). Stakeholder engagement in good faith eliminates power asymmetries and ensures each party safeguards their interests without relying on the benevolence of another party (Freeman & Reed, 1983). The principle of good faith also involves a moral obligation to protect less powerful stakeholders from the business and the more powerful stakeholders (Dawkins, 2014).

Stakeholder engagement in good faith is operationalized through dialogue, negotiation, transparency, and totality of conduct (Dawkins, 2014). Application of the principle does not eliminate conflict but rather offers a mechanism which preserves the independence of parties and their ability to protect their interests. In summary, good-faith stakeholder management is a practical counterweight to management's prerogatives and opportunism and enhances the business's accountability to stakeholders. A fair transaction reputation influences stakeholder cooperation post-business failure ventures.

Entrepreneurial apologies

Entrepreneurial apologies reduce retributive justice in cases where businesses wish to re-establish after violating stakeholder norms and expectations (Pollack & Bosse, 2014; Pollack et al., 2017). Stakeholders perceive unfairness when norms are breached, as in business failures and expect apologies from the business if relationships are to mend (Ashforth & Gibbs, 1990). Apologies may lead to forgiveness, thereby fostering an environment for future cooperation (Clarke & Rhodes, 2020). Apologies may affect future stakeholder cooperation where the business is perceived to have inflicted sufficient self-punishment upon itself (Clarke & Rhodes, 2020). Apologies in forms of compensation, remorse statements, acknowledgment of culpability, and empathy, may be offered (Clarke & Rhodes, 2020).

The effectiveness of apologies depends on the issuer's and recipient's mental and intellectual characteristics (McCullough et al., 1998), severity of failure circumstances, and quality of stakeholder relationship (Clarke & Rhodes, 2020). The extent of forgiveness may also be influenced by the nature of cause of the business failure; moral failures may be harder to forgive than failures arising from incompetence (Kim et al., 2009). Entrepreneurial apologies may thus influence stakeholder behaviours in future business relationships.

Stakeholder class-specific behaviours

Literature notes other, less significant ways of moderating stakeholder management relationship post business failure. The business may advertise and promote the new venture within entrepreneur networks (Alvarez et al., 2020). The business may review internal processes (Shepherd, 2003), adjust stakeholder interactions, and reassess the competitive landscape (Cope, 2011; Shepherd, 2003; Singh et al., 2007). Accepting culpability for the failure may garner sympathy (Harris & Sutton, 1986) and show honesty and a commitment to learning from the failure (Cope et al., 2004). Stakeholders might tolerate failures attributed to factors beyond the business's control (Kirkwood, 2007). Support from committed stakeholders may sway undecided ones to cooperate with the new venture (Cialdini, 2001).

Mechanisms of trust and trustworthiness, stakeholder engagement in good faith, and entrepreneurial apologies foster "jointness" of interest (Civera et al., 2019) and cooperation (Phillips et al., 2019) between parties. Efforts at shaping stakeholder management relationships may produce varied outcomes in view of the diverse and conflicting stakeholder claims on the business.

Stakeholders may terminate relationships after a business failure in order to mitigate future risks and punish the business for violating their expectations (Clarke & Rhodes, 2020). Stakeholders who discontinue ties with the business generally have alternative consumers to whom they reassign resources (Frooman, 1999) and can afford the associated exit costs (Senaux, 2008). Exiting of the business particularly by significant and unilateral stakeholders negatively affects the business's performance outcomes.

Despite past losses, some stakeholders may persist in supporting a business post-failure. Freeman's categorization of stakeholders based on their claims provides insight into understanding and predicting stakeholder behaviour. Stakeholders expect attention commensurate with their contribution to the business while the business may differentiate returns to the stakeholder based on stakeholder salience. The following sections explore potential behavioural postures of stakeholder classes in ventures post-business failure.

Latent/dependent stakeholders

Latent/dependent stakeholders lack tools to influence the business (Dawkins, 2014). These low-power stakeholders may have no influence over the affairs of the business, and their participation may easily be reassigned to another party. This helplessness on the part of the dependent stakeholder creates risk and minimizes trust-based relationships (McAllister, 1995; Greenwood & Van Buren III, 2010). Vulnerable stakeholders may lack choice and consent and are compelled to continue to contribute resources and make sacrifices for the business. The business's moral character may however accommodate latent/dependent stakeholders and offer them the protection they require. The business may reduce power asymmetry and empower low-power stakeholders, making them competent value co-creation partners (Dawkins, 2014). Dependent stakeholders may seek protection from the power and benevolence of other stakeholders (Mitchell et al., 1997).

Definitive stakeholders

Definitive stakeholders possess power, legitimacy, and urgency, making them the most salient for business attention (Mitchell et al., 1997). They significantly influence strategic decision-making, which is crucial for the business's value generation and survival (Manzaneque-Lizano et al., 2019; Gianfelici et al., 2018). Despite potential losses in a business failure, definitive stakeholders have the greatest staying power in ensuring the new venture's survival.

Definitive stakeholders are expected to review their rights and fortify their positions against future failures. Post-failure, they may alter share retention terms and adopt a gradual investment approach where additional investment is contingent upon profitable returns on earlier investments (McGrath, 1999; Magness, 2008). They may demand adherence to reporting standards and accountability in order to reduce information asymmetry (Gianfelici et al., 2018; Assad & Goddard, 2010). Risk in a new venture after a failure may be unquantifiable, leading to stakeholder enrolment challenges (Burns et al., 2016). Human capital replacements mainly at CEO levels may counter uneasiness particularly after a competency failure (Connelly et al., 2016; Davidson III et al., 1995).

Definitive stakeholders may demand appointment of a reputable and independent board of directors (Connelly et al., 2016; Calabrò & Mussolino, 2013). Definitive stakeholders may influence enrollment by creating new business governance structures that have reputation and charisma. The definitive stakeholder is best placed to deal with managerial opportunism and free riding and may advocate for codes of conduct and support the rights of the low-power stakeholders (Dawkins, 2014). While generally associated with positive intentions, definitive stakeholders may pressure the new venture into satisfying inequitable interests (Bond & Saunders, 2005). The significance of the definitive stakeholder class lies in influencing critical aspects of the new venture, particularly strategic decision-making for profitability and growth.

Expectant stakeholders

Expectant stakeholders hold two of the three stakeholder attributes (Mitchell et al., 1997) and are moderately salient. This stakeholder category includes customers, suppliers, and employees, among others. They expect increased responsiveness compared to dependent stakeholders and pose the largest business disruption risk (Mitchell et al., 1997). The new venture must therefore seize every opportunity to mitigate potential dangers that this category of stakeholder may present. The expectant stakeholder appears sensitive to exit costs in future cooperation decisions and may not terminate relationships when exit costs are exorbitant but rather seek legal and other strategic protections (Frooman, 1999). For example, regulators may review frameworks to reduce the impact of failure (Cole et al., 2021) on new ventures. Suppliers may, in either hostile or conciliatory manner, leverage control over resources to extract certain behaviours from the new venture (Frooman, 1999). Specialized and technical skills necessary to maintain the new critical resource dependencies may be required, an outcome which may divert the business's energies from its core performance focus (Pfeffer & Salancik, 2003).

Activism directed at the new venture may be instigated by employees, customers, or the community (Davidson III et al., 1995; Russell et al., 2016; Spar & La Mure, 2003). Where stakeholders remain unsatisfied with a business's behaviour in the aftermath of the business failure, expectant stakeholders may act to boycott the new venture's products. In order to maintain its "social license" to operate, the new venture needs to amass enough reputational capital to counterbalance threats arising from business failure (Fombrun et al., 2000) and seek to avoid activities which, whether prescribed by law or not, are unacceptable to the community (Gunningham et al., 2004).

Conclusion

Stakeholder management relates to the corporate responsibility decisions and actions taken by a business regarding its stakeholders (Freeman et al., 2020b). Business success requires responses that ensure stakeholder satisfaction and ethical considerations. Stakeholders need confidence in management decisions, especially when a business seeks to re-emerge from failure.

Post-failure, stakeholders may protect themselves against potential future failures by terminating relationships or by imposing higher requirements for participation. Power asymmetry can leave some stakeholders, particularly those with low power, vulnerable and with limited alternatives and exposed to potential abuse. The impact of business failure on stakeholder relationships can be moderated by various factors. This chapter emphasizes the influence of trust and trustworthiness, good faith, and entrepreneurial apologies on stakeholder management relationships in ventures established post failure. The study identifies stakeholder salience as a significant factor influencing engagement strategies deployed by both businesses and stakeholders in securing their interests.

The finding offers insights for entrepreneurs managing stakeholder relations after business failure, suggesting embedding trust and trustworthiness, good faith, and entrepreneurial apologies in their strategic approaches. The jointness of interest underlying these mechanisms benefits both stakeholders and business, particularly in weak institutional environments where stakeholder interests may have limited protection.

References

Altman, E. I., Hotchkiss, E. & Wang, W. 2019. *Corporate financial distress, restructuring, and bankruptcy: Analyze leveraged finance, distressed debt, and bankruptcy*. Wiley.

Alvarez, S. A. & Barney, J. B. 2010. Entrepreneurship and epistemology: The philosophical underpinnings of the study of entrepreneurial opportunities. *Academy of Management Annals*, *4*, 557–583.

Alvarez, S. A., Young, S. L. & Woolley, J. L. 2020. Creating the world's deadliest catch: The process of enrolling stakeholders in an uncertain endeavor. *Business & Society*, *59*, 287–321.

Amankwah-Amoah, J. 2015. A unified framework for incorporating decision making into explanations of business failure. *Industrial Management & Data Systems*.

Amankwah-Amoah, J. 2016. An integrative process model of organisational failure. *Journal of Business Research*, *69*, 3388–3397.

Amankwah-Amoah, J. & Debrah, Y. A. 2014. Air Afrique: The demise of a continental icon. *Business History*, *56*, 517–546.

Arditi, D., Koksal, A. & Kale, S. 2000. Business failures in the construction industry. *Engineering Construction and Architectural Management*, *7*, 120–132.

Ashforth, B. E. & Gibbs, B. W. 1990. The double-edge of organizational legitimation. *Organization science*, *1*, 177–194.

Assad, M. J. & Goddard, A. R. 2010. Stakeholder salience and accounting practices in Tanzanian NGOs. *International Journal of Public Sector Management*, *23*, 276–299.

Axelrod, R. & Hamilton, W. D. 1981. The evolution of cooperation. *Science*, *211*, 1390–1396.

Bond, P. & Saunders, R. 2005. Labor, the State, and the Struggle for a Democratic Zimbabwe. *Monthly Review-New York*, *57*, 42.

Brenner, S. N. & Cochran, P. 1991. The stakeholder theory of the firm: Implications for business and society theory and research. *Proceedings of the International Association for Business and Society*, *2*, 897–933.

Bridoux, F. M. & Vishwanathan, P. 2020. When do powerful stakeholders give managers the latitude to balance all stakeholders' interests? *Business & Society*, *59*, 232–262.

Burns, B. L., Barney, J. B., Angus, R. W. & Herrick, H. N. 2016. Enrolling stakeholders under conditions of risk and uncertainty. *Strategic Entrepreneurship Journal*, *10*, 97–106.

Calabrò, A. & Mussolino, D. 2013. How do boards of directors contribute to family SME export intensity? The role of formal and informal governance mechanisms. *Journal of Management & Governance*, *17*, 363–403.

Carroll, A. B. & Näsi, J. 1997. Understanding stakeholder thinking: Themes from a Finnish conference. *Business Ethics: A European Review*, *6*, 46–51.

Cialdini, R. B. 2001. The science of persuasion. *Scientific American*, *284*, 76–81.

Civera, C., De Colle, S. & Casalegno, C. 2019. Stakeholder engagement through empowerment: The case of coffee farmers. *Business Ethics: A European Review*, *28*, 156–174.

Clarke, S. L. & Rhodes, E. S. 2020. Entrepreneurial apologies: The mediating role of forgiveness on future cooperation. *Journal of Business Venturing Insights*, *13*, e00147.

Coase, R. H. 2013. The problem of social cost. *The Journal of Law and Economics*, *56*, 837–877.

Cole, R., Johan, S. & Schweizer, D. 2021. Corporate failures: Declines, collapses, and scandals. *Journal of Corporate Finance*, *67*, 101872.

Connelly, B. L., Ketchen, J. R., Gangloff, K. A. & Shook, C. L. 2016. Investor perceptions of CEO successor selection in the wake of integrity and competence failures: A policy capturing study. *Strategic Management Journal*, *37*, 2135–2151.

Cope, J. 2011. Entrepreneurial learning from failure: An interpretative phenomenological analysis. *Journal of Business Venturing*, *26*, 604–623.

Cope, J., Cave, F. & Eccles, S. 2004. Attitudes of venture capital investors towards entrepreneurs with previous business failure. *Venture Capital*, *6*, 147–172.

Crane, B. 2020. Revisiting who, when, and why stakeholders matter: Trust and stakeholder connectedness. *Business & Society*, *59*, 263–286.

D'Aveni, R. A. 1989. The aftermath of organizational decline: A longitudinal study of the strategic and managerial characteristics of declining firms. *Academy of Management Journal*, *32*, 577–605.

Davidson III, W. N., Worrell, D. L. & El-Jelly, A. 1995. Influencing managers to change unpopular corporate behaviour through boycotts and divestitures: A stock market test. *Business & Society*, *34*, 171–196.

Davis, J. H., Schoorman, F. D., Mayer, R. C. & Tan, H. H. 2000. The trusted general manager and business unit performance: Empirical evidence of a competitive advantage. *Strategic Management Journal*, *21*, 563–576.

Dawkins, C. E. 2014. The principle of good faith: Toward substantive stakeholder engagement. *Journal of Business Ethics*, *121*, 283–295.

Donaldson, T. & Preston, L. E. 1995. The stakeholder theory of the corporation: Concepts, evidence, and implications. *Academy of Management Review*, *20*, 65–91.

Fombrun, C. J., Gardberg, N. A. & Barnett, M. L. 2000. Opportunity platforms and safety nets: Corporate citizenship and reputational risk. *Business and Society Review*, *105*, 85–106.

Freeman, R. E. 1994. The politics of stakeholder theory: Some future directions. *Business Ethics Quarterly*, *4*, 409–421.

Freeman, R. E. 2010. *Strategic management: A stakeholder approach*, Cambridge University Press.

Freeman, R. E., Parmar, B. L. & Martin, K. 2020a. Chapter 4: Stakeholders and shareholders. *The power of and: Responsible business without trade-offs*. Columbia University Press.

Freeman, R. E., Phillips, R. & Sisodia, R. 2020b. Tensions in stakeholder theory. *Business & Society*, *59*, 213–231.

Freeman, R. E. & Reed, D. L. 1983. Stockholders and stakeholders: A new perspective on corporate governance. *California Management Review*, *25*, 88–106.

Frooman, J. 1999. Stakeholder influence strategies. *Academy of Management Review*, *24*, 191–205.

Gianfelici, C., Casadei, A. & Cembali, F. 2018. The relevance of nationality and industry for stakeholder salience: An investigation through integrated reports. *Journal of Business Ethics*, *150*, 541–558.

Greenwood, M. & Van Buren III, H. J. 2010. Trust and stakeholder theory: Trustworthiness in the organisation–stakeholder relationship. *Journal of Business Ethics*, *95*, 425–438.

Gubbins, C., Harney, B., Van Der Werff, L. & Rousseau, D. 2018. Enhancing the trustworthiness and credibility of HRD: Evidence-based management to the rescue? *Human Resource Development Quarterly*, *29*, 193–202.

Gunningham, N., Kagan, R. A. & Thornton, D. 2004. Social license and environmental protection: why businesses go beyond compliance. *Law & Social Inquiry*, *29*, 307–341.

Hambrick, D. C. & D'Aveni, R. A. 1992. Top team deterioration as part of the downward spiral of large corporate bankruptcies. *Management Science*, *38*, 1445–1466.

Harris, S. G. & Sutton, R. I. 1986. Functions of parting ceremonies in dying organizations. *Academy of Management Journal*, *29*, 5–30.

Holmstrom, B. R. & Tirole, J. 1989. The theory of the firm. *Handbook of Industrial Organization*, *1*, 61–133.

Jenkins, A. & McKelvie, A. 2016. What is entrepreneurial failure? Implications for future research. *International Small Business Journal*, *34*, 176–188.

Jenkins, A. & McKelvie, A. 2017. Is this the end? Investigating firm and individual level outcomes post-failure. *Journal of Business Venturing Insights*, *8*, 138–143.

Jensen, M. 2001. Value maximisation, stakeholder theory, and the corporate objective function. *European Financial Management*, *7*, 297–317.

Jensen, M. 2003. The role of network resources in market entry: Commercial banks' entry into investment banking, 1991–1997. *Administrative Science Quarterly*, *48*, 466–497.

Khelil, N. 2016. The many faces of entrepreneurial failure: Insights from an empirical taxonomy. *Journal of Business Venturing*, *31*, 72–94.

Kim, P. H., Dirks, K. T. & Cooper, C. D. 2009. The repair of trust: A dynamic bilateral perspective and multilevel conceptualization. *Academy of Management Review*, *34*, 401–422.

Kirkwood, J. 2007. Igniting the entrepreneurial spirit: Is the role parents play gendered? *International Journal of Entrepreneurial Behaviour & Research*, *13*, pp. 39–59.

Magness, V. 2008. Who are the stakeholders now? An empirical examination of the Mitchell, Agle, and Wood theory of stakeholder salience. *Journal of Business Ethics*, *83*, 177–192.

Manzaneque-Lizano, M., Alfaro-Cortés, E. & Priego de la Cruz, A. M. 2019. Stakeholders and long-term sustainability of SMEs. Who really matters in crisis contexts, and when. *Sustainability*, *11*, 6551.

Mayer, R. C., Davis, J. H. & Schoorman, F. D. 1995. An integrative model of organizational trust. *Academy of Management Review*, *20*, 709–734.

Mcallister, D. J. 1995. Affect-and cognition-based trust as foundations for interpersonal cooperation in organizations. *Academy of Management Journal*, *38*, 24–59.

McCullough, M. E., Rachal, K. C., Sandage, S. J., Worthington, J. R., Brown, S. W. & Hight, T. L. 1998. Interpersonal forgiving in close relationships: II. Theoretical elaboration and measurement. *Journal of Personality and Social Psychology*, *75*, 1586.

Mcgrath, R. G. 1999. Falling forward: Real options reasoning and entrepreneurial failure. *Academy of Management Review*, *24*, 13–30.

Mellahi, K. & Wilkinson, A. 2004. Organizational failure: A critique of recent research and a proposed integrative framework. *International Journal of Management Reviews*, *5*, 21–41.

Mitchell, R. K., Agle, B. R. & Wood, D. J. 1997. Toward a theory of stakeholder identification and salience: Defining the principle of who and what really counts. *Academy of Management Review*, *22*, 853–886.

Peifer, J. L. & Newman, D. T. 2020. Making the business case for corporate social responsibility and perceived trustworthiness: A cross-stakeholder analysis. *Business and Society Review*, *125*, 161–181.

Pejovich, S. 1990. *The economics of property rights: Towards a theory of comparative systems*. Springer Science & Business Media.

Pfeffer, J. & Salancik, G. R. 2003. *The external control of organizations: A resource dependence perspective*. Stanford University Press.

Phillips, R. A. 1997. Stakeholder theory and a principle of fairness. *Business Ethics Quarterly*, *7*, 51–66.

Phillips, R. A., Barney, J., Freeman, R. E. & Harrison, J. S. 2019. Stakeholder chapter. *The Cambridge Handbook of Stakeholder Theory*, *3*.

Pirson, M. & Malhotra, D. 2011. Foundations of organizational trust: What matters to different stakeholders? *Organization Science*, *22*, 1087–1104.

Pollack, J. M., Barr, S. & Hanson, S. 2017. New venture creation as establishing stakeholder relationships: A trust-based perspective. *Journal of Business Venturing Insights*, *7*, 15–20.

Pollack, J. M. & Bosse, D. A. 2014. When do investors forgive entrepreneurs for lying? *Journal of Business Venturing*, *29*, 741–754.

Reynolds, S., Schultz, F. & Hekman, D. 2006. Balancing stakeholder interests: The constraining effects of resource divisibility and stakeholder saliency. *Journal of Business Ethics*, *64*(3), 285–301.

Russell, C. A., Russell, D. W. & Honea, H. 2016. Corporate social responsibility failures: How do consumers respond to corporate violations of implied social contracts? *Journal of Business Ethics*, *136*, 759–773.

Sarasvathy, S. D., Menon, A. R. & Kuechle, G. 2013. Failing firms and successful entrepreneurs: Serial entrepreneurship as a temporal portfolio. *Small Business Economics*, *40*, 417–434.

Sarasvathy, S. D. & Venkataraman, S. 2011. Entrepreneurship as method: Open questions for an entrepreneurial future. *Entrepreneurship Theory and Practice*, *35*, 113–135.

Senaux, B. 2008. A stakeholder approach to football club governance. *International Journal of Sport Management and Marketing*, *4*, 4.

Shane, S. A. 2003. *A general theory of entrepreneurship: The individual-opportunity nexus*. Edward Elgar Publishing.

Shepherd, D. & Haynie, J. M. 2009. Family business, identity conflict, and an expedited entrepreneurial process: A process of resolving identity conflict. *Entrepreneurship Theory and Practice*, *33*, 1245–1264.

Shepherd, D. A. 2003. Learning from business failure: Propositions of grief recovery for the self-employed. *Academy of Management Review*, *28*, 318–328.

Shepherd, D. A., Douglas, E. J. & Shanley, M. 2000. New venture survival: Ignorance, external shocks, and risk reduction strategies. *Journal of Business Venturing*, *15*, 393–410.

Shepherd, D. A. & Wiklund, J. 2006. Successes and failures at research on business failure and learning from it. *Foundations and Trends in Entrepreneurship*, *2*.

Shepherd, D. A., Wiklund, J. & Haynie, J. M. 2009. Moving forward: Balancing the financial and emotional costs of business failure. *Journal of Business Venturing*, *24*, 134–148.

Singh, S., Corner, P. & Pavlovich, K. 2007. Coping with entrepreneurial failure. *Journal of Management & Organization*, *13*, 331–344.

Singh, S., Corner, P. D. & Pavlovich, K. 2015. Failed, not finished: A narrative approach to understanding venture failure stigmatization. *Journal of Business Venturing*, *30*, 150–166.

Spar, D. L. & la Mure, L. T. 2003. The power of activism: Assessing the impact of NGOs on global business. *California Management Review*, *45*, 78–101.

Stevenson, H. H. 1983. *A perspective on entrepreneurship*, Harvard Business School Boston.

Stoney, C. & Winstanley, D. 2001. Stakeholding: Confusion or utopia? Mapping the conceptual terrain. *Journal of Management Studies*, *38*, 603–626.

Ucbasaran, D., Shepherd, D. A., Lockett, A. & Lyon, S. J. 2013. Life after business failure: The process and consequences of business failure for entrepreneurs. *Journal of Management*, *39*, 163–202.

van Buren III, H. J. 2001. Corporate citizenship and obligations of fairness. *Journal of Corporate Citizenship*, *2001*(3), 55–67.

Wheeler, D., Colbert, B. & Freeman, R. E. 2003. Focusing on value: Reconciling corporate social responsibility, sustainability and a stakeholder approach in a network world. *Journal of General Management*, *28*, 1–28.

Wicks, A. C., Berman, S. L. & Jones, T. M. 1999. The structure of optimal trust: Moral and strategic implications. *Academy of Management Review*, *24*, 99–116.

Williams, M. 2001. In whom we trust: Group membership as an affective context for trust development. *Academy of Management Review*, *26*, 377–396.

Xiong, G. & Bharadwaj, S. 2013. Asymmetric roles of advertising and marketing capability in financial returns to news: Turning bad into good and good into great. *Journal of Marketing Research*, *50*, 706–724.

Zakhem, A. & Palmer, D. E. 2017. Normative stakeholder theory. *Stakeholder management*. Emerald Publishing Limited.

17 Entrepreneurial Strategies for Effective Stakeholder Management in Africa

Ernest Kumi, Solomon Tawiah Yeboah and George Kofi Amoako

Introduction

Africa has seen a surge in entrepreneurial ventures, which have become integral players in addressing pressing societal and environmental challenges (Ojong et al., 2021). Effective stakeholder management is crucial for these ventures to succeed, as it helps navigate the complex network of stakeholders' interests, triggers, and expectations. Mismanaged stakeholder engagement strategies can lead to delays in strategy implementation, resource depletion, political interventions, and even strategy termination (AFDB, 2021). To navigate these hurdles and capitalise on stakeholder engagement possibilities, one must comprehend the complex network of stakeholders' interests, triggers, and expectations. This understanding reduces risks and promotes entrepreneurship. Stakeholder management is particularly important in Africa, where development and sustainability face many obstacles and possibilities. Managing stakeholder expectations unlocks access to scarce resources, such as capital, technology, skills, and knowledge, which are often in short supply across the continent (Kujala et al., 2022). By actively engaging stakeholders, businesses can secure essential resources for their activities and goals from investors, donors, partners, suppliers, and customers (Kujala et al., 2022). Efficient stakeholder management enhances an organisation's societal acceptability, building confidence and fostering a positive reputation among communities, government entities, regulatory authorities, and the media (Góes et al., 2023). Stakeholder management solutions assist companies in accomplishing social and environmental goals, which stakeholders increasingly prioritise, especially in Africa (Tsang et al., 2022). However, there is a notable gap in empirical evidence regarding how African entrepreneurs can harness stakeholder engagement to enhance value creation and innovation while mitigating inherent risks and uncertainties. Comparative and cross-cultural studies that examine how stakeholder management practices adapt to varied African markets, sectors, and cultures are lacking (Madumere, 2021). Digital technologies may revolutionise stakeholder management for African entrepreneurs by improving stakeholder efficiency, transparency, and inclusivity, allowing new kinds of co-operation and co-creation (Lockart, 2023). The literature shows that few

DOI: 10.4324/9781003256014-21

studies have examined how African entrepreneurs can use digital technologies to optimise stakeholder management, leaving challenges and opportunities in this transformative digital landscape unexplored. This article examines how innovation and technology adoption affect stakeholder management in African organisations, focusing on local collaborations, social impact prioritisation, cultural diversity, data analytics, and decision-making. The article aims to improve stakeholder management in Africa by illuminating these elements.

Literature review and model development

Stakeholder management

Stakeholder management is pivotal in contemporary business and organisational management, involving the recognition and diligent addressing of the interests, needs, and concerns of individuals, groups, or entities with a stake in an organisation's activities (Eskerod & Jepsen, 2016). Key stakeholders, including workers, consumers, investors, suppliers, government agencies, and communities, must be identified, categorised, and assessed for their influence and significance (Miles, 2017). Thorough analysis is crucial to understanding stakeholders' unique needs, concerns, and expectations, enabling tailored engagement strategies (Kujala et al., 2022). Effective engagement requires open communication, active listening, and a commitment to address concerns through avenues such as meetings, surveys, and social responsibility initiatives (Idowu, Capaldi et al., 2013). Conflict resolution is vital for maintaining positive relationships and averting reputational damage (Pless et al., 2021). Ethical considerations are paramount, with organisations integrating stakeholder management into sustainability and CSR strategies, focusing on the triple bottom line approach (Mendes et al., 2023).

Entrepreneurial strategies for supporting effective stakeholder management

Entrepreneurial strategies are essential for firm success, encompassing opportunity identification, resource allocation, risk management, and innovation (Shepherd & Patzelt, 2021). Entrepreneurs identify market gaps, employing strategies like innovation, imitation, cost leadership, and diversification (Paladino, 2022). Innovation is a key factor for success, spanning product or service innovations, processes, and business models (Satell, 2017). Risk-taking is inherent, necessitating effective risk management strategies (Chanda & Unel, 2021). Effectuation, a decision-making paradigm emphasising resource utilisation to mitigate uncertainty, is crucial (Sarasvathy, 2001). Resource-based-view literature underscores resource acquisition and strategic utilisation (Taher, 2012). Networking and relationship building enhance resource acquisition (Yin et al., 2021). Internationalisation and market expansion are frequent entrepreneurial strategies, bringing challenges and opportunities to entering global markets (Gholizadeh & Mohammadkazemi, 2022).

In summary, stakeholder management is essential for organisational success, requiring effective engagement and conflict resolution.

Innovation, technology, and effective stakeholder management

In the dynamic landscape of global corporations, harnessing creative technology is imperative for organisational success. This paradigm is gaining momentum in Africa as businesses recognise their pivotal role in improving operations and stakeholder engagement (Doe et al., 2022). The advent of innovative technologies, such as mobile applications and internet platforms, has revolutionised communication and accessibility across the continent, enabling organisations to engage effectively with diverse stakeholders, including customers, suppliers, and local communities (Mashiyane & Masuku, 2022). The integration of advanced tools like data analytics and artificial intelligence equips organisations with the capability to amass, analyse, and interpret vast datasets (ZA et al., 2022). This data-driven approach empowers organisations to glean valuable insights into stakeholder preferences and behaviours, facilitating more personalised and effective stakeholder management strategies (Storm & Borgman, 2020). In addition to improving internal operations, innovative technologies have played a pivotal role in elevating service delivery standards across various sectors in Africa, including healthcare, education, and finance (Noorbhai & Ojo, 2023). Organisations leveraging these technologies have gained a reputation for delivering superior services and cultivating trust and loyalty among their stakeholders (Calzon, 2022). Furthermore, those at the forefront of adopting cutting-edge technology often secure a significant competitive advantage, offering unique and convenient solutions that translate into increased market share and fortified stakeholder relationships (Walsh et al., 2020). The transformative potential of innovative technologies in Africa, as evidenced by numerous case studies such as the success story of mobile banking services like M-Pesa in Kenya, underscores the capacity of organisations to effectively engage with stakeholders and address their evolving needs. Thus, we propose that:

Proposition 1: *The level of innovation and technology adoption positively influences the delivery of effective stakeholder management in Africa.*

Local partnerships, alliances, and effective stakeholder management

Organisations that attain notable success often attribute it to adeptly managing stakeholders through fostering local partnerships and alliances (Wells et al., 2020). These intertwined factors play a pivotal role in cultivating trust, garnering support, and nurturing sustainable growth within both the community and the corporate environment. Collaborative engagement with local entities provides organisations with a unique insight into cultural nuances and community values (Ansu-Mensah et al., 2021), forming the foundation for respect and empathy—crucial elements in building trust and eliciting support from stakeholders

(Saenz, 2021). Local partnerships and alliances enable direct engagement with community members, including local leaders, nonprofits, and grassroots organisations. Such collaborations often yield co-created solutions that closely align with the authentic needs and priorities of the community (Sachs et al., 2022). Trust emerges as a linchpin in effective stakeholder management and is established and maintained more readily when organisations engage in collaborative initiatives with local partners who already enjoy the community's trust (Lehtonen et al., 2022). In many African contexts, the concept of the social licence to operate holds paramount significance, particularly in industries like mining and resource extraction (Górski, 2022). Forming alliances with local stakeholders becomes instrumental in gaining and sustaining this social licence, enabling organisations to operate with unequivocal community support (Karanja & Njenga, 2020). Case studies in Africa illustrate the transformative impact of local partnerships, such as collaborations between NGOs and local health workers, addressing healthcare challenges in underserved communities. These partnerships yield improved health outcomes and fortify community relationships (Ahmat et al., 2022). While no universally standardised legislation governs local partnerships, adherence to regulatory obligations in various African countries ensures positive stakeholder relationships (Somo & Onny, 2021). Stakeholder management in Africa relies on local partnerships and alliances to promote cultural awareness, community participation, and trust. Case studies support this idea, and African social dynamics are consistent with it.

Proposition 2: *The establishment of local partnerships and alliances significantly enhances the delivery of effective stakeholder management in Africa.*

Community trust as a moderator in local partnerships and effective stakeholder management in Africa

Community trust, denoting the confidence within a community towards its members and influencing institutions (Pretty & Ward, 2001), plays a pivotal moderating role in the nexus between local partnerships and effective stakeholder management in Africa. First, elevated community trust facilitates collaboration and communication among stakeholders, which is foundational for initiating and sustaining local partnerships and alliances (Mayanja, 2020). Trust encourages information sharing, resource pooling, shared responsibilities, and constructive conflict resolution among stakeholders (Saengsupavanich et al., 2012). Second, increased community trust enhances the legitimacy and accountability of local partnerships and alliances, prerequisites for effective stakeholder management in Africa (Kabahinda & Mwesigwa, 2023). Trust in institutions leads to stakeholder endorsement, compliance with decisions, and active participation in feedback and evaluation processes (Reed et al., 2018). Additionally, heightened community trust nurtures social capital and empowerment, which is advantageous for realising local partnerships and alliances' objectives. Trust in stakeholders' capabilities fosters active engagement in planning and execution, extracting benefits from learning and innovation opportunities within collaborative efforts (Esengulova et al., 2023). In conclusion, community trust enhances local partnerships and stakeholder management in Africa, enabling effective, legitimate, and participatory processes.

Proposition 2a: *Community trust moderates the relationship between the establishment of local partnerships and alliances and the delivery of effective stakeholder management in Africa, such that the relationship is stronger when community trust is high.*

The impact of community support on the relationship between local partnerships and stakeholder management in Africa

In the intricate realm of stakeholder management in Africa, organisations strategically establish local partnerships and alliances to enhance engagement, a strategy whose effectiveness hinges not only on organisational actions but significantly on the support and acceptance garnered from local communities (Mandiriza & Fourie, 2023). The significance of these partnerships cannot be understated, as they provide organisations with insights into the cultural nuances, values, and priorities of the served communities (Soulard et al., 2018), fostering respect, empathy, trust, and support from stakeholders (Sloan and Oliver, 2013). Local partnerships often result in co-created solutions aligned with genuine community needs, proving highly effective in stakeholder engagement (Rabinowitz, 2015). However, their efficacy is intricately tied to the level of community support. Active endorsement and support create a symbiotic relationship benefiting both the organisation and the community (Ansu-Mensah et al., 2021). Community support can manifest through participation, endorsement, and a willingness to collaborate and compromise during conflicts (Lehtonen et al., 2022). In many African contexts, a "social licence to operate" is crucial, especially in industries like mining and resource extraction (Górski, 2022). Community support grants this social licence, enabling smooth operations with community backing (Karanja & Njenga, 2020). Conversely, a lack of or low community support may pose challenges and resistance to local partnerships and alliances, hindering effective stakeholder management (Nuhu et al., 2020). In summary, community support is a critical moderator in the relationship between local partnerships and effective stakeholder management in Africa. High community support is expected to amplify the positive impact of local partnerships on stakeholder engagement, leading to superior stakeholder management outcomes.

Proposition 2b: *Community support moderates the relationship between the establishment of local partnerships and alliances and the delivery of effective stakeholder management in Africa, such that the relationship is stronger when community support is high.*

Social impact initiatives and effective stakeholder management

Organisations emphasising social impact initiatives in Africa align themselves with the social and cultural values of the communities they serve, fostering resonance with stakeholders and showcasing a sincere commitment to addressing issues of significance (Anne, 2021). Demonstrating social responsibility through community development projects, environmental sustainability, and ethical business practices is pivotal in trust-building, laying the foundation for organisational reputation, goodwill, and enduring relationships (Bahadorestani et al., 2020). Social impact initiatives often delve into issues of mutual concern, such as education, healthcare, or poverty alleviation, aligning seamlessly with the aspirations and needs of local communities. This shared interest naturally facilitates collaborative efforts and meaningful engagement (Pishchikova & Izzi, 2020). Adherence to regulatory expectations regarding corporate social responsibility (CSR) in various African countries not only fulfils legal requirements but also showcases an organisation's commitment to ethical conduct, nurturing advantageous stakeholder relationships (Ndong Ntoutoume, 2023). Case studies highlight how organisations prioritising social impact initiatives in Africa enhance stakeholder management. For example, telecommunications companies providing affordable access to mobile phones and internet services contribute to improved communication, economic growth, and social development in many African nations. Additionally, organisations engaging in socially responsible initiatives report increased employee engagement and satisfaction, with engaged employees becoming advocates for the organisation and positively influencing stakeholder relationships (Chatzopoulou et al., 2022). In summary, organisations prioritising social impact initiatives demonstrate enhanced stakeholder management capabilities, aligning with stakeholder interests, and fostering trust, reputation, and a common purpose for elevated stakeholder engagement and proficient management. We therefore propose that:

Proposition 3: *Organisations that prioritise social impact initiatives demonstrate a stronger delivery of effective stakeholder management in Africa, as their commitment to social responsibility aligns with stakeholder interests.*

Cultural diversity and delivery of effective stakeholder management

African countries are renowned for their rich tapestry of diverse cultural landscapes, languages, traditions, and customs. In this multifaceted milieu, organisations that exhibit a high degree of cultural adaptability not only demonstrate sensitivity but also exude profound respect for the intricate nuances of local cultures. This, in turn, serves as the bedrock for cultivating trust and goodwill among stakeholders, who perceive it as a genuine acknowledgment of their unique values and identities (Snowball et al., 2022). The essence of cultural adaptability shines most brilliantly in its ability to enhance communication with stakeholders possessing distinct communication styles or languages (Deal & Prince, 2003). Effective communication stands as a cornerstone of stakeholder engagement, and the capacity to adapt to cultural nuances becomes instrumental in surmounting language and cultural barriers (Molinsky & Gundling, 2016). The diverse cultural contexts within Africa often necessitate bespoke solutions crafted to address stakeholders' unique needs and preferences. Organisations that tailor their products, services, and strategies to align with local cultural norms and expectations invariably find themselves in a more advantageous position to meet stakeholder requirements (Esser, 2021). It is worth noting that cultural diversity, while a source of richness, can occasionally lead to misunderstandings or conflicts. However, organisations with a high degree of adaptability to cultural diversity are distinctly equipped to navigate and amicably resolve such conflicts, thereby preserving positive stakeholder relationships (Shonk, 2020). Numerous case studies present compelling evidence of the positive correlation between cultural adaptability and effective stakeholder management in Africa. For instance, multinational corporations that adeptly tailor their marketing strategies and product offerings to resonate with different cultural groups across the continent have witnessed a significant boost in market share and enhanced customer loyalty (Amoako et al., 2022). Furthermore, organisations that excel in cultural adaptability often foster more robust partnerships with local entities and communities. These partnerships are rooted in mutual respect and a genuine willingness to comprehend and accommodate each other's cultural perspectives, fostering trust and cooperation (Esser, 2021). This article concludes that cultural diversity adaptation improves stakeholder management in Africa. Cultural adaptation improves communication, tailored solutions, trust, and understanding, which are essential to stakeholder involvement in diverse cultures. Therefore, in this article, we propose that:

Proposition 4: *High adaptability to cultural diversity positively correlates with the delivery of effective stakeholder management in Africa, as organisations that tailor their approaches to diverse cultural contexts can better address stakeholders' unique needs.*

Data analytics, decision-making, and delivery of effective stakeholder management

In an era inundated with data, organisations leveraging data analytics gain profound insights into stakeholder behaviour, preferences, and needs, forming a robust foundation for well-informed decision-making and enhancing the precision of stakeholder engagement strategies (Schaninger & Lauricella, 2020). Data analytics enables organisations to segment stakeholders and tailor interactions with surgical precision, creating a more meaningful connection and inevitably boosting stakeholder satisfaction (Lockart, 2023). Advanced data analytics, including predictive modelling, empowers organisations to anticipate stakeholder behaviour and preferences, allowing proactive addressing of needs—a demonstration of exceptional responsiveness (Daudelin, 2022). Additionally, data analytics serves as a potent tool to accurately measure the impact of stakeholder engagement initiatives. By tracking key performance indicators (KPIs) linked to engagement, organisations can refine strategies to effectively meet stakeholder needs (Bal et al., 2013). In the diverse African context, data-driven decision-making helps organisations navigate varied cultures and stakeholders, steering actions based on factual information rather than assumptions (Pillay & Van der Merwe, 2021). Case studies, such as those in the African mobile network sector, emphasise the positive impact of data analytics. Providers optimise network coverage, enhance service quality, and tailor pricing plans, leading to improved customer satisfaction and loyalty (Anne, 2021). Moreover, data analytics aids in resource allocation by identifying high-priority stakeholders and concentrating resources for the most substantial impact (Vanhoucke, 2023). In summary, the strategic use of data analytics empowers organisations to make informed decisions, tailor engagements, and measure the impact of initiatives, enhancing the effectiveness of stakeholder management. The argument presented so far is that data analytics and decision-making improve stakeholder management in Africa. Data-driven initiatives enable personalised, evidence-based, strategic stakeholder interaction, improving stakeholder satisfaction and organisational success. Therefore, in this article, we propose that:

Proposition 5: *Utilising data analytics and decision-making significantly contributes to the delivery of effective stakeholder management in Africa, as data-driven insights enable more personalised and strategic stakeholder engagement.*

Synergistic effects of entrepreneurial strategies on stakeholder management in Africa

The adoption of multiple entrepreneurial strategies empowers organisations to engage stakeholders from diverse perspectives, crafting a comprehensive strategy capable of addressing multifaceted stakeholder needs (Darrell Rigby & O'Keeffe, 2023). In the African landscape, entrepreneurial ventures encounter various risks, and diversifying strategies helps navigate economic, political, and social uncertainties effectively (Ndemo & Smallbone, 2015). The amalgamation of strategies fosters a culture of innovation and adaptability, enabling organisations to experiment and pivot swiftly to align with evolving stakeholder needs (Chen et al., 2022). Combining entrepreneurial strategies also enhances resource utilisation and efficiency. Organisations leverage shared resources and capabilities across strategies, optimising investments and achieving economies of scale (Möller & McCaffrey, 2021). In the African context, integrating social entrepreneurship with commercial activities, as demonstrated in case studies, proves successful. This integration creates economic value and social impact, enhances reputation, and gains stakeholder support (Wanyoike & Maseno, 2021). Addressing diverse stakeholder needs through a well-crafted combination of strategies increases the likelihood of achieving heightened stakeholder satisfaction, fostering loyalty, support, and enduring relationships (Ramkissoon et al., 2020). In conclusion, several entrepreneurial strategies improve stakeholder management in Africa, helping organisations handle risks, encourage innovation, optimise resources, and develop lasting stakeholder connections. This multifaceted strategy helps organisations engage stakeholders, manage risks, innovate, optimise resource use, and increase stakeholder satisfaction and support. We therefore propose that:

Proposition 6: *The combination of multiple entrepreneurial strategies, rather than individual strategies in isolation, leads to a synergistic effect on the delivery of effective stakeholder management in Africa.*

Conceptual framework

The article examines the impact of entrepreneurial strategies, community dynamics, and stakeholder management in Africa. It suggests that organisations that prioritise innovation, technology adoption, local partnerships, community trust, social impact initiatives, and cultural diversity are more effective in managing stakeholders. Data analytics and decision-making processes are crucial for personalising stakeholder engagement efforts. A holistic perspective suggests that combining multiple entrepreneurial strategies can synergise

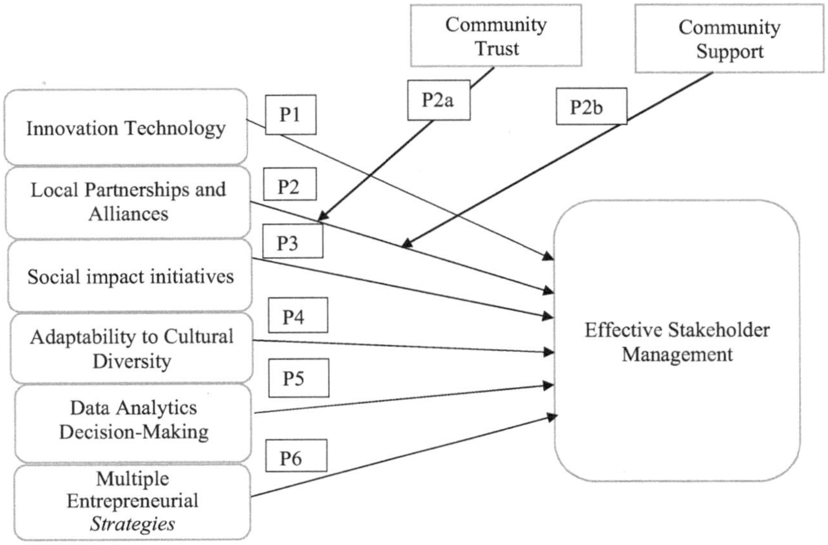

Figure 17.1 Conceptual Model.

effects on stakeholder management. This framework provides a structured foundation for understanding how these factors collectively shape stakeholder management in African businesses (Figure 17.1).

Theoretical implications

This article advocates for the enhancement of stakeholder management in Africa by considering diverse factors influencing stakeholder relationships. It proposes a theoretical framework that integrates multiple entrepreneurial strategies, emphasising cultural adaptability for effective engagement. The role of data analytics and data-driven decision-making in improving stakeholder management is underscored, along with the significance of social impact initiatives aligned with community values. The article contributes insights into the unique challenges and opportunities of stakeholder management in Africa, suggesting refinements and extensions to existing theories for better understanding engagement dynamics in diverse and evolving environments.

Practical implications

The article provides practical implications for enhancing stakeholder management in African organisations. It recommends the adoption of innovative technologies (e.g., mobile apps, internet platforms, data analytics, and artificial intelligence) to improve communication, understand stakeholder preferences, and enhance service delivery. The suggestion includes strategic resource allocation and the establishment of local partnerships to bridge cultural gaps and build trust. Prioritising social impact initiatives aligned with community values is advised to boost organisational reputation. The article emphasises fostering cultural adaptability by respecting diverse cultures, languages, and traditions and adjusting communication styles and offerings to local norms. Finally, it proposes employing a combination of entrepreneurial strategies to address varied stakeholder needs, manage risks, promote innovation, optimise resource utilisation, and enhance stakeholder satisfaction.

Conclusion and direction for future research

This chapter explores using entrepreneurial strategies for effective stakeholder management in Africa, proposing eight propositions with theoretical and managerial implications. The article contributes to stakeholder management, entrepreneurship, and strategic management literature, emphasising the importance of contextual adaptation in Africa. Practical recommendations for organisations operating in the region include leveraging technology, building trust, prioritising social responsibility, cultural adaptation, using data, and combining strategies. These suggestions offer guidance for enhancing stakeholder relationships and achieving success in the dynamic African market. Longitudinal studies on how entrepreneurship affects relationships with stakeholders and the performance of organisations are possible in the future. These could look at different African regions or industries, the views of stakeholders on entrepreneurship strategies, the difficulties and opportunities for African small businesses and startups, how new technologies affect stakeholder participation, and case studies of successful African businesses.

References

AFDB. (2021). Entrepreneurship is critical to Africa's transformation. *African Development Bank.* https://www.afdb.org/en/news-and-events/entrepreneurship-critical-africas-transformation-african-development-bank-44309

Ahmat, A., Okoroafor, S. C., Kazanga, I., Asamani, J. A., Millogo, J. J. S., Illou, M. M. A., Mwinga, K., & Nyoni, J. (2022). The health workforce status in the WHO African Region: findings of a cross-sectional study. *BMJ Global Health*, *7*(Suppl 1), e008317.

Amoako, G. K., Obuobisa-Darko, T., & Ohene Marfo, S. (2022). Stakeholder role in tourism sustainability: The case of Kwame Nkrumah Mausoleum and Centre for Art and Culture in Ghana. *International Hospitality Review*, *36*(1), 25–44.

Anne, D. (2021). The state of mobile internet connectivity in Sub-Saharan Africa: Why addressing the barriers to mobile internet use matters now more than ever. *Mobile for Development.*https://www.gsma.com/mobilefordevelopment/blog/the-state-of-mobile-internet-connectivity-in-sub-saharan-africa/

Ansu-Mensah, P., Marfo, E. O., Awuah, L. S., & Amoako, K. O. (2021). Corporate social responsibility and stakeholder engagement in Ghana's mining sector: A case study of Newmont Ahafo mines. *International Journal of Corporate Social Responsibility*, *6*(1), 1–22.

Bahadorestani, A., Naderpajouh, N., & Sadiq, R. (2020). Planning for sustainable stakeholder engagement based on the assessment of conflicting interests in projects. *Journal of Cleaner Production*, *242*, 118402.

Bal, M., Bryde, D., Fearon, D., & Ochieng, E. (2013). Stakeholder engagement: Achieving sustainability in the construction sector. *Sustainability*, *5*(2), 695–710.

Calzon, B. (2022). Why data driven decision making is your path to business success. *The datapine Blog.* https://www.datapine.com/blog/data-driven-decision-making-in-businesses/

Chanda, A., & Unel, B. (2021). Do attitudes toward risk taking affect entrepreneurship? Evidence from second-generation Americans. *Journal of Economic Growth*, *26*(4), 385–413.

Chatzopoulou, E.-C., Manolopoulos, D., & Agapitou, V. (2022). Corporate social responsibility and employee outcomes: Interrelations of external and internal orientations with job satisfaction and organizational commitment. *Journal of Business Ethics*, *179*(3), 795–817.

Chen, J. S., Elfenbein, D. W., Posen, H. E., & Wang, M. (2022). Programs of experimentation and pivoting for (overconfident) entrepreneurs. *Academy of Management Review*, Working Paper No. 21-001.

Darrell Rigby, Z. F., and O'Keeffe, D. (2023). How to create a stakeholder strategy A data-driven approach to design, measurement, and implementation. *Harvard Business Review.* https://hbr.org/2023/05/how-to-create-a-stakeholder-strategy

Daudelin, D. H. (2022). Stakeholder engagement in predictive model development for clinical decision support. In *Broadly engaged team science in clinical and translational research* (pp. 193–201). Springer.

Deal, J. J., & Prince, D. W. (2003). *Developing cultural adaptability: How to work across differences* (Vol. 105). Center for Creative Leadership.

Doe, J. K., Van de Wetering, R., Honyenuga, B., & Versendaal, J. (2022). Extended contextual validation of stakeholder approach to firm technology adoption: Moderating and mediating relationships in an innovation eco-system. *Society and Business Review*, *17*(4), 506–540.

Esengulova, N., Carella, M. M., & Lopolito, A. (2023). Stakeholder empowerment in sustainable rural development partnerships: Two case studies from Italy. *Sustainability*, *15*(8), 6977.

Eskerod, P., & Jepsen, A. L. (2016). *Project stakeholder management*. Routledge. https://doi.org/10.4324/9781315245881

Esser, J. (2021). The secret of adaptable organizations is trust. *Harvard Business Review*. H05GLB-PDF-ENG.

Gholizadeh, S., & Mohammadkazemi, R. (2022). International entrepreneurial opportunity: A systematic review, meta-synthesis, and future research agenda. *Journal of International Entrepreneurship*, *20*(2), 218–254.

Góes, H. A. d. A., Fatima, G., Santos Jhunior, R. d. O., & Boaventura, J. M. G. (2023). Managing for stakeholders towards corporate environmental sustainability. *Corporate Social Responsibility and Environmental Management*. https://onlinelibrary.wiley.com/doi/10.1002/csr.2448

Górski, J. (2022). *The Palgrave handbook of social license to operate and energy transitions*. Palgrave.

Idowu, S. O., et al. (2013). *Encyclopedia of corporate social responsibility*. Springer. https://link.springer.com/referencework/10.1007/978-3-642-28036-8

Kabahinda, E., & Mwesigwa, R. (2023). Trust mediates the relationship between stakeholder behavior and stakeholder management of public private partnership projects in Uganda. *Public Organization Review*, *23*(1), 245–263.

Karanja, W., & Njenga, N. (2020). Social licence to operate in the energy transition era: Case study of the East African oil and gas sector. In *Energy transitions and the future of the African energy sector: Law, policy and governance* (pp. 341–370). Springer.

Kujala, J., Sachs, S., Leinonen, H., Heikkinen, A., & Laude, D. (2022). Stakeholder engagement: Past, present, and future. *Business & Society*, *61*(5), 1136–1196.

Lehtonen, M., Kojo, M., Kari, M., Jartti, T., & Litmanen, T. (2022). Trust, mistrust and distrust as blind spots of social licence to operate: Illustration via three forerunner countries in nuclear waste management. *Journal of Risk Research*, *25*(5), 577–593.

Lockart, L. (2023). 11 strategies for effective stakeholder management. *Float*. https://www.float.com/resources/stakeholder-management/

Madumere, N. (2021). The impact of stakeholder management on the oil and gas industry in Africa: A case study of oil companies and African host communities. *African Journal on Conflict Resolution*, *21*(2), 8–32.

Mandiriza, T., & Fourie, D. J. (2023). The role of stakeholders in the adoption of public–private partnerships (PPPs) in municipal water infrastructure projects: A stakeholder theory perspective. *World*, *4*(3), 416–430.

Mashiyane, D., & Masuku, M. M. (2022). Resourcing of schools for an inclusive education system: Assistive devices and technologies. In *Handbook of research on creating spaces for African epistemologies in the inclusive education discourse* (pp. 107–118). IGI Global.

Mayanja, S. N. (2020). Impact of E-bills payment on customer satisfaction in Uganda: Stanbic Bank Uganda Limited as the case study. *Science Journal of Business and Management. Special Issue: Business Policy & Strategic Management*, *8*(3), 112–118.

Mendes, T., Braga, V., Correia, A., & Silva, C. (2023). Linking corporate social responsibility, cooperation and innovation: the triple bottom line perspective. *Innovation & Management Review*, *20*(3), 244–280.

Miles, S. (2017). Stakeholder theory classification: A theoretical and empirical evaluation of definitions. *Journal of Business Ethics*, *142*, 437–459.

Molinsky, A., & Gundling, E. (2016). How to build trust on your cross-cultural team. *Harvard Business Review*, *87*(2), 43–49.

Möller, U., & McCaffrey, M. (2021). Entrepreneurship and firm strategy: Integrating resources, capabilities, and judgment through an Austrian framework. *Entrepreneurship Research Journal*, *13*(4), 997–1031.

Ndemo, E. B., & Smallbone, D. (2015). Linkage dynamics between small and large firms in Kenya. *DBA Africa Management Review*, *5*(1), 38–591.

Ndong Ntoutoume, A. G. (2023). Challenges of CSR in sub-Saharan Africa: Clarifying the gaps between the regulations and human rights issues. *International Journal of Corporate Social Responsibility*, *8*(1), 2.

Noorbhai, H., & Ojo, T. A. (2023). mHealth and e-Learning in health sciences curricula: A South African study of health sciences staff perspectives on utilisation, constraints and future possibilities. *BMC Medical Education*, *23*(1), 189.

Nuhu, S., Mpambije, C. J., & Ngussa, K. (2020). Challenges in health service delivery under public–private partnership in Tanzania: Stakeholders' views from Dar es Salaam region. *BMC Health Services Research*, *20*, 1–12.

Ojong, N., Simba, A., & Dana, L.-P. (2021). Female entrepreneurship in Africa: A review, trends, and future research directions. *Journal of Business Research*, *132*, 233–248.

Paladino, A. (2022). Innovation or entrepreneurship: Which comes first? Exploring the implications for higher education. *Journal of Product Innovation Management*, *39*(4), 478–484.

Pillay, K., & Van der Merwe, A. (2021). Big data driven decision making model: A case of the South African banking sector. *South African Computer Journal*, *33*(2), 55–71.

Pishchikova, K., & Izzi, V. (2020). Engaging civil society in peacebuilding. In *Conflict society and peacebuilding* (pp. 41–71). Routledge India.

Pless, N. M., Sengupta, A., Wheeler, M. A., & Maak, T. (2021). Responsible leadership and the reflective CEO: Resolving stakeholder conflict by imagining what could be done. *Journal of Business Ethics*, *180*, 313–337.

Pretty, J., & Ward, H. (2001). Social capital and the environment. *World Development*, *29*(2), 209–227.

Rabinowitz, P. (2015). Section 8. Identifying and analyzing stakeholders and their interests (pp. 8-14). In S. B. Fawcett, C. M. Holt, V. T. Francisco, J. A. Schultz, B. Berkowitz, K. J. Harris, & T. Wolff (Eds.), *Work Group for Community Health and Development*. The University of Kansas.

Ramkissoon, H., Mavondo, F., & Sowamber, V. (2020). Corporate social responsibility at LUX* resorts and hotels: Satisfaction and loyalty implications for employee and customer social responsibility. *Sustainability*, *12*(22), 9745.

Reed, M. S., Vella, S., Challies, E., De Vente, J., Frewer, L., Hohenwallner-Ries, D., Huber, T., Neumann, R. K., Oughton, E. A., & Sidoli del Ceno, J. (2018). A theory

of participation: what makes stakeholder and public engagement in environmental management work? *Restoration Ecology*, *26*, S7–S17.
Sachs, J. D., Kroll, C., Lafortune, G., Fuller, G., & Woelm, F. (2022). *Sustainable development report 2022*. Cambridge University Press.
Saengsupavanich, C., Gallardo, W. G., Sajor, E., & Murray, W. W. (2012). Constraints influencing stakeholder participation in collective environmental management. *Environmental Earth Sciences*, *66*, 1817–1829.
Saenz, C. (2021). The relationship between corporate social responsibility and the social licence to operate: A case study in Peru. *Resources Policy*, *74*, 102399.
Sarasvathy, S. D. (2001). Causation and effectuation: Toward a theoretical shift from economic inevitability to entrepreneurial contingency. *Academy of Management Review*, *26*(2), 243–263.
Satell, G. (2017). The 4 types of innovation and the problems they solve. *Harvard Business Review*, *11*, 2–9.
Schaninger, B., & Lauricella, T. (2020). A data-backed approach to stakeholder engagement. *McKinsey Organization Blog*.
Shepherd, D. A., & Patzelt, H. (2021). *Entrepreneurial strategy: Starting, managing, and scaling new ventures*. Springer Nature.
Shonk, K. (2020). How to resolve cultural conflict: Overcoming cultural barriers at the negotiation table. *Harvard Law School Daily Blog*. https://www.mckinsey.com/capabilities/people-and-organizational-performance/our-insights/the-organization-blog/a-data-backed-approach-to-stakeholder-engagement
Sloan, P., & Oliver, D. (2013). Building trust in multi-stakeholder partnerships: Critical emotional incidents and practices of engagement. *Organization Studies*, *34*(12), 1835–1868.
Snowball, J., Tarentaal, D., & Sapsed, J. (2022). Innovation and diversity in the digital cultural and creative industries. In *Arts, entrepreneurship, and innovation* (pp. 187–215). Springer.
Somo, G., & Onny, M. (2021). Community engagement and the digital economy: Impact on township economic development in the Emfuleni Local Municipality.
Soulard, J., Knollenberg, W., Boley, B. B., Perdue, R. R., & McGehee, N. G. (2018). Social capital and destination strategic planning. *Tourism Management*, *69*, 189–200.
Storm, M., & Borgman, H. (2020). Understanding challenges and success factors in creating a data-driven culture. In T. X. Bui (Ed.), *Proceedings of the 53rd Hawaii International Conference on System Sciences* (pp. 5399–5408). HICSS.
Taher, M. (2012). Resource-based view theory. *Information systems theory: Explaining and predicting our digital society*, *1*, 151–163.
Tsang, A., Frost, T., & Cao, H. (2022). Environmental, social, and governance (ESG) disclosure: A literature review. *The British Accounting Review*, *55*, 101149.
Vanhoucke, M. (2023). The data-driven project manager. *The illusion of control: Project data, computer algorithms and human intuition for project management and control*, 29–48.
Walsh, P. P., Murphy, E., & Horan, D. (2020). The role of science, technology and innovation in the UN 2030 agenda. *Technological Forecasting and Social Change*, *154*, 119957.
Wanyoike, C. N., & Maseno, M. (2021). Exploring the motivation of social entrepreneurs in creating successful social enterprises in East Africa. *New England Journal of Entrepreneurship*, *24*(2), 79–104.

Wells, E. C., Lehigh, G. R., & Vidmar, A. M. (2020). Stakeholder engagement for sustainable communities. In *The Palgrave Handbook of Global Sustainability* (pp. 1–13). Springer International Publishing.

Yin, M., Hughes, M., & Hu, Q. (2021). Entrepreneurial orientation and new venture resource acquisition: why context matters. *Asia Pacific Journal of Management, 38*, 1369–1398.

Za, T., Ga, M. L. L., Ti, N. C., Fos, A., & Villar, C. (2022). *Diversity equity and inclusion in embodied AI.* 4TU.Federation.

18 Stakeholder Management in the Wake of Business Failure

Dacosta Omari and Cai Jin

Introduction

A stakeholder encompasses any group or individual with the potential to exert influence on or be influenced by an organization (Cooper & College, 2014). This comprehensive definition reflects the diverse range of entities involved, including suppliers, customers, shareholders, employees, local communities, political organizations, governments, media, and various others. It underscores the multifaceted nature of an organization's interactions with its external environment. The concept of stakeholder theory is rooted in a set of ideas suggesting that managers of businesses have specific responsibilities toward various groups of stakeholders. This theory challenges traditional economic assumptions by suggesting that firms have broader obligations, as reflected in the term "stakeholder," derived from "stockholder" with an ironic twist (Parmar et al., 2010). It implies that firms must consider the interests of a broader set of stakeholders beyond just their shareholders, thus promoting a more holistic view of corporate responsibility.

While the importance of stakeholders in influencing firm performance is recognized, research in this area has been somewhat limited. The dependence theory highlights the significance of understanding the varying levels of dependence that a business has on its stakeholders. By acknowledging and strategically managing this dependence, businesses can effectively navigate the complexities of their stakeholder environment, aligning stakeholder interests with their own to achieve long-term sustainability (Priego-de-la-Cruz et al., 2020).

However, there remains a noticeable gap in research when it comes to understanding how stakeholder relationships are impacted during and after a business failure. Specifically, it remains unclear how such failures affect an entrepreneur's interactions with individuals or groups connected to their subsequent business endeavours. This is a critical knowledge gap, considering that business failures are inherent and recurrent in entrepreneurial activities (Ucbasaran et al., 2012). Therefore, this chapter seeks to address this knowledge deficit by providing insights into how entrepreneurial failure can influence and reshape relationships with stakeholders.

DOI: 10.4324/9781003256014-22

Defining stakeholder and business failure

Business failures are detrimental occurrences that not only disrupt the ongoing progress of the economy and society but also eradicate the gains of a diverse array of stakeholders, including shareholders, lenders, labour unions, government entities, workers, as well as customers and suppliers (Wu, 2010). Understanding the phenomenon of business failure presents a substantial theoretical challenge that remains insufficiently addressed. According to Pretorius (2009), the existing body of work on business failure is primarily marked by predictive models, but it is fragmented across various areas of investigation. Additionally, the definition of business failure varies significantly among different scholars, making it difficult to establish a unified definition. Cope, Cave, and Eccles (2004) emphasized the need to distinguish between "failure," which denotes a situation where outcomes fall short of initial expectations and may involve some form of loss, and the broader concept of "discontinuance," which may not have the same level of emotional, behavioural, and economic impact and, in some cases, may not even be perceived as a failure. They also caution against conflating the terms "business" failure and "entrepreneurial" failure. Entrepreneurial failure may imply that the venture's downfall is due to the entrepreneur's personal shortcomings, thus equating venture failure with a "failed" entrepreneur. As demonstrated in this article, an entrepreneur who successfully exits a venture during market turbulence can be considered a relative success, even if the outcome results in losses for investors. This distinction is particularly crucial for managing stakeholder relationships, as attitudes toward failure can vary significantly in diverse social contexts and failure scenarios.

Several factors account for business failure. These factors can be categorized into two primary attributes: misfortune and mistake (Cardon et al., 2011). Further, these two categories can be divided into external and internal causes, with each category involving different stakeholders. For instance, internal financial factors may impact stakeholders such as employees, while external funding-related factors may have more relevance for investors. As illustrated in Figure 18.1, the interplay between these two attributes results in diverse impacts of failure for individuals (e.g., emotionally, and socially). These impacts would subsequently affect future stakeholder relationships and the establishment of new ventures.

In the context of stakeholder relationship management, this chapter adopts Cope's (2011) definition of failure, which underscores the concept of business termination resulting from an inability to meet its objectives, consequently disappointing the primary shareholders' expectations. Before formally analysing the interaction between stakeholders and business failure, we first need to provide a clear definition of the concept of stakeholder. Various definitions of stakeholders are presented by different authors, but they generally revolve around the idea of individuals or groups who can affect or are affected by an organization's objectives (Benn et al., 2016). Hence, stakeholders can be individuals, neighbourhoods, institutions, groups, organizations, society, and the environment.

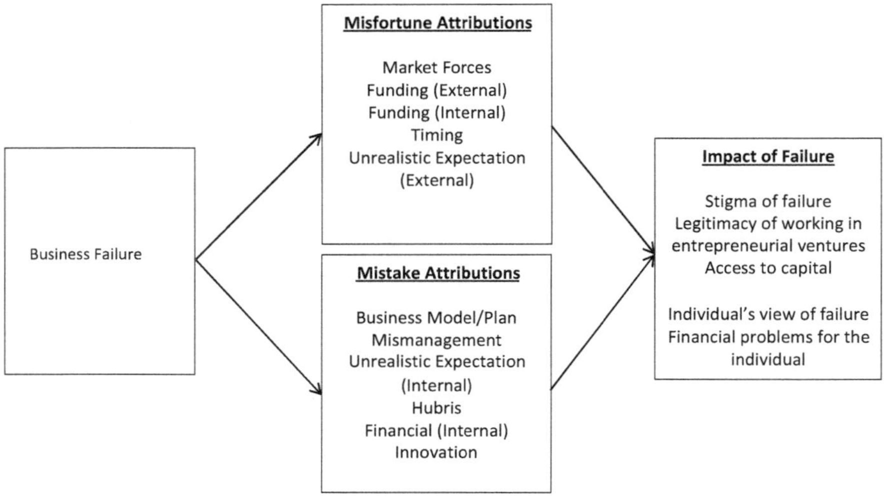

Mistake attributions: Failure caused by circumstances the entrepreneur could not control (external attribution).
Mistake attributions: Failure resulted from avoidable errors on the part of the entrepreneur (internal attribution).

Figure 18.1 Cultural Perceptions of Failure and Their Impact.

Source: Cardon et al. (2011).

According to Clarkson (1995), stakeholder groups can be further classified into primary and secondary stakeholders. Primary stakeholders are defined as "those without whose continuing participation the corporation cannot survive as a going concern." These groups mainly include shareholders, employees, customers, and suppliers, as well as the public sector, including governments and communities that provide infrastructure, regulate organizational activity, and enforce taxes. These are all crucial to the daily operation of a company, so the company needs to pay attention to managing and retaining these relationships. On the other hand, secondary stakeholders are defined as those "who influence or are influenced by the corporation, but they are not engaged in transactions essential for the company's survival." Secondary stakeholder groups include competitors, media, trade associations, and support groups (special interest groups). Although these groups may not have direct contracts or authority over the company, and the company is not dependent on them for survival, they can significantly disrupt the company.

The primary focus of analysis in this chapter will centre on primary stakeholders, as they are often regarded as playing a more pivotal role in corporate activities (Clarkson, 1995). Nevertheless, secondary stakeholders will also be examined when relevant (as it can still affect the context of the business environment). Utilizing the foregoing conceptual framework as a base, this chapter aims to develop a deeper understanding of the connection between business failure and stakeholder management relationships.

The impact of business failure on stakeholders

When investigating the area of business failure, a recurrent and extensively discussed theme is the notion of stigma. Link and Phelan (2001) have provided a comprehensive definition of stigma, characterizing it as a complex amalgamation of interconnected components. Stigma is evident when various aspects, including labelling, stereotyping, separation, status loss, and discrimination, concurrently manifest within a power dynamic that permits their existence. Stigma frequently surfaces in the aftermath of a business failure and wields a profound influence on entrepreneurs and their interactions with stakeholders.

Stakeholders, as a result of the stigma attached to entrepreneurs associated with business failure, may display a proclivity for negative engagement within their relationships. Furthermore, they may encounter challenges when attempting to integrate with these entrepreneurs. This dynamic has a cascading effect, leading to a deterioration in the overall quality of the relationship and resulting in adverse consequences for employment opportunities. Moreover, it also limits the firm's access to future resources, encompassing financial support and network connections. It is important to note that stigma-related factors collectively contribute to our understanding of why some entrepreneurs tend to exhibit social withdrawal attitudes subsequent to a business failure, as highlighted by Ucbasaran et al. (2012). The culmination of these elements can adversely affect prospects for future venture activities.

However, it's important to note that not all business failures necessarily lead to a stigma event. In other words, the consequential outcome of business failure heavily depends on the context. In light of this, the negative impact of the stigma is also situation-specific. According to Simmons, Wiklund, and Levie (2013), the experience of business failure can be associated with stigma attitudes, sanctions, and behaviours under three conditions:

1. *Cultural sense-making*: Entrepreneurial failure is perceived as stigmatizing when it deviates from societal norms and expectations. This perception can vary across countries due to differing social norms and institutions, affecting the magnitude of business failure rates and the association with stigma.
2. *Acceptance of stigma*: Stigmatized entrepreneurs may accept the stigma imposed on them, leading to performance pressures and social isolation. This acceptance can influence their willingness to start new ventures or engage in risky activities.
3. *Discoverable stigma*: Stigma becomes relevant when social audiences can access information about business failure through formal or informal institutions that serve as repositories and carriers of such information. This is likely to have a direct connection with secondary stakeholders, as suggested by Clarkson (1995). Secondary stakeholders include competitors, media, trade associations, and support groups (special interest groups). While they may not have the sole ability to lead to stigma after a business failure, they

certainly play a facilitating role. For example, negative comments on business failure from sources like social media or competitors can increase the accessibility of such information, making it more challenging for subsequent business activities.

The aforementioned elements imply that stigma arises when there is both social and individual recognition of the stigma, and when the general public has access to such stigma-related information and therefore would vary across regions. This perspective finds further support in the work of Ucbasaran et al. (2012), suggesting that regions such as Silicon Valley might exhibit varying levels of stigma potential based on their social environment and bankruptcy laws.

Additionally, insights from Simmons, Wiklund, and Levie (2013) shed light on the intricate interplay between negative social judgment and the regulated disclosure of historical business data:

- Negative social judgment often acts as a deterrent for entrepreneurs re-entering entrepreneurial activities due to the fear of stigma and the demoralization stemming from past failures.
- Regulated disclosure of historical business data has the potential to alter this dynamic. When entrepreneurs are aware that their past failures are already part of the public record due to regulatory requirements, the personal stigma associated with failure tends to diminish. This transparency reduces the apprehension of social judgment.

Consequently, some entrepreneurs may be more inclined to re-enter entrepreneurial activities, as they perceive that since their past failures are already in the public domain, there is less at stake. Regulated disclosure essentially "levels the playing field" by making everyone cognizant of their past failures, thereby reducing the fear of social judgment. This interplay of factors significantly influences the decisions of entrepreneurs who have experienced business failure in the past, motivating them to approach stakeholders with the aim of re-entering the market.

As discussed previously, it is evident that business failure and its associated stigma have an impact on stakeholder management in subsequent business activities. However, whether this impact is negative or positive heavily depends on the context.

Another way to explain the consequences of business failure is through the explanation of the interactions between social, psychological, and financial costs (Ucbasaran et al., 2012). Among these three costs, the social cost is particularly relevant to stakeholder relationships and, therefore, will be the primary analytical focus. In real-world settings, these three different costs are often interconnected. Therefore, the remaining two costs will also be analysed to help understand their mutual impact on the business and its stakeholders.

Cope's (2011) research findings shed light on the intricate relationship between the negative emotional impact of failure and its multifaceted social cost. For some entrepreneurs, the difficulty in coming to terms with failure is rooted in their strong commitment to investors, making it challenging to accept the reality that investors may not recoup their investments. Consequently, the emotional aftermath of failure can intensify feelings of isolation, heightened anxiety, and withdrawal, as individuals find it challenging to share their concerns with others. This, in turn, adversely impacts subsequent stakeholder relationships, as they find it difficult to turn to certain network contacts and established social support mechanisms that are typically part of regular business operations.

Furthermore, Cope (2011) argues that participants in such situations may experience a loss of confidence and optimism. While this loss may initially deter entrepreneurs from approaching and actively engaging with stakeholders, it is not necessarily an entirely negative outcome of failure. Entrepreneurs who recognize the mistakes and challenges and work on improving them can become valuable assets, enabling more thoughtful, anticipatory, and affirmative actions in the future. This, in essence, can help counterbalance the social cost element mentioned earlier.

While this research reveals that only one of the participants has ventured into a new business, the subsequent career paths of the majority demonstrate their continued involvement in the broader entrepreneurial landscape. They retain the ability to apply and share the lessons learned from failure. Thus, from a different perspective, although entrepreneurs may have lost some of their initial stakeholder connections in their original industries, they may have opened doors to engage with stakeholders in other industries and possibly initiate new ventures.

Taking into account the other two types of costs (financial cost and psychological cost), Ucbasaran et al. (2012) note that the first interaction effect is where higher financial cost leads to greater emotional cost in the context of business failure. Second, Ucbasaran and colleagues emphasize that the social costs of failure can have financial implications, even when the direct financial costs of failure are not exceptionally high at the moment. Entrepreneurs may still face challenges in raising funds for future ventures and securing subsequent employment. However, there are still ways to make up for this situation. For example, Sutton and Callahan's (1987) research on impression-management strategies used by leaders of firms undergoing bankruptcy found that accepting at least partial responsibility for failure helps create an illusion of control for entrepreneurs, garnering sympathy, and presenting them as individuals who have done their best and learned from their mistakes. Such impression-management tactics can enhance external stakeholders' willingness to maintain relationships with these entrepreneurs in the future, thereby reducing both the social and financial costs of business failure for the entrepreneurs.

In a nutshell, while it is evident that business failure can to some extent have negative effects on future business stakeholder relationships and new venture development, it is undeniable that contemporary literature offers numerous insights into how entrepreneurs can learn and progress positively from business failure. Factors such as stigma and the business environment can interact, and stakeholders may value an entrepreneur's ability to learn from failure, among other things. In other words, stakeholder relationships may potentially experience positive development as entrepreneurs engage in further learning, compensating for the previously discussed negative effects. The next section delves into how different types of failure can trigger entrepreneurial learning and examines the interactions that may affect stakeholders' relationships specifically in relation to new venture development.

Setting up new venture after business failure

As discussed in the previous section, the impact of business failure can yield both positive and negative outcomes on future business and new venture development. While the debilitating consequences of business failure are well acknowledged, contemporary literature provides a compelling body of evidence suggesting that business failure can serve as a catalyst for entrepreneurial relearning and positive outcomes. Various interconnected factors such as stigma and the entrepreneurial environment play pivotal roles in shaping these outcomes. Furthermore, stakeholders, who are deeply intertwined with an entrepreneur's journey, often place significant value on the entrepreneur's ability to derive essential lessons from failure. In essence, stakeholder relationships can undergo positive development as entrepreneurs continue to learn, effectively offsetting previous negative effects. This section aims to delve into the dynamics of how different types of failures trigger entrepreneurial learning and explore the resulting interactions that may or may not culminate in future venture development.

The notion that business and venture activities are fundamentally grounded in the establishment and nurturing of relationships has garnered increasing recognition (Taylor & Thorpe, 2004). This acknowledgement underscores the significance of comprehending the dynamics of relationships following a business failure, particularly in the context of launching a new venture. It's essential to recognize that contemporary business environments are characterized by intricate webs of connections and interdependencies. Entrepreneurs do not operate in isolation; they engage with various stakeholders, including customers, suppliers, investors, and partners. These relationships play a pivotal role in shaping the success or failure of a venture. Understanding how these relationships evolve and how entrepreneurs adapt following a business failure is of paramount importance for those embarking on new entrepreneurial endeavours. Thus, post-failure relationship dynamics can nurture a fertile ground for learning and growth, ultimately contributing to the success of future ventures.

Traditionally, business failure has been perceived as having predominantly negative impacts on both firms and entrepreneurs. These repercussions include substantial financial costs, emotional toll, and social ramifications.

More specifically, the emotional aspect of experiencing failure is connected to a sense of social obligation and the resulting tension it can generate. These societal expectations originate from various stakeholders, such as investors, staff members, lenders, and family members (Ucbasaran et al., 2012; Shepherd et al., 2009a). Nevertheless, on the strength of failure theorists, Cope (2011) introduced a distinctive perspective by arguing that individuals who have experienced failure are prime candidates for future ventures due to their heightened knowledge and resilience. The research further emphasizes that entrepreneurs who manage to overcome social, financial, and emotional costs would gain valuable insights, not only into their personal growth and the intricacies of their ventures downfall but also into the dynamics of relationships, the broader business environment, and the critical stress points within the entrepreneurial journey. This would not only mean that they develop the capabilities of repairing stakeholder relationships but also the competencies and experiences to effectively manage future ventures.

In addition to the points mentioned earlier, Cope (2011) draws on the concept of "grief recovery" introduced by Shepherd, Covin, and Kuratko (2009b) to shed further insights. This concept refers to the time and process required for individuals to acknowledge and accept failure, which is crucial because the learning process and the initiation of new ventures only commence after this phase. Within the learning process, entrepreneurs gain a deeper understanding of the nature and management of stakeholder relationships and new venture management. This is why Cope argues that in such situations, business failure may benefit entrepreneurs in new venture settings rather than negatively impacting them.

Cope (2011) underscores the significance of considering the contextual factors and feedback from social environments in the evaluation of entrepreneurial endeavours. This perspective finds further validation in the work of Ucbasaran et al. (2012), who emphasize the pivotal role of specific social groups for entrepreneurs, particularly when they plan to engage in business activities within the same industries (e.g., new ventures). Venture capitalists and other funders of entrepreneurial initiatives, including business angels, emerge as critical constituents of these groups. Notably, in such environments, there is a heightened acceptance of failure, accompanied by a more forgiving attitude toward it, as observed in countries like the United Kingdom and the United States.

However, it is essential to acknowledge that this leniency may not always be uniformly applicable. Entrepreneurs who have experienced failure may still face scepticism, particularly if their demeanour reflects flamboyance and machismo or if they appear to lack a profound understanding of the complexities involved in entrepreneurial endeavours (Cope et al., 2004). Conversely, acceptable failures often involve entrepreneurs who earnestly attempt to build successful companies but encounter setbacks primarily due to factors beyond their control, such as luck or timing. Furthermore, when all other factors are held constant, prior failure experiences do not significantly deter venture capitalists from investing in an entrepreneur. Overall, the body of evidence suggests that the venture capitalist community, notably in the United States and the United Kingdom, approaches venture failure with a degree of tolerance, acceptance, and an open-minded perspective.

However, under certain circumstances, the concept of "learning from failure" may face significant barriers. These barriers primarily revolve around the balance between the costs and benefits associated with failure. While the previous discussion highlights the valuable insights and positive impacts that entrepreneurs can gain from learning through failure, it's crucial to acknowledge the factors that can tip the scales in the opposite direction, causing entrepreneurs to abandon their entrepreneurial endeavours.

First, the financial costs of failure can be substantial. Entrepreneurs may have invested significant resources, both personal and external, into their ventures. When the financial losses are too overwhelming, it can be financially unsustainable for entrepreneurs to continue on their current path. If the debt accumulates or the financial stability of the entrepreneur is severely compromised, it may become a compelling reason to exit the entrepreneurial career.

Second, social costs constitute another critical impediment. The stigma associated with business failure can extend beyond personal and emotional repercussions. Entrepreneurs may face social isolation and damaged relationships with stakeholders, including investors, employees, creditors, and even their families. These social pressures can create a heavy burden and stress, making it difficult to carry on with the learning process after a failure. It may lead entrepreneurs to discontinue their entrepreneurial journey to escape from this social pressure.

Finally, psychological costs play a significant role in this decision-making process. The emotional toll of failure can be substantial, impacting an entrepreneur's mental well-being. Feelings of guilt, shame, and inadequacy can be overwhelming, making it challenging to initiate the learning process. Entrepreneurs who experience severe psychological distress may decide that the costs of persisting in entrepreneurship outweigh the potential benefits of learning from their failure.

In such cases, when entrepreneurs reach a tipping point where the combined financial, social, and psychological costs outweigh the expected benefits of learning from failure, they might make the difficult decision to exit their entrepreneurial careers. This decision can lead to missed opportunities for gaining valuable experience and insights, as discussed earlier. It underscores the delicate balance that entrepreneurs must navigate when weighing the costs and benefits of learning from failure in the pursuit of new ventures.

Overall, this section explores the complex consequences of business failure on future entrepreneurial ventures. It highlights that contemporary literature presents both positive and negative outcomes of failure, with an emphasis on the potential for entrepreneurial relearning and growth. Stakeholders and their evolving relationships play a pivotal role, offering opportunities for learning and positive development. The text challenges the traditional view of failure as purely negative, with an argument that overcoming its social, financial, and emotional costs can result in valuable insights and improved stakeholder relationships. Additionally, the text discusses the importance of considering contextual factors and the role of specific social groups, such as venture capitalists. However, it also acknowledges that some entrepreneurs may face barriers to learning from failure, such as substantial financial, social, and psychological costs, which may lead to the abandonment of entrepreneurial endeavours. Overall, the passage underscores the delicate balance entrepreneurs must strike when weighing the costs and benefits of learning from failure in their pursuit of new ventures.

Conclusion and implications

This chapter offers valuable insights and implications for entrepreneurs facing business failure and embarking on future venture. Entrepreneurs are encouraged to delve into the concepts of stakeholder theory and dependence theory, which can significantly heighten their understanding of the critical role stakeholders play in the aftermath of business failure. Recognizing that many of their business activities are fundamentally relationship-based and often entail dependencies on resources held by stakeholders, entrepreneurs are prompted to acknowledge the utmost importance of maintaining these relationships even after experiencing a business failure (Priego-de-la-Cruz et al., 2020). This heightened awareness empowers entrepreneurs to approach post-failure scenarios with a strategic focus on preserving and nurturing stakeholder relationships, which will ultimately contribute to future venture success.

It is imperative for businesses to comprehend that stakeholders do not uniformly hold negative attitudes toward all instances of business failure. This understanding can alleviate the pressure that entrepreneurs often feel when interacting with stakeholders following a failure. While social withdrawal behaviours are not uncommon among entrepreneurs after a business failure, given the associated psychological, financial, and social costs, it's important to realize that context plays a pivotal role in shaping stakeholders' perceptions (Ucbasaran et al., 2012). Certain stakeholders, such as venture investors, often exhibit a higher tolerance for business failure, recognizing it as an inherent element of normal business activities (Cope et al., 2004). Furthermore, entrepreneurs who learn from their mistakes and adapt may be perceived as more valuable and have a positive impact (Cope, 2011). This knowledge enables entrepreneurs to approach stakeholder interactions with greater optimism and adaptability. Understanding the principles of the grief recovery theory concerning entrepreneurial learning is crucial for entrepreneurs. It emphasizes that the process of recovering from business failure takes time and is akin to healing from emotional grief. This insight enables entrepreneurs to navigate the recovery process more effectively by comprehending its nature and stages. By doing so, they can potentially expedite the healing process and gather positive feedback from various groups, aiding their recovery and growth in the aftermath of a business failure.

In practical terms, entrepreneurs are advised to consider prioritizing the interests of specific stakeholders, particularly during periods of financial difficulty. When businesses face resource constraints after a failure, it becomes essential to make judicious decisions regarding which stakeholders to cultivate valuable relationships with, such as venture investors. These strategic choices are instrumental in ensuring that limited resources are allocated to stakeholders who can offer substantial support and opportunities for future ventures (Cope, 2011).

Building effective mutual communication is vital in the realm of stakeholder management relationships. As put forth by Cooper and College (2014), sustainable success is only achievable when relationships evolve to a level of mutual communication. This mutual understanding and engagement facilitate smoother interactions, collaboration, and the alignment of stakeholder interests with those of the entrepreneur, ultimately contributing to long-term success. Entrepreneurs are encouraged to prioritize building and nurturing robust relationships with relevant stakeholders, recognizing their fundamental role in achieving sustainable success in future ventures. These implications are likely to equip entrepreneurs with a comprehensive perspective on navigating the complex landscape of business failure, emphasizing the significance of stakeholders, relationships, and recovery in shaping future entrepreneurial endeavours.

References

Benn, S., Abratt, R., & O'Leary, B. (2016). Defining and Identifying stakeholders: Views from management and stakeholders. *South African Journal of Business Management*, *47*(2), 1–11. https://doi.org/10.4102/sajbm.v47i2.55

Cardon, M. S., Stevens, C. E., & Potter, D. R. (2011). Misfortunes or mistakes? *Journal of Business Venturing*, *26*(1), 79–92. https://doi.org/10.1016/j.jbusvent.2009.06.004

Clarkson, M. B. E. (1995). A stakeholder framework for analyzing and evaluating corporate social performance. *The Academy of Management Review*, *20*(1), 92–117. https://www.jstor.org/stable/258888

Cooper, C. L., & College, O. (2014). *Wiley encyclopedia of management. 2, Business ethics*. Wiley.

Cope, J. (2011). Entrepreneurial learning from failure: An interpretative phenomenological analysis. *Journal of Business Venturing*, *26*(6), 604–623.

Cope, J., Cave, F., & Eccles, S. (2004). Attitudes of venture capital investors towards entrepreneurs with previous business failure. *Venture Capital*, *6*(2–3), 147–172. https://doi.org/10.1080/1369106041000 1675965

Link, B. G., & Phelan, J. C. (2001). Conceptualizing stigma. *Annual Review of Sociology*, *27*(1), 363–385. https://doi.org/10.1146/annurev.soc.27.1.363

Parmar, B. L., Freeman, R. E., Harrison, J. S., Wicks, A. C., Purnell, L., & de Colle, S. (2010). Stakeholder theory: The state of the art. *Academy of Management Annals*, *4*(1), 403–445.

Pretorius, M. (2009). Defining business decline, failure and turnaround: A content analysis. *The Southern African Journal of Entrepreneurship and Small Business Management*, *2*(1), 1. https://doi.org/10.4102/sajesbm.v2i1.15

Priego-de-la-Cruz, A. M., Alfaro-Cortés, E., & Manzaneque-Lizano, M. (2020). Understanding the stakeholders' role in a business failure situation: An empirical boosting approach. *Revista de Contabilidad*, *23*(1), 113–126. https://doi.org/10.6018/rcsar.369321

Shepherd, D. A., Covin, J. G., & Kuratko, D. F. (2009a). Project failure from corporate entrepreneurship: Managing the grief process. *Journal of Business Venturing*, *24*(6), 588–600. https://doi.org/10.1016/j.jbusvent.2008.01.009

Shepherd, D. A., Wiklund, J., & Haynie, J. M. (2009b). Moving forward: Balancing the financial and emotional costs of business failure. *Journal of Business Venturing*, *24*(2), 134–148. https://doi.org/10.1016/j.jbusvent.2007.10.002

Simmons, S. A., Wiklund, J., & Levie, J. (2013). Stigma and business failure: implications for entrepreneurs' career choices. *Small Business Economics*, *42*(3), 485–505. https://doi.org/10.1007/s11187-013-9519-3

Sutton, R. I., & Callahan, A. L. (1987). The stigma of bankruptcy: Spoiled organizational image and its management. *Academy of Management Journal*, *30*(3), 405–436. https://doi.org/10.2307/256007

Taylor, D. W., & Thorpe, R. (2004). Entrepreneurial learning: a process of co-participation. *Journal of Small Business and Enterprise Development*, *11*(2), 203–211. https://doi.org/10.1108/14626000410537146

Ucbasaran, D., Shepherd, D. A., Lockett, A., & Lyon, S. J. (2012). Life after business failure. *Journal of Management*, *39*(1), 163–202. https://doi.org/10.1177/0149206312457823

Wu, W.-W. (2010). Beyond business failure prediction. *Expert Systems with Applications*, *37*(3), 2371–2376. https://doi.org/10.1016/j.eswa.2009.07.056

Index

Pages in *italics* refer to figures and pages in **bold** refer to tables.